# NAVIGATING DIGITAL TRANSFORMATION IN MANAGEMENT

T0313129

*N*avigating Digital Transformation in Management provides a thorough introduction to the implications of digital transformation for leaders and managers. The book clearly outlines what new or enhanced roles and activities digital transformation requires of them. The book takes a practical approach and shapes an actionable guide that students can take with them into their future careers as managers themselves.

With core theoretical grounding, the book explains how the digital transformation imperative requires all organizations to continuously undertake digital business transformation to adapt to ongoing digital disruption and to effectively compete as digital businesses. The book discusses the critical roles managers need to play in establishing, facilitating, and accelerating the day-to-day activities required to build and continuously upgrade these capabilities.

Drawing on cutting edge research, this textbook:

- Explains how digital technology advancements drive digital disruption and why digital business transformation and operating as a digital business are critical to organization survival
- Unpacks the different digital business capabilities required to effectively compete as a digital business
- Considers the new or digitally enhanced competencies required of leaders, managers, and their supporting professionals to effectively play their roles in digital transformation

- Discusses how leaders, managers, and their supporting professionals can keep up with digital technology advancements
- Unpacks key digital technology advancements, providing a plain language understanding of what they are, how they work, and their implications for organizations.

Enriched with pedagogical features to support understanding and reinforce learning, such as reflective questions, learning summaries, and case studies, and supported by a suite of instructor materials, this textbook is an ideal choice for teachers that want to enable their information systems, information technology, and digital business students to compete and thrive in the contemporary business environment.

**RICHARD BUSULWA** (PhD, MBA, B.Info.Sys) researches and teaches in the Business School at Swinburne University of Technology, home to Australia's first fully immersed Industry 4.0 facility. His digital transformation research explores different digital technology advancements, how they drive disruption, and their implications for particular industries, business functions, and professions. He is the author of *Strategy Execution and Complexity: Thriving in the Era of Disruption* (2018); *Start-up Accelerators: A Field Guide* (2020); *Digital Transformation and Hospitality Management* (2021); and *Digital Transformation in Accounting* (2022). Before entering academia, Richard worked as managing director, COO, CFO, middle manager, and frontline manager. He is co-founder of Digital Keys, the world's first NBIoT smart lock platform.

# Business and Digital Transformation

Digital technologies are transforming societies across the globe, the effects of which are yet to be fully understood. In the business world, technological disruption brings an array of challenges and opportunities for organizations, management and the workplace.

This series of textbooks provides a student-centred library to analyse, explore and critique the evolutionary effects of technology on the business world. Each book in the series takes the perspective of a key business discipline and examines the transformational potential of digital technology, aided by real world cases and examples.

With contributions from expert scholars across the globe, the books in this series enable critical thinking students to excel in their studies of the new digital business environment.

**Digital Transformation in Accounting**
*Richard Busulwa and Nina Evans*

**Demand-Driven Business Strategy**
Digital Transformation and Business Model Innovation
*Cor Molenaar*

**Navigating Digital Transformation in Management**
*Richard Busulwa*

For more information about this series, please visit www.routledge.com/ Routledge-New-Directions-in-Public-Relations – Communication-Research/ book-series/BAD

# NAVIGATING DIGITAL TRANSFORMATION IN MANAGEMENT

**Richard Busulwa**

Routledge
Taylor & Francis Group

LONDON AND NEW YORK

Cover image: © Getty Images

First published 2023
by Routledge
4 Park Square, Milton Park, Abingdon, Oxon, OX14 4RN

and by Routledge
605 Third Avenue, New York, NY 10158

*Routledge is an imprint of the Taylor & Francis Group, an informa business*

© 2023 Richard Busulwa

*British Library Cataloguing-in-Publication Data*
A catalogue record for this book is available from the British Library

*Library of Congress Cataloguing-in-Publication Data*
Names: Busulwa, Richard, 1980– author.
Title: Navigating digital transformation in management / Richard Busulwa.
Description: First Edition. | New York, NY : Routledge, 2023. |
Series: Business and digital transformation | Includes bibliographical references and index.
Identifiers: LCCN 2022016411 (print) | LCCN 2022016412 (ebook) |
ISBN 9781032184043 (hardback) | ISBN 9781032184043 (paperback) |
ISBN 9781003254614 (ebook)
Subjects: LCSH: Management—Technological innovations. |
Leadership. | Organizational change.
Classification: LCC HD30.2 .B887 2023 (print) | LCC HD30.2 (ebook) |
DDC 658.4/0380285—dc23/eng/20220406
LC record available at https://lccn.loc.gov/2022016411
LC ebook record available at https://lccn.loc.gov/2022016412

ISBN: 978-1-032-18407-4 (hbk)
ISBN: 978-1-032-18404-3 (pbk)
ISBN: 978-1-003-25461-4 (ebk)

DOI: 10.4324/9781003254614

Typeset in Minion Pro
by Apex CoVantage, LLC

Access the Support Material: www.routledge.com/9781032184043

# CONTENTS

# CONTENTS

# FIGURES

# TABLES

# Part I

# Digital Disruption and the Digital Transformation Imperative

# CHAPTER 1

# Need for This Book and Research for This Book

DOI: 10.4324/9781003254614-2

# NEED FOR THIS BOOK

The computing field (comprising the disciplines of information systems, information technology, computer science, computer engineering, and software engineering) is renowned for its specialized terminology, jargon, acronyms, and abbreviations. These can often make it challenging, even for professionals within the field, to cut through the jargon in order to clearly understand critical issues. This challenge is particularly accentuated for the topic of digital transformation. For example, digital transformation encompasses terms such as digitization, digitalization, digital business transformation, digital business, digital business strategy, and digital transformation strategy. Each of these terms has a distinct meaning, yet they have overlaps, which can impact what is meant in conversations or literatures using the terms. In addition, digital transformation encompasses equally similar slippery terms relating to a range of digital technologies, digital assets, digital capabilities, and digital concepts that an organization may need to adopt, apply, or understand as part of its digital business strategy or digital transformation strategy (e.g., cloud computing, IoT, blockchain, artificial intelligence, digital platforms, digital ecosystems, digital culture, digital ethics, APIs). Further, digital transformation is at the nexus of change management, strategic management, and digital technology. This can add confusion to leaders', managers', and supporting professionals' understanding of digital transformation – with the juxtaposition of concepts from two or more of these fields or disciplines seeming like new age spin or mere smoke and mirrors. For example, experienced leaders/managers may roll their eyes and not see the concepts of digital leadership or digital business strategy as being significant relative to traditional leadership and strategy. Such attitudes are mostly reflections of easy misunderstandings. Unfortunately, so much is at stake for leaders who misunderstand digital transformation. Depending on leaders' level of influence over the organization, their attitudes resulting from misunderstandings of digital transformation can put their organizations' survival in jeopardy.

Given the importance of digital transformation to organizations' survival, it is critical that leaders cut through the noise and understand it. There are five key aspects to this understanding: making sense of the slippery terminology, understanding the digital business and digital transformation imperatives, understanding digital business capabilities, understanding what is involved in making and executing digital transformation strategy, and having sufficient understanding of critical digital technologies driving the digital imperatives (e.g., which technologies, how they conceptually work, how they can impact business strategy, how they are currently being used). The aim of this book is to impart this understanding as simply as possible and to do so as concisely as possible. To this end, the book has dedicated sections for each of these five key aspects. Leaders, managers, and supporting professionals who take the time to read these sections will find an invaluable lens for understanding digital transformation and digital business that will serve their careers and leadership undertakings well.

# RESEARCH FOR THIS BOOK

The research for this book consisted of five stages. In stage one, a review was undertaken of the relevant and seminal information systems research on digital technology advancements, digital disruption, digital transformation, and digital business. The purpose of this stage was to understand the implications of these concepts for organization strategy and operations in general, and for leaders and managers in particular. In stage two, key practitioner literature on digital technologies, digital transformation, digital business, and digital business strategy was reviewed. The aim of this stage was to understand how organizations were undertaking digital transformation, what digital strategies and digital business models they were pursuing, what digital capabilities they were building, and how they were safeguarding themselves against disruption risks. In stage three, case studies were sought out of organizations successfully leveraging digital technologies, digital transformation strategies, and digital business strategies. The aim of this stage was to provide practical examples of technologies,

**Table 1.1** *Key literatures reviewed at each research stage for this book and the focus of each literature review*

| Research stage | Research activity |
| --- | --- |
| Stage 1 | Review of the **information systems academic research** for discussions of:<br>• The relationship between traditional information systems concepts and contemporary digital business concepts<br>• The link between digital technology advancements and digital disruption<br>• The need for digital transformation and digital business<br>• The capabilities required for digital transformation and digital business<br>• The overlapping and/or slippery terms that get in the way of understanding digital transformation and digital business<br>• The managerial competencies required for digital transformation and digital business |
| Stage 2 | Review **key practitioner literature** on digital technologies, digital transformation, digital business, and digital business strategy for discussions of:<br>• How organizations are undertaking digital transformation<br>• What digital business strategies and digital business models are being pursued by organizations<br>• What digital business capabilities organizations are building<br>• How organizations are safeguarding themselves against disruption risks |
| Stage 3 | Review digital transformation and digital business-related **case studies** focusing on:<br>• Digital transformation initiatives<br>• Digital business capability building initiatives<br>• Optimal digital business competencies for leaders, managers, and supporting professionals<br>• Digital transformation and digital business challenges, benefits, and lessons learned |
| Stage 4 | Review relevant and seminal entrepreneurship, innovation, change management, and general management literature discussing:<br>• Digital transformation or the impact of digital technology advancements on organization strategy or organization capabilities |

| Research stage | Research activity |
|---|---|
| Stage 5 | Synthesize and organize findings so as to: <br> • Clarify slippery terminologies <br> • Explain the digital business and digital transformation imperatives <br> • Explain digital business capabilities <br> • Provide a high-level overview of what is involved in making and executing digital transformation strategy <br> • Provide sufficient understanding of critical digital technologies driving the digital imperatives |

concepts, and strategies in practice across industries. In stage four, relevant and seminal entrepreneurship, innovation, change management, and general management literature discussing digital transformation or the impact of digital technology advancements on organization strategy or organization capabilities was reviewed. It was reasoned that these literatures may have additional digital transformation insights. Finally, in stage five, the varied findings were synthesized and organized into the book sections focusing on clarifying slippery terminologies, explaining the digital business and digital transformation imperatives, explaining digital business capabilities, providing a high-level overview of what is involved in making and executing digital transformation strategy, and providing sufficient understanding of critical digital technologies driving the digital imperatives.

## STRUCTURE OF THIS BOOK

This book is organized into five parts. Part I discusses the nature of digital technology advancements, how they drive digital disruption, the threats and opportunities of digital disruption, and the digital business and digital transformation imperatives. This part links contemporary digital business and digital transformation concepts/terms to traditional information technology and information systems concepts/terms. In doing so, it resolves commonly confusing definitional ambiguity that can get in the way of making sense of digital technology, digital business, and digital transformation conversations. Part II provides an overview of the formation and execution of digital transformation strategy. It first discusses the aims of digital transformation strategy, the arenas/focus areas/levers critical to forming digital transformation strategy, and the outputs of the digital transformation strategy formation process. Subsequently, the different approaches to executing digital transformation strategy are discussed. Common caveats and principles to keep in mind when forming and executing digital transformation strategy are also discussed.

Part III provides an overview of the diverse expertise and roles required on the team driving the digital transformation strategy. It also discusses how digital transformation impacts management practice – specifically, how it changes the roles of line managers or other leaders and the competencies required by these line managers/leaders. This part also discusses the challenge of keeping up with digital technology advancements, the risks of not doing so, and what strategies managers/leaders/supporting professionals can adopt to keep up with accelerating digital technology advancements. Part IV provides an overview of the different digital business capabilities that are important building blocks of digital business competitiveness and longevity. It discusses what each capability means, how it differs from its traditional counterpart where one exists, how it impacts organization competitiveness and longevity, the roles of leaders/managers in building/sustaining/optimizing the capability, and the competencies required of leaders/managers to play such roles. Finally, Part V unpacks more than 36 digital technologies, explaining what they are, how they work, their implications for operations and strategy, current and future use cases, and implications for leaders and managers.

# HOW TO USE THIS BOOK
## LEADERS, MANAGERS, AND SUPPORTING PROFESSIONALS

The book will provide a great working understanding of the interrelationships between IT, information systems, digital technologies, digital disruption, digital transformation, digital business, digital business capabilities, and leadership/managerial roles and competencies if read from end to end. However, it has been written in such a way that each chapter can be read as a stand-alone chapter. Thus, leaders/managers/ professionals only seeking an explanation of digital disruption can go straight to Chapter 3. And leaders/managers/professionals only seeking to understand a particular digital business capability can go straight to the chapter on that capability. Alternatively, leaders/managers/professionals who already have a good understanding of digital transformation and digital business but need a reference book explaining different digital technologies (e.g., blockchain, mixed reality, IoT, data science etc.) and their implications for strategy, operations, and management can skip to the chapter on that specific digital technology in Part V of the book. Readers should notice that each part and chapter has been unpacked extensively in the Table of Contents to enable them to efficiently find and go straight to the specific information they need (e.g., concepts, technologies, issues).

## INSTRUCTORS

Instructors can use this book as the principal book for digital transformation and digital business-related focused subjects or courses at postgraduate and undergraduate level to give students a simple, broad enough, and sufficiently deep digital transformation and digital business foundation. For example, select chapters can be combined in such a way as to form a topic to be covered each week over a 12-week study period. Used this way, the book will provide leaders/managers/ supporting professionals with a comprehensive, practical and integrated understanding of important digital transformation and digital business concepts, as well as working knowledge of relevant digital technologies. Alternatively, instructors can use the book as a supplementary text in any leadership/management/supporting professional subject or course which may need to discuss a particular digital technology (e.g., artificial intelligence, augmented reality), a particular digital technology issue (e.g., digital ethics, cybersecurity), or a particular digital transformation and digital business issue (e.g., digital business models, digital business capabilities). The book can also be used as an invaluable reference book for definitions of slippery terms and concepts, which are explained in as simple a way as possible throughout the book.

## STUDENTS

Students doing assessments on digital technology, digital transformation or digital business-related topics will find this book an invaluable reference book. It explains key terms, concepts, and issues in simple terms and from a business and strategic perspective. Students can use the book as a resource for understanding specific digital technologies where these come up in an assessment exercise (e.g., researching how the Internet of Things works and the implications of Internet of Things technologies for organizations). For more interested and proactive students, a cover-to-cover read of the book would provide an invaluable framework for understanding digital technologies, digital transformation, and digital business. Such a framework would, in turn, provide an invaluable lens for leadership/managerial/professional decision making and be an invaluable weapon in career progression.

## RESEARCHERS

Finally, researchers investigating a particular digital technology or a particular digital transformation and digital business issue may find this book an invaluable starting point. The book provides a plain language explanation and an integrated picture of how that technology or digital business issue fits with related technologies and digital business issues as well as with the broader strategic and operational aims of organizations. Researchers may also find the review of different technologies invaluable for identifying unresolved digital transformation/digital business research questions or other research questions at the intersection between strategy, digital technology, and management/leadership.

# CHAPTER 2

# Getting Out of the Digital Terminology Zoo

DOI: 10.4324/9781003254614-3

# INTRODUCTION

Although digital transformation is interdisciplinary, it has strong roots in the disciplines of information systems, information technology, computer science, computer engineering, and software engineering.[1] These disciplines are notorious for their specialized terminology, jargon, acronyms, and abbreviations. The resultant obfuscation of meaning is compounded by the proliferation in digital technologies and the pace with which innovations in these technologies are occurring. Even information technology (IT) professionals can easily get overwhelmed by the slippery terminology, concepts, and issues. It can be akin to getting trapped in a tech jargon zoo where the noise obfuscates one's ability to hear and have meaningful conversations. Unsurprisingly, not understanding or misunderstanding some critical terminologies, jargon, acronyms, and abbreviations can get in the way of understanding digital transformation and its implications. It is this lack of understanding or misunderstanding of the slippery and overlapping terms that often drives some leaders/managers/supporting professionals to trivialize, or only see a part of, the importance and value of information systems and digital technologies to business operations and strategy. In turn, this can lead them to misunderstand their role in digital transformations and digital technology issues (and therefore sideline them) or to see them as issues that only belong to the IT/information systems (IS)/Technology function. This misunderstanding and the resultant attitudes and actions can pose grave risks to organizations' adaptability, agility, and therefore, longevity. This chapter starts from scratch and provide a reintroduction to the key foundational concepts and definitions from these disciplines that are critical to understanding digital transformation and digital business. The chapter finishes by explaining the important and growing role of leaders, managers, and supporting professionals in information systems and digital technology issues.

**LEARNING OBJECTIVES**

- Understand what an information system is what its key elements and roles are
- Understand key terminology used in relation to information systems and their boundaries

- Apply information systems definitions and concepts to explain the interactions between digital technologies, information systems, and organization strategy
- Analyze and evaluate the implications of the aforementioned interactions for managers, leaders, and their supporting professionals.

## INFORMATION SYSTEMS (IS)

An information system is a collection of interrelated components (hardware, software, data, networks, processes, and people – see Figure 2.1) that work together to perform a specific role for an organization. These roles include

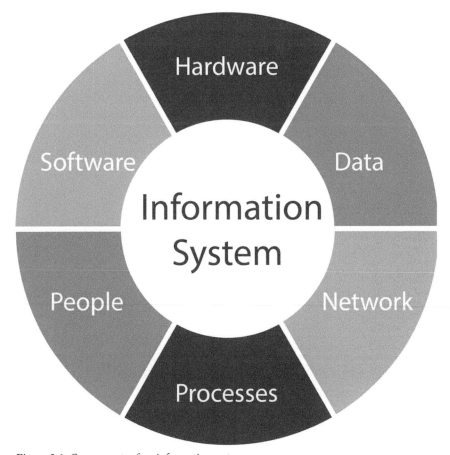

*Figure 2.1* *Components of an information system*

the collection, storage, organization, and transformation of data into information and knowledge, as well as the distribution of that information and knowledge throughout the organization.[2] The distributed information and knowledge play a crucial role in the operations and strategy of an organization (e.g., supporting decision making and supporting coordination and control at all levels and in all parts of an organization).[3]

## COMPONENTS OF AN INFORMATION SYSTEM

The hardware component of an information system includes all the physical components used by an organization for collecting, storing, organizing, transforming, and distributing data and information. For example, hardware includes physical computers and computer components, smart phones, servers and server components, sensors, physical robots, drones, and more. The software component of information systems refers to sets of instructions, software algorithms, code for controlling or telling the hardware what to do. Software includes systems software (which operates the hardware and coordinates instructions between application software and the hardware). Examples of systems software includes operating system software, utilities software, compilers, assemblers, debuggers, and drivers. Popular operating systems software includes Microsoft Windows operating systems, Mac operating systems, Linux operating systems, and Android operating systems. The software component also includes application software (the software most people are familiar with and interact with to perform tasks or work). Examples of application software include word processing software, spreadsheets, and other applications or apps. The data component of information systems refers to what data is collected or created (e.g., text, videos, images, etc.), how that data is stored (e.g., in what systems/databases, in which locations, etc.), how it is organized, how it is transformed into information, how it is presented for understandability, and how it is distributed throughout the organization. For more information, see the chapter on data and data management technologies in Part V of this book. The network component of information systems refers to the technology that enables devices and other entities within an information system to communicate with each other and for communication between different information systems to occur. The network component includes networking hardware and software (e.g., servers, coaxial cables, network interface cards, hubs, routers, LAN cables, network operating systems, etc.).

Although many people tend to focus on the technology aspects of information systems (i.e., hardware, software, data, and network technology), the process and people components are an important aspect of information systems that should not be overlooked. Regarding the process component, organizations have a range of processes for getting organization work done and meeting organization objectives. Examples of these include product development processes, procurement processes, customer acquisition processes, customer support processes, accounting processes, marketing processes, HR processes, strategy making processes, governance processes, risk management processes, and more. Technology is increasingly becoming integrated into these processes and used to design, facilitate, manage, and optimize processes. For example, hardware and software are used to detect when particular processes have not occurred or to trigger particular processes to occur (e.g., sensors can detect an unsafe change in temperature and initiate building evacuation processes; or video monitoring hardware and software may spot vandalism and automatically request security or police attendance). Hardware and software are also used to provide the data used to perform many processes (e.g., data driven operational decisions), alert people to events that have occurred or failed to occur (e.g., patients missed during ward rounds at a hospital), orchestrate or perform processes (e.g., driving vehicles), provide the platforms on which people perform processes (e.g., workflow management platforms), automate processes (e.g., robotic process automation or workflow automation), and more. Used in the right processes and in the right ways, both software and hardware can optimize process efficiency (e.g., speed and cost), effectiveness (e.g., customer satisfaction, stakeholder satisfaction, and competitive advantage), adaptability (e.g., ability to adapt processes to unexpected internal and external events), and agility (e.g., capacity for flexibility and speed in sensing and responding to external changes).

Regarding the people component of information systems, it is people who are creators of information systems (e.g., imagining, designing, developing information systems); people are mostly the operators of information systems (e.g., implement, trouble shoot, maintain, train users, support users); people are the administrators of information systems (e.g., undertaking specific systems upkeep, configuration, database maintenance); and people are mostly the managers of information systems (e.g., governance, performance management, risk management, project management). And it is people who are typically the users of information systems, who experience the benefits or challenges of using information systems, and who are ultimately served by the outputs of information systems. The people aspect of information systems is typically concerned with the different formal and informal roles involved in the creation, operation/administration, management, use, and value of information systems. Examples of information systems creation roles include systems analysts, systems architects, systems engineers, programmers, software engineers, hardware engineers, and network engineers. Examples of systems operators include hardware technicians, helpdesk analysts, security analysts/engineers, IS product managers, and IS trainers. Examples of information systems administration roles include systems administrators, database administrators, and network administrators. Examples of managers of information systems include the Chief Information Officer (CIO), the Chief Technology Officer (CTO), the Chief Digital Officer (CDO), and IS functional or specialist managers (e.g., application managers, network services managers, desktop support managers, systems design and development managers, ERP managers, IS security managers, IS project managers, and digital risk managers). As noted earlier, the people component of information systems is also concerned with users of information systems. An important focus of this aspect is how users adopt new information systems. Frameworks such as Everett Rogers' Diffusion of Innovations categorizes user adoption behavior or approaches into innovators, early adopters, early majority, late majority, and laggard adoption behaviors or adoption approaches. Understanding the different types of adopters, adoption approaches, and adoption behaviors is often instrumental in planning the speed and effectiveness with which information systems can be implemented.

## ROLES OF INFORMATION SYSTEMS

Information systems play three key roles in organizations. First, as noted earlier, the components of an information system work together to capture data, store it, organize it, transform it into information, and organize that information into organizational knowledge. Second, the information and knowledge produced by information systems is distributed throughout the organization to support decision making (e.g., day-to-day operational decisions and more long-term strategic decisions). Operational decisions include decisions such as how much inventory to buy and from whom, who to put on what shifts, which customers to serve and when. Strategic decisions include decisions such as what business models and revenue models to use, what technology infrastructure to use, and how to combine business models and technology infrastructure to optimize competitiveness, adaptability, and agility. Third and finally, information systems facilitate operational and strategic processes (e.g., enabling a range of organization processes and workflows such as product development, procurement, customer acquisition, customer support, accounting, marketing, HR, strategy making, risk management, and governance). Almost all organization work is informed, facilitated, and supported by information systems.

## TYPES OF INFORMATION SYSTEMS

The term information systems is often combined with other terms to refer to subsets of information systems, or particular types of information systems. These subsets, or typologies, are usually based on what technologies are used or not used, processes those information system subsets focus on, stakeholders the specific information systems subsets serve in the organization hierarchy, or specific organization functions the subset information systems focus on. Subsets or types of information systems focusing on the technologies used or not used include computer-based information systems and manual-based information systems. Computer-based information systems are information systems that use computer hardware and software to capture data, store it, organize it, transform it into information, organize that information into organizational knowledge, and disseminate it throughout the organization. In contrast, manual-based information systems are information systems that perform the role of information systems without computer hardware and software (e.g., using paper, filing cabinets, people's memories, etc.). Types of information systems focusing on stakeholders in the organization hierarchy include transaction processing systems (e.g., those used by operational level employees to serve customers), management information systems and decision support systems (e.g., those used by middle managers and senior managers to monitor and manage performance), and executive information systems (those used by the top management team or executive team to monitor organization-wide performance and risk, and to inform strategic decision making). Types of information systems focusing on specific organization processes/activities include data warehousing systems, enterprise resource planning systems, and office automation systems. Types of information systems focusing on specific organization functions include operational information systems, property management systems, customer relationship management systems, marketing information systems, accounting information systems, HR information systems, procurement systems, and more. See Figure 2.2 for examples of types of information systems and users.

Information systems specialists typically study degrees in information systems that focus on systems design and development methodologies, enterprise information management, enterprise architecture and governance, database systems and information modeling, business process management, project and change management, IS security, and IS strategy and governance. They often specialize in areas such as IS infrastructure management, IS project and change management, business analysis, business analytics, and functional IS areas (e.g., accounting information systems, HR information systems). IS specialists enter careers

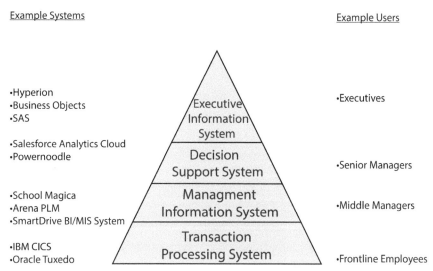

Example Systems

Example Users

- Hyperion
- Business Objects
- SAS

- Salesforce Analytics Cloud
- Powernoodle

- School Magica
- Arena PLM
- SmartDrive BI/MIS System

- IBM CICS
- Oracle Tuxedo

Executive Information System

Decision Support System

Managment Information System

Transaction Processing System

- Executives

- Senior Managers

- Middle Managers

- Frontline Employees

**Figure 2.2** *Types of information systems, including example systems and example users*

such as business systems analysts, solution architects, data and analytics managers, data engineers, IS project managers, consultants and functional system managers (e.g., finance systems manager, HR information systems managers, property information systems managers).

# INFORMATION TECHNOLOGY (IT) AND INFORMATION COMMUNICATIONS TECHNOLOGY (ICT)

Although people use the terms IT and information systems interchangeably, information technology is actually a subset of information systems. As a subset, it typically only focuses on the technology component of information systems. IT specialists focus on ensuring the organization has the right hardware and software products, installing them, customizing them, integrating them with existing products, maintaining them, supporting users to use them, and ensuring that the security, availability, and accessibility of each product and of the information system as a whole, is optimized. IT specialists typically require degrees in information technology or computer science. Within such degrees, they often specialize in hardware and/or software areas such as network design, hardware design, software design, software development, cybersecurity, artificial intelligence, and the Internet of Things. And they enter jobs such as network architects, software developers, IT systems analysts, security analysts, web developers, systems administrators, software product managers, and IT managers.

The term ICT (information communications technology) is sometimes used interchangeably with IT. It refers to the convergence or integration of IT with audiovisual technologies and telephone networks (e.g., media broadcasting technologies, audio and video transmission, and telephony). Thus, the term ICT can be thought of as an extended synonym for the term IT.

# STRATEGIC INFORMATION SYSTEMS AND DIGITAL TECHNOLOGIES
## STRATEGIC INFORMATION SYSTEMS

Strategic information systems are information systems that can significantly transform the strategic position of an organization in its external environment. Such transformation can be in the form of breakthroughs in efficiency, differentiation, innovation, adaptability, or agility. Efficiency breakthroughs include dramatically speeding up or enabling cost leadership in processes such as product and service delivery processes, customer engagement and support processes, and strategy execution processes. For example, in its early days, Dell Technologies leveraged web/internet technology to be able to offer custom, built-to-order computers to customers at a cost of 10% of its revenue.[4] In contrast, dominant industry competitors such as Hewlett-Packard, Gateway, and Cisco could only do this at a cost of 20% to 50% of their revenue.[5] This improved Dell's strategic position (i.e., Dell had cost leadership as a competitive advantage), enabling it to grow into a dominant player in the industry. Differentiation breakthroughs include being able to offer products and services that, relative to competitors, have unique benefits that are important to customers. For example, Apple has leveraged a closed technology ecosystem and greater investment in product design to differentiate its products from competitors. As a result, Apple is able to charge two to three times as much as its competitors' products? and also enjoys cult-like customer loyalty. Innovation breakthroughs relate to breakthroughs in the rate at which new and better products/services are created and delivered. For example, Amazon's first product was an online bookstore platform, but it has since leveraged its information systems (technology infrastructure, processes, and people) to globally deliver a consistent stream of products including Kindle, Amazon Web Services, Amazon Prime, Amazon Publishing, and Amazon Robotics. These innovation breakthroughs have propelled Amazon to become a dominant leader in a range of industries. Adaptability refers to an organization's ability to adapt its operations to surprising events in its external environment (e.g., financial crises, pandemics, disruptive competition). And agility refers to an organization's capacity for flexibility and speed in sensing and responding to external changes. Companies such as Google and Intel configure their information systems to enable them to maximize their adaptability and agility. For example, Google uses its sophisticated information systems to sense changes in its external environment (e.g., collect and interpret data on search patterns and online ad performance), and then uses the insights to drive operational responses to external events.[6] Furthermore, both Google and Intel use investment arms such as Google Ventures and Intel Capital to discover and profit first from the next breakthrough product and market innovations.[7] Thus, when they are designed or configured appropriately, information systems (different combinations of technology, networks, people, and business processes) can be very powerful strategic weapons, capable of transforming the fortunes of organizations.

## DIGITAL TECHNOLOGIES

The term digital technologies refers to combinations of information (or data), computing (or computation), communication, and connectivity technologies.[8] Digital technologies include all types of electronic hardware and software that use information in the form of binary code (information represented by strings of 0s and 1s). Digital technologies include electronic tools, systems, devices, personal computers, calculators, traffic light controllers, mobile telephones, satellite technology, high definition television, the internet and other networks, software applications, email, mobile apps, etc. Digital technologies generate, receive, store, process, transmit, and even act on data. Increasingly, digital technologies are enabling all manner of things (e.g., people, organizations, physical products, physical infrastructure, software, etc.) to capture data within and around them, communicate that data with other things locally or globally, receive information from other things, use sophisticated computation/algorithms to gain insights from that information (e.g., spot patterns, understand instructions), and use combinations of algorithms and robotics capabilities to act on that information in the same way that a person can (e.g., call the police on capturing or receiving information that a known fugitive is nearby).

It was noted earlier that, used the right way, information systems can become very powerful strategic weapons capable of conferring often insurmountable strategic advantages. The right digital technologies can supercharge this strategic power of information systems by drastically enhancing how efficiently and effectively such information systems function. For example, the right combination of digital technologies can speed up the rate at which data flows between hardware, software, networks, business processes, and people – making it near instant. The right combination of digital technologies can transform all of an organization's infrastructure (buildings, machinery, furniture, cars, stationery, etc.) into smart things capable of collecting data, communicating data, acting on data insights, and doing all of these things autonomously. The right combination of digital technologies can enable an organization's employees to work from anywhere in the world, collaborate with any of the organization's infrastructure and other physical things, and serve large numbers of customers globally in real time, irrespective of their location. The right combination of digital technologies can enhance the efficiency and effectiveness of interactions between people, technology, and processes. These examples only scratch the surface of the power of digital technologies to supercharge the strategic power of information systems. Microsoft, Google, Amazon, and other global giants are leveraging combinations of digital technologies and breakthroughs in these digital technologies to create strategic information systems that enable them to efficiently and effectively serve billions of people globally every day. Doing so has conferred significant wealth and global influence to the owners, employees, and strategic partners of these organizations.

# IMPLICATIONS FOR LEADERS, MANAGERS, AND SUPPORTING PROFESSIONALS

So far, this chapter has unpacked the terms IT, information systems, strategic information systems, and digital technologies. It has delineated the overlaps and boundaries between them. It has also explained the importance of digital technologies to information systems and how they can supercharge the efficiency, effectiveness, and strategic value of information systems. Ensuring the effective design, implementation, operation, maintenance, and optimization of information systems is not just the responsibility of the IT/IS or similar function, but a shared responsibility of leaders, managers, and supporting professionals at all levels. For example, leaders, managers, and supporting professionals need to work as a team to ensure that the right digital technologies are used, that the right operational and strategic processes are in place, and that these processes leverage digital technologies for optimal efficiency and effectiveness. They also need to ensure that the right talent and the supporting infrastructure are in place to ensure information systems function optimally, that the right strategic partnerships are in place to optimize the strategic value of IS, and that employees throughout the organization continuously upgrade their technology skills and keep up with digital technologies. In order to deliver on this responsibility, leaders, managers, and supporting professionals need to first be able to make sense of the often confusing terminology and acronyms related to information systems and digital technologies. This will position them to make clear sense of what they read/hear about different digital technologies and their implications for information systems (e.g., what they read in product brochures, consultant proposals, whitepapers, books and what they hear in meetings, conferences, etc.), and it will position them to constructively engage in conversations with stakeholders about digital technologies and information systems (e.g., stakeholders such as strategic leaders, employees, IT/IS professionals, IT/IS consultants, IT/IS vendors and strategic partners). They will then be in a position to leverage resultant insights to spot opportunities for improving their organizations' information systems and to effectively participate in and play a leadership role in necessary IS related changes.

# GOOGLE AND REFLECT

To improve your comfort with IT/IS/digital technology terminology, try Googling the following terms to find a credible and complete definition that makes better sense to you.

Chief Information Officer (CIO), Chief Technology Officer (CTO), Chief Digital Officer (CDO), IT Manager, IS Manager, Digital Strategist, Business Systems Analyst, ERP Systems administrator, IT Strategy, Information Systems Strategy, Information Systems Governance, Information Systems Assurance, Information Systems Security, Technology Governance, Digital Governance, Digital Technology Device, Digital Technology Platform, Digital Convergence

# DISCUSSION QUESTIONS

To check your understanding of the concepts covered in this chapter, please reflect on or discuss what constitutes concise answers to the following questions.

1 What is the difference between IT and ICT?

2 What is the difference between IT and Information Systems?

3 Is Information Systems a part of IT, or is IT a part of information systems? Does it matter which is a part of which?

4 What is the best metaphor you can think of to explain the interrelationship between digital technologies and information systems?

5 Are digital technologies a part of IT, or is IT a part of digital technologies?

6 What is the role of digital technologies in information systems?

7 What are five different types of digital technologies?

8 Assuming that an organization is not already using the digital technologies you identified above, how could using them improve each component of an information system?

9 Assuming that an organization is not already using the digital technologies you identified above, how could using them improve the functioning of its information systems? (e.g., How would using them impact efficiency, effectiveness, strategic position?)

10 What are strategic information systems? How can they transform the strategic positioning of an organization? (Identify five ways they can transform it.)

11 Identify two organizations that are exemplar users of information systems as powerful strategic weapons.

12 What is the role of leaders and managers in the efficient and effective functioning of information systems?

13 Identify five actions that a leader or manager can take to improve the effectiveness and efficiency of information systems at their organization.

# NOTES

1 Chapter is an adaptation of Busulwa, R., Evans, N., Oh, A., & Kang, M. (2020). *Hospitality management and digital transformation: Balancing efficiency, agility and guest experience in the era of disruption* (1st ed.). Routledge. https://doi.org/10.4324/9780429325205. pp 9–17.

2   Bourgeois, D. (2014). *Information systems for business and beyond*. The Saylor Foundation.

3   Laudon, K.C., & Laudon, J.P. (2019). *Management information systems: Managing the Digital firm*. Pearson.

4   The Power of Virtual Integration: An Interview with Dell Computer's Michael Dell. (1998, March). Retrieved April 21, 2020, from Harvard Business Review website: https://hbr.org/1998/03/the-power-of-virtual-integration-an-interview-with-dell-computers-michael-dell

5   What You Don't Know About Dell. (2003, November 3). Retrieved April 21, 2020, from Bloomberg.com website: www.bloomberg.com/news/articles/2003-11-02/what-you-dont-know-about-dell

6   Adaptability: The New Competitive Advantage. (2011, July). Retrieved April 21, 2020, from Harvard Business Review website: https://hbr.org/2011/07/adaptability-the-new-competitive-advantage

7   Rowley, J. (2018, February 17). A peek inside Alphabet's investing universe. Retrieved April 21, 2020, from TechCrunch website: https://techcrunch.com/2018/02/17/a-peek-inside-alphabets-investing-universe/; Burgelman, R. A., & Grove, A. S. (2007). Let chaos reign, then rein in chaos – repeatedly: Managing strategic dynamics for corporate longevity. *Strategic management Management Journal*, 28(10), 965–979.

8   Bharadwaj, A., El Sawy, O., Pavlou, P., & Venkatraman, N., 2013. Digital business strategy: Toward a next generation of insights. *MIS Quarterly*, 37(2), 471–482.

# CHAPTER 3

# Understanding Digital Disruption

DOI: 10.4324/9781003254614-4

# INTRODUCTION

This chapter discusses how digital technology advancements cause digital disruption, the different types of disruption they create, and the risks of not responding to this disruption effectively and in a timely manner.[1] The chapter then discusses the types of game changing opportunities presented by digital technology advancements and how organizations can leverage digital technology advancements to both adapt to disruption and also to seize the game changing opportunities digital technology advancements present. Case studies of organizations that were unable to guard against or effectively respond to digital disruption are discussed (e.g., organizations such as Kodak,[2] Blockbuster Video,[3] and Borders bookstores[4]). Contrasting cases of organizations that adapted to disruption and seized the game changing opportunities offered by digital technology advancements to transform their operations and their product/service offerings for significantly enhanced agility, adaptability, scalability, and profitability are also discussed (e.g., organizations such as Netflix, Caterpillar, Walmart, and Disney). Understanding the ongoing dynamics of disruption and the associated opportunities and threats is critical to understanding the ongoing digital transformation imperative.

---

**LEARNING OBJECTIVES**

- Understand digital disruption and how digital technology advancements drive digital disruption
- Understand different manifestations of digital disruption and their implications
- Analyze and evaluate the existential threats and gam- changing opportunities created by digital disruption
- Analyze and evaluate the implications of digital disruption for managers, leaders, and their supporting professionals.

# DIGITAL TECHNOLOGY ADVANCEMENTS AND DIGITAL DISRUPTION

## DIGITAL TECHNOLOGY ADVANCEMENTS

In Chapter 2, digital technologies were defined as technologies that combine information (or data), computing (or computation), communication, and connectivity technologies. Digital technologies include social, mobile, analytics, cloud, internet, Internet of Things (IoT), software, platform, artificial intelligence, robotics, drones, satellite, blockchain, and other technologies.[5] Innovations in these technologies have been advancing and continue to advance at an exponential rate. Such advancements include ongoing breakthroughs in processing speeds, memory capacity, number and size of pixels in digital cameras, computational capacity, network capacity, and sophistication of software algorithms.[6] Further examples include the introduction and commercial adoption of technologies like blockchain, edge computing, 5G and 6G technology, brain-computer interfaces, 4D printing, Neuromorphic hardware, exoskeletons, and quantum computing. Consider that all these advancements, and more, have occurred in just over 40 years since the introduction of the IBM PC. Thus, in referring to advances in digital technologies or digital technology innovations, the chapter is referring to the introduction of new digital technologies or to breakthroughs in the capacity of existing digital technologies. For instance, the introduction of new digital technologies like 3D printing and 5G or significant improvements in existing technologies like computational power, cloud computing capacity, or artificial intelligence capabilities.

## DIGITAL TECHNOLOGY ADVANCEMENTS AS A SOURCE OF DIGITAL DISRUPTION

The term disruption refers to preventing something (e.g., routines, processes, events) from continuing as usual or as expected. Put another way, it refers to interrupting the normal course of action or throwing the status quo into disorder. Digital disruption, then, refers to digital technology-induced disruption. Digital disruption is often discussed from the perspective of incumbent organizations that are heavily invested in established ways of doing things and whose established way of operating is interrupted or made irrelevant.[7] But digital disruption can also occur at an industry, sector, and/or societal level.[8] That is, the established way of doing things in a whole industry, sector, or society can be disrupted. For example, the introduction of electronic health records can render hospitals' and medical clinics' prior processes for storing, retrieving, and transmitting patient information obsolete (an industry level disruption). And the introduction of, and improvements in, telehealth can increase the availability and quality of healthcare services to rural and emerging economies, reduce the need to travel for some patients, and reduce the cost of certain types of care (an industry and society level disruption).

# UNPACKING DIGITAL DISRUPTION

The introduction of new digital technologies or breakthroughs in existing digital technologies results in three types of disruptions: disruption of consumer or customer expectations and behaviors, disruption of the competitive landscape, and disruption of available data.[9] Each of these disruptions is unpacked in more detail below.

## DISRUPTION OF CUSTOMER EXPECTATIONS AND BEHAVIORS

Businesses make money and are able to continue their existence if they cost effectively provide products and/or services that customers want and choose to buy from them. Customers typically want and choose to buy products that they expect to provide the best cost/benefit proposition (e.g., most accessible, best quality, best brand image, most compatible with other products, and best suited for the particular job the customer is trying to get done, at a particular price). Using search engine, social media, data analytics, artificial intelligence, and other digital technologies, consumers have access to an unprecedented amount of information about available product and service options and the differences in benefits and costs of these options. For example, at the push of a button, they can see almost all available options for a particular product or service and compare their benefits and costs. In addition, consumers can easily access information on what accessibility, convenience, and other benefits are possible from substitute products/services. For example, when it comes to banking services, most consumers can easily check whether online banking, mobile banking, blockchain-based payment, email-based payment, and cardless cash withdrawal services are possible. The easy access to product/service information and options, as well as knowledge of what is possible, shapes consumer expectations and behavior. Continuing with the banking services example, banks that are either not competitive on price and/or don't provide online banking, mobile banking, blockchain-based payment, email-based payment, and cardless cash withdrawal services (for example), may gradually find themselves unable to attract new customers and also find their existing customers choosing to go with banks that live up to these consumer expectations. Thus, digital technology advancements (the introduction of new digital technologies or improvements in existing ones) change consumer expectations.[10] They also change consumer behaviors, either due to changed expectations or due to changes in consumer routines and habits.[11] For example, the introduction of driverless cars (a digital technology advancement) may significantly reduce consumer driving, car purchasing, car parts purchasing, and other related consumer routines. This may disrupt operations of organizations providing products and services used in those consumer routines (e.g., significantly reduced demand, inability to satisfy customers). Broadly, digital disruption manifests itself as diminishing business results (e.g., loss of customers, falling prices, diminished availability of product/service input suppliers, loss of talented staff, challenges accessing funding etc.).

## DISRUPTION OF THE COMPETITOR FIELD
## AND BASES OF COMPETITION

The introduction of new digital technologies or improvements in existing digital technologies can lower barriers to entry into an industry, allowing new startups to enter that industry as competitors, as well as allowing existing organizations in different industries to enter the industry. For example, digital technology advancements enabled startups like Spotify (in 2006), Soundcloud (in 2007), and Tidal (in 2014) to enter and become dominant players in the music industry. And such advancements enabled Apple (iTunes/Apple Music), Google (YouTube Music), and Amazon (Amazon Music) to leverage the digital platforms used in different industries (e.g., cloud infrastructure, search, and device platforms) to become dominant players in the music industry. Digital technology advances lower barriers to new competitors entering an industry by lowering the cost to produce and distribute products, as well as to acquire customers, support them, and manage relationships with them. For example, by leveraging cloud infrastructure to record and stream music, new entrants in the music industry were able to offer music to customers instantly (instead of waiting for physical CD delivery), offer it at a better price (since cost was low), and offer it to almost everyone with an internet connection (significantly expanded distribution). They were able to have significantly greater margins, as digital technologies enabled them to circumvent costly activities traditionally associated with music production and distribution (e.g., signing artists; managing artists; operating recording venues; promoting artists; setting up and managing live shows; producing CDs; packaging, marketing, and distributing artist music; and manually managing intellectual property rights).

Digital technologies also disrupt incumbent organization's bases, or sources, of competitive advantage.[12] For example, over a long period of time, incumbent organizations dominating the music industry had established competitive advantages such as locking in key strategic partners (e.g., companies doing artist scouting, recording, live venue management, packaging, marketing, and distribution), cost leadership (e.g., from using their size to negotiate the lowest fees for artists, recording, packaging, marketing, and distribution), and brand differentiation (e.g., being more attractive to top artists due to their brands being more recognized, better financed, and having greater album sales capability). Digital technology advancements removed the potency of these advantages by making them much less relevant to music sales. By leveraging digital technology infrastructure, new competitors could circumvent the need for traditional strategic partners (e.g., companies providing recording, packaging, marketing, and distribution services); they could also reach anyone around the world with an internet connection (minimizing the need to rely on the established sales infrastructure of traditional record labels). New competitors then leveraged search engine optimization (SEO), social media, artificial intelligence, mobile, and other digital technologies to acquire customers, provide them with the songs they wanted instantly, and do all this at a fraction of the cost that traditional record labels provided their music for. The bases or sources of competition then evolved to include, for example, the quality and availability of digital music platforms, the number of consumers active on those platforms, and the ease with which artists could get their music onto those platforms.

## DISRUPTION OF DATA AVAILABILITY

Organizations that leverage new or improved digital technologies are able to capture and have access to more data (e.g., data about consumers and consumption experiences, data about processes for creating and providing products/services, and data about the market dynamics of their industries).[13] This data provides them with additional strategic advantages. For example, they can monetize it by selling it to third parties (e.g., Facebook and Google monetize their user data by selling user targeted advertising; Amazon uses its data for targeted adverts as well as dynamic product pricing). Outside such monetization, organizations can employ sophisticated analytics to optimize consumer experience, operational efficiency, and effectiveness and for strategic sensing of market and other external environment trends. They can also use collected data, in combination with sophisticated artificial intelligence algorithms, to provide automated consumer experiences. For example,

Google and Apple leverage their data, along with sophisticated artificial intelligence, to offer chatbots and virtual assistants like Siri and Google Assistant. In the hotel industry, organizations like Hilton augment their customer service with robots like Connie, the robot concierge. The data available from digital technologies includes data captured by the organization, as well as data captured by external organizations (e.g., governments, suppliers, platform organizations, etc.). Savvy competitors can clean, store, organize, and integrate external and internal data, then leverage it for real-time operational insights, as well as for strategic insights. By doing so, they have an additional basis of competitive advantage. The additional data availability digital technologies enable disrupts existing ways of doing things by necessitating that organizations change what data they are capturing themselves, what data they are pulling in from external sources, how they integrate this data, and how they optimize the insights available to operational and strategy processes. That is, organizations can't continue as they have been, as they risk losing competitive positioning.

# EXISTENTIAL THREATS AND GAME CHANGING OPPORTUNITIES

The introduction of new digital technologies, and/or improvements in existing digital technologies, creates existential threats for organizations; but it also offers game changing opportunities.[14] The paragraphs that follow unpack the nature of the existential threats and the game changing opportunities for alert and proactive organizations.

## EXISTENTIAL THREATS

By disrupting customer expectations and behaviors, disrupting the competitor makeup and bases of competition, and disrupting data availability, digital technology advancements create an ultimatum for incumbent organizations in an industry – adapt to the disruption

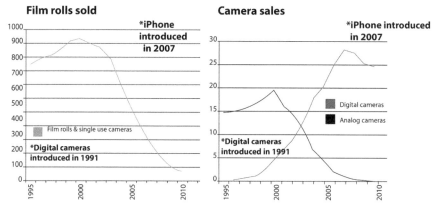

**Figure 3.1** *Kodak failed to effectively respond to disruption from digital cameras and smartphones, despite creating the technology behind them (Kodak invented the first digital camera in 1975)[20]*

or risk your survival. This survival risk is the existential threat. If organizations continue to do what they have always done (or only make tokenistic changes) and don't adapt their product and service offering to changed customer expectations and behaviors, existing customers will start going to other organizations with better value or more convenience. In addition, organizations that continue to operate the way they always have will struggle to attract new customers. In less extreme cases, the effect of disruption may play out as gradual customer attrition, gradual price erosion, gradual decline in revenue, decreasing margins, and loss of profitability, until a point at which it is no longer worth sustaining the business. In more extreme cases, the effect of disruption can manifest itself much more rapidly, resulting in sudden and significant financial losses that bring about heavy layoffs, fire sale acquisition, or even insolvency. This can occur for particular organizations, it can occur for an industry, or it can occur for a whole sector or geography. For example, digital technology advancements brought about the slow, but eventual demise of Kodak[15] – see Figure 3.1. In contrast, digital disruption brought about the sudden demise of many organizations in the taxi industry.[16] Organizations can ignore or deny the existential threat created by digital technology advancements, or they can leverage digital technologies to reconfigure their product and service offerings, redesign their operational processes, and reform their medium and long-term strategy for continuous adaptation to certain future disruption. For example, Walmart has managed to adapt to the disruption of retail by leveraging digital technologies to transform its products/services, distribution approach, and customer relationships and experiences.[17] Other retailers, such as Borders,[18] either ignored, denied, or were not quick enough to understand and leverage the power of digital technologies to adapt to the disruption of retail.[19]

## GAME CHANGING OPPORTUNITIES

Proactive organizations can leverage new digital technologies or improvements in existing digital technologies to seize three common types of game changing opportunities. Effectively seizing one or more of these opportunities can safeguard their market position for a period or enable them to leapfrog competitors to become a market leader. The first type of game changing opportunity is leveraging digital technologies to introduce new or significantly enhanced products and services that meet or exceed customer expectations.[21] Netflix's business model was originally based on renting out movies stored on physical media (e.g., VHS, DVD, Blu-Ray). The company recognized the game changing opportunities in internet and cloud computing digital technologies. Netflix leveraged these digital technologies to transform its product offering and business model into a web-based video streaming service. Blockbuster Video, the industry leader with more than 10,000 retail stores and a turnover of more than $5 billion, clung onto its established business model until it was untenable. It eventually attempted to leverage digital technologies to revamp its offering, but by then it was too late. In 2010, the industry leader declared bankruptcy and no longer exists. Netflix, in the meantime, has gone from strength to strength, continuing to embrace digital technologies such as mobile streaming, artificial intelligence based personalized recommendation algorithms, set top boxes, smart TVs, Xbox/PlayStation/Wii consoles, and virtual private networks. Netflix also leveraged the data collected from different digital technologies to better understand what consumers like to watch, when they like to watch it, and how they like to watch it. This, in turn, continuously feeds its programming and service delivery. Today Netflix has a turnover of more than $20 billion and annual income/profit of more than $2 billion.

Other proactive organizations are leveraging digital technologies to transition from product to platform organizations. That is, rather than just being sellers of products, providing the infrastructure that other entities (e.g., businesses, contractors, consumers) can use to create, market, sell, or enhance their products and customer experiences more conveniently and at lower cost. For example, Caterpillar, the heavy equipment manufacturer, leveraged digital technologies to offer a vehicle management platform that users of its equipment can draw on for vehicle utilization, health, location, servicing, and longevity insights.[22] In addition to quality equipment, such a platform makes it difficult for customers to switch from Caterpillar in the absence of breakthrough competitor offerings.

The second type of game changing opportunity available to proactive organizations is leveraging digital technologies to bypass intermediaries and interact directly with consumers,[23] to enhance collaboration and coordination between strategic partners in the value chain,[24] or to create and manage an ecosystem-based business model.[25] Microsoft had traditionally distributed its hardware and software through resellers but has recently started to also sell direct to consumers its surface hardware and cloud services.[26] This direct interaction with customers enables greater understanding of the customer, greater control of the customer experience, and greater customer engagement opportunities.[27] Organizations can also leverage digital technologies for more effective and faster collaboration and coordination with strategic value chain partners.[28] For instance, organizations integrate aspects of their information systems with those of strategic partners and have shared systems for collaboration and coordination that draw on the data from both sets of systems. This can improve data visibility, workflow visibility, engagement, incentives, and more. Organizations can also leverage digital technologies to create and manage an ecosystem of suppliers, consumers, and other stakeholders.[29] For example, Uber continues to build and manage an evolving ecosystem of transportation made up of self-employed drivers, restaurants, hospitals and medical clinics, end consumers, certifiers, and other stakeholders. Digital technologies expand the number of possible consumer engagement channels from traditional physical mail, phone, and email to online live chat, social media, mobile, mobile app, IoT devices, and more. These expanded engagement channels bring about opportunities to engage with customers via their dominant or preferred engagement channels. And improved engagement can lead to better customer acquisition and retention.

Finally, the third type of game changing opportunity available to organizations is leveraging digital technologies to improve their adaptability, agility, and ambidexterity. Adaptability was defined in Chapter 2 as the ability to reconfigure routines, processes, and practices to suit the demands of unexpected internal and external changes. For example, reconfiguring an organization's product development and delivery processes to suit changes in customer expectations and behaviors as Netflix did. And agility was defined as the capacity for flexibility and speed in sensing and responding to external changes. For example, through sophisticated data analytics, as well as their Google Ventures and Intel Capital arms, Google and Intel are highly agile organizations able to continuously adapt and thrive in industries characterized by an extraordinary rate of change, unpredictability, growing convergence and an assault on technology standards.[30] In contrast to adaptability and agility, ambidexterity is concerned with having processes to ensure existing process efficiency in parallel with processes to undertake exploratory activities so as to discover new products and services. For example, for a long time, Intel has operated both efficiency and exploratory activities. Efficiency activities have enabled it to maximize revenue and profitability from its existing products and processes. At the same time, exploratory activities have enabled Intel to discover the next breakthrough products prior to the decline of their existing core products.[31] Organizations can leverage digital technologies to configure their operations and strategy for optimal adaptability, agility and ambidexterity.

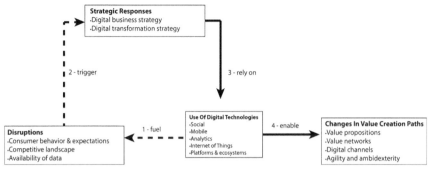

**Figure 3.2** *Digital technology advancements cause digital disruption but can be leveraged to respond to disruption and recreate value offerings and capabilities*[32]

Figure 3.2 shows how digital technology advancements drive disruption but can also be leveraged to respond to disruption and recreate value offerings.

# IMPLICATIONS FOR THE LEADERS, MANAGERS, AND SUPPORTING PROFESSIONALS

The disruption experience to date in most industries is just the beginning, in the same way that early disruptions of the digital camera, video rental, taxi, and photography industries were just the beginning.[33] Accelerating digital technology advancements will continue to raise customer expectations and change customer behaviors, introduce new competitors and raise the capabilities of existing competitors, change the bases of competition, and expand data availability. To remain competitive and ensure their continued existence, organizations must keep up with evolving digital technologies and find ways to leverage them to better respond to changing customer expectations and behaviors, counter changes in the competitive landscape and competitive dynamics, and adapt to unexpected changes in the external environment. This requires leaders, managers, and supporting professionals to continuously make sense of evolving digital technologies and to continuously explore how they can be used for breakthroughs in product/ service offerings, operational processes, and strategy.

# GOOGLE AND REFLECT

Disruptive technology, disruptive innovation, Digital Disruption, Digital innovation, Digital Platform, Digital Technology Infrastructure, Cloud Infrastructure, Bimodal IT, Operational Backbone, Digital Backbone, Business Ecosystem, Adaptability, Agility, Ambidexterity

# DISCUSSION QUESTIONS

1 What is the difference between the terms digital disruption, disruptive technology, and disruptive innovation?
2 How do digital technology advancements cause disruption?
3 What are the three types of disruption caused by the introduction of new digital technologies or breakthroughs in existing ones?
4 What are the different ways digital disruption manifests itself in an organization's financial performance?
5 What digital technology advancement has had the most disruptive impact on your industry in the last 10 years?
6 What digital technology trend is likely to have the most disruptive impact on your industry in the next 10 years?
7 What are the three common types of game changing opportunities that can be seized by leveraging digital technology advancements?
8 What is the difference between adaptability, agility, and ambidexterity?
9 How can an organization use digital technologies to enhance its adaptability?
10 How can an organization use digital technologies to enhance its agility?
11 How can an organization use digital technologies to enhance its ambidexterity?
12 What is the role of leaders, managers, and supporting professionals in guarding against digital disruption at their organizations?
13 What can management graduates do to contribute to the adaptability, agility, and ambidexterity of their organization?

# NOTES

1 Chapter is an adaptation of Busulwa, R., Evans, N., Oh, A., & Kang, M. (2020). Hospitality management and digital transformation: Balancing efficiency, agility and guest experience in the era of disruption (1st ed.). Routledge. https://doi.org/10.4324/9780429325205. pp 9–17.

2 Satell, G. (2018). How blockbuster, kodak and xerox really failed (It's not what you think). Retrieved April 25, 2020, from Inc.com website: www.inc.com/greg-satell/pundits-love-to-tell-these-three-famous-innovation-stories-none-of-them-are-true.html

3 Downes, L. & Nunes, P. (2013). Blockbuster becomes a casualty of big bang disruption. Retrieved April 26, 2020, from Harvard Business Review website: https://hbr.org/2013/11/blockbuster-becomes-a-casualty-of-big-bang-disruption

4 Frazier, M. (2011). The three lessons of the borders bankruptcy. *Forbes*. Retrieved April 25, 2020, from www.forbes.com/sites/myafrazier/2011/02/16/the-three-lessons-of-the-borders-bankruptcy/#3c1218242a1a

5 Vial, G. (2019). Understanding digital transformation: A review and a research agenda. *The Journal of Strategic Information Systems*, 28(2), 118–144.

6 Roser, M., & Ritchie, H. (2013). Technological progress. Retrieved April 23, 2020, from Our World in Data website: https://ourworldindata.org/technological-progress

7 Skog, D. A., Wimelius, H., & Sandberg, J. (2018). Digital disruption. *Business & Information Systems Engineering*, 60(5), 431–437. https://doi.org/10.1007/s12599-018-0550-4

8 Skog, D. A., Wimelius, H., & Sandberg, J. (2018). Digital disruption. *Business & Information Systems Engineering*, 60(5), 431–437. https://doi.org/10.1007/s12599-018-0550-4

9 Vial, G. (2019). Understanding digital transformation: A review and a research agenda. *The Journal of Strategic Information Systems*, 28(2), 118–144.

10 Vial, G. (2019). Understanding digital transformation: A review and a research agenda. *The Journal of Strategic Information Systems*, 28(2), 118–144.

11 Vial, G. (2019). Understanding digital transformation: A review and a research agenda. *The Journal of Strategic Information Systems*, 28(2), 118–144.

12 Vial, G. (2019). Understanding digital transformation: A review and a research agenda. *The Journal of Strategic Information Systems*, 28(2), 118–144. Reeves, M., & Deimler, M. (2009). New bases of competitive advantage. Retrieved April 26, 2020, from www.bcg.com website: www.bcg.com/

en-au/publications/2009/business-unit-strategy-new-bases-of-competitive-advantage.aspx

13 Vial, G. (2019). Understanding digital transformation: A review and a research agenda. *The Journal of Strategic Information Systems*, 28(2), 118–144.

14 Vial, G. (2019). Understanding digital transformation: A review and a research agenda. *The Journal of Strategic Information Systems*, 28(2), 118–144.

15 Satell, G. (2018). How blockbuster, kodak and xerox really failed (It's not what you think). Retrieved April 25, 2020, from Inc.com website: www.inc.com/greg-satell/pundits-love-to-tell-these-three-famous-innovation-stories-none-of-them-are-true.html

16 Goldstein, M. (2018). Dislocation and its discontents: Ride-sharing's impact on the taxi industry. *Forbes*. Retrieved from www.forbes.com/sites/michaelgoldstein/2018/06/08/uber-lyft-taxi-drivers/#6a5415559f0d

17 Danziger, P. N. (2018). Walmart doubles down on its transformation into a technology company. *Forbes*. Retrieved from www.forbes.com/sites/pamdanziger/2018/10/22/walmart-doubles-down-on-its-transformation-into-a-technology-company/#408a349b404c

18 Frazier, M. (2011). The three lessons of the borders bankruptcy. *Forbes*. Retrieved April 25, 2020, from www.forbes.com/sites/myafrazier/2011/02/16/the-three-lessons-of-the-borders-bankruptcy/#3c1218242a1a

19 Frazier, M. (2011). The three lessons of the borders bankruptcy. *Forbes*. Retrieved April 25, 2020, from www.forbes.com/sites/myafrazier/2011/02/16/the-three-lessons-of-the-borders-bankruptcy/#3c1218242a1a; Streitfeld, D. (2017). Bookstore chains, long in decline, are undergoing a final shakeout. *The New York Times*. Retrieved April 25, 2020, from www.nytimes.com/2017/12/28/technology/bookstores-final-shakeout.html; Abramovich, G. (2017). 5 Ways ways Amazon has disrupted retail – So so Farfar. (2020). Retrieved April 25, 2020, from CMO.adobe.com website: https://cmo.adobe.com/articles/2017/10/two-ways-amazon-is-disrupting-retail-and-advice-for-the-way-forward.html#gs.4zgb8m

20 Alley. (2011). You press the button. Kodak used to do the rest. Retrieved June 18, 2020, from MIT Technology Review website: www.technologyreview.com/2011/12/09/189254/you-press-the-button-kodak-used-to-do-the-rest/

21 Vial, G. (2019). Understanding digital transformation: A review and a research agenda. *The Journal of Strategic Information Systems*, 28(2), 118–144.

22 Vial, G. (2019). Understanding digital transformation: A review and a research agenda. *The Journal of Strategic Information Systems*, 28(2), 118–144.

23 Calder, N., Parvarandeh, S., & Brady, M. (2018). Building a direct-to-consumer strategy without alienating your distributors. Retrieved April 26, 2020, from Harvard Business Review website: https://hbr.org/2018/12/building-a-direct-to-consumer-strategy-without-alienating-your-distributors; Vial, G. (2019). Understanding digital transformation: A review and a research agenda. *The Journal of Strategic Information Systems*, 28(2), 118–144.

24 Vial, G. (2019). Understanding digital transformation: A review and a research agenda. *The Journal of Strategic Information Systems*, 28(2), 118–144.

25 Vial, G. (2019). Understanding digital transformation: A review and a research agenda. *The Journal of Strategic Information Systems*, 28(2), 118–144; Ref, R. (2019). How ecosystems create value for their members |. *Accenture*. Retrieved April 26, 2020, from Accenture.com website: www.accenture.com/au-en/insights/strategy/how-ecosystems-create-value-members

26 Foley, M. (2019). Microsoft to start selling more Azure services directly starting in March. Retrieved April 25, 2020, from ZDNet website: www.zdnet.com/article/microsoft-to-start-selling-more-azure-services-directly-starting-in-march/; Warren, T. (2013). Microsoft is now selling its Surface tablets direct to businesses. Retrieved April 25, 2020, from The Verge website: www.theverge.com/2013/3/19/4124400/microsoft-surface-business-order-site; Burke, S. (2013). Microsoft partners fuming at surface slight. Retrieved April 25, 2020, from CRN Australia website: www.crn.com.au/news/microsoft-partners-fuming-at-surface-slight-348654

27 Calder, N., Parvarandeh, S., & Brady, M. (2018). Building a direct-to-consumer strategy without alienating your distributors. Retrieved April 26, 2020, from Harvard Business Review website: https://hbr.org/2018/12/building-a-direct-to-consumer-strategy-without-alienating-your-distributors

28 Andal-Ancion, A., Cartwright, P.A., & Yip, G.S. (2003). The digital transformation of traditional business. Retrieved April 26, 2020, from MIT Sloan Management Review website: https://sloanreview.mit.edu/article/the-digital-transformation-of-traditional-business/

29 Ref, R. (2019). How ecosystems create value for their members. *Accenture*. Retrieved April 26, 2020, from Accenture.com website: www.accenture.com/au-en/insights/strategy/how-ecosystems-create-value-members

30 Eisenhardt, K. M., & Sull, D. N. (2001). Strategy as simple rules. *Harvard Business Review*, 79(1), 107–116; OptiStructure, Optimal. Market dynamism and the strategy of simple rules. Davis, Jason, Eisenhardt and Bingham. *Administrative Science Quarterly* 54(2009), 413–452; Davis, J., Eisenhardt, K. M.,

& Bingham, C. B. (2009) Optimal structure, market dynamism, and the strategy of simple rules. *Administrative Science Quarterly*, 54, 413–452.

31 Burgelman, R. A., & Grove, A. S. (2007). Let chaos reign, then rein in chaos – repeatedly: Managing strategic dynamics for corporate longevity. *Strategic Management Journal*, 28(10), 965–979; Busulwa, R., Tice, M., & Gurd, B. (2018). *Strategy execution and complexity: Thriving in the era of disruption.* Routledge.

32 Vial, G. (2019). Understanding digital transformation: A review and a research agenda. *The Journal of Strategic Information Systems*, 28(2), 118–144.

33 Satell, G. (2018). How blockbuster, kodak and xerox really failed (It's not what you think). Retrieved April 25, 2020, from Inc.com website: www.inc.com/greg-satell/pundits-love-to-tell-these-three-famous-innovation-stories-none-of-them-are-true.html

# CHAPTER 4

# The Digital Business and Digital Transformation Imperatives

DOI: 10.4324/9781003254614-5

# INTRODUCTION

No industry is immune to digital disruption. Customers expect organizations to deliver on the consumer benefits and promises of digital business. For example, customers expect benefits such as much higher levels of personalization, convenience and value, instantaneous customer service, novel experiences, and platforms that automatically integrate with their devices/apps and follow them everywhere. Digital business offers much more scope for customer value creation and experience, operational efficiency, new market creation, scalability, adaptability and agility, and staff satisfaction. But realizing the promise and benefits of digital business requires leaders, managers, and supporting professionals to understand the vision of digital business, the nature of business transformation required to realize this vision, and how to undertake such transformation successfully and safely. This chapter unpacks the nature, characteristics, and promise of digital business. It then explains the imperative for organizations to become digital businesses. It discusses digital business transformation and the challenges and risks associated with the journey to become a digital business. Finally, it discusses the implications for leaders, managers, and supporting professionals – that is, the unique roles they can play in accelerating and enhancing the success rate of digital business transformation efforts. On completion of this chapter, readers can expect to understand what they can do now and in future to build their digital business and digital transformation knowledge and competencies, leverage the knowledge and competencies to effectively lead or participate in digital transformation efforts at their current and future organizations, and leverage their knowledge, competencies, and digital leadership experiences to supercharge their career development.

## LEARNING OBJECTIVES

- Understand digital business and digital business transformation
- Understand the digital business and digital transformation imperatives

- Analyze and evaluate challenges and risks associated with digital business transformation
- Analyze and evaluate the implications of digital business transformation for managers, leaders, and their supporting professionals.

# DIGITAL BUSINESS
## PINNING DOWN A SLIPPERY TERM

World leading IT research firm, Gartner, defines digital business as the creation of new business designs by blurring the digital and physical worlds.[1] Forrester, another leading technology research firm, defines digital business as the use of digital assets and ecosystems to continually improve customer outcomes while, at the same time, continuously increasing operational agility. Yet another IT research firm, Aragon Research, defines a digital business as an organization with business models that enable it to proactively reach, serve, and support their customers and partners from their contextual perspective (i.e., from each customer's unique setting or environment, device, timing, etc.), rather than restricting them to what is defined by the business' traditional infrastructure.[2] Digital business has also been defined more simply as the use of digital technologies to enable major business improvements, such as enhancement of customer experience, operations optimization, and creation of new business models.[3]

Gartner's Jorge Lopez proposes that what makes digital business different from prior terms such as e-business, for example, is the presence and integration of connected and intelligent things with business processes and with people.[4] He adds that once objects (things) start to negotiate among themselves, as well as communicate with business processes and people, an entirely new world of potential becomes possible.[5] In the past, people were required to be proxies for objects at certain stages (e.g., turn them on, sense for them, transfer data to/from them, perform actions that required intelligence); but increasingly, human proxies are required less and less, as things become more intelligent (e.g., using data analytics, artificial intelligence), able to sense (e.g., using a vast array of sensors), able to communicate (e.g., exchange information with other things, processes and people via the cloud), able to take physical action (e.g., using robotic and drone capabilities), and more autonomous (e.g., aware of themselves and others, aware of the environment around them, and able to independently determine the optimal actions to take).[6]

Karel Dörner, a Senior Partner at McKinsey & Company, proposes that the promise of digital business is a universe of applications and digitized assets that almost automatically work together to deliver value and yield competitive advantage.[7] He adds that this promise requires companies to understand where the new frontiers of value are and to be open to reexamining their entire way of doing business.[8] Forrester's Nigel Fenwick puts it another way, saying that companies must think of their businesses as being part of a dynamic ecosystem that connects digital resources inside and outside the firm to create value for customers.[9] That is, not as a set of products and services, but as a personal value ecosystem that customers can assemble to suit their unique needs and desires. And that companies create greater value by increasing their role and value in customers' personal value ecosystems.[10] Either way, Karel Dörner adds that being a digital business, and realizing the promise of digital business, requires sophisticated engineering, integration, and orchestration capabilities.[11]

## DIGITAL BUSINESS AS A FUTURE STATE

Digital business is often described as a future state (i.e., how business should function once it becomes a digital business and what characteristics or capabilities it should have in order to function this way). Such characteristics and capabilities discussed to date include having a frictionless operating system (e.g., one that delivers easy communication/ interaction/engagement and collaboration across the value chain and between internal and external stakeholders).[12] They also include having a competitive digital platform strategy[13] (e.g., one that enables rapid value delivery, other stakeholders' technologies or platforms to integrate/

interact with the digital platform in a simple "plug and play" manner, easy self-service access to data insights, and stakeholders to run value creation improvement experiments safely and that ensures consistent/dependable customer experience). They further include designing products and customer experiences based on value as defined by the customer (e.g., leveraging technology to be where customers are, do things with them, walk in their shoes, and understand their preferences and habits). The characteristics and capabilities of a digital business include intelligence driven decision making or weaponization of data for competitive advantage (e.g., collecting, storing, cleaning, curating, featurizing, modeling, productionalizing, and leveraging to support operational and strategic execution). An increasingly discussed characteristic or capability of digital businesses is combining technical excellence and an engineering culture that gets things done/delivered (e.g., upgrading engineering skills and capabilities to world class level and cultivating an engineering culture that enables engineering to be more integrated into the business).

## DIGITAL BUSINESS AS A CHANGE JOURNEY OR CHANGE PROCESS

Digital business has also been described as a journey or process of change (i.e., what activities a business should undertake, and in what sequence, in order to become a digital business, to realize the promise of digital business, or to avert the dangers of not becoming a digital business). Such discussed required changes have included digitalizing stakeholder interactions/communications, business processes, business functions, and business models (i.e., turning them into more digital ones), then connecting and integrating them internally and externally, as well as with digitalized things internal and external to the organization.

They've also included enhancing the sensing (e.g., sensors), computational capacity (e.g., computation speed, sophistication), connectivity (e.g., connection speed, strength, distance, reliability), intelligence (e.g., data analytics, data science, artificial intelligence), autonomy (e.g., applications and things that can sense, make decisions, and take corresponding action independently – without human intervention), and scalability of business models/processes/technology platforms (e.g., being able to serve many more customers around the world quickly and at acceptable cost and risk). More recently, they have included activities such as enhancing customer engagement across a range of platforms and channels (e.g., desktop, mobile, social, video, IoT, video) and building digital strategy and digital innovation capability to be able to better sense, adapt to, and capitalize on new customer expectations and preferences.

Whether viewed as a future state or a change process, most organizations' digital business capability, functioning, or change journey exist across a digital business maturity continuum. On one end are digital natives like Google, Amazon, Microsoft, and Apple, who are very advanced in their digital business capabilities and functioning. On the other end of the continuum are businesses either turning a blind eye to advancing digital disruption or realizing the need for change but moving glacially to digitize, let alone digitalize most of their processes. The first category of organizations typically grow rapidly from strength to strength, entering new markets, disrupting dominant incumbents, making outsized profits, and expanding their influence and power. Of the second category of organizations, some are lucky enough to survive disruption when it eventually reaches them, and others experience a slow loss of relevance and finally death or sudden collapse. Most organizations are somewhere between these two extremes. Digital business maturity models, such as the one in Figure 4.1, attempt to measure and map an organization's digital business maturity across various digital business capabilities or outcome areas.

## BENEFITS OF BEING A DIGITAL BUSINESS

Organizations that undertake the journey to become digital businesses and compete as digital businesses open themselves up to a range of benefits. From a customer perspective, they expand their ability to engage with their customers, understand them, have an expanded understanding of their needs and preferences, offer them better value, and be able to enter other markets to acquire new customers. From a product

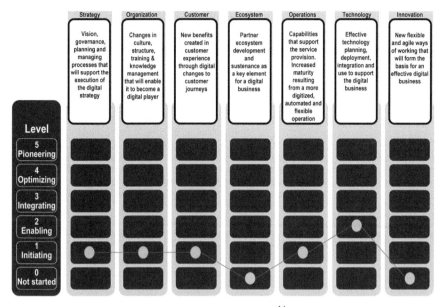

**Figure 4.1** *Digital business maturity models, like this one,[14] attempt to map where an organization is along various digital business capabilities or outcome areas*

perspective, digital businesses are better able to identify and act on new product/service/value delivery opportunities or to digitally enhance existing products/services. From an operations perspective, digital businesses can realize efficiency and effectiveness breakthroughs that nondigital businesses can't dream of (e.g., a nondigital business couldn't dream of the speed to market, employee productivity, process efficiency, or asset utilization of, say, Amazon or Google).

From a strategy perspective, digital businesses are able to employ novel, highly agile, and highly scalable business models (e.g., marketplaces, ecosystem platforms), unbundle offerings to offer customization/remove non-value adding aspects of a product (e.g., so customers can buy the one song they like for $2 instead of a whole album they won't listen to for $30), and unconstrain supply (e.g., have access to all suppliers rather just a few). From a decision-making perspective, digital businesses are able to access massive amounts of data from within and outside of the firm; they are able to optimally manage and use this data to make better and faster decisions (e.g., through access to real-time insights). In doing so, they weaponize data and make it a strong competitive capability. From a technology infrastructure perspective, digital businesses are able to assemble and integrate hardware, things, networks, software, and platforms to enable them to function optimally as a digital business. Finally, from a people perspective, digital businesses have enough people in the organization with the right digital mindsets (attitudes and behaviors) and skills (e.g., digital technology, digital business, and communication/influence skills) to effect a digital business culture (collective appreciation of the importance and urgency of becoming a digital business).

# THE DIGITAL BUSINESS IMPERATIVE

Chapter 3, on digital disruption, explained how digital technology advancements disrupt customer expectations and behaviors, the competitive field and bases of competition, and data availability. The chapter noted that this disruption creates existential threats for organizations not able to guard against it or adapt to it in a timely manner. It pointed to examples of disrupted organizations and industries such as Kodak, Blockbuster Video, Borders bookstores, the taxi industry, and the newspaper industry. The chapter also explained the game changing opportunities presented by digital technology advancements, which are essentially the promise of or opportunities available to digital businesses. The digital business imperative, then, is a four-pronged ultimatum for businesses. The first such ultimatum is to guard against and have the capacity to adapt to disruption (e.g., like Intel, Disney, and Caterpillar) or face certain death.[15] The second is to become a digital business so as to realize the promise of being a digital business or become sidelined by competitors who do so (ultimately leading to certain death).[16] The third is to continuously and sufficiently upgrade and leverage digital business capabilities to become the disruptor or still risk disruption from companies with superior digital business capabilities.[17] This is despite being a digital business. Finally, even though businesses may initiate efforts to guard against disruption, to build their capacity to adapt to disruption, to become digital businesses, and to leverage their digital business capabilities in order to become a disruptor, if they can't do it fast enough (relative to the speed of technology changes and/or the speed of existing competitors and new entrants), they may still risk disruption and death.[18]

# DIGITAL BUSINESS TRANSFORMATION
## DEFINING DIGITAL BUSINESS TRANSFORMATION

Like digital business, the term digital business transformation, often used interchangeably with digital transformation, is also a term with often opaque definitions. Gartner defines it as:

> . . . the process of exploiting digital technologies and supporting capabilities to create a robust new business model.[19]

Synthesizing the extant definitions of digital business transformation, University of Montreal Assistant Professor Gregory Vial defined it as:

> . . . a process that aims to improve an entity by triggering significant changes to its properties through combi-nations of information, computing, communication, and connectivity technologies.[20]

Michael Wade, Professor of Innovation and Strategy as well as Cisco Chair in Digital Business Transformation at IMD business school, and Donald Marchand, Professor of Strategy Execution and Information Management, offer a simpler definition of digital business transformation as:

> . . . organizational change through the use of digital technologies to materially improve performance.[21]

ZDNet's Mark Samuels adds that although the idea is to use digital technologies to make processes more efficient and effective, it's not just replicating those processes into digital form, rather, it is transforming them and, in turn, transforming the product/the business' offering into something significantly better.[22]

Salesforce, a leading cloud customer relationship management (CRM) platform, proposes this definition of digital transformation:

Digital transformation is the process of using digital technologies to create new – or modify existing – business processes, culture, and customer experiences to meet changing business and market requirements. This reimagining of business in the digital age is digital transformation.[23]

## DIGITAL BUSINESS TRANSFORMATION IS NOT JUST ABOUT DIGITAL TECHNOLOGIES

Bringing together the different definitions above, as well as the earlier definition of digital business, digital business transformation can be defined yet another way as the change process involved in becoming a digital business – thus, realizing the promise of being a digital business. Digital transformation researchers and practitioners point out the transformation to a digital business is not just about changes to the digital technologies used. It is also about changes to an organization's strategy (e.g., business models, bases of competition, strategy execution approach, adaptability, and agility), changes to its structure (e.g., organization hierarchy, business functions, roles, and responsibilities), changes to its processes (e.g., operational, functional, and strategic processes), changes to its workforce at all levels (e.g., hiring and retention choices, roles and responsibilities, hire and cultivate appropriate competencies, attitudes, and behaviors), and changes to its culture (e.g., collective attitudes and behaviors).[24]

## CHALLENGES AND RISKS OF DIGITAL BUSINESS TRANSFORMATION

In general, such all-encompassing change and transformation efforts have a low success rate, with management consultancy firm McKinsey estimating this success rate at about 30%. This means up to 70% of such change and transformation efforts fail to deliver. McKinsey further points out that the success rate of digital transformation efforts is even lower, at about 16%. A range of potential causes for this low success rate have been discussed. These include unspoken disagreement among senior managers about the goals and approach to digital transformation,[25] organizations not having the supporting

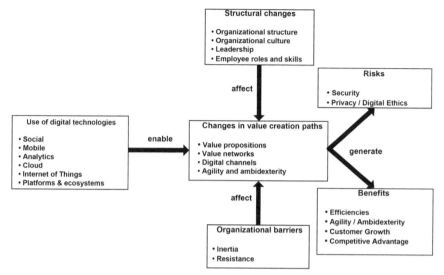

**Figure 4.2** *Digital business transformation is not just about using digital technologies; it is also about changing organization structures, overcoming change barriers, and managing both digital risks and change risks*[30]

digital capabilities to support the transformation (e.g., appropriately skilled people, technology infrastructure),[26] lack of a clear strategy and CEO sponsorship of it,[27] falling into the "let's wait and see" trap, not understanding what needs to change and how to go about it, challenges getting the right technology and/or the right talent to operate it, employee resistance to change or efforts to undermine the change, obsession with technology tools that don't meaningfully improve customer value, not changing fast enough, challenges sourcing top talent (e.g., technology leaders, digital strategists, designers, DevOps engineers, data scientists, artificial intelligence specialists, etc.),[28] and not dealing with employees' fears of being replaced.[29]

Successful digital transformation is the barrier between the existential threats of disruption and the promise or benefits of being a digital business. Thus, in spite of the low success rate, organizations invest in digital business transformation and navigate the obstacles and challenges because the alternative, digital disruption, has little upside. Figure 4.2 summarizes how use of digital technologies combines with structural changes to overcome organizational barriers to digital business transformation and to enable changes in value creation paths.

# THE DIGITAL TRANSFORMATION IMPERATIVE

The digital business imperative is the ultimatum for a business to become a digital business and leverage digital technologies to effectively compete as a digital business or risk their continued survival. Related to this imperative, the digital transformation imperative is the ultimatum for a business to undertake the change process of becoming a digital business safely, efficiently, and effectively or risk their continued survival. The business must safely, efficiently, and effectively undertake the structural, cultural, digital infrastructure, competency, and other changes. These changes are a prerequisite to delivering the necessary digitalization of business models, business processes, and products/services, as well as the optimization of digital business capabilities. As noted earlier, there are risks involved in undertaking digital transformation. If businesses don't undertake digital transformation, they open themselves to risk of disruption. If they undertake digital transformation but don't do so safely, the associated landmines in undertaking it can accelerate the organization's demise. If businesses undertake digital transformation but don't do it as fast as competitors and/or as fast as digital technologies are changing the business environment, then they still risk their competitiveness and future survival. The change process involved in becoming a digital business may be unique to each organization; each organization likely has unique structure, culture, capabilities/competencies, existing digital infrastructure, and environmental factors.

# IMPLICATIONS FOR LEADERS, MANAGERS, AND SUPPORTING PROFESSIONALS

Leaders at all levels are critical to effective responses to the digital business and business transformation imperatives. Only they can realign and sustain the investments in money, talent, time, incentives/disincentives, and organization attention that are necessary for such all-encompassing change and transformation undertakings. Absent their playing this role, digital transformation initiatives have very low odds of success. Professionals supporting leaders and managers are also critical to digital business and digital transformation efforts. For example, technology specialists can help ensure leaders and managers within the organization understand the ongoing threat of digital disruption from new or emerging technologies. They can help leaders/managers ensure that the organization adopts effective technology infrastructure to enable it to adapt to disruption. And they can help leaders/managers ensure that the organization is architecturally positioned to capitalize on emerging technology trends and opportunities. Technology specialists can also support leaders and managers to overcome any blockers or barriers they face in leveraging digital technologies to transform processes/products/business models. And they support leaders and managers to ensure the organization has effective data and cybersecurity capabilities for digital transformation to be undertaken safely and efficiently.

Similarly, line managers are vital links between the top management team and frontline employees. They translate top management team intentions to frontline and other employees. They translate top management team strategic initiatives into the component day-to-day actions that enable realization of those initiatives. They are responsible for hiring, performance development, and retention choices that impact organization culture and competencies within the organization. And they are responsible for modeling attitudes and behaviors aligned with top management team intentions. They also typically have a more intimate knowledge of internal processes, products/services, and customer relationships. Given this vital position they occupy and roles they play, they are critical to the success of digital transformation efforts. Through their actions (or lack of action) they can significantly enhance the chance of success or significantly derail it.

To leverage these important roles to enhance the odds of digital transformation success, leaders, managers, and supporting professionals can develop their digital business and digital transformation competencies, and then leverage these competencies to effectively lead or support digital transformation efforts. To develop their digital transformation competencies, they need to do the ongoing groundwork to understand and keep up with digital technology advancements (e.g., IoT, blockchain, artificial intelligence, satellite, and cloud computing advancements), understand and keep up with digital business and digital transformation (e.g., digital business characteristics, digital business strategy, digital business models, successful digital transformation approaches and cases, digital transformation leadership roles and responsibilities, etc.), and understand effective change and transformation methodologies (e.g., Agile, Lean, change management methodologies). Building on this groundwork, they can then develop digital technology, digital business, and digital transformation competencies (e.g., deep and broad technical technology and data skills, strategic technology skills, digital leadership skills, strategic thinking skills, cross functional leadership and change management skills, etc.). Further, they can build informal networks vertically and across the organization that are important for accelerating strategy execution.

Having developed the aforementioned digital business and digital transformation competencies, leaders, managers, and support professionals can then leverage these competencies to accelerate and improve the odds of success of digital transformation efforts. For example, they can use their digital transformation and digital business knowledge and skills to cultivate the digital business and digital transformation competencies of their direct reports and other people across the organization. They can shape appropriate digital business and digital transformation attitudes and behaviors, thus helping nurture the digital culture to support digital business transformation efforts. They can ensure the hiring of direct reports and other employees with appropriate digital business and digital transformation attitudes and skills. They can leverage their digital business and digital transformation knowledge/skills to take on and successfully carry out one or more key digital transformation leadership roles (e.g., Chief Digital Officer, Project/Program Manager, Operating Model Lead, Customer Engagement Lead, Digital Product Manager, Ethics Compliance Lead, UX Designer, Change and Transformation specialist, etc.).[31] They can leverage their informal networks to accelerate implementation of transformation initiatives, and to encourage frontline staff to understand and accept transformation related changes. Finally, they can leverage their technology and data skills to work hand in hand with technologists, service delivery staff, and the rest of the executive team to accelerate and minimize the risks of transformation efforts. The alternative to building and leveraging the digital business and digital transformation knowledge and competencies we've described above is for leaders, managers, and support professionals to become one more of the many bottlenecks or barriers to overcome in digital transformation efforts.

# GOOGLE AND REFLECT

Digitization, digitalization, digital business, digital business transformation, digital transformation, digital business capabilities, digital business competencies, digital platforms, digital strategy, omnichannel strategy, scalability, digital customer engagement, digital customer experience, Agile methodologies, Lean methodologies, digital accelerator, user story, customer touch point, digital business imperative, digital transformation imperative, user-centered design

# DISCUSSION QUESTIONS

1. What is the difference between the terms digital transformation and digital business transformation?
2. What is the difference between the terms digital business and digital business transformation?
3. Which of the definitions of digital business transformation provided in this chapter makes the most sense to you? Why?
4. What does the common assertion that "digital transformation is not about technology" mean?
5. Are any businesses you know of fully digital businesses? If not, what can make them fully digital businesses?

6 Once an organization becomes a digital business, does it have any need for digital transformation?

7 What is meant by the assertion that digital business is ". . . a change process or a journey"?

8 What is meant by the assertion that digital business is ". . . a future state"?

9 What are the top four benefits of being a digital business? Why are they more important than other benefits?

10 What is the digital business imperative?

11 People often talk about digital business imperative and digital transformation imperative. Are these the same or different?

12 What are some challenges and risks of digital business transformation?

13 What is the success rate for transformation efforts in general? What is the success rate for digital transformation efforts? Why is the success rate for digital transformation efforts much worse?

14 What are two important implications of digital business and digital business transformation for leaders, managers, and support professionals?

15 What are five things leaders, managers, and support professionals can do to maximize their organizations' chances of succeeding at digital transformation?

# NOTES

1 Gartner Inc. (2014). Digital business. Retrieved April 28, 2020, from Gartner website: www.gartner.com/en/information-technology/glossary/digital-business

2 Aragon Research. (2020). Defining digital business – Business and IT glossary. (2019). Retrieved May 20, 2020, from Aragon Research website: https://aragonresearch.com/glossary-digital-business/

3 Chaffey, D. (2015). *Digital business and e-commerce management: Strategy, implementation and practice* (6th edn). Financial Times Prentice Hall

4 Lopez, J. (2014). Digital business is everyone's business. *Forbes.* Retrieved from www.forbes.com/sites/gartnergroup/2014/05/07/digital-business-is-everyones-business/#636bd0da7f82

5 Lopez, J. (2014). Digital business is everyone's business. *Forbes*. Retrieved from www.forbes.com/sites/gartnergroup/2014/05/07/ digital-business-is-everyones-business/#636bd0da7f82

6 Lopez, J. (2014). Digital business is everyone's business. *Forbes*. Retrieved from www.forbes.com/sites/gartnergroup/2014/05/07/ digital-business-is-everyones-business/#636bd0da7f82

7 Dörner, K., & Edelman, D. (2015). What 'digital' really means. Retrieved April 28, 2020, from McKinsey & Company website: www.mckinsey.com/ industries/technology-media-and-telecommunications/our-insights/ what-digital-really-means

8 Dörner, K., & Edelman, D. (2015). What 'digital' really means. Retrieved April 28, 2020, from McKinsey & Company website: www.mckinsey.com/ industries/technology-media-and-telecommunications/our-insights/ what-digital-really-means

9 Sacolick, I. (2017). *Driving digital: The leader's guide to business transformation through technology*. Amacom.

10 Fenwick, N. (2015). Unleash your digital predator. Retrieved May 22, 2020, from Forrester website: https://go.forrester.com/ blogs/15-12-09-unleash_your_digital_predator/

11 Dörner, K., & Edelman, D. (2015). What 'digital' really means. Retrieved April 28, 2020, from McKinsey & Company website: www.mckinsey.com/ industries/technology-media-and-telecommunications/our-insights/ what-digital-really-means

12 Swords, J. (2020). Becoming a modern digital business in 2020. *Thoughtworks*. Retrieved May 22, 2020, from Thoughtworks.com website: www. thoughtworks.com/perspectives/edition8-modern-digital-business-article

13 Swords, J. (2020). Becoming a modern digital business in 2020. *Thoughtworks*. Retrieved May 22, 2020, from Thoughtworks.com website: www. thoughtworks.com/perspectives/edition8-modern-digital-business-article; Gupta, S. (2018). *Driving digital strategy: A guide to reimagining your business*. Harvard Business Press.

14 Valdez-de-Leon, O. (2016). A digital maturity model for telecommunications service providers. *Technology Innovation Management Review*, 6(8).

15 Stanek, R. (2018). Council post: Why it's important to make your company the disruptor, not the disrupted. *Forbes*. Retrieved from www.forbes.com/sites/ forbestechcouncil/2018/06/04/why-its-important-to-make-your-company-the-disruptor-not-the-disrupted/#4ddb3e8331a6; Vial, G. (2019). Understanding

digital transformation: A review and a research agenda. *The Journal of Strategic Information Systems*, 28(2), 118–144; Schadler, T., Fenwick, N. (2017) The digital business imperative. Retrieved May 22, 2020, from Forrester.com website: www.forrester.com/report/The+Digital+Business+Imperative/-/E-RES115784

16  Schadler, T., Fenwick, N. (2017) The digital business imperative. Retrieved May 22, 2020, from Forrester.com website: www.forrester.com/report/The+Digital+Business+Imperative/-/E-RES115784; Stanek, R. (2018). Council post: Why it's important to make your company the disruptor, not the disrupted. *Forbes*. Retrieved from www.forbes.com/sites/forbestechcouncil/2018/06/04/why-its-important-to-make-your-company-the-disruptor-not-the-disrupted/#4ddb3e8331a6; Vial, G. (2019). Understanding digital transformation: A review and a research agenda. *The Journal of Strategic Information Systems*, 28(2), 118–144.

17  Stanek, R. (2018). Council post: Why it's important to make your company the disruptor, not the disrupted. *Forbes*. Retrieved from www.forbes.com/sites/forbestechcouncil/2018/06/04/why-its-important-to-make-your-company-the-disruptor-not-the-disrupted/#4ddb3e8331a6; Fenwick, N. (2015). Unleash your digital predator. Retrieved May 22, 2020, from Forrester website: https://go.forrester.com/blogs/15-12-09-unleash_your_digital_predator/; Stanek, R. (2018). Why it's important to make your company the disruptor, not the disrupted. *Forbes*. Retrieved from www.forbes.com/sites/forbestechcouncil/2018/06/04/why-its-important-to-make-your-company-the-disruptor-not-the-disrupted/#4ddb3e8331a6

18  Ross, J. (2018). Jeanne Ross | digital is about speed – but it takes a long time. Retrieved May 22, 2020, from MIT Sloan Management Review website: https://sloanreview.mit.edu/article/digital-is-about-speed-but-it-takes-a-long-time/; Brown, S. (2020). Strategy at the speed of digital. Retrieved May 22, 2020, from McKinsey & Company website: www.mckinsey.com/business-functions/strategy-and-corporate-finance/our-insights/strategy-at-the-speed-of-digital

19  Gartner. (2018). Gartner glossary: Digital business transformation. Retrieved May 22, 2020, from Gartner website: www.gartner.com/en/information-technology/glossary/digital-business-transformation

20  Vial, G. (2019). Understanding digital transformation: A review and a research agenda. *The Journal of Strategic Information Systems*, 28(2), 118–144.

21  Marchand, D. A., & Wade, M. R. (2014). Digital business transformation: Where is your company on the journey. Retrieved May 22, 2020, from

IMD business school website: www.imd.org/research-knowledge/articles/ digital-business-transformation-where–is-your-company-on-the-journey/

22  Samuels, M. (2018). What is digital transformation? Everything you need to know about how technology is reshaping business. Retrieved May 22, 2020, from ZDNet website: www.zdnet.com/article/what-is-digital-transformation-everything-you-need-to-know-about-how-technology-is-reshaping/

23  Salesforce. (2018). What is digital transformation? A definition by salesforce. Retrieved May 22, 2020, from Salesforce.com website: www.salesforce.com/ products/platform/what-is-digital-transformation/

24  Vial, G. (2019). Understanding digital transformation: A review and a research agenda. *The Journal of Strategic Information Systems*, 28(2), 118–144.

25  Sutcliff, M., Narsalay, R., & Sen, A. (2019). The two big reasons that digital transformations fail. *Harvard Business Review*. Retrieved May 22, 2020, from Harvard Business Review website: https://hbr.org/2019/10/ the-two-big-reasons-that-digital-transformations-fail

26  Sutcliff, M., Narsalay, R., & Sen, A. (2019). The two big reasons that digital transformations fail. *Harvard Business Review*. Retrieved May 22, 2020, from Harvard Business Review website: https://hbr.org/2019/10/ the-two-big-reasons-that-digital-transformations-fail

27  Boulton, C. (2019). 12 reasons why digital transformations fail. *CIO*. Retrieved May 22, 2020, from CIO website: www.cio.com/article/3248946/ 12-reasons-why-digital-transformations-fail.html

28  Boulton, C. (2019). 12 reasons why digital transformations fail. *CIO*. Retrieved May 22, 2020, from CIO website: www.cio.com/article/3248946/ 12-reasons-why-digital-transformations-fail.html

29  Tabrizi, B., Lam, E., Girard, K. & Irvin, V. (2019). Digital transformation is not about technology. *Harvard Business Review*. Retrieved May 22, 2020, from Harvard Business Review website: https://hbr.org/2019/03/ digital-transformation-is-not-about-technology

30  Vial, G. (2019). Understanding digital transformation: A review and a research agenda. *The Journal of Strategic Information Systems*, 28(2), 118–144.

31  Boulton, C. (2018). 8 essential roles for a successful digital transformation. Retrieved May 22, 2020, from CIO website: www.cio.com/article/3258767/8-essential-roles-for-a-successful-digital-transformation.html

# Part II

# Forming and Executing Digital Transformation Strategy

# CHAPTER 5

# Forming Digital Transformation Strategy

DOI: 10.4324/9781003254614-7

# INTRODUCTION

Digital transformation strategy and digital business strategy are inextricably linked. Whereas the former focuses on how to best undertake the change process involved in becoming a digital business, the latter focuses on the type of digital business an organization should become. Without effective digital transformation strategy, digital business strategy is unlikely to be realized. And without a clear digital business strategy, the change process involved in becoming a digital business lacks clear vision/direction. Ultimately though, both digital transformation strategy and digital business strategy have the shared aim of effecting the building and optimization of digital business capabilities – capabilities that enable an organization to repeatedly and reliably function as a competitive digital business. This chapter discusses the aims of, and interrelationships between, digital transformation strategy, digital business strategy, and digital business capabilities. It then provides an approach to initially forming the digital transformation strategy when an organization may not have a digital business strategy. As well, the chapter provides an approach for ongoing digital transformation strategy making.

---

### LEARNING OBJECTIVES

- Understand digital business and digital transformation strategy formation
- Analyze digital business and digital transformation strategy needs
- Apply digital business and digital transformation strategy formation concepts to form digital business and digital transformation strategies
- Evaluate digital business and digital transformation strategies

---

# DIGITAL TRANSFORMATION STRATEGY VS DIGITAL BUSINESS STRATEGY

Digital transformation strategy is strategy that focuses on how to best undertake the change process involved in becoming a digital business.[1] This seems straightforward enough – except that there are different types of digital businesses[2] (i.e., if we consider the digitalization of their products/services, their business models, and their digital business capabilities). Also, digital businesses are typically on a digital maturity continuum[3] (with some being nascent digital businesses that may have just completed their first digital transformation, and others being more mature digital businesses with sophisticated digital business models and digital capabilities – like those of Netflix, Google, or Facebook). This digital maturity continuum conceptualization of a digital business is perhaps why digital business is also defined as an ongoing change process or ongoing journey to become more digitally mature. The implication of this conceptualization of a digital business for digital transformation strategy is that digital transformation strategy is strategy that focuses on undertaking the ongoing change process involved in becoming both a particular type of digital business, and also of a becoming a more digitally mature version of that type of digital business. For example, one business may choose to become a digital disruptor business, another may choose to become a digital platform business or ecosystem orchestrator business, and yet another may choose to be a proudly analog business with select digital business capabilities or processes. In this example, digital transformation refers to the ongoing change process involved in becoming one of the aforementioned types of digital businesses, and also the ongoing change process involved in becoming a more digitally mature version of that type of digital business.

There is often confusion about which comes first – digital transformation strategy or digital business strategy. It was noted earlier that digital business strategy refers to the making and execution of strategy that leverages digital resources and assets to create strategic benefits such as efficiency, differentiation, adaptability, agility, and longevity.[4] These strategic benefits are often incapsulated in the type of digital business an organization is or seeks to become, and the intended digital maturity level of that type of digital business that an organization is pursuing. Thus, digital transformation strategy can be thought of as an enabler or a subset of digital business strategy. Viewed this way, digital business strategy specifies the type of digital business an organization should or aims to become, the characteristics and capabilities it should develop to become so, and what of the desired future state the organization should pursue in particular time periods given the internal and external constraints of that time period. Digital transformation strategy then specifies how to best undertake the change process involved in becoming that type of digital business in the long term and in achieving the desired future digital business strategy prescribes for particular time periods.

Many strategic leaders may start pursuing digital transformation prior to having a digital business strategy or perhaps even before understanding what digital business strategy is. In such cases, while considering how to best undertake the change process involved in becoming a digital business, strategic leaders are likely to be drawn into envisioning the digital business future state they should transform to – that is, into thinking through the nature or type of digital business they should become after the transformation. And, further, they may be drawn into thinking through how that digital business should function, what value it should create and for whom, and what digital business capabilities it should have in order to function as desired or to create the desired value. Not everything envisioned will be achievable at once, thus strategic leaders will be forced to stage or phase the journey to the envisioned future state –that is, to consider what aspects of the envisioned future state will be pursued in different time periods given the internal and external constraints of that time period (e.g., funding, talent availability, customer readiness, competitor activity, political/legal/economic/social/ethical issues). In being drawn into envisioning the desired digital business future state, strategic leaders are essentially undertaking some level of digital business strategy formation, or an iteration of digital business strategy formation. The level of digital business strategy formation they undertake is likely to be limited by their understanding of digital transformation and digital business. Thus, digital transformation strategy ideally first involves having or forming an iteration of digital business strategy formation. The term iteration is used to suggest that digital business strategy is an ongoing and iterative process of forming strategy, executing it, learning from the results of execution and using that learning in the next iteration (e.g., which would restart with refining the strategy or discarding it and forming a better one).

# DIGITAL TRANSFORMATION STRATEGY CAVEATS

## DIGITAL TRANSFORMATION IS NOT A SINGLE INITIATIVE AND DOES NOT HAVE AN OVERALL END STATE

"Before further discussing how strategic leaders can go about forming digital transformation strategy, the paragraphs that follow outline some important caveats any digital transformation strategy should accomodate."

It is important to define the type of digital business an organization aims to become and to establish a clear future state of that digital business. But the change process involved in becoming that type of digital business and realizing the future state digital business envisioned is unlikely to occur in a single initiative. Typically, it occurs through the delivery of a range of related initiatives that build on one another to bring about the desired future state (e.g., recruit and incentivize the team to drive digital transformation, undertake sufficient culture change to enable the implementation of the core digital platform, acquire and implement a core digital platform for the organization to induce more extensive cultural and process changes). Pursuit of these initiatives typically also needs to dynamically be adapted to changing internal and external conditions (e.g., digital technology advancements, customer needs, competitor and vendor actions, economic and financial constraints). Initiatives are typically grouped into related workstreams, and their occurrence scheduled or staged for occurrence in the most optimal sequence. Thus, it is unlikely for digital transformation to successfully be undertaken as a single big initiative. Also, while staged delivery of a program or collection of initiatives may get the organization to its desired future state, that is not necessarily an end state to the organization's digital transformation imperative. Digital technology advancements will continue to drive digital disruptions, which will require corresponding changes to the type and maturity of digital business an organization needs to be. Thus, it makes sense that digital transformation needs to be an ongoing and never-ending process in line with ongoing and never-ending digital disruption driven by digital technology advancement. Where digital transformation isn't an ongoing and never-ending process, significant and dangerous transformations (e.g., bigger, or much faster, or much riskier than ideal) may be needed to make up for periods of inaction.

There are a range of implication for digital transformation leaders from this caveat. For example, one is that they don't need to try and do it all at once – in fact, this may be more dangerous than not doing anything. Two, they can strategically divide the transformation strategy into initiatives and innitiative groups; they can strategically sequence the execution of those initiatives; and they can dynamically adapt the execution of initiatives to changing internal and external opportunities/threats. Three, leaders need to ensure that digital transformation efforts undertaken today optimally position the organization for future and ongoing digital transformations.

## SOLUTIONS, REQUIREMENTS, AND TECHNOLOGIES CHANGE FAST AND CONTINUOUSLY DURING DIGITAL TRANSFORMATIONS

Digital technology advancements are occurring at an exponential rate, are increasingly more pervasive, and increasingly require greater integration. From a technology adoption perspective, this means that leaders should expect their digital transformation efforts to continuously be disrupted (e.g., by the introduction of new or better technologies than the ones they are adopting, by the expansion of digital solution requirements, by the rise of new or better technology vendors, and by the emergence of better ways of undertaking digital transforming [e.g., Agile, Lean startup, change acceleration, accelerator, hackathon methods]). One implication of this caveat for leaders/managers/professionals is that taking action and making progress is generally more beneficial than waiting to do things perfectly (e.g., getting a viable digital platform in place this year is better than taking 3 years to find the "perfect" one). Another implication is that the chosen strategy and platforms should be flexible to change without significant waste. For example, if the viable digital platform implemented in year 1 needs to be changed in year 3 it should be able to be changed without prohibitive costs (e.g., perhaps the organization acquired a platform in such a way as not to have huge contract cancellation costs, perhaps it acquired a platform that is integration friendly so as to allow integration of a range of other technologies and vendor products, or perhaps the platform was acquired on a month-by-month subscription basis allowing scalable consumption in line with the organization's changing service provision levels). Yet another implication for digital transformation leaders is that they should effect digital transformation or organization readiness for digital transformation in such a way as to not materially erode the organization's will for future and ongoing digital transformation (e.g., leaders could ensure that employees see any solution, requirement, or technology as an iteration in an ongoing quest to have solutions and technologies that optimize competitiveness and organization longevity).

## IT'S EXTRAORDINARILY EASY AND DANGEROUS TO BUY INTO THE HYPE OR CYNICISM RELATING TO ONE OR MORE DIGITAL TECHNOLOGY ADVANCEMENTS

The Gartner Hype Cycle depicts the typical stages new or significant digital technology advancements go through during adoption in terms of overall awareness of them, expectations of what they can do, what they can actually do, the types of customers adopting them, and the number of customers adopting them. The Gartner Hype Cycle highlights how initially when a new digital technology is introduced, awareness of it and expectations of it grow almost exponentially to reach a "peak of inflated expectations". This is a point at which the expectations of what the technology can do far exceed what it can actually do. Subsequent adoption and disappointment by organizations when the technology does not deliver anywhere near the inflated expectations leads to a crash in expectations or what the model refers to as the "trough of disillusionment" – where the expectations of the technology are likely well below its actual potential. In spite of the crash in expectations, iterations and improvements in the technology and its use cases continue until more and more businesses and consumers start to see the "aha" moment in terms of the technology's true business value and impact – what the model refers to as the "slope of enlightenment". After the "aha" moment, businesses find more and better ways to use the technology to enhance competitiveness. In contrast to Gartner's Hype Cycle, Rogers' Diffusion of Innovations model depicts how in the early days of a technology (e.g., from its introduction to the slope of enlightenment), it is usually mostly innovators and early adopters (e.g., mostly the highly curious, the technology enthusiasts, or those with faith in the technology's potential) who are the initial adopters and who stick with the technology long enough to see it through various iterations until it reaches mainstream acceptance. Eventually mainstream adoption occurs. However, even after all the time it typically takes for mainstream acceptance and adoption to occur, there are still organizations who don't adopt a technology almost until everyone has done so – who the model refers to as the "laggards".

There can be a competitiveness and organization survival risk to not adopting necessary technologies or adopting them too late (e.g., consider the cases of Kodak, Blockbuster, Borders). Typically, this lack of adoption is due to organization leaders becoming cynical about the business value or reliability of one or more technologies (perhaps due to past adoption efforts that didn't deliver – maybe due to adoption at the peak of inflated expectations). This cynicism can blind leaders to ongoing and rapid advances in the capacity, reliability, and business value of these technologies.

Their cynicism may eventually be broken by digital disruption that forces the organization to fight for its survival in a high stakes transformation imperative. Related to this cynicism and its risks, famed management theorist Clayton Christensen warns leaders against ignoring technologies that don't initially meet the needs of their mainstream customers.[5] In contrast to buying into cynicism, leaders can also buy into the hype (or the inflated expectations). This can cause them to over invest in, or over rely on, one or more digital technologies, resulting in financial losses, customer disappointment, talent losses, and workforce cynicism when such investments fail and put the organization in a difficult position (e.g., where it has to lay off staff, restructure, get acquired, or fight for its survival). Thus, it is extraordinarily easy and dangerous to buy into the hype or cynicism. Leaders must maintain an open, reality informed, and evolving understanding of technology advancements to make the most of them.

## AMONG ALL THE CHANGES REQUIRED, PEOPLE AND CULTURAL CHANGES ARE THE MOST IMPORTANT

Ultimately, the right people enable an organization to adopt new digital technologies, leverage digital technologies to effect more sophisticated processes (e.g., intelligent, automated, autonomous processes), and to transform products/services. If you don't have the right people to lead digital transformation and the right people to use the technology in the way it should be used, the technology may be useless. The right people are typically existing leaders and employees who deeply understand business processes and the needs of organization stakeholders and are equipped with the skills required to adopt and use the new technologies in the right way. These people can be contrasted to new hires who may have the required technology skills but not the deep knowledge of business processes and stakeholder needs. Alternatively, the right people may be a mixture of both of the aforementioned groups. But they need to be able to coexist and work together effectively. Getting existing employees to acquire needed skills, disrupt their existing ways of working, and optimally leverage digital technologies requires cultural, attitudinal, and behavioral changes. With the right culture, attitudes, and behaviors, digital transformation can occur faster and with far greater success odds. Without the right Culture, attitudes, and behaviors, digital transformation efforts may be doomed to failure – in spite of the sophisticated technologies acquired, the imperative to transform processes, and the needs of customers for digital products/services. The implication for leaders is that they must understand the people and cultural change needs, hone and apply their change management skills to effectively facilitate people and cultural change, and optimally invest in having the right skills for digital transformation.

## KNOWING THE POINT AT WHICH THINGS ARE MATURE ENOUGH AND SHOULD SCALE IS A TEST OF REAL UNDERSTANDING

As noted earlier, digital technologies typically go through cycles of inflated expectations, disappointment and disillusionment, and finally delivering on, or even overdelivering on, the original inflated expectations. This has important implication for organizations taking an experiment, embed, and scale approach to the adoption of digital technologies. Their experimentation may reveal that a technology has real and significant business value for the organization right now. However, the technology may not be yet advanced enough or reliable enough – or customers may not be ready to embrace it. Alternatively, the technology may be advanced enough and reliable enough, but customers may not be ready to embrace it, or employees may not have the requisite skills to use the technology. Therefore, leaders have to keep their finger on the pulse of advancements/ developments in that technology to know when it is matured enough for scaled adoption, they have to keep their finger on the pulse of internal readiness to scale successful experiments with that technology, and they have to keep their finger on the pulse of customer or stakeholder readiness to adopt products/services incorporating that technology. This is a test of real ongoing understanding of the technology, the organizations adoption readiness, and customer or stakeholder adoption readiness.

## DIGITAL TRANSFORMATIONS CAN'T WAIT AND WON'T HAPPEN OVERNIGHT

As discussed earlier, digital technology advancements are occurring at an exponential rate and are increasingly more pervasive across societies, industries, markets, and technology standards. This means digital disruption is likely occurring faster and from all directions (e.g., it could drive or manifest itself as industry disruption, geographic disruption, product disruption, technology standards disruption, customer disruption, societal disruption). Even for organizations at which it might not seem like digital disruption is occurring, this non-apparent disruption will gradually manifest itself as gradual instability (e.g., in revenues, product/service quality, staff satisfaction, crises) until a bifurcation point is reached, at which the organization has to pull off an emergency and high stakes transformation or cease to exist.[6] Whether ongoing and accelerating digital disruptions driven by exponential digital technology advancements are obvious or not, organizations need to undertake ongoing digital transformation. Thus, digital transformation can't wait; any waiting is likely to need a correspondingly bigger transformation which comes with a correspondingly bigger risk of failure. While digital transformation should be done as fast as digital technology advancements are occurring and as fast as the organization is able to be prepared to effectively undertake digital transformation, attempting to do it all at once or doing too much too fast may create more risks than not undertaking it at all. The implications for leaders are that they should remember that they need to digitally transformation straight away, that they should plan and execute with the understanding that they are starting an ongoing and never-ending process, and that they need to keep the initiatives they are undertaking aligned with what technologies are really able to deliver and what initiatives the organization is really in a position to deliver on in the particular timeframe.

## DIGITAL TRANSFORMATION CAN BE FINANCIALLY RUINOUS, BUT IT DOESN'T HAVE TO BE

There are ample case studies of digital transformations that involved massive technology investments and disrupted revenue from traditional operations, only to be abruptly scrapped partway through to avoid the risk of their dragging the business down with them. But digital transformations don't have to occur on such a large scale, involve massive investments, or disrupt operations in such a financially costly way.[7] In fact, most organizations are moving away from such "big bang" transformations and the big risks they come with.[8] They are instead favoring (and having more success with) dividing digital transformation objectives into smaller, less resource intensive, and more manageable streams of initiatives that can be pursued in a measured, iterative manner to build on each other and effect staged delivery of transformation objectives.[9] This better enables easier adaptation to the changing internal and external context in which digital transformation occurs (e.g., a context of ongoing talent departures, changing customer needs, economic and social disruptions).

## DIGITAL TRANSFORMATION ISN'T JUST FOR BIG COMPANIES

The digital transformations that usually make case studies and newspaper or blog front pages are usually those of large complex organizations. While such transformations may be more noteworthy and gain more attention, the digital transformation imperative applies to all organizations. Small businesses in particular may have far more to gain from digital transformation given they typically have more limited access to large workforces, professional talent, specialist departments, and big growth budgets. Digital transformation can enable small businesses to circumvent such limitations (e.g., by accessing global talent remotely at a fraction of the cost, enabling 24/7 work, overcoming geographic limitations, and scaling the business to previously unimaginable levels). For example, in 2019 Craigslist operated in over 70 countries, turned over more than $1 billion, and yet had an estimated workforce of only 50 employees. Effectively used, digital technology advancements offer this type of scalability and/or efficiency/effectiveness opportunity for small businesses. Although they may lack the big budgets and large teams, undertaking digital transformation is likely to be much simpler for small businesses. For example, preparing a workforce of 10–20 people to undertake digital transformation is likely to be much simpler than doing the same for a workforce of thousands who are dispersed across the globe and who use thousands of legacy systems to carry out many opaque yet interconnected processes.

## TRADITIONAL IT DEPARTMENTS OR EQUIVALENT TECHNOLOGY TEAMS ARE VITAL TO DIGITAL TRANSFORMATION

As digital transformation leaders envision the type of digital business they want to become, the role of traditional IT departments or teams may not factor into those visions. And it may be tempting for digital transformation leaders to disregard or even shun traditional IT departments or technology teams' involvement in digital transformation efforts – favoring instead more inspiring digital leaders such as chief digital officers, digital business/transformation consultants, or technology evangelists. But not involving the IT department or its equivalent in the organization would be a terrible mistake. First, the IT department understands the technology and vendor landscape, the skills needed/available/accessible to deploy new technologies, and the likely implementation impacts/landmines/opportunities. Second, IT departments and their equivalents are optimally positioned to play critical roles in data management and analytics, technology architecture and infrastructure management, technology sourcing and vendor management, and management/oversight of software development efforts. Third, IT departments or teams often have strong relationships/goodwill with people across the broad organization and intimate understanding of processes across the organization. Disregarding such an in-house blend of technical and business expertise would be folly, even in organizations where such departments may have limited versions of that expertise. Digital transformation is an opportunity to reorient attitudes toward IT, better engage and involve the IT department or equivalent teams in business partnering, and better leverage the IT team's technical expertise/technical support capability/technology implementation leadership capability. Engaged and involved effectively, IT can play a vital role in effectively transitioning between where the business has been, where it currently is, and where it aims to be. For example, IT may intuitively understand where the operational bottlenecks, customer pain points, or cybersecurity issues relating to new digital platforms are likely to lie and take action to plug them. They are likely to understand aspects of legacy technologies or systems that need to be transitioned with care. And they are likely to know the typical organization barriers and effective approaches to technology adoption.

## DIGITAL TRANSFORMATION IS ULTIMATELY ABOUT BOTH KEEPING AND CREATING CUSTOMERS THROUGH OFFERING BETTER VALUE

Digital transformation is ultimately about sustainably delivering competitive or differentiated customer experience and value – which keeps customers and bringing in new customers. Technology adoption and the organization transformation it enables have the ultimate aims of having more resources available to invest in customer experience and value creation/delivery, better carrying out customer experience and value delivery processes, and enhancing the organization's ability to adapt to events that risk disrupting the organization's future value creation/delivery. Thus, any digital transformation objective or initiative should have the overarching aim of optimizing current and long-term customer experience and value and, where unavoidable, limiting negative impacts on customer experience and value.

# FORMING THE INITIAL AND SUBSEQUENT STRATEGY
## FORMING THE INITIAL DIGITAL BUSINESS STRATEGY AND DIGITAL TRANSFORMATION STRATEGY

The initial digital business strategy and digital transformation strategy formed by leaders are likely to have significant limitations. Thus, it is henceforth referred to as preliminary – since it can be thought of as an initial draft that needs many ongoing markups, additions, and refinements prior to becoming the final version. Many of the insights driving changes to the initial or preliminary digital business strategy and digital transformation strategy will occur during execution, as strategic leaders better understand the line between the ideals and realities of digital transformation and digital business strategy (e.g., what is really technically possible, what will customers/stakeholders accept, what is too dangerous to attempt, what is do or die). In the sections that follow, a simple outline of one approach to forming both the initial and subsequent digital business strategy and digital transformation strategy is provided. This approach envisions a strategic leader or a group of strategic leaders forming and leading the execution of digital business strategy and digital transformation strategy without the support of consultants who may be able to make the strategy formation process easier. It assumes that they have already undertaken strategic analysis of the external and internal environment and are clear on the organization's strengths and weaknesses, as well as opportunities and threats.

### Forming the Initial Digital Business Strategy
Forming the initial digital business strategy first requires choosing and envisioning the type of digital business the organization should/will become (e.g., an analog product/service business, a digitally enhanced product/service business, a digital and/or online product/service provider, a marketplace or platform operator, an ecosystem orchestrator, a sharing economy business, an as-a-service/subscription business, a free or freemium product/service provider). As pointed

out earlier, the different types of digital businesses are differentiated by the nature of their products/services, their business models, and their digital business capabilities – or the unique ways they combine these three characteristics. Once leaders decide on and envision the type of digital business they want to become, they need to translate that decision and vision into specific objectives and goals. They can do this by focusing on five key digital business strategy arenas or focus areas. These arenas include digital business strategy, products/services, business model, DT infrastructure and digital platform, and data analytics. Within each of these arenas, they can first ask and answer the questions: *What do we need to get done in this arena in the long term in order to realize our desired digital business future state?* Answering this question effectively can result in formation of strategic objectives for that arena. Following this, leaders can then proceed to answering the next question: *Given our medium- and short-term constraints (e.g., financial, talent, customer, infrastructure constraints), what of our strategic objectives in this arena can we get done in the medium/short term.* Answering this question can enable them to translate strategic objectives into achievable specific medium/short-term goals. As noted earlier, in translating strategic objectives into specific goals to achieve in those timeframes, leaders can consider what is achievable given constraints related to those timeframes (e.g., financial, talent, customer, infrastructure constraints). After completing the strategic objectives and translating them into short/medium-term goals for each of the five initial digital business strategy formation arenas, leaders will have a "beachhead" digital business strategy. This strategy can be thought of like the strategy to land invading sea troops onto a beach from where subsequent land invasions can occur. Realization of the beachhead strategy will maximize the chances of the organization realizing its desired digital business future state. In Table 5.1, the five arena initial digital business strategy formation framework has been used to create the beachhead strategy for the hypothetical building/construction firm "Smart Construct". Let's assume Smart Construct's strategic leaders have decided they want to become a digitally enhanced product and services business. They envision the business' products being connected/smart buildings, modularized and smart building components, and including real-time building information as-a-service leveraging a to-be-built analytics platform. They also envision all the businesses' processes (except the actual building construction) being digitally facilitated, but the building construction process itself being as digitally enhanced as possible (e.g., with real-time monitoring using sensors and analytics, predictive and prescriptive workflow scheduling etc.). As can be seen in Table 5.1, Smart Construct's leaders have answered questions within each of the five initial digital business strategy formation arenas, resulting in strategic objectives and medium/short-term goals within each arena. Collectively, the strategic objectives and goals make up the beachhead digital business strategy. If Smart Construct realizes the beachhead digital business strategy, they will be in a similar position to invading sea troops landing on the beachhead. From that point, Smart Construct leaders will be well positioned to pursue more significant digital transformation and digital business competitiveness pursuits and to execute these faster.

It is possible that some organizations may be unclear about the type of digital business they should become. Or they may have an idea of the type of business they may want to become but be hesitant to modify products/services, business models, or core operational processes. Such firms may feel more comfortable having the digital transformation of support functions and services (e.g., accounting/finance, HR, marketing, logistics, administration) as their beachhead strategy. Perhaps followed by customer driven digital transformation of products/services, processes, and channels that function in parallel with traditional ones until they eventually come to include most of the organization's customers. The five initial digital business formation arenas can be adapted to substitute or include additional arenas that may be critical to particular organizations (for example, in some organizations arenas like cybersecurity management and digital governance may be important additions or substitutes). Typically, the additional arenas will be an aspect of one or more of the digital business capabilities discussed in Part IV of this book.

Table 5.1 Example initial digital business strategy for a building/construction firm

| Arena | Objectives | Medium-term goals | Short-term goals |
|---|---|---|---|
| Digital business strategy | • Choose the type of digital business we want to become or choose a general digital transformation direction and digital transformation initiatives to undertake until we choose a digital business type to become<br>• Envision the desired future state digital business we want to become, including the desired digital business capabilities<br>• Translate the envisioned digital business into more specific medium- and short-term goals<br>• Identify the necessary changes in products/services, business model, DT infrastructure/digital platform, operational processes, and data analytics | • Choose the type of digital business we want to become or choose a general digital transformation direction and digital transformation initiatives to undertake until we choose a digital business type to become<br>• Envision the desired future state digital business we want to become and required digital business characteristics/capabilities<br>• Form an initial beachhead strategy (i.e., decide on strategic objectives and medium/short-term goals that need to be achieved in order to maximize chances of achieving the desired future state – do this by making explicit decisions about objectives and goals within the strategic arenas of digital business strategy, products/services, business model, DT infrastructure/digital platform, operational processes, and data analytics)<br>• Execute the initial beachhead strategy<br>• Continuously and/or iteratively stress test, adapt, and refine the envisioned future state digital business and related beachhead strategy as implementation occurs to its optimized strategic potential and executability | • Choose the type of digital business we want to become or choose a general digital transformation direction and digital transformation initiatives to undertake until we choose the type of digital business we want to become<br>• Form the initial beachhead strategy<br>• Form a plan for the execution/implementation of the beachhead strategy |

| Products and services | • Leverage DTs to become an industry leader in the incorporation of digital/physical, programmable/reprogrammable, connected/smart characteristics that benefit customers into our products<br>• Leverage DTs to become an industry leader in the digital customer experience characteristics of reachability, convenience, simplicity, personalization, digital channel flexibility, and brand consistency | • Benchmark our products currently against our overall objectives to identify gaps and improvement opportunities<br>• Benchmark our customer experience currently against our overall objectives to identify gaps and improvement opportunities<br>• Prepare a staged plan for achieving our overall objectives for leveraging DTs to optimize our product/services and customer experience | • Benchmark our products currently against our overall objectives to identify gaps and improvement opportunities<br>• Benchmark our customer experience currently against our overall objectives to identify gaps and improvement opportunities |

*(Continued)*

**Table 5.1** (*Continued*)

| Arena | Objectives | Medium-term goals | Short-term goals |
|---|---|---|---|
| Business model | • Experiment with business model enhancement and/or transformation opportunities such as digital/physical channels, information-based service extensions, multi-sided platforms, and participation in platforms operated by others, so as to understand their adaptability, scalability, profitability, and sustainable business model benefits/opportunities.<br><br>• Leverage business model enhancement or transformation experiments to settle on an adaptable, scalable, profitable, and sustainable business model with a competitive customer experience | • Experiment with business model enhancement and/or transformation opportunities such as "as-a-service", digital/physical channels, information-based service extensions, multi-sided platforms, and participation in platforms operated by others | • Explore different "as-a-service" and digital/physical channels enhancements to business models and curate those that are possible within our industry and for our product/service offerings<br><br>• Engage an accelerator program manager to run internal accelerators and/or hackathons to derive "as-a-service" and digital/physical channel business model enhancement ideas |

| Operational processes | • Digitize and/or digitalize all organization processes, records, and capturable knowledge so they can be accessed or carried out remotely anytime and anywhere in the world with an online connection (except for the physical construction/home build itself)<br>• Ensure DT infrastructure and digital platforms enable full digitization and/or digitalization of all relevant processes, records, and capturable knowledge being transformed<br>• Develop the vision and future state for digitalized, connected/integrated, dynamic, automatable, intelligent, partially autonomous operations | • Ensure the DT infrastructure and digital platforms necessary for digitizing and/or digitalizing all relevant processes, records, and capturable knowledge are funded and can be available in time<br>• Build the rationale and task each manager with the responsibility to digitize and/or digitalize all relevant processes, records, and capturable knowledge<br>• Design the incentives and disincentives to motivate managers to digitize or digitalize all relevant processes, records, and capturable knowledge they have oversight of or interface with | • Identify the DT infrastructure and digital platforms necessary for digitizing and/or digitalizing all relevant processes, records, and capturable knowledge<br>• Build the rationale for digitizing and/or digitalizing all relevant processes, records, and capturable knowledge<br>• Prepare managers for the change process involved in digitalizing all relevant processes, records, and capturable knowledge |

*(Continued)*

**Table 5.1** (*Continued*)

| Arena | Objectives | Medium-term goals | Short-term goals |
|---|---|---|---|
| DT infrastructure and digital platform | • Have the necessary DT infrastructure in place to enable efficient and effective realization of the organization's desired digital transformation and digital business competitiveness<br>• Wherever possible, ensure the DT infrastructure adopted can serve future digital transformation and digital business strategies in addition to immediate change/transformation needs and strategies<br>• Have a clean, integrated, and user/management friendly digital platform for effectively facilitating internal workflows, effectively facilitating interactions with and by external customers and ecosystem partners, and effectively enabling the management and harnessing data to enable data driven decision making | • Have the necessary DT infrastructure in place to enable ongoing organization digital transformation and implementation of the initial beachhead strategy<br>• Wherever possible, ensure the DT infrastructure adopted can serve future digital transformation and digital business strategies in addition to immediate change/transformation needs and strategies<br>• Define the requirements for the organization's digital platform, and get the business case for its implementation approved/funded | • Understand the current DT infrastructure, the value it creates, and its limitations<br>• Design target enterprise architecture (EA) options and select the optimal one for both the beachhead strategy and longer-term digital transformation strategy<br>• Define future state DT infrastructure, identify target DTs to acquire to achieve future state DT infrastructure, and prepare plan for funding and sourcing relevant DTs |

| Data and analytics | • Build a world class management, data analytics, and data science capability<br>• Weaponize this world class capability by leveraging it to drive operational efficiency/ effectiveness breakthroughs and strategic differentiation | • Benchmark current data management, data analytics, and data science capability against world class capabilities to identify the capability gap<br>• Prepare and get approval for the business case to build the world class capability<br>• Find and hire the leadership talent to lead building of the capability | • Commission internal or external experts to benchmark current data management, data analytics, and data science capability against world class capabilities to identify the capability gap<br>• Commission a team of internal and external experts to prepare the business case for closing the identified capability gap |

## Forming the Initial Digital Transformation Strategy

Being clear on the type of digital business to become and the envisioned future state of that digital business better informs how to best undertake the change process involved in becoming that digital business (i.e., better informs digital transformation strategy). Similar to the process undertaken to form the digital business strategy, Table 5.2 identifies critical arenas that can be used to form digital transformation strategy. These include organization change and transformation, funding and financial risk management, and management of key stakeholder impacts and risks. As done with forming the digital transformation strategy, these arenas can be used to think through and answer questions such as: *What leadership and governance/talent/incentives and disincentives/engagement and communication structures and processes need to be in place to best position the organization's digital business strategy to succeed? What needs to be done funding wise to resource digital business strategy initiatives? What financial risks will be involved and how will these be mitigated, or their impacts managed? How will key stakeholder impacts and risks be managed?* Using the digital transformation strategy arenas, strategic leaders can identify strategic objectives for each arena and translate those into specific medium/short-term goals. As can be seen in Table 5.2, Smart Construct's leaders have answered most of these questions within each of the five initial digital transformation strategy formation arenas, resulting in strategic objectives and medium/short-term goals within each arena. The collective strategic objectives and their related medium/short-term goals across the three arenas become the initial beachhead change strategy or initial digital transformation strategy. Effectively executing this beachhead change strategy should prepare the organization to execute its digital business strategy. This initial digital transformation strategy needs to be continuously adapted, expanded, and refined based on learning that occurs during its execution and during execution of the digital business strategy. These adaptations, expansions, and refinements will accelerate organization readiness to execute the digital business strategy – hence maximizing chances of success in realizing the desired future state digital business. The arenas within Table 5.2 can be added to or substituted for other arenas that may be more critical to particular organizations. For example, some of the traditional organization change and transformation elements (e.g., culture, talent) may become arenas as they may require expanded focus in some organizations.

**Table 5.2** Example initial digital transformation strategy for a building/construction firm

| Arena | Objectives | Medium-term goals | Short-term goals |
|---|---|---|---|
| Organization change and transformation:<br>– leadership and governance<br>– culture<br>– talent<br>– engagement and communication<br>– incentives and disincentives | • Form the initial beachhead change strategy (specifying how to best undertake the change process necessary to enable the organization to pursue and realize the digital business strategy; to become the desired future state digital business, and to continuously and effectively compete as a digital business)<br>• Implement the initial beachhead change strategy to build the organization's readiness for undertaking the initial digital business strategy to maximize that digital business' longevity<br>• Continuously undertake the change process involved in realizing the initial digital business strategy | • Establish effective structures and resources for continuously keeping track of and optimizing organization readiness for undertaking the initial digital business strategy (e.g., implementing necessary policies/procedures, implementing necessary governance mechanisms, establishing necessary roles/reporting relationships, nurturing the necessary culture, proving optimal budgets, engaging and communicating effectively with all stakeholders, ensuring effective incentives/disincentives)<br>• Implement the initial beachhead change strategy and learn from the implementation<br>• Ensure optimal communication with, and engagement of, key stakeholders prior to and during implementation of the initial digital business strategy | • Understand the change process involved in becoming a digital business<br>• Understand digital cultures and how to build a digital culture<br>• Get the right leadership and governance structures in place to drive the digital transformation<br>• Assemble the right team to drive digital transformation, implement the beachhead change strategy, and achieve the initial digital business strategy<br>• Ensure optimal buy-in to the digital vision by key stakeholders<br>• Identify the required talent to maximize chances of successful digital transformation<br>• Hire or upskill for the required talent below the leadership and governance team to enable short, medium, and/or long-term digital transformation aims<br>• Have the right incentives to drive enabling behaviors and to discourage unsupportive or undermining behaviors<br>• Develop a plan for effecting the required digital culture |

*(Continued)*

**Table 5.2** (*Continued*)

| Arena | Objectives | Medium-term goals | Short-term goals |
|---|---|---|---|
| Funding and financial risk management | • Ensure adequate funding for each beachhead digital business strategy and beachhead digital transformation strategy<br><br>• Closely monitor progress of initiatives to ensure they succeed within budget and pay back sufficiently to help fund subsequent transformation initiatives | • Prepare validated and stress-tested budgets for the beachhead digital business strategy and beachhead digital transformation strategy<br><br>• Prepare effective reporting and monitoring mechanisms to ensure initiatives remain within budget and deliver on expected benefits (e.g., revenue growth, efficiency gains, risk reduction) | • Identify a strategic lead for each arena and task them to work with the accounting/finance team to prepare validated and stress-tested budget/financial plans to achieve that arena's objectives and medium/short-term goals |
| Management of key stakeholder impacts and risks:<br>– operational risks and impacts<br>– customer risks and impacts<br>– employee risks and impacts<br>– other stakeholder risks and impacts | • Put in place a system for continuously identifying, evaluating, and proactively managing key stakeholder impacts/risks<br><br>• Closely monitor progress of initiatives and changes in key stakeholder impacts/risks | • Investigate typical stakeholder impacts/risks<br><br>• Identify best practice systems/approaches to continuously identifying, evaluating, and proactively managing key stakeholder impacts/risks<br><br>• Prepare possible options for a system to put in place for continuously identifying, evaluating, and proactively managing key stakeholder impacts/risks | • Investigate typical stakeholder impacts/risks<br><br>• Identify best practice systems/approaches to continuously identifying, evaluating, and proactively managing key stakeholder impacts/risks |

# SUBSEQUENT DIGITAL BUSINESS STRATEGY AND DIGITAL TRANSFORMATION STRATEGY

Subsequent digital business strategy and digital transformation strategy largely involve building and optimizing digital business capabilities – which include the digital business strategy and digital transformation strategy capabilities. Digital business capabilities are organization structures, processes, and/or routines or activities that work together and leverage digital assets to enable an organization to digitally do particular things or to digitally achieve particular outcomes repeatably and reliably.[10] For example, digital innovation capability refers to the organization routines/activities, structures, and/or processes that work together and leverage digital assets to digitally innovate (e.g., use DT facilitated distributed innovation, open innovation, and network-centric innovation practices to produce new digital or hybrid digital/physical products). Each digital business capability is explained further in the chapters on digital business capability primers (Part IV). To form ongoing digital business and digital transformation strategy, each digital business capability can be used as an arena for which strategic objectives can be set and subsequently translated into medium and short-term goals. Alternatively, organizations can select particular digital business capabilities that are critical to them and focus their digital business and digital transformation strategy on optimizing those capabilities. Either way, the more sophisticated, repeatable, and reliable each relevant capability is, the greater will be an organization's digital business maturity and digital business competitiveness. For example, the more sophisticated an organization's ability to devise and execute digital business strategy (digital business strategy capability), the better positioned it is to become the type of digital business it seeks to become and to effectively compete as a digital business. There are two important challenges to address in building and optimizing the various digital business capabilities. The first is prioritization since all required digital business capabilities can't be invested in and built at once. The second is ensuring that prioritized capabilities are sequenced, integrated, and reinforce each other to

**Table 5.3** *Subsequent digital business and digital transformation strategy is largely about building and optimizing prioritized digital business capabilities*

| Digital business strategy arena | Strategic objectives | Medium-term goals | Short-term goals |
|---|---|---|---|
| Digital transformation strategy | | | |
| Digital business strategy | | | |
| Digital leadership | | | |
| Digital culture | | | |
| Accelerated change and transformation | | | |
| Enterprise architecture management | | | |
| Digital technology adoption and use | | | |
| Data management/data analytics/ data science | | | |
| Digital innovation | | | |
| Adaptability, agility, and ambidexterity | | | |
| Workforce digital competencies | | | |
| Digital customer experience management | | | |
| Digital customer and stakeholder engagement | | | |
| Cybersecurity management | | | |
| Digital ethics | | | |
| Digital risk management and governance | | | |

maximize overall impact. For example, prioritizing digital technology adoption/use and digital innovation without corresponding investments in workforce digital technology competencies is likely to limit the chances of success and the impact of those capabilities. But ensuring workforce digital technology competencies align with digital technology adoption/ use and digital innovation strategic objectives and goals will enhance integration among the three capability areas and maximize their impact. Table 5.3 shows the different digital business capability areas framed as digital business strategy formation arenas.

# NOTES

1 Busulwa, R., Pickering, M., & Mao, I. (2022). Digital transformation and hospitality management competencies: Toward an integrative framework. *International Journal of Hospitality Management*, 102, 103132.

2 Tekic, Z., & Koroteev, D. (2019). From disruptively digital to proudly analog: A holistic typology of digital transformation strategies. *Business Horizons*, 62(6), 683–693.

3 Valdez-de-Leon, O. (2016). A digital maturity model for telecommunications service providers. *Technology Innovation Management Review*, 6(8).

4 Busulwa, R., Pickering, M., & Mao, I. (2022). Digital transformation and hospitality management competencies: Toward an integrative framework. *International Journal of Hospitality Management*, 102, 103132; Bharadwaj, A., El Sawy, O. A., Pavlou, P. A., & Venkatraman, N. (2013). Digital business strategy: Toward a next generation of insights. *MIS Quarterly*, 471–482.

5 Christensen, C. M., & Bower, J. L. (1995). Disruptive technologies: Catching the wave *Harvard Business Review*.

6 Leifer, R. (1989). Understanding organizational transformation using a dissipative structure model. *Human Relations*, 42(10), 899–916.

7 Kark, K. (2020, January 29). 7 digital transformation myths. *CIO*. www.cio.com/article/201558/7-digital-transformation-myths-2.html

8 Collett, S. (2019, February 20). IT shifts away from "Big Bang" digital transformations. *CIO*. www.cio.com/article/219746/it-shifts-away-from-big-bang-digital-transformations.html

9 Salinas, S. (2019, January 24). Craigslist is raking in $1 billion a year, according to one researcher's estimates. *CNBC*. www.cnbc.com/2019/01/24/craigslist-posts-annual-revenue-of-1-billion-study.html

10 Busulwa, R., Pickering, M., & Mao, I. (2022). Digital transformation and hospitality management competencies: Toward an integrative framework. *International Journal of Hospitality Management*, 102, 103132.

# CHAPTER 6

# Executing Digital Transformation Strategy

DOI: 10.4324/9781003254614-8

# INTRODUCTION

U nless it is executed effectively, digital transformation strategy may just be a meaningless distraction. And executing it effectively warrants careful consideration of the different ways strategy execution can be undertaken and what ways are most optimal for the digital transformation leadership team and for the broader organization. This is because the execution of digital transformation strategy differs from the execution of other strategies due to the dynamic, high velocity, and discontinuous nature of changes within the digital technology ecosystem (e.g., the ecosystem that includes inventors, component manufacturers and integrators, hardware and software vendors, platforms). These changes result in constant changes in the nature and availability of digital technologies and their vendors (see further discussion of this in the Simple Rules Process section in this chapter). And the changes introduce significant uncertainty and risk in the choice and adoption of digital technologies (e.g., what ones are adopted, how they are adopted). This challenge is in addition to the earlier discussed challenges and risks associated with transformations in general, and digital transformations in particular. Together, these changes/challenges/risks form the contextual background to digital transformation undertakings – it needs to be considered seriously, as it can result in disruption and derailment of the digital transformation effort. For example, it can result in a technology becoming irrelevant just after acquisitions costs are incurred; it can result in customer digital channel preferences changing mid-way through realignment of an organization's processes to those channels; or it can result in negative attitudes to digital transformation initiatives in the workplace as a result of technology adoptions that over promise and under deliver. This chapter first reviews some important principles for leaders to keep in mind before and during the execution of digital transformation strategy. These principles are helpful for getting transformation efforts off to the right start, keeping them aligned with business needs, and keeping key stakeholders engaged. The chapter then provides an overview of key strategy execution processes or approaches that are proposed to be most effective for the execution of digital transformation strategy, given the dynamic and rapidly changing context in which such transformation efforts are undertaken. Strategy execution effectiveness in such a context requires strategy execution approaches amenable to speed, flexibility, ambidexterity, and customer/stakeholder focus.

---

**LEARNING OBJECTIVES**

- Understand how the execution of digital transformation strategy differs from the execution of typical business strategies
- Understand common principles and rules of thumb to keep in mind when executing digital transformation strategy
- Understand different approaches to executing digital transformation strategy
- Analyze and select optimal approaches for executing digital transformation strategy
- Apply effective principles and approaches to lead, facilitate, and/or participate in the execution of digital transformation
- Evaluate the effectiveness of different digital transformation approaches and the likely causes
- Understand the implications of using different strategy execution processes/approaches for leaders, managers, and other professionals

---

# PRINCIPLES FOR EXECUTING DIGITAL TRANSFORMATION STRATEGY

## SECURE OWNERSHIP AND/OR TOP MANAGEMENT TEAM COMMITMENT

It's true that most change agendas in organizations just can't get enough ownership and/or top management team commitment. Thus, competition for ownership and/or top management team commitment is likely to be strong in most organizations. And it can be convincingly argued that there just isn't enough ownership and/or top management team commitment to go around. Even so, given its organization-wide and all-encompassing nature, ownership and/or top management team commitment is critical to digital transformation. Most digital transformation undertakings without such commitment are most likely to be costly to those pursuing them and eventually moot or short lived until such commitment is secured. The ownership and/or top management team needs to play very critical roles in digital transformation including communicating the digital transformation vision, building the rationale for change, funding the change, prioritizing the change ahead of pressing operational demands, incentivizing and disincentivizing behaviors of key people, shepherding the change from powerful opposition, and reinvigorating change leaders when particular initiatives under deliver. Without the funding and prioritization, digital transformation initiatives may not even be able to start. Without ownership and/ or top management's direct involvement in communicating the vision and in building the rationale for the transformation, the transformation may struggle to gain the attention and engagement of powerful stakeholders and the wider organization. Without the right incentives and disincentives, people may passive aggressively ignore the transformation or actively thwart it. And without shepherding of the transformation, any number of change related landmines may sideline it or kill it off altogether. How leaders go about securing ownership and/ or top management team commitment may vary from organization to organization. But it is a critical prerequisite to the execution of digital transformation initiatives.

## SECURE ADEQUATE INVESTMENT[1]

Digital transformation will be challenging enough without the added pressures of not having sufficient budget to adopt critical digital infrastructure, not having sufficient access to key internal talent, and not having sufficient budget to respond to unexpected disruptions of the transformation (e.g., security breaches, key changes in technology standards, departure of key personnel). Thus, it is important to ensure access to sufficient financial, talent, and other resources. It is also important to ensure that access to these resources is set up in such a way that it can't just be suddenly cut or reallocated to emerging crises in other parts of the organization. Although transformation leaders can always do with more resources and are likely always seeking ways to do more with existing resources, there should be a clear investment level at which point which they acknowledge is insufficient for the transformation to succeed. Leaders also need to ensure that this point reflects investment needed for today's transformation initiatives and for future initiatives that will proceed them. As the transformation proceeds, leaders can look to become self-sufficient with new revenues from the transformation or to use new revenues driven by the transformation as the basis for increased levels of investment in the transformation.

## SET CLEAR TARGETS OR DELIVERABLES THAT ARE EXTERNALLY BENCHMARKED WHEREVER POSSIBLE

It can be easy for digital transformation undertakings to appear ambiguous, like fluffy visions/unrealistic posturing, smoke and mirrors work with no measurable benefits, or new hire aggrandizement work that just gets in the way of people doing their actual work. Therefore, where there is lack of clarity regarding what is required, what the outcomes are, and who is accountable for different aspects of the requirements and outcomes, it is understandable why and how work in service of digital transformation initiatives may be evaded. To resolve such issues, it is important for digital transformation objectives to be translated into clear targets or deliverables that are externally benchmarked. Clear targets and deliverables make the required work and results, as well as the people charged with delivering the work and results, clear for everyone – enhancing accountability and progress visibility.[2] They also help clarify the effectiveness or ineffectiveness of actions that people may take in pursuit of those targets or deliverables. And they can enhance motivation.[3] Finally, external benchmarking of targets can build employees' self-efficacy and conviction that they can do it since their peers in similar organizations have done so or have similar targets.[4]

## FIND WAYS TO CONTINUOUSLY AND EFFECTIVELY INVOLVE, ENGAGE, AND REGULARLY COMMUNICATE WITH ALL INTERNAL AND EXTERNAL STAKEHOLDERS

Digital transformation eventually impacts all of an organization's varied stakeholders albeit in different ways. And these varied stakeholders may use their influence to assist or sabotage digital transformation efforts – intentionally or unintentionally. Thus, it is important to understand and address their concerns, educate them about the purpose and rationale for the transformation, keep them apprised of current and pending changes as well as their potential positive or negative impacts, and incorporate their ideas. Doing so will both diffuse resistance and build coalitions of support to accelerate the transformation. It is true that it is a significant challenge for leaders to involve and engage every stakeholder. But leaders can find creative ways to achieve this (e.g., finding and involving leaders/ influencers of different stakeholder groups, finding and participating in key stakeholder communication and consultation forums, leveraging internal and even external social and communication platforms, etc.).

## SEQUENCE INITIATIVES SO AS TO CONTINUOUSLY DELIVER VALUE AND TO BUILD THE CONFIDENCE OF THE WIDER ORGANIZATION

To overcome cynicism within the wider organization and build organization confidence in the transformation (e.g., that the transformation can deliver tangible outcomes, that it is gaining unstoppable momentum, and that it will eventually succeed), leaders need to deliver visible and increasing value (e.g., revenue growth, channel adoption by customers, cost reductions, resolved organization problems). To achieve this, leaders need to sequence the delivery of digital transformation initiatives in such a way as to continuously maximize visible value delivered and to continuously remove obstacles or enhance support for the pursuit of subsequent initiatives. Leaders can start by identifying and pursuing high reward/low failure risk activities to inspire early confidence and support (e.g., projects that will delight customers, staff, and stakeholders with profit responsibility, so they see the potential of digital transformation efforts). And leaders can anticipate and plan for dampening or turning around the impact of projects that fail to deliver, or the unintended negative impacts of the transformation on the organization. They can also keep a watchful eye on initiatives nearing completion or that have already started delivering business value so these can be celebrated at opportune times.

## GET IMPLEMENTATION FEEDBACK EARLY AND CONTINUOUSLY

When implementing digital transformation initiatives or products, it is better to err on the side of smaller and faster iterations that enable fast evaluation of results/effects, incorporation of stakeholder feedback, and improvement of subsequent iterations. Once a change has gone through these iterations and its results and impacts have been understood, validated, and shown to be consistently repeatable, then they can be scaled to the wider organization with confidence. The alternative, pursuing bigger implementations with long lags between completion of implementation and collection of results/impacts and stakeholder feedback, can result in significant waste of limited resources if the results/impacts and/or feedback are negative. It may then be too late and/or too expensive to iterate. The bigger implementation can be broken down into a smaller collection of initiatives that result in faster delivery, faster collection of results/impact data, and faster collection of stakeholder feedback.

## OBSERVE AND MEASURE THE RIGHT THINGS, THEN LEVERAGE INSIGHTS TO INFORM TRANSFORMATION DECISIONS

To track progress to targets; track the impact of, and feedback on, initiatives; and make data-informed decisions or make data-backed arguments/cases; digital transformation leaders need to ensure they have systems in place to capture or access the right data, undertake relevant and reliable analysis of the data, and leverage the derived insights to inform transformation decisions. For example, initiatives directed at improving digital customer experience and growing new revenue ought to have readily available and timely access to relevant customer experience and new revenue growth metrics.

## ENCOURAGE AND PROMOTE FAST, ADAPTABLE, AND CUSTOMER CENTRIC WAYS OF WORKING

The required scale and speed with which digital transformation needs to occur mandates the use of strategy execution approaches that are designed for contexts characterized by high dynamism, high uncertainty, rapid technological changes, and disruption. As well as enabling faster and more adaptable change and transformation, such approaches typically put the customer front and center of changes. Examples of these approaches include Lean startup, Agile, design thinking, hackathons, and blitz-scaling approaches.[5] Digital transformation leaders can encourage, promote, and support the use of these approaches in the wider organization. For example, they may do so by adopting Agile approaches to executing digital transformation. Or they can fund or advocate for Agile training of leaders within the organization. Or they can hire leaders with backgrounds in Agile/Lean startup/accelerator/hackathon methods.

## APPOINT A LEADERSHIP TEAM THAT CAN EFFECTIVELY INFLUENCE/LEAD STAKEHOLDERS, CAN ATTRACT TOP TALENT, AND CAN EXECUTE THE DIGITAL TRANSFORMATION STRATEGY

The team leading digital transformation is critical to the transformation's success. To succeed, it needs to be able to effectively influence and lead the organization's varied stakeholders directly or indirectly. That is, it has to ensure understanding, involvement, buy-in, and commitment of key leaders and the wider organization to the digital transformation. The team also needs to be able to attract and engage top digital talent to play key roles in the transformation (e.g., help with forming digital business strategy, identify the key digital technologies and platforms to adopt, design digital products or integrate digital into existing products, engage customers in and across digital channels, build digital capabilities). Further, the team needs to be able to lead execution and deliver on the promises of digital transformation. In recruiting/appointing the team to lead the transformation, leaders need to ensure the leadership team has plentiful capacity in these areas.

# EFFECTIVE PROCESSES OR APPROACHES FOR EXECUTING DIGITAL TRANSFORMATION STRATEGY

Formed digital transformation strategies, also referred to as deliberate or intended digital transformation strategies, are effected or realized through one or more different strategy execution processes or approaches. Strategy execution processes or approaches, also referred to as strategy making processes or strategy realization processes, refer to the integrated set of activities that enable deliberate and/or emergent strategies (or intended and/or unintended strategies) to be realized. Strategy execution has evolved over the last 30 years from identifying factors for successful strategy execution to integrating those factors into cause-and-effect frameworks for guiding strategy execution to processes with clear steps and activities for executing strategy that are guided principles. A range of different strategy execution processes or approaches exist, each with unique strengths for realizing either deliberate strategy or emergent strategy, or for optimally balancing the level to which deliberate strategy is realized and emergent strategy is realized. Each strategy execution approach's effectiveness at realizing deliberate and/or emergent strategy varies across different types of environments. For example, some are more effective at realizing deliberate strategy in stable environments, but ineffective at realizing either deliberate strategy or emergent strategy in dynamic and fast changing and unpredictable environments. In contrast, particular strategy execution processes are highly effective in fast changing and unpredictable environments.

The IT industry has been shown to be characterized by extraordinary complexity, high velocity change, fleeting opportunity windows, as well as constant obsolescence in the products/services or product/service components of organizations in the industry. This has important implications for digital transformation strategy. Specifically, many of these industry issues are manifested in digital transformation efforts. For example, while an organization is attempting to adopt/build/configure its digital platform or component products/services, these may be opaque, constantly changing, and subject to obsolescence in the platforms/platform components or in technology standards. Similarly, the preferred channels through which customers are engaged or consume a company's products are typically undergoing constant change with certain channels or vendors falling out of favor and new ones emerging. So, leaders overseeing both the formation and/or execution of digital transformation initiatives must constantly keep a vigilant eye on such changes and execute in such a way as to be able to make rapid changes in the strategy and its execution – or they are likely to face certain failure. A selection of strategy execution processes or approaches have been shown to be much more effective in environments characterized by the type of dynamism and change surrounding digital transformations undertakings. The most common ones are briefly summarized below to aid leaders in choosing one or more, and there is an abundance of readily available resources on each one that leaders can draw from (e.g., books, scholarly and online articles, videos, consulting/advisory services). The approach or process selected by each leader may be dependent on each leader's ability to use and preference for a particular process, the potential capacity for, or ease of, adoption of the process by an organization, the alignment of the process or approach with an organization's particular digital transformation strategy, and other issues. Each of the approaches below can be operated in parallel with one or more structured and instituted processes traditionally used to execute strategy.[6]

## AGILE PROGRAM AND PROJECT MANAGEMENT APPROACHES

Agile program and project management approaches are approaches that apply Agile principles and values to the practice of program and project management.[7] Examples of Agile principles include customer satisfaction through continuous delivery, accommodating changing customer requirements throughout the project, simplicity, self-organizing teams, and regular reflection on how to become more effective.[8] And examples of Agile values include engaging and collaborating with the customer throughout the project, embracing and incorporating change over following a plan that may no longer be relevant, and valuing individuals and interactions over processes and tools.[9] The benefits of an Agile project can be contrasted to a project in which it isn't discovered until too much time and money has been spent that what is delivered or going to be delivered is not actually what the customer wants, or that it is no longer needed due to external changes (e.g., changes in technology standards, changes in the customer's needs, or changes in the external environment). Applying Agile principles and values minimizes the risk of such situations occurring and maximize customer satisfaction.

To use Agile program and project management approaches, digital transformation strategy objectives and/or goals are translated into a collection of specific projects that, if delivered, would result in realization of those objectives and/or goals. Each project's deliverables are then delivered iteratively through iterations or deliverables packages known as sprints. The customer is involved in reviewing the outputs of these iterations or sprints and providing feedback or change suggestions. The team involved in the delivery of an iteration or sprint also reviews/reflects on the performance/success of that iteration. Customer reviews/change suggestions and sprint team reflections then inform subsequent iterations. The ability to adjust and improve with each iteration minimizes risk (e.g., of waste), drives speed, enhances adaptability, and enhances customer satisfaction. In Agile program or project management, the customer can be thought of as the sponsor or owner of a particular digital transformation program or project. At a very high level, the main aspects of an Agile project can be conceptualized as consisting of (1) identifying the project sponsor or owner, (2) creating an outcome delivery roadmap, (3) creating an outcome release plan, (4) undertaking or forming a sprint plans, (5) initiating execution of the first sprint plan, (6) holding regular sprint team standup meetings to inspect progress, resolving bottlenecks, making decisions, and aligning subsequent actions, (7) undertaking sprint reviews involving customers, (8) undertaking sprint retrospectives, and (9) incorporating sprint learnings into the next sprint plan.[10] Steps 4 to 9 can be repeated as needed until the project requirements are fully delivered. Steps 1 to 4 can be updated continuously to reflect learnings from each sprint, as well as to reflect external and internal environment changes.

In contrast to Agile project management, Agile program management applies Agile principles and values at a more macro level. That is, applying the principles and values with a focus on enhancing the visibility, alignment, integration, and coordination of multiple interrelated projects and sprint teams to optimize organization value delivery (e.g., what value, how much, when) and return on project investments. An amazon.com search for "Agile project management" or "Agile program management" will reveal an abundance of books providing guidance on how to optimally use Agile program and project management approaches.

## HOSHIN KANRI OR LEAN STRATEGY DEPLOYMENT

Lean Strategy Deployment (also referred to as Hoshin Planning, Hoshin Kanri, Direction Management, or Policy Deployment), is a process for forming and actioning "breakthroughs" that significantly change the position of an organization in its external environment through strategically aligned business objectives and metrics that are driven from

## The Hoshin Planning or Lean Strategy Deployment Process

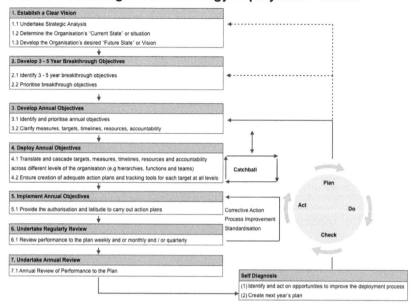

**Figure 6.1** *The Hoshin Planning, Hoshin Kanri, or Lean Strategy Deployment process*[15]

both top-down and bottom-up activity.[11] While the way this process is used can vary from organization to organization, in general, high-level steps common to it include: (1) establish a clear organization vision, (2) develop 3–5 year breakthrough objectives, (3) develop annual objectives, (4) deploy annual objectives, (5) implement annual objectives, (6) undertake regular progress review, and (7) undertake annual review – see Figure 6.1.[12] Typically, during step 4, an important and unique component of this process, each leader or manager conducts continuous "catchball" dialogues with their direct reports about the targets or tasks being allocated to them, the resources required to achieve those targets or tasks, and the opportunities or barriers to achieving them.[13] For example, if the organization's Head of Customer Experience was allocated the annual objective of "achieving a 10% improvement in the organization's Net Promoter score across each digital channel", she may deploy this objective through catchball dialogues with her team members. These dialogues would focus on what each team member can contribute to the achievement of her goal, what each team member needs from her in order to make that contribution, and what obstacles each team member may face in making their contribution. Her team members can, in turn, undertake the same process with their teams, thus deploying (i.e., translating and cascading) the strategic objective all the way to the frontline. An amazon.com search for "Hoshin Kanri" or "Hoshin Planning" or "Lean strategy" will reveal an abundance of books providing guidance on how to optimally use this approach.[14]

## CHANGE ACCELERATION PROCESS

The Change Acceleration Process was developed by John Kotter, Emeritus professor of leadership at Harvard Business School, *New York Times* best-selling author on change management, and founder of the change management consulting firm Kotter International.[16] The process draws on, and perhaps evolved from, John Kotter's long established and tested body of research into change management.[17] The process is designed to work in parallel with more structured strategy execution processes that organizations may already use to drive operational efficiency and the pursuit of deliberate strategies in line with the organization's instituted execution routines and timeframes.[18] Working in parallel, the process enables organizations to pursue more exploratory strategies, strategies that need to be executed in much shorter timeframes, or strategies that would otherwise disrupt traditional operations. The process is made up of eight "accelerators," or concurrent and ongoing collections of activities that operate as network-like structure in parallel with the traditional hierarchy-based process.[19] The eight accelerators are: (1) create a sense of urgency around a single big opportunity, (2) build and maintain a guiding coalition, (3) form the strategic vision and initiatives, (4) enlist a volunteer army, (5) enable action by removing barriers, (6) generate short-term wins, (7) sustain acceleration, and (8) institute change – see Figure 6.2.[20] The accelerators are also guided by these five principles: (1) have many change agents rather than the usual appointees, (2) create a "want to" and "get to" rather than "have to" mindset, (3) engage both head and heart rather than just head, (4) have much more leadership rather

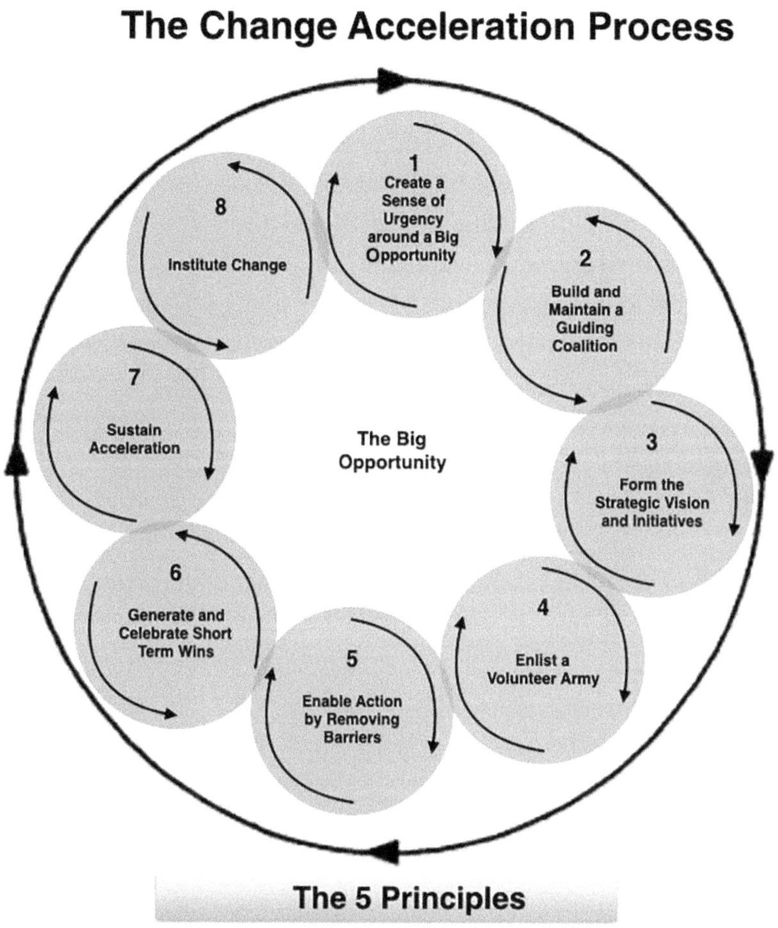

# The Change Acceleration Process

**1** Create a Sense of Urgency around a Big Opportunity

**2** Build and Maintain a Guiding Coalition

**3** Form the Strategic Vision and Initiatives

**4** Enlist a Volunteer Army

**5** Enable Action by Removing Barriers

**6** Generate and Celebrate Short Term Wins

**7** Sustain Acceleration

**8** Institute Change

The Big Opportunity

**The 5 Principles**

*Figure 6.2* The Change Acceleration Process[22]

than just management, and (5) ensure the change acceleration and the traditional hierarchy-based processes work as one rather than as silos.[21]

## SIMPLE RULES PROCESS

The Simple Rules process was developed by Kathleen Eisenhardt and Donald Sull in the course of their research on why certain technology firms thrived while others did not. This research led them to discover the challenges of the environments in which these technology firms operated.

Specifically, the discovered that these environments were characterized by high dynamism, high uncertainty, rapid technological obsolescence, and discontinuous change.[23] They turned their attention to trying to understanding how effective firms navigate and thrive in such environments. They discovered that sustained effectiveness in such environments required enabling leaders to make on-the-spot decisions and adapt to rapidly changing circumstances while, simultaneously, keeping these decisions and actions aligned to the organization's big picture strategy.[24] They translated their findings into the Simple Rules process or approach. The key steps in the Simple Rules process are: (1) set clear direction by clarifying the priority strategic objectives, (2) identify bottlenecks that may keep the organization from achieving strategic objectives, and (3) effect simple rules for dealing with the bottlenecks – see Figure 6.3.[25] In their book *Simple Rules: How to Thrive in a Complex World*, they unpack each element of the process in much more detail and share extensive case studies of the process in action in a range of different organizations. Eisenhardt and Sull propose that the Simple Rules process provides a solution to another important but unaddressed strategy issue. They argue that for strategy to influence action, it has to be remembered; for it to be remembered, it has to first be understood; and for it to be understood, it has to be simple. Thus, the Simple Rules process provides a solution to the common challenge of strategies being too complicated to be understood. It does this by providing a way for strategic leaders to distill a potentially complicated strategy into a simple set of rules that can be understood, remembered, and acted on by people in all parts of the organization as they make on-the-spot decisions and adapt to changing circumstances.[26] Some complementary methods/tools which can be used as sub-methods within each strategy execution process or as part of strategy formation include Lean startup, design thinking, accelerator, hackathon methods/approaches, and many others.

## REVERSE ACQUISITION APPROACHES

An alternative, although potentially much more expensive, approach to executing on particular digital transformation strategies and eventually building particular digital business capabilities is to strategically acquire

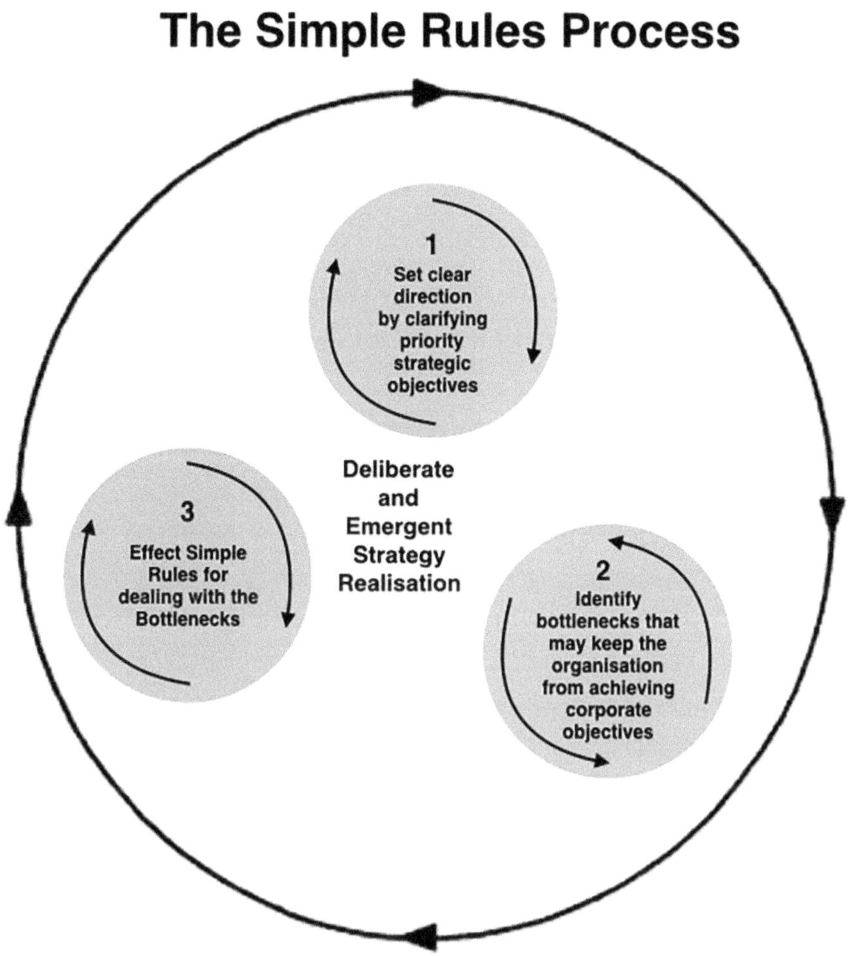

# The Simple Rules Process

**Figure 6.3** *The Simple Rules process*[27]

complementary businesses that already have those digital business capabilities an organization is seeking. And rather than integrating the acquired organization, instead let that organization's leaders take over that aspect of the organization. An example of this is how Disney acquired Pixar and then proceeded to give Pixar's leadership control of Walt Disney Animation Studios. Pixar's leadership proceeded to transform Walt Disney Animation Studios without destroying its unique culture and advantageous existing practices. This brought in a new era of growth and profitability to Disney.[28] In a similar way, an organization seeking to build its digital business strategy or digital innovation capabilities could acquire a digital business strategy firm or a digital innovation firm and give the leaders of the acquired business control of the acquiring organization's strategy or innovation functions.

# IMPLICATIONS FOR LEADERS, MANAGERS, AND SUPPORTING PROFESSIONALS

There are two common ways leaders, managers, and supporting professionals participate in digital transformation. One is by occupying a specific role on the digital transformation leadership team (e.g., chief digital officer, change manager). And the other is by being a supporter and ally to the digital transformation effort (e.g., by adapting their leadership/management/professional services activities to have maximum positive impact on digital transformation efforts). In either of these situations, it is important for leaders/managers/supporting professionals to understand the digital transformation strategy and the effective strategy execution approaches that should or are likely to be used in efforts to effect the strategy. A leader/manager recognizing that their strategic leaders are adopting Agile methods/approaches can move quickly to upskill themselves and their teams on the methods/tools. And they may ensure that they and their teams understand and are able to effectively participate in Agile programs and projects. This is likely to catalyze the success and impact of the methods/approaches as well as the delivery of the projects being undertaken. Such a manager can be contrasted to one who does nothing, resulting in her and her direct reports inadvertently slowing down and potentially derailing the effectiveness of methods/approaches used and/or the projects those approaches aim to deliver. For example, direct reports of such a manager are unlikely to optimally contribute to Agile projects or sprints; they are likely to feel out of touch and left out in Agile projects or sprints; and they are likely to disengage or even become resistant/obstructive to digital transformation efforts. In playing a specific role on the digital transformation leadership team, understanding the strategy execution processes being used or choosing the best one to use is critical to getting things done and being an effective contributor to the digital transformation leadership team.

# NOTES

1 Catlin, T., Lorenz, J.-T., Sternfels, B., & Willmott, P. (2017, March). *A roadmap for a digital transformation*. McKinsey & Company. www.mckinsey.com/industries/financial-services/our-insights/a-roadmap-for-a-digital-transformation

2 Catlin, T., Lorenz, J.-T., Sternfels, B., & Willmott, P. (2017, March). *A roadmap for a digital transformation*. McKinsey & Company. www.mckinsey.com/industries/financial-services/our-insights/a-roadmap-for-a-digital-transformation

3 Catlin, T., Lorenz, J.-T., Sternfels, B., & Willmott, P. (2017, March). *A roadmap for a digital transformation*. McKinsey & Company. www.mckinsey.com/industries/financial-services/our-insights/a-roadmap-for-a-digital-transformation

4 Catlin, T., Lorenz, J.-T., Sternfels, B., & Willmott, P. (2017, March). *A roadmap for a digital transformation*. McKinsey & Company. www.mckinsey.com/industries/financial-services/our-insights/a-roadmap-for-a-digital-transformation

5 Busulwa, R., Evans, N., Oh, A., & Kang, M. (2020). *Hospitality management and digital transformation: Balancing efficiency, agility and guest experience in the era of disruption*. Routledge.

6 Busulwa, R., Tice, M., & Gurd, B. (2018). *Strategy execution and complexity: Thriving in the era of disruption*. Routledge.

7 Alexander, M. (2018, June 19). Agile project management: 12 key principles, 4 big hurdles. *CIO*. www.cio.com/article/237027/agile-project-management-a-beginners-guide.html; Sliger, M. (2011). Agile project management with Scrum. Paper presented at PMI® Global Congress 2011 – North America, Dallas, TX. Newtown Square, PA: Project Management Institute.

8 Alexander, M. (2018, June 19). Agile project management: 12 key principles, 4 big hurdles. *CIO*. www.cio.com/article/237027/agile-project-management-a-beginners-guide.html

9 Alexander, M. (2018, June 19). Agile project management: 12 key principles, 4 big hurdles. *CIO*. www.cio.com/article/237027/agile-project-management-a-beginners-guide.html

10 Busulwa, R., Tice, M., & Gurd, B. (2018). *Strategy execution and complexity: Thriving in the era of disruption*. Routledge.

11  Ouda, H., & Ahmed, K. (2016). A proposed systematic framework for applying hoshin kanri strategic planning methodology in educational institutions. *European Scientific Journal*, 12(16), 158–194; Pejsa, P., & Eng, R. (2011). Lean strategy deployment delivers customer satisfaction at GE healthcare. *Global Business and Organizational Excellence*, 30(5), 45.

12  Busulwa, R., Tice, M., & Gurd, B. (2018). *Strategy execution and complexity: Thriving in the era of disruption*. Routledge.

13  Busulwa, R., Tice, M., & Gurd, B. (2018). *Strategy execution and complexity: Thriving in the era of disruption*. Routledge.

14  Busulwa, R., Tice, M., & Gurd, B. (2018). *Strategy execution and complexity: Thriving in the era of disruption*. Routledge.

15  Busulwa, R., Tice, M., & Gurd, B. (2018). *Strategy execution and complexity: Thriving in the era of disruption*. Routledge.

16  Busulwa, R., Tice, M., & Gurd, B. (2018). *Strategy execution and complexity: Thriving in the era of disruption*. Routledge.

17  Busulwa, R., Tice, M., & Gurd, B. (2018). *Strategy execution and complexity: Thriving in the era of disruption*. Routledge.

18  Busulwa, R., Tice, M., & Gurd, B. (2018). *Strategy execution and complexity: Thriving in the era of disruption*. Routledge.

19  Adapted from Kotter, J.P. (2014) *Accelerate: Building strategic agility for a faster-moving world*. Harvard Business School Publishing.

20  Adapted from Kotter, J.P. (2014) *Accelerate: Building strategic agility for a faster-moving world*. Harvard Business School Publishing.

21  Adapted from Kotter, J.P. (2014) *Accelerate: Building strategic agility for a faster-moving world*. Harvard Business School Publishing.

22  Busulwa, R., Tice, M., & Gurd, B. (2018). *Strategy execution and complexity: Thriving in the era of disruption*. Routledge.

23  Busulwa, R., Tice, M., & Gurd, B. (2018). *Strategy execution and complexity: Thriving in the era of disruption*. Routledge.

24  Busulwa, R., Tice, M., & Gurd, B. (2018). *Strategy execution and complexity: Thriving in the era of disruption*. Routledge.

25  Busulwa, R., Tice, M., & Gurd, B. (2018). *Strategy execution and complexity: Thriving in the era of disruption*. Routledge.

26  Sull, D., & Eisenhardt, K. (2012). Simple rules for a complex world. *Harvard Business Review*. https://hbr.org/2012/09/simple-rules-for-a-complex-world

27 Busulwa, R., Tice, M., & Gurd, B. (2018). *Strategy execution and complexity: Thriving in the era of disruption*. Routledge.

28 Sanders, P. (2008, October 27). Disney learns lessons from pixar. *The Wall Street Journal*. www.wsj.com/articles/SB122506337211970383; Sanders, P. (2008, October 27). Disney learns lessons from pixar. *The Wall Street Journal*. www.wsj.com/articles/SB122506337211970383

# Part III

# Leadership and Management of Digital Transformation

# CHAPTER 7

# Building and Leading the Digital Transformation Team

DOI: 10.4324/9781003254614-10

# INTRODUCTION

At the heart of most successful digital transformations is a highly effective digital transformation team – the collection of people architecting and driving the digital transformation. Such a team requires people with particular knowledge and abilities, experience, influence, personality, and positions or roles within the organization's formal and/or informal hierarchy. While it may be a challenge for some digital transformation teams to tick off all these requirements, the absence of particular requirements or of too many requirements may doom the transformation from the start – for example, resulting in the team's efforts being ignored and sidelined, resulting in an inability to get adequate funding, resulting in the digital transformation falling prey to organization politics, or resulting in the transformation proceeding at such a glacial speed as to stunt its impact. Given these types of risks to the transformation, understanding the talent requirements of the digital transformation team and being able to effect them within the team is critical. In this chapter, the required roles and competencies of the digital transformation team are discussed.

---

**LEARNING OBJECTIVES**

- Understand the type of roles and expertise required for an effective digital transformation team
- Analyze and select optimal members for the digital transformation team
- Apply understanding to build an effective digital transformation team
- Evaluate the strengths and shortcomings of digital transformation teams
- Understand how the absence of particular roles and expertise can impact the success prospects of digital transformation efforts

---

# REQUIRED TYPES OF ROLES AND EXPERTISE FOR THE DIGITAL TRANSFORMATION TEAM

The expertise required by the digital transformation team can be grouped into six areas: (1) strategic leadership, (2) technology leaders and technology specialists, (3) process transformation leaders and process specialists, (4) specialist professional services leaders and specialists, (5) program and project management specialists, and (6) change management specialists. A high-level overview of each area is provided below, in particular the common types of roles involved, example responsibilities of those roles, and example competencies required by people filling those roles. The job titles delivering required expertise may vary across organizations. And some organizations may be lucky enough to have individuals able to deliver expertise across several roles. Where several individuals possess particular expertise, selection of the individual or individuals to include on the digital transformation team should aim to broaden representativeness of the diverse viewpoints of the organization (e.g., by including people across hierarchies, across the value chain, across business units, across customer segments, and across geographies).

## STRATEGIC LEADER OR PRINCIPAL DIGITAL TRANSFORMATION LEADER (E.G., CDO, COO, CIO, CTO)

Most digital transformations need an influential strategic leader as the principal digital transformation leader. A strategic leader is someone on the executive team and/or on the dominant coalition of the organization (e.g., a key owner of the business or someone who wields significant power in the organization).[1] This individual is typically commissioned by the CEO and/or owners of the organization to form, lead, and deliver the effective digital transformation of the organization. A commonly associated job title for the principal digital transformation leader is Chief Digital Officer (CDO). But in some organizations the role may also be performed by a Chief Transformation Officer (CTO), a Chief Information Officer (CIO), a Chief Technology Officer (CTO), a Chief Operating Officer (COO), or another strategic leader.

One crucial responsibility of the principal digital transformation leader is leading, educating, coaching, and doing whatever else is necessary to help other executives understand the digital transformation imperative, relevant digital technologies and their implications, and digital business and digital transformation strategy options and choices. The leader must help other executives remain apprised of the status of transformation efforts and to understand and play the roles they need to play to effectively support digital transformation. Another crucial responsibility of the principal digital transformation leader is to build and manage the digital transformation team (e.g., attracting required talent, continuously engaging them, aligning their motivations/behaviors/actions with the digital transformation and digital business strategy objectives, line managing diverse leaders and specialists) and to ensure it receives sufficient funding and other resources necessary for its full success. Yet another critical responsibility of the principal digital transformation leader is to form or lead the formation of the digital vision, the digital business strategy, and the digital transformation strategy. The principal digital transformation leader also needs to lead the continuous and never-ending work of engaging, educating, and communicating the digital transformation imperative, the digital business strategy, and the digital transformation strategy to the broader organization (e.g., maintaining and enhancing buy-in to the digital vision and the organization change requirements, continuously communicating the transformation imperative and strategy vertically/horizontally/laterally/formally/informally, and being the digital transformation/digital business/digital technology evangelist in chief). Finally, the principal digital transformation leader needs to lead the effective execution and realization of deliberate and emergent digital business and digital transformation strategies so that the organization can realize the desired value from digital transformation efforts (e.g., this may involve effectively translating deliberate strategies into strategic initiatives and cascading those strategic initiatives to all levels/all parts of the organization, it may involve effectively incentivizing the pursuit of strategic initiatives, it may involve effectively reviewing progress and taking corrective actions, and it may involve effectively enabling the emergence of autonomous initiatives in support of the digital transformation).

The ideal principal digital transformation leader will have a potent blend of business acumen (e.g., understanding the inner workings of a business and how it creates value, being able to lead an organization transformation), technology acumen (e.g., understanding different digital technologies and the business value that can genuinely be realized from them, understanding how to effectively lead technology teams, understanding technology methodologies and practices), and strategy acumen (e.g., understanding business strategy and the strategic advantages possible from effectively leveraging different digital technologies). Other competencies that would be invaluable to them include being able to engage and lead the executive team (e.g., having respectable experience, having sufficient personality power, and having sufficient position power), being able to engage and lead the broader organization (e.g., communicating effectively across diverse employee groups, inspiring/energizing employees across diverse communication mediums), being able to attract and engage technology and digital transformation leaders, and proficiency with forming and executing both digital business strategy and digital transformation strategy.

## TECHNOLOGY LEADERS AND TECHNOLOGY SPECIALISTS

A critical part of digital transformation is optimizing the composition and configuration of technology infrastructure, technology assets, and digital ecosystems adopted by an organization to maximize their strategic impact. The diversity in technologies, technology infrastructure, technology assets, and digital ecosystems creates a talent issue for organizations adopting them – how to how to attract, retain, and optimally motivate the necessary technical and strategic talent necessary to enable successful adoption and leveraging of value from the adoption. Typically, such people come in two groups – technical technology specialists (e.g., the people to actually do the technical work involved in identifying vendors to use, configuring acquired technologies/assets for use, providing technical support to users of the technologies/assets, and keeping the technologies/assets in an up-to-date and secure state) and technical technology leaders (e.g., people who are able to effectively attract and line manage technical technology specialists). Either of these two groups of experts may be required to make, advise, and provide assurance on technology issues relating to the digital transformation.

Digital transformations may vary across organizations in the choice of technology infrastructure/technology assets/digital ecosystems to be adopted or enhanced and how these are intended to be leveraged to optimize value creation. Therefore, the technology leaders and technology specialists they need will vary. For example, one organization may require technology leaders and technology specialists across cloud ecosystems, Internet of Things, and artificial intelligence. Whereas another organization may require technology leaders and technology specialists across blockchain, fintech ecosystems, and data science/data analytics technologies.

## TECHNOLOGY IMPLEMENTATION LEADS

The adoption or implementation of new or enhanced technology infrastructure or assets requires careful planning and execution to avoid issues such as new systems/applications/devices not integrating with existing systems, legacy data being lost or subsequent data not being captured properly, impedance of critical processes and workflows, systems availability and security issues, and lack of sufficient training to enable employees to use the new systems/applications/devices. Technology implementation leaders and specialists are required who understand how to carefully plan and execute technology adoptions and implementations. Typically, such people come in two categories – those with strengths and abilities geared toward getting the technologies deployed, and those with strengths and abilities geared toward facilitating the associated process/workflow changes and managing the corresponding change risks. Leaders/managers who can effectively lead and line manage technology implementation leads are also important.

## CUSTOMER EXPERIENCE AND ENGAGEMENT SPECIALISTS

Enhanced customer value, customer experience, and customer engagement are overarching aims of most digital transformation efforts. In fact, digital transformation efforts can hasten an organization's demise if, rather than enhancing, they negatively impact customer value, experience, and engagement. Thus, the digital transformation team should have experts on board who deeply understand the organization's customers, their wants and needs, how to best engage and involve them in the value creation, and their preferences in relation to experiences across channels and devices. Such team members can be experts in these customer aspects by virtue of their experiences and track record, and/ or they may be experts in contemporary customer involvement and engagement approaches like design thinking, user experience design, Lean startup, customer development, and digital customer engagement practices. Customer experience and engagement specialists can play a critical role in ensuring that customer value/experience/engagement remain at the center of digital business and digital transformation strategies. Without them, there is a risk that what the strategies deliver does not enhance customer value or even destroys customer value and results in the loss of important customers.

## SECURITY AND COMPLIANCE SPECIALISTS

As noted in earlier chapters, both the adoption of new or enhanced digital technologies and the transformation of organization processes/ workflows interfacing with those digital technologies can come with significant cybersecurity and digital ethics risks. Without adequate foresight, proactive action, and continuous/near real-time adaptation, these risks may materialize and force cessation of the transformation all together and require its leaders to go back to the drawing board. At worst, the materialization of the risks may put the organization's very survival in jeopardy. Therefore it is important for the digital transformation team to have security and compliance specialists on the team who understand the different types of risks, how to effectively monitor for their manifestations, how to ensure the digital transformation team remains compliant with policies/procedures aimed at mitigating/recovering from those risks, and how to ensure that neither compliance with policies/procedures or noncompliance with policies/procedures don't slow down or stifle digital transformation efforts.

## BUSINESS-TECHNOLOGY LIAISONS

While technology specialists have deep understanding of particular digital technologies and their value, often they have shallow knowledge of the intricacies of the business (e.g., the core work of different business units, how operational and specialist functional processes/workflows work, the key players in different teams, customer wants/needs/behaviors, market trends). Similarly, while operational and functional specialists have a deeper understanding of the intricacies of operational and functional processes and people, they often have shallow knowledge of the intricacies of digital technologies and related issues. Unfortunately, maximizing value from digital technologies requires both technology and business knowledge. Consequently, it requires business and technology teams to be able to be able to sufficiently understand each other and effectively collaborate together. Business-technology liaisons can play an important role as interpreters and facilitators between these parts of the organization that often speak differently, see the world differently, and act differently. In this role, the liaisons can help technology specialists understand the issues/concerns of different parts of the business, the impacts of technology decisions on different processes or people, and how to effectively work with people in different parts of the organization. Similarly, the liaisons can help people outside of the technology team understand the perspectives of technology specialists, how what they do can help the business, and how to best work with them. Liaisons can also help bridge the gap between technology specialists and business people's understanding of how technology can be used to transform processes and customer value.

## PROJECT MANAGERS AND CHANGE MANAGERS

Sooner or later in most digital transformations, the digital transformation team will be involved in leading or participating in the delivery of one or more projects. For example, this might be because it is using one or more project management methodologies for executing digital transformation strategy (e.g., Agile project management) or because a particular digital transformation strategy objective is best suited to use of a particular project management methodology for its realization (e.g., implementation of a software system), or even because use of a particular vendor/ other stakeholder necessitates use of a particular project management methodology. Having appropriately skilled project managers on the digital transformation team will ease leadership or delivery of those projects. In turn, that will enhance the odds of success of the digital transformation. Similarly, absent preventative measures, the digital transformation is likely to face varied resistance to its proposed changes. Specialist change managers can play critical roles in effectively preparing the organization to accept and adapt to proposed changes. Even without resistance to change, such managers can be instrumental in helping cultivate a digital culture. As a result, they are also critical members of the digital transformation team.

## DIGITAL BUSINESS CAPABILITY LEADERS AND SPECIALISTS

Digital business strategy and digital transformation strategy have shared aims of enabling the organization to become a digital business and to effectively compete as a digital business. Ultimately, these aims are enabled by the building, maintenance, continuous upgrading, and optimization of digital business capabilities (these capabilities are discussed further in the section on digital business). As building and optimizing the effectiveness and sustainability of these capabilities is a central aim of digital transformation efforts, it makes sense to have experts in the aims, functioning, and building of these capabilities on the digital transformation team. They can serve to educate the digital transformation team and the wider organization on relevant digital business capabilities, set the vision for relevant capabilities, and advise and/or lead on the formation and execution of strategies to realize relevant capabilities.

## SPECIALIST PROFESSIONAL SERVICES

Finally, the digital transformation team requires specialist advice and support from functional or professional services teams. Digital transformation initiatives have financial, legal, HR, procurement/sourcing, and marketing related issues, needs, and impacts. The digital transformation team therefore needs effective financial, legal, HR, procurement/sourcing, and marketing representatives on the team. Without representatives and supports from these functional areas, the transformation team may find itself unable to access sufficient funding or wasting precious financial resources; it may find key initiatives exposing the organization to significant legal risks; it may find itself unable to access critical talent from business units for particular initiatives; it may find itself in technology procurement/sourcing situations that negatively impact the digital transformation; or it may find itself unable to align customer behavior to changes in product offerings and channels/devices.

# IMPLICATIONS AND CAVEATS

While the list of expertise required is extensive and diverse, not every digital transformation needs every item of expertise. And strategically selected individuals may be able to play several roles and tick off several expertise requirements. Some may even be able to do this while still undertaking their day jobs. It is up to digital transformation leaders to sniff out talent, access opportunities, and use their influence to access required talent from both internally within the organization and externally where needed. Also, digital transformation leaders have to balance the opportunities and challenges that come with building a larger team with all required expertise vs a smaller team that may be deficient in some expertise areas. For example, a smaller team may move faster but have particular blind spots. Whereas a larger team with all relevant expertise may eliminate blind spots but move slower. It is rare for cost limitations to not be a factor when seeking out top talent; leaders may need to find creative ways to access relevant talent in cost effective ways. Finally, as they pursue particular expertise and build the digital transformation team, leaders need to keep in mind the importance of adding people who will contribute their expertise as well as enhance or at least not disrupt team functioning.

# NOTE

1   Boal, K. B., & Hooijberg, R. (2000). *Strategic leadership research: Moving on.* *The Leadership Quarterly*, 11(4), 515–549; Cyert, R. M., & March, J. G. (1963). *Behavioral theory of the firm.* Prentice – Hall Inc.

# CHAPTER 8

# The Digital Disruption and Digital Transformation of Management

DOI: 10.4324/9781003254614-11

# INTRODUCTION

The digital disruption and digital transformation of organizations disrupt managerial practice[1] by changing the nature of organizational work, how management functions or roles can best be undertaken, the optimal tools for undertaking managerial work, and the competencies required to effectively undertake managerial work.[2] Digitally transformed management adopts the optimal approaches for performing management functions, the optimal tools for carrying out managerial work, and the required competencies to use new managerial approaches and tools to accelerate the digital transformation, digital business, and adaptability/agility capabilities of their organizations. This chapter discusses established managerial functions/roles and their digital disruption and transformation. It then discusses the implications of this digital disruption and transformation for managerial effectiveness. The subsequent chapters build on this chapter with a dedicated chapter on each key digital transformation and digital business capability – discussing what it means, the roles managers can play in its building and optimization, and the competencies they require to effectively play their roles in each organization digital business capability.

---

**LEARNING OBJECTIVES**

- Understand key management functions/roles and their evolution
- Understand how the digital disruption and digital transformation of organizations disrupt and transform managerial functions/roles
- Understand how the digital disruption and transformation of managerial functions/roles shapes required managerial competencies
- Apply knowledge and understanding of the digital transformation of management to improve managerial practice in digitally transforming or digital business contexts

---

# MANAGEMENT FUNCTIONS AND ROLES

## RESILIENCE OF FAYOL'S MANAGEMENT FUNCTIONS

Practitioners and researchers have long been interested in the job functions or roles of managers, the corresponding competencies required to carry out those functions and roles, and how both functions/roles and competencies evolve in response to the different management challenges facing organizations.[3] Although there have been debates about meaningfulness and completeness, the management functions of planning, organizing, coordinating, leading, and controlling are still widely accepted.[4] These are based on adaptations and extensions of French management theorist Henri Fayol's ideas from as far back as 1916 (these functions and their interrelationships are shown in Figure 8.1).[5] The planning function involves deciding what needs to happen and how to make it happen (e.g., what objectives/steps/activities to carry out, in what order, by whom, when, and with what resources).[6] It includes activities such as setting objectives, forecasting, budgeting, scheduling, and forming policies and procedures.[7] The organizing function involves allocating human and other resources, assigning work, and granting authority.[8] It includes activities such as establishing/configuring organization structures, delegating work, and building relationships.[9] It also includes staffing activities such as recruiting, training, and developing employees. The coordinating function involves aligning the actions and efforts of people contributing to the plan across functional, department, and hierarchical groups.[10] The leading function involves communicating, motivating, guiding, encouraging, influencing, coaching, and mentoring[11] activities. The controlling function involves activities such as continuously monitoring performance to plan, identifying deviations, and taking corrective actions.[12]

## MINTZBERG'S TEN MANAGERIAL ROLES

Contending that the functions discussed in the previous section didn't really make it clear what day-to-day roles and activities managers undertook, renowned management thinker Henry Mintzberg offered

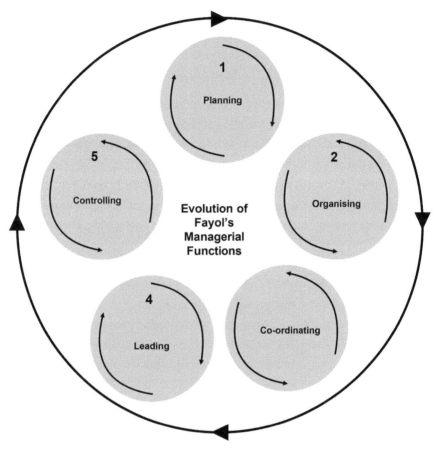

**Figure 8.1** *Managerial functions as commonly conceptualized today evolved from Fayol's research introduced in 1916*

a different view of the job of manager. He proposed that managers are people vested with formal authority over a team or unit. That formal authority enables managers to have status, particular relationships, and access to particular information.[13] This formal authority can be used to fulfill ten roles of managers. Mintzberg organized these ten roles into three categories: interpersonal, informational, and decision roles (see Figure 8.2).[14] In the interpersonal roles category, the manager fulfills figurehead, leader, and liaison roles.[15] Being a figurehead involves representational activities such as performing ceremonial or symbolic duties, signing legal documents, and greeting dignitaries.

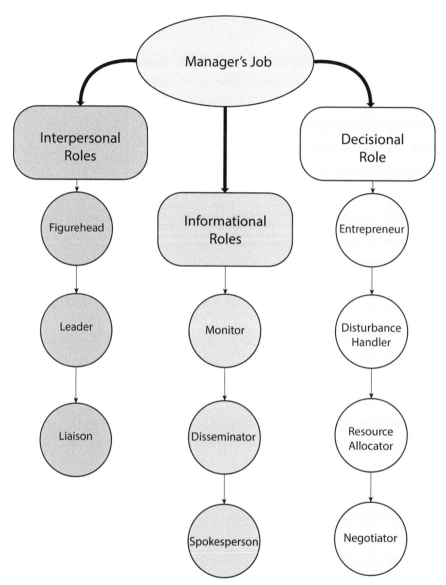

**Figure 8.2** *Mintzberg's ten roles of managers*[25]

Being a leader involves traditional leadership activities like hiring, developing, influencing, and directing staff and other stakeholders.[16] Being a liaison involves facilitating and maintaining information links across formal and informal organization structures and inside and outside the organization. In the informational roles category, the manager fulfills monitor, disseminator, and spokesperson roles.[17] Being a monitor involves constantly scanning the internal and external environment for information about risks and opportunities facing the team. For example, external monitoring may involve reviewing relevant information platforms for political, economic, social, technological, ethical, and legal opportunities and threats that may face the team. Internal monitoring may involve formal and informal interactions such as catch-ups with people up the hierarchy, across functions and business units, and in other subgroups. In carrying out monitoring activities, the manager may come across information about opportunities for, and threats to, the team and its efforts. Being a disseminator involves sharing information between team and organization members (e.g., via emails, reports, memos, meetings).[18] Being a spokesperson involves speaking on behalf of the team members and the team (e.g., speaking up for team members unable to do so by themselves or speaking for the team up the hierarchy, across functions, and outside the organization).[19] In the decisional roles category, the manager fulfills entrepreneur, disturbance handler, resource allocator, and negotiator roles.[20] Being an entrepreneur involves constantly seeking out new ideas and approaches to improve the team's effectiveness and to adapt it to changing internal and external conditions.[21] Being a disturbance handler involves responding to disruptions, crises, and pressures (e.g., a key employee abruptly quits, a financial crisis or pandemic occurs, a key customer goes out of business).[22] As resource allocator, the manager decides how to allocate their time and their financial, talent, attention, and other resources.[23] As a negotiator, the manager represents the team in negotiations (e.g., with senior managers, other departments, unions, other team members).[24] Managerial functions and roles discussed have also included innovation (which can be included in Mintzberg's entrepreneur role or in the leadership role), decision making (which can be included in the planning or leading functions), communicating (which can be included in the leading functions or in Mintzberg's informational roles category), and others.

# DIGITAL DISRUPTION AND DIGITAL TRANSFORMATION OF MANAGEMENT FUNCTIONS, ROLES, AND COMPETENCIES

Organization digital disruption, digital transformation, and digital business disrupt management practice in four ways. First, they disrupt the nature of the work that managers have to manage as well as the outputs of this work. They do this by digitalizing the processes/workflows making up the work and the outputs of the work. For example, whereas once customer support processes and workflows may have been carried out in person or over the phone, digital disruption and digital transformation may now require them to be carried out online (e.g., through live chat or though chatbots) and from more diverse locations and devices (e.g., employee homes, smartphones, PCs). And the outputs of the work may be digital products or digital experiences. This disruption of the nature of the work and the outputs of the work managed prevents managers from managing how they have always managed (e.g., instead of spending time in store with retail employees to improve their customer service, a manager may now need to digitally monitor service delivery occurring across many locations and across many different platforms).

Second, organization digital disruption, digital transformation, and digital business disrupt the nature of the infrastructure and tools used to undertake both managerial work and the work of their direct reports. For example, managers may have to use new data analytics tools to understand and manage employee performance. And both managers and their direct reports may have to communicate using new digital tools such as Zoom or Microsoft Teams. Similarly, managerial workflows may have to occur though digital infrastructure such as cloud computing and mobile platforms or intelligent algorithms (e.g., that check whether employees have taken certain actions and prompt them to do so if needed).

Third, the competencies required to undertake managerial work are disrupted. Managers need new and/or enhanced digital competencies to effectively participate in their organization's digital transformation and digital business change initiatives, manage the increasingly digital/ intelligent/integrated processes and workflows that underpin digital businesses, and use the new and/or enhanced digital infrastructure and tools facilitating digital business processes and workflows. Examples of the types of new or enhanced digital competencies managers require include knowledge and/or understanding of established and emerging digital technologies and assets, knowledge and/or understanding of digital transformation and digital business concepts and capabilities, understanding of and ability to use new digital technology tools, and understanding of and ability to use digital transformation/digital business/digital technology related methods and techniques (e.g., Agile methodologies, accelerators, hackathons, data analytics, and data visualization methods/techniques).

Finally, the optimal ways of undertaking managerial functions/roles are disrupted. Digital processes and workflows, new digital tools, and digital infrastructure/assets, as well as new digital competencies, provide opportunities for managers to undertake managerial functions/roles in more efficient and effective ways. For example, being competent in digital stakeholder engagement tools/platforms like Jira, Trello, Zoom, Microsoft Teams, Zendesk, LiveChat, Slack, and Culture Amp can enable a manager to perform coordination, communication, and liaison activities much more efficiently and effectively – especially at scale, across hybrid work settings, and across time zones. And digital leadership competencies enable managers to create, communicate, and engage employees around a digital vision; they can be an effective interpreter between strategic leaders and direct reports with regard to the digital transformation change and digital business agenda, diagnose and report on/resolve barriers to the change agenda, and better align employee and strategic leadership interests. Alternatively, digital leadership competencies can better enable a manager to shape both a digital culture and a data driven culture. In each of these examples provided, managers are able to draw on more efficient and effective ways of undertaking managerial functions and roles.

Thus, the digital transformation of management refers to the new and/
or enhanced ways of undertaking managerial functions and roles, the
new and/or enhanced tools managers can use for managerial work,
and the digitally transformed work and work outputs that managers
have to manage (i.e., the more digital/intelligent/integrated processes
and workflows as well as their outputs). The digital transformation
of management is critical to enabling organizations to respond to the
digital transformation imperative and to enabling them to build digital
business capabilities like digital transformation strategy,[26] digital
business strategy,[27] digital leadership,[28] digital innovation,[29] digital
customer engagement, digital stakeholder engagement,[30] digital customer
experience,[31] digital technology adoption, digital learning,[32] enterprise
architecture management, digital risk management, digital governance,
digital ethics, adaptability/agility,[33] and cybersecurity management.

Managers who adapt their managerial practice accordingly (i.e.,
who adopt the new ways of undertaking managerial functions/roles,
develop their ability to leverage the new and/or enhanced tools,
and develop their understanding of and ability to manage digitally
transformed workflows) stand to positively transform their efficiency
and effectiveness. In contrast, managers who do not adapt face limited
and declining effectiveness and relevance (e.g., they may find themselves
unable to understand digital work, unable to use necessary digital
tools and infrastructure, and therefore unable to optimize employee
and organization performance in digitally transforming and/or digital
businesses). The chapters that follow will unpack each of the new or
enhanced digital transformation and digital business-related capabilities
required to effectively compete as a digital business. For each capability,
the chapter will discuss the related roles managers need to play, the
new or enhanced managerial competencies they require to play such
roles, and some of the challenges/strategies/benefits of acquiring and
using the new competencies. The chapters will also discuss the risks
of not doing so to both organizations' survival and to managerial
career prospects.

# NOTES

1   Araujo, C. (2019, January 9). The "future of work" in the digital era may not be what you think. Retrieved May 29, 2020, from CIO website: www.cio.com/article/3332203/the-future-of-work-in-the-digital-era-may-not-be-what-you-think.html; Gleeson, B. (2017, March 28). The future of leadership and management in the 21st-century organization. *Forbes*. Retrieved from www.forbes.com/sites/brentgleeson/2017/03/27/the-future-of-leadership-and-management-in-the-21st-century-organization/#2ff06d1b218f; Grant, R. M. (2008). The future of management: Where is Gary Hamel leading us? *Long Range Planning*, 41(5), 469–482. https://doi.org/10.1016/j.lrp.2008.06.003

2   Weill, P. (2018, June 28). Why companies need a new playbook to succeed in the digital age. Retrieved May 29, 2020, from MIT Sloan Management Review website: https://sloanreview.mit.edu/article/why-companies-need-a-new-playbook-to-succeed-in-the-digital-age/; Busulwa, R., Pickering, M., & Mao, I. (2022). Digital transformation and hospitality management competencies: Toward an integrative framework. *International Journal of Hospitality Management*, 102, 103132.

3   Giddens, A. (1981). *A contemporary critique of historical materialism* (Vol. 1). University of California Press; Lynch, F. M. (1997). Management, labour and industrial politics in Modern Europe: The quest for productivity growth during the twentieth century. *Business History*, 39(2), 138–140; Waring, S. P. (2016). *Taylorism transformed: Scientific management theory since 1945*. UNC Press Books; Carroll, S. J., & Gillen, D. I. (1987). Are the classical management functions useful in describing managerial work? *Academy of Management Review*, 12(1), 38–51.

4   Levin, J. S. (2019, April 17). Council post: The role of the successful manager in four simple functions. *Forbes*. Retrieved from www.forbes.com/sites/forbescoachescouncil/2019/04/17/the-role-of-the-successful-manager-in-four-simple-functions/#1c1b22721b12

5   Mintzberg, H. (1990). The manager's job: Folklore and fact. *Harvard Business Review*. Retrieved June 18, 2020, from Harvard Business Review website: https://hbr.org/1990/03/the-managers-job-folklore-and-fact

6   Peaucelle, J. L. (2015). *Henri Fayol, the manager*. Routledge.

7   Levin, J. S. (2019, April 17). Council post: The role of the successful manager in four simple functions. *Forbes*. Retrieved from www.forbes.com/sites/forbescoachescouncil/2019/04/17/the-role-of-the-successful-manager-in-four-simple-functions/#1c1b22721b12

8  Peaucelle, J. L. (2015). *Henri Fayol, the manager*. Routledge.

9  Levin, J. S. (2019, April 17). Council post: The role of the successful manager in four simple functions. *Forbes*. Retrieved from www.forbes.com/sites/forbescoachescouncil/2019/04/17/the-role-of-the-successful-manager-in-four-simple-functions/#1c1b22721b12

10  Peaucelle, J. L. (2015). *Henri Fayol, the manager*. Routledge.

11  Levin, J. S. (2019, April 17). Council post: The role of the successful manager in four simple functions. *Forbes*. Retrieved from www.forbes.com/sites/forbescoachescouncil/2019/04/17/the-role-of-the-successful-manager-in-four-simple-functions/#1c1b22721b12

12  Peaucelle, J. L. (2015). *Henri Fayol, the Manager*. Routledge; Levin, J. S. (2019, April 17). Council post: The role of the successful manager in four simple functions. *Forbes*. Retrieved from www.forbes.com/sites/forbescoachescouncil/2019/04/17/the-role-of-the-successful-manager-in-four-simple-functions/#1c1b22721b12

13  Mintzberg, H. (1990). The manager's job: Folklore and fact. *Harvard Business Review*. Retrieved June 18, 2020, from Harvard Business Review website: https://hbr.org/1990/03/the-managers-job-folklore-and-fact

14  Mintzberg, H. (1990). The manager's job: Folklore and fact. *Harvard Business Review*. Retrieved June 18, 2020, from Harvard Business Review website: https://hbr.org/1990/03/the-managers-job-folklore-and-fact

15  Mintzberg, H. (1990). The manager's job: Folklore and fact. *Harvard Business Review*. Retrieved June 18, 2020, from Harvard Business Review website: https://hbr.org/1990/03/the-managers-job-folklore-and-fact

16  Mintzberg, H. (1990). The manager's job: Folklore and fact. *Harvard Business Review*. Retrieved June 18, 2020, from Harvard Business Review website: https://hbr.org/1990/03/the-managers-job-folklore-and-fact

17  Mintzberg, H. (1990). The manager's job: Folklore and fact. *Harvard Business Review*. Retrieved June 18, 2020, from Harvard Business Review website: https://hbr.org/1990/03/the-managers-job-folklore-and-fact

18  Mintzberg, H. (1990). The manager's job: Folklore and fact. *Harvard Business Review*. Retrieved June 18, 2020, from Harvard Business Review website: https://hbr.org/1990/03/the-managers-job-folklore-and-fact

19  Mintzberg, H. (1990). The manager's job: Folklore and fact. *Harvard Business Review*. Retrieved June 18, 2020, from Harvard Business Review website: https://hbr.org/1990/03/the-managers-job-folklore-and-fact

20  Mintzberg, H. (1990). The manager's job: Folklore and fact. *Harvard Business Review*. Retrieved June 18, 2020, from Harvard Business Review website: https://hbr.org/1990/03/the-managers-job-folklore-and-fact

21  Mintzberg, H. (1990). The manager's job: Folklore and fact. *Harvard Business Review*. Retrieved June 18, 2020, from Harvard Business Review website: https://hbr.org/1990/03/the-managers-job-folklore-and-fact

22  Mintzberg, H. (1990). The manager's job: Folklore and fact. *Harvard Business Review*. Retrieved June 18, 2020, from Harvard Business Review website: https://hbr.org/1990/03/the-managers-job-folklore-and-fact

23  Mintzberg, H. (1990). The manager's job: Folklore and fact. *Harvard Business Review*. Retrieved June 18, 2020, from Harvard Business Review website: https://hbr.org/1990/03/the-managers-job-folklore-and-fact

24  Mintzberg, H. (1990). The manager's job: Folklore and fact. *Harvard Business Review*. Retrieved June 18, 2020, from Harvard Business Review website: https://hbr.org/1990/03/the-managers-job-folklore-and-fact

25  Mintzberg, H. (1990). The manager's job: Folklore and fact. *Harvard Business Review*. Retrieved June 18, 2020, from Harvard Business Review website: https://hbr.org/1990/03/the-managers-job-folklore-and-fact

26  Vial, G. (2019). Understanding digital transformation: A review and a research agenda. *The Journal of Strategic Information Systems*, 28(2), 118–144. https://doi.org/10.1016/j.jsis.2019.01.003

27  Vial, G. (2019). Understanding digital transformation: A review and a research agenda. *The Journal of Strategic Information Systems*, 28(2), 118–144. https://doi.org/10.1016/j.jsis.2019.01.003

28  Cortellazzo, L., Bruni, E., & Zampieri, R. (2019). The role of leadership in a digitalized world: A review. Retrieved from www.frontiersin.org/articles/10.3389/fpsyg.2019.01938/full; Avolio, B. J., Sosik, J. J., Kahai, S. S., & Baker, B. (2014). E-leadership: Re-examining transformations in leadership source and transmission. *The Leadership Quarterly*, 25(1), 105–131.

29  Demirkan, H., Spohrer, J. C., & Welser, J. J. (2016). Digital innovation and strategic transformation. *IT Professional*, 18(6), 14–18; Warner, K. S., & Wäger, M. (2019). Building dynamic capabilities for digital transformation: an ongoing process of strategic renewal. *Long Range Planning*, 52(3), 326–349.

30  Eigenraam, A. W., Eelen, J., Van Lin, A., & Verlegh, P. W. (2018). A consumer-based taxonomy of digital customer engagement practices. *Journal of Interactive Marketing*, 44, 102–121.

31  Bolton, R. N., McColl-Kennedy, J. R., Cheung, L., Gallan, A., Orsingher, C., Witell, L., & Zaki, M. (2018). Customer experience challenges: Bringing together digital, physical and social realms. *Journal of Service Management*, 29(5), 776–808; Nadeem, A., Abedin, B., Cerpa, N., & Chew, E. (2018). Digital

transformation & digital business strategy in electronic commerce: The role of organizational capabilities. *Journal of Theoretical and Applied Electronic Commerce Research*, 13(2), i – viii; Betzing, J. H., Beverungen, D., & Becker, J. (2018). Design principles for co-creating digital customer experience in high street retail. *Proceedings of the Multikonferenz Wirtschaftsinformatik, MKWI*, 18; Parise, S., Guinan, P. J., & Kafka, R. (2016). Solving the crisis of immediacy: How digital technology can transform the customer experience. *Business Horizons*, 59(4), 411–420.

32 Sousa, M. J., & Rocha, Á. (2019). Digital learning: Developing skills for digital transformation of organizations. *Future Generation Computer Systems*, 91, 327–334.

33 Cozzolino, A., Verona, G., & Rothaermel, F. T. (2018). Unpacking the disruption process: New technology, business models, and incumbent adaptation. *Journal of Management Studies*, 55(7), 1166–1202; Busulwa, R., Tice, M., & Gurd, B. (2018). *Strategy execution and complexity: Thriving in the era of disruption*. Routledge; Burgelman, R. A. (1991). Intraorganizational ecology of strategy making and organizational adaptation: Theory and field research. *Organization Science*, 2(3), 239–262; Birkinshaw, J., Zimmermann, A., & Raisch, S. (2016). How Do firms adapt to discontinuous change? Bridging the dynamic capabilities and ambidexterity perspectives. *California Management Review*, 58(4), 36–58.

CHAPTER 9

# Keeping Up With the Pace of Technology Changes

DOI: 10.4324/9781003254614-12

# INTRODUCTION

O rganization digital transformation and digital business capabilities depend on leadership/managerial/other professional digital business competencies (e.g., to lead digital transformation and digital innovation efforts and apply new digital technology tools and assets). These competencies, in turn, depend on leaders/ managers/supporting professionals' ability to keep up with and, therefore, be able to leverage digital technology advancements. Keeping up with digital technologies is increasingly becoming a critical component of "expert leadership" in digitalizing and fully digital businesses. As a result, it is increasingly critical to the effectiveness of leaders/managers/supporting professionals. In this chapter, keeping up with digital technologies is conceptualized as an accelerated learning practice. That is, leaders/managers/supporting professionals can keep up with digital technologies to the extent that they can accelerate or align their learning rate to the rate of change in digital technologies. Accelerated learning, or learning efficiency, has individual beliefs/attitudes/traits levers which can be influenced, and it has learning strategies/practices/habits levers which can be adopted/learned. This chapter unpacks each of these lever types and explains how they interact together to drive the accelerated learning/ learning efficiency necessary to keep up with digital technology advancements.

---

**LEARNING OBJECTIVES**

- Understand the importance and challenge of keeping up with digital technology advancements
- Understand different types of strategies that can be used to keep up with digital technology advancements
- Apply different types of strategies to keep up with digital technology advancements

---

# IMPORTANCE AND CHALLENGE OF KEEPING UP WITH DIGITAL TECHNOLOGIES

Chapter 8 outlined the threat of digital disruption, the pressing need for digital transformation, and the digital capabilities required by organizations to effectively compete as a digital business. For each of these organization digital capabilities, required leadership/managerial competencies (knowledge, skills, abilities) were highlighted. A recurring theme in all organization digital capabilities is the need for leaders/managers/supporting professionals to have sufficient technical and strategic knowledge of, and proficiency with, a range of different digital technologies. Without this knowledge/skills/ability across different digital technologies, leaders/managers/supporting professionals can become key impediments to their organizations' digital transformation and digital business competitiveness efforts – in addition to limiting their own careers. However, leaders/managers/professionals face challenges effectively acquiring the required working knowledge of different digital technologies and keeping it relevant. For example, the range of digital technologies to have working knowledge and skills in is broad; it's ever changing and seems to expand in breadth and depth at an exponential rate. As a result, keeping up with it can easily overwhelm even the most enthusiastic of leaders/managers/ professionals. Leaders/managers/professionals who succeed at it recognize that technology learning is a never-ending process that combines effective technology learning habits/practices with effective strategies to maximize both what is learned and the efficiency with which it is learned.

# COMMON STRATEGIES AND PRACTICES FOR KEEPING UP WITH DIGITAL TECHNOLOGIES

The challenge of keeping up with digital technologies is not a leader/ manager/professional's industry, job function, profession, or location in the organization hierarchy. Across different industries, job functions, professions, and organization hierarchy, a range of strategies and practices are employed to keep up with digital technologies. In the remainder of this chapter, you will find a curated a list of commonly used strategies and practices from both the academic research and from practitioners. This list is just a starting point, and what works for one leader/manager/professional may not work for another. The aim in putting together this list is to start leaders/managers/professionals on the never-ending journey of seeking out effective strategies and practices to add to their repertoire and leveraging the right strategy or practice for them, at the right time, and for the right technology, to maximize their learning and learning efficiency.

# STRATEGIES AND PRACTICES FROM THE RESEARCH ON TECHNOLOGICAL KNOWLEDGE RENEWAL EFFECTIVENESS

Framing it as technological knowledge renewal effectiveness, researchers exploring challenges and drivers of effectiveness at keeping up with digital technologies have identified three individual beliefs/attitudes/traits and two technology learning strategies. The identified individual beliefs/attitudes/traits are (1) perceived need for digital technology competencies, (2) sufficient appreciation of the technology learning challenge, and (3) tolerance for ambiguity.[1] The identified technology learning strategies are learning from external experts and learning from internal experts.[2] Each of these is explained below. Each of these individual beliefs/attitudes/traits and learning strategies can be thought of as a lever that can be turned one way to accelerate technology learning or turned another way to decelerate it.

## PERCEIVED NEED FOR DIGITAL TECHNOLOGY COMPETENCIES, APPRECIATION OF THE TECHNOLOGY LEARNING CHALLENGE, AND TOLERANCE FOR AMBIGUITY

A leader/manager/professional's perceived need for digital technology competencies refers to a leader/manager/professional's belief or lack of belief that digital technology competencies materially impact their job performance and career prospects.[3] Leaders/managers/professionals who don't believe that digital technology competencies materially impact their job performance and career prospects have been shown to lack sufficient motivation to make or sustain the necessary investments in time and effort required to learn and keep up with digital technologies. On the contrary, leaders/managers/professionals who see digital technology competencies as being a significant driver of job performance and career success have been shown to have far greater motivation and persistence in pursuing these competencies. Fortunately for the latter leaders/managers/professionals, the research on expert leadership has reinforced the importance of technical expertise to leadership effectiveness.[4] For leaders/managers/supporting professionals, this technical expertise used to only be expert knowledge of their functional area, and perhaps of their organization and industry. But with the digital transformation of products/services and operational/management processes, technical expertise now also includes technical and strategic digital technology and digital business expertise.

A leader/manager/professional's appreciation of the true challenge of keeping up with digital technologies refers to how accurately they understand and take seriously the rate of change in digital technologies and the resultant disruption threats.[5] The more fully leaders/managers/professionals appreciate and take seriously the rate of change, the more serious has been their approach and effort to keep up with digital technologies. Leaders/managers/professionals underestimating the nature of the challenge in front of them have been found to make insufficient efforts to keep up with digital technologies.[6] Tolerance for ambiguity refers to a leader/manager/professional's tendency to perceive ambiguous situations as tolerable or even desirable.[7] For example, leaders/managers/professionals with higher tolerance for ambiguity are more willing to cope with change, modify their opinions in the face of new information, embrace new experiences, and renew their knowledge.[8] Tolerance for ambiguity has been shown to have a positive impact on the ability to learn new technology[9] and, thus, to keep up with digital technologies.

Leaders/managers/supporting professionals can leverage these three research findings to enhance their and their direct reports' motivation to keep up with digital technologies and resilience in the face of setbacks or overwhelm. For example, they can ensure that they and their direct reports fully understand and are continuously reminded of the value of digital technology competencies to their organizations and careers; they can ensure that they and their direct reports understand the true challenge of keeping up with digital technologies and how this challenge is evolving; and they can ensure that they continuously work on improving their and their direct reports' tolerance for ambiguity (e.g., through work assignments and other learning activities that expand tolerance to ambiguity). For example, they can influence employees to see technological change and dynamism as an opportunity rather than a burden. And they can cultivate a culture that encourages and incentivizes employees to take on and overcome challenges, embrace change, and deal with uncertainty. Through recruiting processes, leaders/managers can ensure that they hire for ambiguity tolerance and motivation to learn and keep up with digital technologies.

## LEARNING FROM EXTERNAL EXPERTS AND LEARNING FROM INTERNAL EXPERTS

Learning from external experts refers to acquiring new knowledge and skills from professional entities outside the organization. The learning activities can be in the form of reading professional literature (e.g., consulting firm research reports on a topic, professional/academic journals on a topic), attending conferences (e.g., a vendor IoT conference), attending networking events (e.g., an information ethics professional's dinner), participating in online forums and discussion boards, signing up for electronic newsletters, or some other form. The amount of time spent on such learning activities, and the choice of learning activities, are strongly associated with effectiveness in learning new digital technologies,[10] and thus with keeping up with digital technologies. In the research, learning from external experts is also referred to as "professional delegation" as the learner "delegates" the identification/curation of what to learn and how to learn it to an expert (typically a professional entity). For example, a learner wanting to learn more about artificial intelligence may seek out leading associations, vendors, and research organizations in that area and make a point of reading as much of their content (e.g., blogs, videos, reports) and attending as many of their conferences and networking events as possible. Learning from internal experts refers to acquiring new knowledge and skills from units or departments or individuals within the organization with that expertise.[11] Typically, this might be the IT/IS/technology function. So, for example, a leader/manager may learn through informal conversations with employees from the IT/IS/technology function. Or they may learn through seeking out the support of, or collaborating on projects with, employees in the IT/IS/technology function. Leaders/ managers/supporting professionals can leverage both external and internal experts in both professional and social contexts to improve what they learn and how efficiently and effectively they learn it.

# STRATEGIES AND PRACTICES FROM PRACTITIONERS

## HAVE AN EVOLVING PLAN FOR MANAGING INFORMATION OVERLOAD

The relentless torrent of information on just about any technology topic, the proliferation of information sources, the blurring boundaries between credible and non-credible information, and the growth of misinformation can leave leaders/managers/professionals feeling overwhelmed. Navigating this situation requires leaders/managers/professionals to make decisions about when to pay attention, what information to pay attention to, what information sources to trust, and when to trust both the information and the information sources. Fortunately, there is no shortage of strategies, habits, and tools that practitioners prescribe for dealing with information overload. These include filtering or explicitly deciding which information sources to pay attention to and which to ignore, [12] having a process for prioritizing and sequencing information consumption[13] (e.g., scanning selected information sources in the morning for the day's content and then curating and scheduling when important items[14] will be read and in what order), implementing automated information filtering tools[15] (e.g., recommendation engines, search tools, email inbox rules), and learning to skim read fast and effectively.[16] Other strategies include curating or eliminating push notification on smart devices, limiting the amount of incoming information[17] (e.g., via email, social media, push notifications, adverts, search engine recommendations, smart devices, computers, etc.), and enhancing the ability to effectively process incoming information.[18] It is important for leaders/managers/supporting professionals to devise their own plan (a combination of strategies, practices, and tools that are effective for them), and that they continuously adapt/evolve this plan to maximize its effectiveness at both enabling optimal learning and offsetting information overload related anxiety/stress.

## CONTINUOUSLY UPGRADE YOUR LEARNING EFFICIENTLY

Learning efficiency refers to a learner's rate of learning and retention.[19] It can also be thought of as a combination of degree of difficulty of what is being learned, the accuracy of learning, and the quantity of learning that takes place per unit of time.[20] Or, put another way, it is the amount and quality of learning that occurs per unit of time, assuming what is being learned is the same. Researchers have linked learning efficiency to attentional control,[21] working memory capacity,[22] learning strategy use (e.g., which strategy and how well it is applied),[23] curiosity,[24] and constructive self-talk.[25] In addition, "learning to learn" and "accelerated learning" are burgeoning fields with contributions from practitioners, social scientists, and educators across a range of industries. Leaders/ managers/supporting professionals can leverage this burgeoning content to dramatically improve focus, memory, curiosity, constructive self-talk, and learning strategy literacy. In doing so, they can dramatically expand the effectiveness and speed with which they learn new digital technologies and related issues.

## CHOOSE THE RIGHT LEARNING PLATFORMS

Learning platforms continue to grow in popularity based on their ability to drive learning efficiency (e.g., through benefits such as curation and serving up content, personalized learning recommendations, behavioral nudges, learning analytics, device flexibility).[26] Platforms can differ in the type of content offered, the way in which the content is delivered, cost, learner experience, certification, device flexibility, and more. For example, there are course style platforms (e.g., CodeSchool, Udemy, Coursera, Job Ready Programmer, Pluralsight, Cloud Academy, Katacoda, DataCamp, Cybrary, Udacity, Linux Academy, Lynda, Skillshare, Code Academy, GoSkills, Edx, Future Learn); there are coaching/mentoring-oriented platforms (e.g, Masterclass, CrossKnowledge); there are technology-oriented content platforms (e.g., MIT Technology Review, ZNet, Engadget, Thenextweb, Wired, Arstechnica, Techcrunch, Tomshardware, Gizmodo, Forbes); there are specialist industry technology content platforms (e.g., hospitalitytech.com, medicalfuturist.com, talkinghealthtech.com, retailitinsights.com); and many more – see Tables 9.1–9.3 for specific examples. By finding and leveraging the right platforms, leaders/managers/supporting professionals can significantly improve their ability to discover which technologies to learn, what issues to focus on in relation to use of that technology within and outside of the industry, what technical and strategic skills to develop, and how to develop skills. In addition, the platforms can make the learning process much more enjoyable.

## EMBRACE OMNICHANNEL LEARNING

Learning can take place in a variety of environments, on a variety of platforms and devices, and at a variety of times. For example, while waiting for a client to arrive, a learner may have 20 minutes to spend on learning activities. Having mobile access to the relevant learning content (e.g., Kindle book, Audible book, YouTube video, LinkedIn article) can result in seized learning opportunities. And these seized opportunities can accumulate over years to represent significant differences in time

*Table 9.1* Top learning tools by category and change in ranking from year to year – Part 1[27]

| 2019 Ranking | Change from 2018 | Tool | Learning tool type |
|---|---|---|---|
| 181 | NEW | Filtered | AI-powered learning platform |
| 182 | NEW | Docebo | AI-powered LMS |
| 67 | down 22 | Powtoon | animated explainer tool |
| 61 | up 33 | Audible | audio books platform |
| 191 | NEW | Fleeq | bite-size training video tool |
| 116 | up 74 | getAbstract | book abstracts |
| 138 | down 17 | Blinkist | book abstracts |
| 165 | down 15 | Omnigraffle | diagramming tool |
| 25 | up 13 | Evernote | digital notebook |
| 71 | down 7 | Kindle App | e-books reader |
| 6 | same | Google Docs and Drive | file sharing and collaboration |
| 17 | down 4 | Dropbox | file sharing platform |
| 55 | down 5 | OneDrive | file sharing platform |
| 91 | down 30 | Quizlet | flashcard app |
| 164 | down 3 | PebblePad | learning journey platform |
| 179 | NEW | EdCast | learning platform |
| 65 | down 18 | Degreed | lifelong learning platform |
| 134 | NEW | Meetup | local community events app |
| 174 | up 9 | Office Lens | makes photos of whiteboards readable |
| 158 | up 4 | Highbrow | micro-course platforms |
| 39 | up 12 | Google Scholar | web search engine |
| 64 | down 15 | Webex | webinar platform |
| 113 | NEW | Jamboard | whiteboard collaboration |
| 197 | NEW | Drafts | writing automation tool |

spent learning. This a key benefit of embracing learning across a range of channels (e.g., across mobile, desktop, other smart devices, social, web, email marketing, digital and physical books, etc.). Omnichannel learning can maximize learning flexibility (e.g., there is always a right channel for the situation), learning availability (e.g., the right content

*Table 9.2* Top learning tools by category and change in ranking from year to year – Part 2[28]

| 2019 Ranking | Change from 2018 | Tool | Learning tool type |
|---|---|---|---|
| 128 | down 10 | Axonify | micro-learning platform |
| 170 | same | Freemind | mind mapping app |
| 133 | BACK | XMind | mind mapping tool |
| 63 | up 39 | Mindmeister | mind mapping app |
| 139 | down 17 | Google Alerts | monitor the Web |
| 15 | down 1 | Feedly | news aggregator |
| 76 | up 48 | Inoreader | news aggregator |
| 183 | BACK | Notability | note-taking app |
| 151 | NEW | Mind Tools | online business resources |
| 121 | down 14 | CodeCademy | online coding courses |
| 13 | up 21 | LinkedIn Learning [Lynda] | online courses |
| 29 | up 7 | Udemy | online courses |
| 53 | down 22 | Coursera | online courses |
| 101 | down 20 | edX | online courses |
| 103 | down 17 | FutureLearn | online courses |
| 115 | up 43 | Udacity | online courses |
| 173 | up 2 | Khan Academy | online courses |
| 176 | up 23 | Alison | online courses |
| 156 | down 43 | Pluralsight | online IT courses |
| 24 | up 6 | TED Talks | online talks |
| 54 | NEW | Apple Podcasts | podcast platform |
| 105 | BACK | Pocket Casts | podcast player |
| 146 | down 16 | Overcast | podcast player |

is always accessible), and learning efficiency (e.g., the most efficient channel in a situation can be used, and there are less wasted learning opportunities). It would be highly advantageous for leaders/managers/supporting professionals to make deliberate efforts to effect and maximize omnichannel learning (e.g., signing up to platforms across a range of channels, downloading relevant apps, and ensuring online/

**Table 9.3** *Top learning tools by category and change in ranking from year to year – Part 3*[30]

| 2019 Ranking | Change from 2018 | Tool | Learning tool type |
|---|---|---|---|
| 155 | down 22 | Castro | podcast player |
| 157 | NEW | Podcast Addict | podcast player |
| 107 | BACK | Quora | Q&A website |
| 177 | BACK | Quizizz | quizzing app |
| 178 | BACK | Zotero | research management app |
| 56 | down 21 | Pocket | save for later app |
| 27 | down 2 | Snagit | screen capture tool |
| 110 | NEW | Loom | screen recorder |
| 148 | NEW | Screencastify | screen recorder |
| 92 | down 15 | Screencast-O-matic | screen casting app |
| 23 | up 1 | Camtasia | screen casting tool |
| 77 | down 11 | Google Maps | searchable/zoomable maps |
| 32 | up 17 | Diigo | social bookmarking |
| 1 | same | YouTube | video platform |
| 66 | down 13 | Vimeo | video platform |
| 159 | up 34 | Kaltura | video platform |
| 129 | NEW | Microsoft Stream | video streaming service |
| 99 | down 16 | Adobe After Effects | visual effects app |
| 35 | up 19 | Google Chrome | web browser |
| 125 | up 13 | Firefox | web browser |
| 167 | down 14 | Microsoft Edge | web browser |
| 81 | down 21 | Adobe Connect | web conferencing platform |
| 142 | BACK | Big Blue Button | web conferencing platform |
| 94 | down 24 | Sway | web content app |
| 2 | up 1 | Google Search | web search engine |

offline availability, sufficient data, access to optimal smart devices, etc.). It would also be highly advantageous for leaders/managers/supporting professionals to invest time in constantly improving their omnichannel learning approach (e.g., adding new tools, reconfiguring content access processes, integrating content across channels, etc.).

## BUILD AND LEVERAGE THOUGHT LEADERS ON SOCIAL NETWORKS

Besides their published works, social media provides one of the greatest vehicles to access the insights and latest thinking of digital technology, digital transformation, and digital business thought leaders. Through following digital strategy, AI, data science, and blockchain thought leaders on Twitter, LinkedIn, Facebook, and other social networks, leaders/managers/supporting professionals can access cutting edge information directly from people shaping the evolution of these digital technologies. In contrast, this information may take decades to filter down through other information channels like published books and courses. A range of strategic leaders of world leading technology companies, technical specialists and futurists, and industry technology specialists post regularly on Twitter, LinkedIn, Facebook, and other social media sites (e.g., Bill Gates, Cathy Hackl, Michael Krigsman, QuHarrison Terry, Paul Graham, Lisa Seacat Deluca, Tom Davenport, Michael Fauscette, Brian Solis, Bill Marriott, Daniel E. Craig, Jason Q. Feed, Craig Rispin). Through regularly following the posts of these thought leaders on social networks, leaders/managers/supporting professionals can learn first, spot technology opportunities first, and ensure their organizations profit first. For example, one early-stage company participating in a seed accelerator to raise funding struggled to raise a million dollars in startup funding through conventional venture capitalists. In contrast, a cohort company participating in the same seed accelerator acted on a tweet suggesting that there was not an easier fundraising opportunity than ICOs (initial coin offerings at that time). The startup, spotting and acting on this thought leader's insight, spent its time setting up an ICO instead of pursuing venture capitalists. As a result, it raised millions of dollars in the course of a month without having to give up any ownership in the company.[29]

## CONFIGURE YOUR SEARCH ENGINES, SOCIAL MEDIA, AND EMAIL SUBSCRIPTIONS

Suggested news articles, social media feeds, and subscription emails can be distractions, drawing time away from learning activities. Google's search engine app, for example, automatically suggests news articles a searcher might be interested in. And social media platforms like LinkedIn and Twitter have automatic news/post feeds that platform users see as soon as they log in. Similarly, the majority of people are likely to scroll through a bunch of subscription emails before getting to a personal or work email. But rather than being distractions, suggested news articles, social media feeds, and emails can be configured to be content discovery and learning prompts. For example, Google-suggested news articles can be configured to suggest news articles related to desired technology learning topics (e.g., configured to automatically search and suggest news article for "digital business model" and "digital innovation"; each time a user opens the search app it can automatically deliver the latest news about new digital business models or digital innovation practices). Search results can also be configured to automatically be emailed monthly/weekly/daily. For example, a user may configure weekly alerts for "new digital business model" and receive an email with links to the latest information containing those keywords as soon as such information goes online somewhere in the world. Similarly, social media feeds can be configured so that they automatically serve up information on particular learning topics. For example, on LinkedIn and Twitter you can subscribe to/follow certain hashtags (e.g., #artificialintelligence, #digitalleadership, #digitalinnovation) to automatically receive the latest news and posts relating to these topics. And you can also use those hashtags to filter for and follow particular thought leaders for each hashtag. By configuring the platforms they access most regularly, leaders/managers/supporting professionals have access to cutting edge news and insights on technology topics, as well as near daily curiosity, reflection, and learning prompts for their targeted learning topics.

## HAVE AN EFFECTIVE AND SUSTAINABLE PERSONAL INFORMATION MANAGEMENT STRATEGY

After configuring channels, platforms, and devices to deliver the best information, then comes the challenge of capturing each information item, storing each information item, organizing it so it can be found, and leveraging tools that can enable near-instant retrieval of the desired article as and when needed. Doing so can significantly enhance learning efficiency by minimizing retrieval time and the chance of the desired information may not be found, thereby losing the learning opportunity or at least making it suboptimal. But having an effective system for storing and retrieving information can be challenging. One issue is the number of channels in which information can be sourced (e.g., social media, YouTube, search engines, email, conversations with people, conferences, etc.). For example, it can be challenging to remember which channel the information resides. Or it can be time consuming to transfer information across channels in order to have all information on a single platform or device. Another issue is that some content requires platform specific storage (e.g., YouTube videos may be better stored on YouTube). Yet another issue is that some platforms and devices significantly simplify the retrieval and learning experience but are limited in their ability to integrate information from other platforms/devices. Further, settling on a particular platform or device, and building learning routines around it, needs careful consideration since the device or platform can be discontinued. Or it may not be updated regularly enough to keep with changes across other platforms, hence limiting integrability. Fortunately, a range of personal information management platforms and tools exist. Leaders/managers/supporting professionals can curate or architect a combination of platforms, devices, and apps that fit perfectly into their routines to maximize learning effectiveness. For example, one manager may decide on the following configuration/architecture: email (use Gmail for personal emails and set up email folders by technology topic; then drag and drop information into relevant folders for ease of retrieval [e.g., new digital innovation practice related emails can be dragged and dropped into "digital innovation practices" folder, whereas digital business model related emails can go into the "digital strategies" folder]); articles (use Instapaper to save articles for later reading and set up folders in Instapaper [e.g., a "digital innovation practices" folder or a "new digital tech to explore" folder]; Instapaper is available on almost all devices, can be integrated into almost all browsers to enable single button addition of articles, and has inbuilt search in addition to a folder structure to enable even faster retrieval of articles); video (establish a YouTube account and follow key thought leaders' channels, set up folders to save videos [e.g., "digital innovation practices" and "digital strategies"]); audio (set up Audible and Blinkist to be able to listen to books and book summaries; make these apps available on mobile, desktop, carplay); books (set up Kindle app and Apple books to purchase any book and have lifetime access to it; the search function in these apps can enable in-book search; the apps have inbuilt note taking); TV (set up technology related channels and apps on the smart TV to enable watching of interesting tech documentaries); notes (set up Apple Notes or Evernote to enable digital note taking; these have highly effective inbuilt search functions to enable fast access to past notes); transcription (set up audio recording and transcription apps on mobile and desktop [e.g., Otter Voice Meeting]; integrate these with virtual meeting apps such as Microsoft Teams and Google Meet); desktop/ laptop (ensure all selected platforms/applications are cloud based and can be replicated onto a desktop/laptop/web environment); and smart device (ensure apps for as many of the platforms used as possible are also installed on every possible smart device so that if one device is down, learning can switch to another device). What has just been outlined is one example of a personal information management approach; it can be configured differently to suit each individual (e.g., more or better channels, platforms, apps, devices can be added; and perhaps a better plan for integrating information across channels, devices, platforms, and apps). The most effective strategies/approaches are those undergoing continuous adaptation/improvement as users gauge their effectiveness, as users discover better tools, and as users evolve their learning behaviors. Deliberately designing/architecting/configuring a system and continuously improving it can supercharge learning efficiency and effectiveness.

## PARTICIPATE IN HACKATHONS AND ACCELERATORS

Hackathons originated as computer-programming events in which a small group of people work intensely together (sometimes around the clock to solve a difficult programming problem in a fixed [and often very short] amount of time).[31] For example, they could work on "hacking" or solving a complex security problem over the course of a weekend, whereas this problem might otherwise take months or years via traditional approaches. Due to their success, hackathons have been applied to solve a range of problems across sectors, industries, and disciplines.[32] Many hackathons focus on leveraging digital technologies and digital business models to solve organization, government, community, and state problems. Many are run in a competitive style format (different teams competing to solve a problem first or come up with the best solution in the timeframes allowed) for a prize and are open to teams or individual volunteers who are then allocated into teams by the hackathon organizers. For example, some nation states have "govhack" style hackathons in which volunteer teams are formed to leverage publicly available government data to build innovative new products over the course of a weekend (e.g., these products could be mobile apps, smart devices, cloud platforms, etc.). These particular types of hackathons have a big data focus, but there are others that focus on leveraging different digital technologies. Leaders/managers/supporting professionals can build practical working knowledge of digital technologies, digital strategy, and digital innovation participating as members of a hackathon team, by volunteering as hackathon organizers/facilitators, or by volunteering as judges of hackathon innovations/solutions. In any participation form, leaders/managers/professionals can gain a lot of practical know-how about the digital technologies leveraged in that hackathon, about digital innovation and digital strategy issues, and about digital leadership.

In contrast to a hackathon, an accelerator (e.g., seed accelerator, startup accelerator, corporate accelerator), is a fixed-term, cohort based, accelerated learning program that typically focuses on accelerating product development and commercialization processes.[33] An accelerator program is typically run over a 3–6-month period that culminates in a "Shark Tank" style public pitch event known as demo day.[34] In this time accelerated or compressed learning occurs through a combination of iterative experimentation, intensive mentoring and coaching, customer and investor feedback, and product/business model pitching. Accelerators usually bring together a network of investors, entrepreneurs, potential strategic partners, and potential customers that cohort companies can draw on to accelerate their learning, product development, and commercialization outcomes. Leaders/managers/supporting professionals can participate in accelerators as volunteer organizers, industry or function specific coaches/mentors, demo day judges, or just as demo day observers. There are even industry tech-focused accelerators which would expose leaders/managers/supporting professionals to emerging industry technologies and business models, potential areas of industry disruption, and innovation opportunities or challenges. Leaders/managers/supporting professionals can also leverage the accelerator model to drive innovation at their organization (e.g., partnering with an organization such as TechStars to invite teams of internal and external people to participate in an accelerator program focused on developing innovative new products for the organization or that the organization can acquire and commercialize).

## VOLUNTEER FOR A STARTUP

Similar to the learning benefits of hackathons and accelerators, leaders/managers/supporting professionals can volunteer to be on the boards of technology startups. For example, a manager could join an early-stage custom software development firm as an industry advisor or provide other advice in the manager's other specialist area of expertise. In return, that manager would have the opportunity to accelerate their learning of different digital technologies and of operational and strategic technology issues. They would also have an informal sounding board to run ideas or questions by.

# IMPLICATIONS FOR LEADERS/ MANAGERS/SUPPORTING PROFESSIONALS

This chapter had three aims; first, it sought to highlight the importance of accelerated learning or learning efficiency as an important leadership/managerial/professional competence for keeping up with digital technologies. Second, it sought to highlight the importance of taking a strategic approach to managing accelerated learning and to provide an example framework of such an approach. Finally, it aimed to provide some example strategies, practices, and habits that leaders/managers/supporting professionals can leverage to accelerate their learning. But all this is just a starting point; and our hope is that leaders/managers/supporting professionals use this starting point to begin the career-long process of seeking out accelerated learning practices and tools and leveraging these to adapt and optimize their accelerated learning strategy. Doing so is crucial to keeping up with exponential advancements in digital technologies and to growing leaders/managers/professionals' performance demands.

## GOOGLE AND REFLECT

Accelerated learning, learning efficiency, learning science, content curation, expert leadership, tolerance for ambiguity, learner self-talk, constructive self-talk, experiential learning, learning platform, learning experience platform (LXP), attention control, memory capacity, learning strategy, curiosity, learning to learn, omnichannel learning, thought leader, futurist, personal information management strategy (PIM), hackathon, accelerator, project-based learning, inquiry based learning

## DISCUSSION QUESTIONS

1  What is accelerated learning?
2  What is learning efficiency?
3  What is the difference between accelerated learning and learning efficiency?
4  What personal three characteristics drive learning efficiency?
5  What are the top four drivers of learning efficiency?
6  What is the role of digital technologies in learning efficiency?
7  How do digital technologies enhance learning efficiency?

8　What is the relationship between digital technologies, learning efficiency, and a leader/manager/professional's ability to keep up with digital technologies?

# NOTES

1　Rong, G., & Grover, V. (2009). Keeping up-to-date with information technology: Testing a model of technological knowledge renewal effectiveness for it professionals. *Information & Management*, 46(7), 376–387.

2　Rong, G., & Grover, V. (2009). Keeping up-to-date with information technology: Testing a model of technological knowledge renewal effectiveness for it professionals. *Information & Management*, 46(7), 376–387.

3　Rong, G., & Grover, V. (2009). Keeping up-to-date with information technology: Testing a model of technological knowledge renewal effectiveness for it professionals. *Information & Management*, 46(7), 376–387.

4　Markman, A. (2017). *Can you be a great leader without technical expertise.* Harvard Business Review; Goodall, Amanda H., & G. Pogrebna. Expert leaders in a fast-moving environment. *The Leadership Quarterly*, 26(2), 123–142.

5　Rong, G., & Grover, V. (2009). Keeping up-to-date with information technology: Testing a model of technological knowledge renewal effectiveness for it professionals. *Information & Management*, 46(7), 376–387.

6　Rong, G., & Grover, V. (2009). Keeping up-to-date with information technology: Testing a model of technological knowledge renewal effectiveness for it professionals. *Information & Management*, 46(7), 376–387.

7　Rong, G., & Grover, V. (2009). Keeping up-to-date with information technology: Testing a model of technological knowledge renewal effectiveness for it professionals. *Information & Management*, 46(7), 376–387.

8　Rong, G., & Grover, V. (2009). Keeping up-to-date with information technology: Testing a model of technological knowledge renewal effectiveness for it professionals. *Information & Management*, 46(7), 376–387.

9　Rong, G., & Grover, V. (2009). Keeping up-to-date with information technology: Testing a model of technological knowledge renewal effectiveness for it professionals. *Information & Management*, 46(7), 376–387.

10　Rong, G., & Grover, V. (2009). Keeping up-to-date with information technology: Testing a model of technological knowledge renewal effectiveness for it professionals. *Information & Management*, 46(7), 376–387.

11 Rong, G., & Grover, V. (2009). Keeping up-to-date with information technology: Testing a model of technological knowledge renewal effectiveness for it professionals. *Information & Management*, 46(7), 376–387.

12 Lavenda, D. (2012). 7 time-proven strategies for dealing with information overload. Retrieved June 15, 2020, from Fast Company website: www. fastcompany.com/3002467/7-time-proven-strategies-dealing-information-overload; Asay, M. (2009). Shirky: Problem is filter failure, not info overload. *CNet*. Retrieved June 15, 2020, from CNet website: www.cnet. com/news/shirky-problem-is-filter-failure-not-info-overload/; Beaton, C. (2017). The single most effective way to deal with information overload. Retrieved June 15, 2020, from Inc.com website: www.inc.com/caroline-beaton/the-single-most-effective-way-to-deal-with-information-overload. html

13 Lavenda, D. (2012). 7 time-proven strategies for dealing with information overload. Retrieved June 15, 2020, from Fast Company website: www.fastcompany. com/3002467/7-time-proven-strategies-dealing-information-overload

14 Lavenda, D. (2012). 7 time-proven strategies for dealing with information overload. Retrieved June 15, 2020, from Fast Company website: www.fastcompany. com/3002467/7-time-proven-strategies-dealing-information-overload

15 Lavenda, D. (2012). 7 time-proven strategies for dealing with information overload. Retrieved June 15, 2020, from Fast Company website: www.fastcompany. com/3002467/7-time-proven-strategies-dealing-information-overload

16 Lavenda, D. (2012). 7 time-proven strategies for dealing with information overload. Retrieved June 15, 2020, from Fast Company website: www.fastcompany. com/3002467/7-time-proven-strategies-dealing-information-overload

17 Soucek, R., & Moser, K. (2010). Coping with information overload in email communication: Evaluation of a training intervention. *Computers in Human Behavior*, 26(6), 1458–1466.

18 Soucek, R., & Moser, K. (2010). Coping with information overload in email communication: Evaluation of a training intervention. *Computers in Human Behavior*, 26(6), 1458–1466.

19 Zerr, C. L., Berg, J. J., Nelson, S. M., Fishell, A. K., Savalia, N. K., & McDermott, K. B. (2018). Learning efficiency: Identifying individual differences in learning rate and retention in healthy adults. *Psychological Science*, 29(9), 1436–1450. https://doi.org/10.1177/0956797618772540

20 Bruce, G. S. (2004). Learning efficiency goes to college. In *Evidence-based educational methods* (pp. 267–275). Academic Press. https://doi.org/10.1016/ b978-012506041-7/50016-4

21 Zerr, C. L., Berg, J. J., Nelson, S. M., Fishell, A. K., Savalia, N. K., & McDermott, K. B. (2018). Learning efficiency: Identifying individual differences in learning rate and retention in healthy adults. *Psychological Science*, 29(9), 1436–1450. https://doi.org/10.1177/0956797618772540

22 Zerr, C. L., Berg, J. J., Nelson, S. M., Fishell, A. K., Savalia, N. K., & McDermott, K. B. (2018). Learning efficiency: Identifying individual differences in learning rate and retention in healthy adults. *Psychological Science*, 29(9), 1436–1450. https://doi.org/10.1177/0956797618772540

23 Zerr, C. L., Berg, J. J., Nelson, S. M., Fishell, A. K., Savalia, N. K., & McDermott, K. B. (2018). Learning efficiency: Identifying individual differences in learning rate and retention in healthy adults. *Psychological Science*, 29(9), 1436–1450. https://doi.org/10.1177/0956797618772540

24 Andersen, E. (2016). Learning to learn. *Harvard Business Review*. Retrieved June 15, 2020, from Harvard Business Review website: https://hbr.org/2016/03/learning-to-learn

25 Andersen, E. (2016). Learning to learn. *Harvard Business Review*. Retrieved June 15, 2020, from Harvard Business Review website: https://hbr.org/2016/03/learning-to-learn

26 Gullotti, D. (2019, November 26). Leveraging technology platforms for the best learning experiences. *Harvard Business Publishing*. Retrieved June 15, 2020, from Harvard Business Publishing website: www.harvardbusiness.org/leveraging-technology-platforms-for-the-best-learning-experiences/

27 Hart. J. (2019). Top 200 learning tools for 2019: Results of the 13th Annual Learning Tools Survey published 18 September 2019. Retrieved June 20, 2020, from Toptools4learning.com website: www.toptools4learning.com/

28 Hart. J. (2019). Top 200 learning tools for 2019: Results of the 13th Annual Learning Tools Survey published 18 September 2019. Retrieved June 20, 2020, from Toptools4learning.com website: www.toptools4learning.com/

29 Busulwa, R., Birdthistle, N., & Dunn, S. (2020). *Startup accelerators: A field guide*. John Wiley & Sons.

30 Hart. J. (2019). Top 200 learning tools for 2019: Results of the 13th Annual Learning Tools Survey published 18 September 2019. Retrieved June 20, 2020, from Toptools4learning.com website: www.toptools4learning.com/

31 Lara, M., & Lockwood, K. (2016). Hackathons as community-based learning: A case study. *TechTrends*, 60(5), 486–495. https://doi.org/10.1007/s11528-016-0101-0

32 Lara, M., & Lockwood, K. (2016). Hackathons as community-based learning: A case study. *TechTrends*, 60(5), 486–495. https://doi.org/10.1007/s11528-016-0101-0

33 Busulwa, R., Birdthistle, N., & Dunn, S. (2020). *Startup accelerators: A field guide*. John Wiley & Sons.

34 Busulwa, R., Birdthistle, N., & Dunn, S. (2020). *Startup accelerators: A field guide*. John Wiley & Sons.

# Part IV

# Understanding Digital Business Capabilities

## Primers for Leaders, Managers, and Supporting Professionals

CHAPTER 10

# Digital Transformation Strategy and Digital Business Strategy Capabilities

DOI: 10.4324/9781003254614-14

# INTRODUCTION

This primer looks at two organization capabilities that shape how organizations become and effectively compete as digital businesses. The first capability, digital transformation strategy, refers to the organization routines/activities, structures, and/or processes that work together to enable an organization to safely, effectively, and efficiently undertaking the change processes involved in becoming a digital business. And the second capability, digital business strategy, refers to the routines/activities, structures, and/or processes that work in concert to enable an organization to effectively compete as a digital business. The focus of the primer is on ensuring leaders, managers, and supporting professionals understand what each capability means, what its significance is, what roles they need to play in it, and what competencies they need to play required roles in catalyzing the building, maintenance, and optimization of the capability.

---

**LEARNING OBJECTIVES**

- Develop knowledge of the key definitions and concepts related to digital transformation strategy and digital business strategy capabilities
- Understand the meaning and role of these capabilities in the digital transformation strategy and digital business strategy of organizations
- Understand the roles that leaders and managers can play in these digital capabilities
- Understand the competencies required by leaders and managers to maximize their roles in these digital capabilities
- Analyze and evaluate the implications of these capabilities, as well as related leadership or management roles and competencies, for organizations' digital transformation strategy and digital business strategy
- Apply knowledge and understanding to participate in, support, or lead workstreams or initiatives related to the building and optimization of these capabilities

---

# UNDERSTANDING DIGITAL BUSINESS STRATEGY

Digital business strategy is strategy formed and realized by leveraging digital resources to achieve breakthroughs in efficiency, differentiation, adaptability, and agility.[1] It fuses together the domains of information systems and business strategy so that, rather than being positioned below business strategy or being a component of business strategy (like traditional IT strategy), digital business strategy becomes business strategy itself.[2] This is because digital technology advancements continue to rapidly fuse together people, processes, technologies, networks, and things inside and outside organizations (or blur the boundaries between them) to such a degree that conceiving strategy separately is increasingly becoming counterproductive. When digital business strategy becomes the business strategy itself, it is able to be a strategic dynamic capability that enables organizations to dynamically configure and orchestrate diverse digital assets to respond to and shape changes in marketplaces.[3]

Jeanne Ross and Ina Sebastian, researchers at the MIT Center for Information Systems Research, and Cynthia Beath, emerita professor of information systems at the University of Texas, propose that a great digital business strategy sets a clear direction.[4] In doing so, it enables leaders/managers to form and lead digital initiatives, assess their progress against the set direction, and adapt their efforts as required.[5] Sunil Gupta, professor of business administration at Harvard Business School and chair of the executive program on driving digital strategy, warns that digital business strategy shouldn't just be thought of as having an independent digital unit or running digital experiments. That the former is like launching a speedboat to turn around a large ship (lots of activity and speed but it does not move the ship); and the latter, without a clear roadmap, may result in proliferation of disjointed ideas that don't address fundamental strategic issues.[6] He also cautions that, while organizations should always pursue cost reduction and operational efficiency, viewing digital business strategy solely as leveraging technology to reduce costs and improve operational efficiency ignores the potential (and high likelihood) of technology fundamentally disrupting the business and its industry.[7] This is consistent with the thinking of MIT researchers Jeanne Ross and Ina Sebastian, and Cynthia Beath, who clarify that operational excellence (efficiency and effectiveness) is a digital business commodity, not a basis for competitive advantage. These three researchers also argue that organizations should choose between a customer engagement strategy (one that ". . . targets superior, personalized experiences that engender customer loyalty") or a digitized solutions strategy (one that ". . . targets information-enriched products and services that deliver new value for customers") – but not attempt both, as they risk doing both badly.

Digital business strategy is about leaders/managers determining what combination of digital assets to leverage and how to leverage them to effectively compete as a digital business. Effectively competing as a digital business requires competing on new and evolving bases of competition such as being able to rapidly flex operations up or down in response to disruptions or changes in demand (e.g., elastic cloud infrastructure),[8] benefiting from network effects and multi-sided business models,[9] being able to scale rapidly (e.g., between 1996–1999 Amazon grew from 151 employees generating US$5.1 million revenue to 7,600 employees generating $1.64 billion revenue),[10] shared digital asset alliances and partnerships (e.g., hospitality and leisure organizations that share reservation systems, loyalty programs, and online cross selling – such as Star Alliance and OneWorld), speed (e.g., speed to market of new products, match speed of complementary product partners and of competitors, speed of decision making, real-time customer sensing and responsiveness, speed of supply chain orchestration, speed of network formation and adaptation, etc.),[11] expanded value creation/capture opportunities (e.g., leveraging growing data availability for product innovation, creating and capturing value from coordinating different business models in networks, building and controlling industry platforms and ecosystems).[12]

# UNDERSTANDING DIGITAL TRANSFORMATION STRATEGY

Whereas digital business strategy focuses on identifying effective future states that optimize competitiveness as a digital business, digital transformation focuses on forming and effecting the blueprint for becoming a digital business,[13] that is, forming and effecting the blueprint for how to undertake the necessary changes to the organization's structures, digital infrastructure, culture, and capabilities/competencies. For example, this blueprint can address how to build a guiding coalition to drive necessary changes and overcome barriers to change, how to reconfigure internal structures to catalyze necessary changes (e.g., reconfiguring business functions or units, leadership roles, reporting relationships), and how to how to bring about necessary cultural change (e.g., changes in attitudes, beliefs, behaviors). As noted earlier, digital transformation is an all-encompassing change and undertaking that comes with significant risks. Examples of manifestations of these risks include significant investments in digital transformation that don't bring about the desired transformation, mishandled digital infrastructure or technology tool changes that result in data breaches, loss of key talent who may become frustrated with how the change is undertaken, and short-term financial risks that may threaten the continued survival of the organization.

# IMPLICATIONS FOR LEADERS, MANAGERS, AND SUPPORTING PROFESSIONALS

Leaders, managers, and supporting professionals need to play critical roles in building, sustaining, and optimizing digital business strategy and digital transformation strategy capabilities. These roles include leading the formation and realization of a digital business strategy (e.g., establishing a clear mission/vision/direction for digital business, identifying and leading digital business initiatives, motivating people at different levels and in different parts of the organization to participate in the building and leveraging of digital business capabilities, aligning digital business efforts, etc.). They include participating in digital business strategy formation (e.g., contributing ideas for business model innovations, digital assets to implement and leverage, networks/ecosystems/communities to participate in, product/service innovations, customer experience innovations, etc.), and championing and supporting digital business strategy initiatives and cultural changes (e.g., leveraging their formal and informal networks to encourage employees to understand and embrace digital business strategy initiatives, ensuring their direct reports have relevant knowledge and skills, and modeling appropriate attitudes and behaviors).

To effectively lead, participate in, and/or champion digital business strategy and digital transformation strategy efforts, leaders, managers, and supporting professionals need corresponding digital competencies. Examples of these digital competencies include having an understanding of different digital technology advancements and their strategic implications (e.g., what digital assets do advancements in IoT, AI, blockchain, robotics, and drones present) and having working knowledge of the technical aspects of these digital technologies (e.g., how do they work; what are the limitations and issues; what is really involved in implementing and using them; what is hype and what is reality in their value proposition; etc.). Further examples of required competencies include having a working understanding of different digital business strategy approaches and benefits (e.g., different business models and approaches to digital infrastructure configuration, alliances and partnerships, network and ecosystem participation, product innovation and enhancement, and adaptability and agility, etc.), having a working understanding of digital business bases of competition and the value of key platforms and ecosystems, and having a working understanding of digital transformation strategies and accelerated change/transformation approaches (e.g., speed is critical to digital business and digital transformation strategy, so leaders/managers/supporting professionals leading digital strategy initiatives need to understand effective approaches for rapidly implementing and instituting digital business strategy initiatives so they aren't undermined, rejected, or killed off by the wider organization – examples of these approaches include Agile,[14] Lean thinking,[15] Lean startup,[16] design thinking,[17] accelerators,[18] change acceleration,[19] etc.).

# GOOGLE AND REFLECT

| Digital capability | Common terminology |
|---|---|
| Digital business strategy | Digital asset, digital infrastructure, elastic Infrastructure, business model innovation, digital capability, network effects, digital ecosystem, API economy, digital heart, digital footprint, digital platform, growth hacking, mobile first, MVP, platform economy, touchpoints, composable business, Omnichannel, Interoperability |
| Digital transformation strategy | Technical debt, inclusivity, employee engagement, cross – functional collaboration, digital strategist, chief digital officer, Multidisciplinary team, agile, business led IT, digital dexterity, digitalization, digitization, shadow IT, change management, change acceleration |

# DISCUSSION QUESTIONS

1 How is digital business strategy different from traditional strategy?
2 How is digital transformation strategy different to digital business strategy?
3 What leadership or management role in digital business strategy is the most critical to building and maintaining that capability? Why?
4 What digital business strategy related competency is likely to have the greatest positive impact on a leader/manager/supporting professional's career?

# NOTES

1 Bharadwaj, A., El Sawy, O. A., Pavlou, P. A., & Venkatraman, N. (2013). Digital business strategy: Toward a next generation of insights. *MIS Quarterly*, 471–482.
2 Bharadwaj, A., El Sawy, O. A., Pavlou, P. A., & Venkatraman, N. (2013). Digital business strategy: Toward a next generation of insights. *MIS Quarterly*, 471–482.

3  Bharadwaj, A., El Sawy, O. A., Pavlou, P. A., & Venkatraman, N. (2013). Digital business strategy: Toward a next generation of insights. *MIS Quarterly*, 471–482.

4  Ross, J. W. (2016, November 8). How to develop a great digital strategy. Retrieved May 31, 2020, from MIT Sloan Management Review website: https://sloanreview.mit.edu/article/how-to-develop-a-great-digital-strategy/

5  Ross, J. W. (2016, November 8). How to develop a great digital strategy. Retrieved May 31, 2020, from MIT Sloan Management Review website: https://sloanreview.mit.edu/article/how-to-develop-a-great-digital-strategy/

6  Gupta, S. (2018). *Driving digital strategy: A guide to reimagining your business.* Harvard Business Press.

7  Gupta, S. (2018). *Driving digital strategy: A guide to reimagining your business.* Harvard Business Press.

8  Bharadwaj, A., El Sawy, O. A., Pavlou, P. A., & Venkatraman, N. (2013). Digital business strategy: Toward a next generation of insights. *MIS Quarterly*, 471–482.

9  Bharadwaj, A., El Sawy, O. A., Pavlou, P. A., & Venkatraman, N. (2013). Digital business strategy: Toward a next generation of insights. *MIS Quarterly*, 471–482.

10  Hoffman, R., & Yeh, C. (2018, October). The blitzscaling basics. Retrieved June 1, 2020, from strategy+business website: www.strategy-business.com/article/The-Blitzscaling-Basics?gko=3ebb0; Hoffman, R., & Yeh, C. (2018). *Blitzscaling: The lightning-fast path to building massively valuable businesses.* Broadway Business.

11  Hoffman, R., & Yeh, C. (2018). *Blitzscaling: The lightning-fast path to building massively valuable businesses.* Broadway Business.

12  Hoffman, R., & Yeh, C. (2018). *Blitzscaling: The lightning-fast path to building massively valuable businesses.* Broadway Business.

13  Vial, G. (2019). Understanding digital transformation: a review and a research agenda. *Journal of Strategic Information Systems*, 28 (2) (2019), pp. 118–144

14  Rigby, D. K., Sutherland, J., & Takeuchi, H. (2016). Embracing agile. *Harvard Business Review*, 94(5), 40–50; Busulwa, R., Tice, M., & Gurd, B. (2018). *Strategy execution and complexity: Thriving in the era of disruption.* Routledge.

15  Haque, B., & James-Moore, M. (2004). Applying lean thinking to new product introduction. *Journal of Engineering Design*, 15(1), 1–31; Womack, J. P., & Jones, D. T. (1997). Lean thinking – banish waste and create wealth in your corporation. *Journal of the Operational Research Society*, 48(11), 1148–1148;

Melton, T. (2005). The benefits of lean manufacturing: What lean thinking has to offer the process industries. *Chemical Engineering Research and Design*, 83(6), 662–673.

16 Ries, E. (2011). *The lean startup: How today's entrepreneurs use continuous innovation to create radically successful businesses.* Crown Books.

17 Martin, R., & Martin, R. L. (2009). *The design of business: Why design thinking is the next competitive advantage.* Harvard Business Press.

18 Busulwa, R., Birdthistle, N., & Dunn, S. (2020). *Startup accelerators: A field guide.* John Wiley & Sons.

19 Kotter, J. P. (2014). *Accelerate: Building strategic agility for a faster-moving world.* Harvard Business Review Press.

# CHAPTER 11

# Digital Innovation, Digital Learning, and Adaptability/Agility Capabilities

DOI: 10.4324/9781003254614-15

# INTRODUCTION

This primer unpacks three organization capabilities that are critical to adapting to ongoing and accelerating disruption as well as to building digital business competitive advantages. These capabilities are digital innovation, digital learning, and adaptability/agility capabilities. The chapter discusses what the capabilities mean, how they differ from their traditional or nondigital counterparts, and what their value is to organization performance and longevity. The chapter then identifies the key roles leaders, managers, and supporting professionals can play in building and optimizing these organization capabilities. It also discusses what competencies leaders, managers, and supporting professionals require to perform those particular roles. Each of these capabilities can be a complex area with lots of depth, interdisciplinary knowledge, slippery terms and concepts, and practice challenges. The chapter's aim is to provide a meaningful introduction to the digital capability, required roles, and competencies so leaders/managers/other professionals can have a starting point and a contextual framework to support further and lifelong learning/competency development in these important capability areas. Figure 11.1 shows how traditional business capabilities and digital business capabilities have similar aims (improved business performance and longevity). However, they differ in their ability to deliver on those common aims. Digital transformation is required to effect digital business capabilities. And effecting digital transformation requires particular capabilities (e.g., digital business transformation strategy, digital leadership, digital innovation).

---

**LEARNING OBJECTIVES**

- Develop knowledge of the key definitions and concepts related to digital innovation, digital learning, adaptability, and agility capabilities
- Understand the meaning and role of these capabilities in the digital transformation strategy and digital business strategy of organizations

---

- Understand the roles leaders and managers can play in these digital capabilities
- Understand the competencies required by leaders and managers to maximize their roles in these digital capabilities
- Analyze and evaluate the implications of these capabilities, as well as related leadership or management roles and competencies, organizations' digital transformation strategy, and digital business strategy
- Apply knowledge and understanding to participate in, support, or lead workstreams or initiatives related to the building and optimization of these capabilities

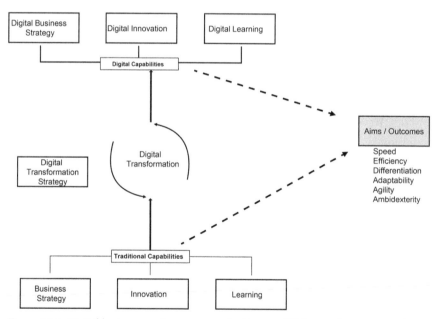

**Figure 11.1** *Digital business requires new organization capabilities or enhancements of traditional capabilities*

*Note*: These new or enhanced capabilities are effected through digital transformation, which in turn requires new capabilities like digital transformation strategy. The aims of traditional and digital business are similar, although some aims become much more important to digital business.

# DIGITAL INNOVATION

From an organization perspective, innovation refers to the introduction and application of new products, processes, and ideals that have a significant and positive net impact on organization performance.[1] This definition of innovation refers to both the process or practice of innovating and the outcomes of the innovation process. Thus, innovation discussions or efforts can focus on how innovation occurs (e.g., what processes, activities, stakeholders, tools) or what types of new products/services/other benefits are realized from innovation efforts. Digital technology advancements, digital transformation, and digital business change or expand the nature of innovation and the potential impact of innovation. That is, they change or expand how innovation can be done (i.e., innovation processes/practices), the nature of innovation outcomes (i.e., new products/processes/value created), and the impact of innovation outcomes (e.g., enabling near-instant global scalability to billions of consumers). This new or expanded way that innovation can occur, the types of new products/services/value creations that can occur, and the speed/scope of their impact is what is referred to as digital innovation. Digital innovation has been formally defined by researchers as both the new products/services/business processes/models and other forms of stakeholder value created through the use of digital technologies, and the process of using digital technologies to create (and subsequently change) these new products/services/business processes/models and other forms of stakeholder value.[2] Other formal definitions include that it is "the carrying out of new combinations of digital and physical components to produce novel products,"[3] that it is "the use of digital technologies in the process of innovating," and that it is the infusion of digital technologies into innovation outcomes and processes.[4]

## DIGITAL INNOVATION VS TRADITIONAL INNOVATION

Digital innovation differs from traditional innovation in four important ways. First, the nature of innovation outputs differs in that the outputs have digital or digital/physical hybrids that are programmable/reprogrammable.[5] Thus they are malleable, editable, open, transferable, and continuously shifting. They can, and often need to, continue to be improved even once they are in customer's hands. This continued evolution/improvement can even be done by customers[6] or other stakeholders outside of the organization.[7] The outputs can be both products and platforms. The outputs can have several layers (e.g., device layer, network layer, service layer, content layer) with an organization competing on one layer but collaborating on another.[8] They can be made to think for themselves, continue to work for their creators (e.g., collecting data), improve themselves (e.g., using AI), collaborate with other outputs (e.g., AI/IoT products), exist as orchestrated collections of other outputs, and more (e.g., Apple's iPhone can tick most of these characteristics). Second, the nature of the innovation process differs in that digital innovation processes are digitized, have blurred boundaries between stages of the innovation process (e.g., continuous iterative cycles of empathizing, defining, testing, releasing a new innovation), are much more fluid and nonlinear, and more open.[9] For example, digital innovation processes can be both intra- and/or inter-organizational and leverage community-based generativity and platform-based network effects (e.g., crowdsourcing, crowdfunding, network-centric innovation platforms). Third, digital innovation differs from traditional innovation in that the innovation actors, or the people/entities/things doing the innovation, aren't just employees. Instead, they can also include dynamic and often unexpected collections of actors (or innovation collectives) with different interests, motivations, abilities, and tools.[10] Concepts such as distributed innovation, open innovation, network-centric innovation, shared cognition, and joint sense-making reflect different approaches to facilitating innovation among diverse actors.[11] Fourth, digital innovation involves use of different tools to facilitate the innovation process and as components in innovation outputs: for example, a broad swath of new digital technologies (e.g., 3D/4D printing, AI, blockchain, big data) and tools (e.g., crowdsourcing/crowdfunding platforms, smart devices and algorithms, data analytics/data science models).[12] Exponential growth in the number and abilities of these tools is rapidly expanding their role in facilitating innovation processes/practices and as key components of innovation outputs.[13] Fortunately for innovation leaders and innovators, digital innovation can simplify, democratize, and drastically lower the cost of innovation outputs. Table 11.1 provides

*Table 11.1* Impact of digital technology advancements on digital innovation and examples of opportunities that can be leveraged[14]

| Impact type | Impact description | Examples |
|---|---|---|
| Industry transformation | industry and market convergence; transformation of whole industries | Apple, Bonnier, Netflix, GM OnStar, 3D printing, digital convergence |
| Distinctive diffusion dynamics | standards wars, risk of stranding | VHS vs Beta; Apple Mac vs Windows; iPhone vs Android; HD DVD vs Blu-ray |
| Greater diversity of products and services | greater diversity of products and services developed and offered ("long tail" effect) | Netflix, Amazon, Hulu's customized ads, Zara's quicker and more localized market, social media/user-generated content |
| Greater personalization of products and services | greater personalization of novel processes, products, and services | Personalization, mass customization, gamification |
| Faster innovation cycles and processes | more rapid development and evolution of innovative processes and products | Capital One, Shinsei Bank, Enterprise IT at SYSCO, Zara's Fast Fashion, CVS |
| Faster/broader product diffusion | accelerated emergence and faster/broader diffusion of new products and business models | DVD players, iPhone/ smartphones, tablet computers, Facebook/ social networking |
| Product pricing and delivery flexibility | increased control over how digital products are used, when, and by whom (e.g., bundling, trials, "freemium" models); greater pricing flexibility (e.g., how much is charged, to whom, when, by what mechanism, and for what level of functionality) | Napster, Rhapsody, Hulu, YouTube |

| Impact type | Impact description | Examples |
|---|---|---|
| New ways to market new products | new avenues for marketing and supporting new products | Google, Facebook, Twitter |
| Move to smart technologies and servitization | widespread emergence of "smart" technologies; accelerated move to servitization (converting products into services) and other kinds of new business models enabled by smart technologies | Rolls-Royce "power by the hour," Progressive Insurance Snapshot program, Zipcar, RFID, smart hospitals |
| Move to real-time question answering systems | new organizational process and business models based on generalized real-time question answering systems | Apple Siri, streaming data analytics, IBM Watson |
| Creation of analytics-driven digital innovation opportunities | increased opportunities for process and product/business model innovation | Amazon, Capital One, Harrah's, business analytics |
| Democratized innovation | process and product innovation discovery and development become more open, democratized, and user-driven | InnoCentive, P&G Connect and Develop, open prize competitions, Dell Ideastorm, Whirlpool's Innovation E-Space, Threadless |

examples of the different ways digital technology advancements impact digital innovation and provides examples of these impacts in action.

## IMPLICATIONS FOR LEADERS, MANAGERS, AND SUPPORTING PROFESSIONALS

Leaders, Managers, and Supporting Professionals at all levels can play a range of critical roles in digital innovation. Examples of these roles include setting or clarifying the innovation vision and direction, effectively leading/

managing/facilitating innovation processes, identifying/ensuring use of the right tools for optimizing innovation process and outcomes, effectively engaging innovation collectives across relevant networks and ecosystems, instituting the right mindsets and behaviors for digital innovation, building/continuously upgrading organization innovative capacity, and ensuring effective capture of organization value from innovation efforts and outputs. To play such roles, leaders and managers need to understand digital innovation, have working knowledge of different digital innovation platforms/tools/methodologies, have a working knowledge of digital innovation collectives and how to best leverage them, have working knowledge of important digital technologies to the innovation process and innovation outputs, and have strong digital leadership skills.

# DIGITAL LEARNING

Organizations have long been interested in employee/workforce/workplace-based learning as a driver of competitive advantage and a safeguard to disruption or loss of competitiveness. To this end, they have always been interested in how to optimize learning (maximize the knowledge/skills/abilities derived by employees from learning efforts and the value created from that learning) and invested in upgrading their workforce learning capability. But for each gain they have made, digital technology advancements, in combination with unprecedented growth in complexity/uncertainty, regulation, compliance requirements, globalization, and competition, have exponentially expanded the nature and amount of learning required. This has resulted in many employees finding themselves unable to keep up with technological advances that affect their everyday work processes as their knowledge/skills become obsolete quickly and new knowledge/skill requirements increase[15] (e.g., new skills with big data, data analytics and artificial intelligence). In response, companies have sought ways to close the learning gap (the gap between actual and required workforce knowledge/skills/abilities).[16] As a result, workforce learning has evolved from traditional, instructor-centered, class-style delivery to become much more online, interactive, multidisciplinary, multiplatform, multi-device, portable, user-centered/personalized, self-directed, gamified, always on anywhere/anytime/real time, immersive, social, and so forth.[17] These evolutions have largely been made possible by digital technology advancements.

Digital learning, then, is employee learning that leverages digital technologies in the learning process, learning content, and/or learning outcomes. It has been described as a both planned and/or unplanned, implicit and/or explicit, multi-technology and/or multi-device, intentional and/or unintentional, spontaneous/unconscious and/or planned/defined, independent/autonomous and/or directed/controlled, and occurring in the workplace or outside it.[18]

## DIGITAL LEARNING VS TRADITIONAL LEARNING

Digital learning differs from traditional learning in that the nature/characteristics of the learning process is significantly transformed; the learning context is significantly transformed; the teaching methodologies are significantly transformed; the learning participants are expanded; and the learning systems and tools are significantly transformed. As noted above, the nature and characteristics of digital learning include being much more online, interactive, multidisciplinary, multiplatform, multi-device, portable, user-centered/personalized, self-directed, gamified, always on anywhere/anytime/real time, immersive, social, and so forth. As to teaching methods, digital learning differs from traditional learning in that new teaching methods/approaches are used that better involve learners in the learning process and optimize learning efficiency and effectiveness.[19] Examples of these methodologies/approaches include project-based learning, problem-based learning, digital stories, online learning environments, digital moments, technology-integrated teaching methods, digital storytelling, educational games, and authentic learning.[20] As to learning contexts, digital learning differs from traditional learning in that learning contexts that support new and more effective pedagogical models are used. Examples of these include collaborative communities, cooperative learning, collaborative learning, digital combinational systems, digital media-based flipped classrooms, online spaces, experiential online development, open educational practice, and network participation.[21] As to learning participants, digital learning differs from traditional learning in that the participants are expanded to include collaborative community participants, cooperative/collaborative learning participants, network participants, and software algorithms.[22] Finally, digital learning differs from traditional learning in that it leverages a diverse collection of digital technology platforms and tools to provide/maintain the learning context, facilitate the learning process, support learners, and report on the effectiveness of both learning processes and learning outcomes. Examples of such tools include web-based video applications, narrated stop-motion animation applications, augmented reality applications, webinar applications, learning management systems (LMS), YouTube, Facebook, Instagram, Wikipedia, LinkedIn, Google/other search engines, mobile learning apps, learning object repositories, Blackboard, Moodle Learning Manager, Collaborate Ultra, Zoom, Twitter, and massive open online course (MOOC).[23]

## Implications for Leaders, Managers, and Supporting Professionals

Effective digital learning can engage, empower, motivate, and retain employees. In turn, this can accelerate organization efficiency, adaptability, and agility and become a strong base for competitive advantage. Leaders, managers, and supporting professionals at all levels can play important roles in optimizing digital learning. Examples of these roles include setting or clarifying the digital learning vision and direction, effectively leading/managing/facilitating digital learning processes, identifying/ensuring use of the right tools for optimizing digital learning process and outcomes, ensuring access to the best content, identifying/ensuring use of the most effective teaching methodologies and pedagogical models, inspiring and motivating employees to make the most of available learning opportunities, instituting the right mindsets and behaviors for digital learning, building/continuously upgrading organization digital learning capacity, and ensuring effective capture of organization value from digital learning efforts and outputs. To play such roles, leaders/managers/supporting professionals need to understand digital learning, have working knowledge of different digital learning platforms/tools/methodologies/pedagogical models, have working knowledge of important digital technologies to the digital learning process and digital learning outputs, and have strong digital leadership skills.

# ADAPTABILITY AND AGILITY

Adaptability was earlier defined as the ability to dynamically reconfigure routines, processes, and practices to suit the demands of unexpected internal and external events or disruptions. And agility was defined as the capacity for flexibility and speed in sensing and responding to such events and disruptions, especially external ones. For example, an agile organization is able to anticipate/spot/understand disruptions early (e.g., COVID-19) and is able to efficiently and effectively redeploy/redirect its resources to value creating/value capturing/value protecting activities dynamically as the situation warrants.[24] In contrast, ambidexterity was defined as having the ability to ensure efficiency/effectiveness in the organization's existing products/services while also ensuring the organization undertakes the exploratory activities to discover future winning products and services.[25]

It was noted that adaptability capabilities are critical to enabling organizations to reconfigure their operations and offerings to surprising internal and external events, such as the financial crisis (which resulted in lack of access to new credit, the clawing back of approved credit facilities, growth in payment defaults, a sharp decline in consumer demand, and drying up working capital) or the COVID-19 pandemic (which resulted in social distancing and travel restrictions, inability of staff to attend workplaces, procurement challenges, sharp declines in product/service demand, restrictions on ways in which organizations could serve customers, etc.).[26] Organizations with established adaptability capabilities would have had the relevant infrastructure, processes, talent, culture, and financial resources to enable them to reconfigure their operations in response to the surprising events or disruptions. For example, during the COVID-19 pandemic, organizations that had made significant progress with their digital transformation efforts were able to have their workforce work from home, undertake meaningful work that contributed to the organization's future adaptive capacity, offer existing or new products virtually, and do all of this without compromising customers' and employees' safety and privacy. Organizations with established agility capabilities are able to sense/anticipate surprising events and disruptions, are able to effect fast responses to seize the corresponding opportunities or react to the threats, and have the flexibility to dynamically vary their responses as the situation requires.[27] Organizations with established ambidexterity capabilities are able to build, maintain, and use their adaptability and agility capabilities without those capabilities materially compromising their established operational processes.[28]

Digital technology advancements are key drivers of the need for adaptability, agility, and ambidexterity. But paradoxically, they offer unparalleled opportunities to build, maintain, and use adaptability, agility, and ambidexterity capabilities. For example, big data/data analytics/ AI technologies and tools can be used for digital scouting and digital scenario planning. Cloud/AI/learning platforms can be used for digital learning and digital mindset shaping. Elastic/anywhere/anytime/any device digital infrastructure can be used to enable dynamic flexing of resources in response to customer/demand side changes or supplier/ supply side changes. Combinations of digital technologies can be brought together to assemble highly efficient and scalable business models, build smart products that can sense and report on consumer behavior changes, or build smart and autonomous processes that can independently flex with demand and supply side changes. Combinations of digital technologies can be used to effect bimodality (e.g., digital infrastructure to facilitate/support established processes and digital infrastructure to facilitate/support exploratory or experimental products/services).

## IMPLICATIONS FOR LEADERS, MANAGERS, AND SUPPORTING PROFESSIONALS

Leaders, managers, and supporting professionals at all levels can play important roles in leveraging digital technologies to building, maintaining, and optimizing the adaptability, agility, and ambidexterity capabilities of their organizations. Examples of these roles include setting or clarifying a vision for firm adaptability/agility/ambidexterity (e.g., what does the future state of this capability look like in practice), maintaining both efficiency and exploratory digital infrastructure and processes, ensuring the right combination of technologies are used and configured in the right way to maximize adaptability/agility/ambidexterity capabilities, instituting conditions/mindsets/attitudes that provide impetus for both exploration and exploitation actions, and cultivating and using ambidextrous leadership styles.

# GOOGLE AND REFLECT

| Digital capability | Common terminology |
|---|---|
| Digital business strategy | Digital business strategy, digital transformation strategy, digital asset, network effects, elastic infrastructure, dynamic capability, digital infrastructure |
| Digital innovation | Crowdsourcing, crowdfunding, network-centric innovation platform, innovation collective, shared cognition, joint sense-making, design thinking, layered modular architecture |
| Digital learning | Digital learning context, digital learning systems/platforms, gamification, self-directed learning, immersive learning, autonomous learning, learning efficiency, multidisciplinary knowledge, multidisciplinary teaching, interdisciplinary teaching, pedagogical model, collaborative communities, cooperative learning, collaborative learning, digital combinational systems, flipped classroom, experiential online development, open educational practice, narrated stop-motion animation application, augmented reality application, webinar application, learning management system (LMS), learning object repository, massive open online course (MOOC) |
| Adaptability, agility, ambidexterity | adaptability, agility, ambidexterity, bimodal IT |

# DISCUSSION QUESTIONS

1 How is digital innovation different from traditional innovation?
2 Which leadership/managerial/supporting professional role in digital innovation is the most critical to building and maintaining that capability? Why?
3 How is digital learning different from traditional learning?
4 Which leadership/managerial/supporting professional role in digital learning is the most critical to building and maintaining that capability? Why?
5 Which is more important to organization longevity: adaptability, agility, or ambidexterity?
5 What are some examples of digital technologies being used to effect adaptability, agility, and ambidexterity?
6 Which of the capabilities discussed in this chapter is the most important to optimizing digital business competitiveness?

# NOTES

1 West, M., & Farr, J. (1989). Innovation at work: Psychological perspectives. *Social Behavior*, 4, 15–30.
2 Nambisan, S., Lyytinen, K., Majchrzak, A., & Song, M. (2017). Digital innovation management: Reinventing innovation management research in a digital world. *MIS Quarterly*, 41(1).
3 Yoo, Y., Henfridsson, O., & Lyytinen, K. (2010). Research commentary – The new organizing logic of digital innovation: An agenda for information systems research. *Information Systems Research*, 21(4), 724–735.
4 Nambisan, S., Lyytinen, K., Majchrzak, A., & Song, M. (2017). Digital innovation management: Reinventing innovation management research in a digital world. *MIS Quarterly*, 41(1).
5 Nambisan, S., Lyytinen, K., Majchrzak, A., & Song, M. (2017). Digital innovation management: Reinventing innovation management research in a digital world. *MIS Quarterly*, 41(1).
6 Bradonjic, P., Franke, N., & Lüthje, C. (2019). Decision-makers' underestimation of user innovation. *Research Policy*, 48(6), 1354–1361. https://doi.org/10.1016/j.respol.2019.01.020

7  Nambisan, S., Lyytinen, K., Majchrzak, A., & Song, M. (2017). Digital innovation management: Reinventing innovation management research in a digital world. *MIS Quarterly*, 41(1); Yoo, Y., Henfridsson, O., & Lyytinen, K. (2010). Research commentary – The new organizing logic of digital innovation: An agenda for information systems research. *Information Systems Research*, 21(4), 724–735; Lee, J., & Berente, N. (2012). Digital innovation and the division of innovative labor: Digital controls in the automotive industry. *Organization Science*, 23(5), 1428–1447.

8  Nambisan, S., Lyytinen, K., Majchrzak, A., & Song, M. (2017). Digital innovation management: Reinventing innovation management research in a digital world. *MIS Quarterly*, 41(1).

9  Nambisan, S., Lyytinen, K., Majchrzak, A., & Song, M. (2017). Digital innovation management: Reinventing innovation management research in a digital world. *MIS Quarterly*, 41(1).

10 Nambisan, S., Lyytinen, K., Majchrzak, A., & Song, M. (2017). Digital innovation management: Reinventing innovation management research in a digital world. *MIS Quarterly*, 41(1); Yoo, Y., Henfridsson, O., & Lyytinen, K. (2010). Research commentary – the new organizing logic of digital innovation: An agenda for information systems research. *Information Systems Research*, 21(4), 724–735; Lee, J., & Berente, N. (2012). Digital innovation and the division of innovative labor: Digital controls in the automotive industry. *Organization Science*, 23(5), 1428–1447.

11 Nambisan, S., Lyytinen, K., Majchrzak, A., & Song, M. (2017). Digital innovation management: Reinventing innovation management research in a digital world. *MIS Quarterly*, 41(1); Yoo, Y., Henfridsson, O., & Lyytinen, K. (2010). Research commentary – the new organizing logic of digital innovation: An agenda for information systems research. *Information Systems Research*, 21(4), 724–735; Lee, J., & Berente, N. (2012). digital innovation and the division of innovative labor: Digital controls in the automotive industry. *Organization Science*, 23(5), 1428–1447.

12 Nambisan, S., Lyytinen, K., Majchrzak, A., & Song, M. (2017). Digital innovation management: Reinventing innovation management research in a digital world. *MIS Quarterly*, 41(1); Yoo, Y., Henfridsson, O., & Lyytinen, K. (2010). Research commentary – the new organizing logic of digital innovation: An agenda for information systems research. *Information Systems Research*, 21(4), 724–735; Lee, J., & Berente, N. (2012). Digital innovation and the division of innovative labor: Digital controls in the automotive industry. *Organization Science*, 23(5), 1428–1447.

13 Nambisan, S., Lyytinen, K., Majchrzak, A., & Song, M. (2017). Digital innovation management: Reinventing innovation management research in a digital world. *MIS Quarterly*, 41(1).

14 Fichman, R. G., Dos Santos, B. L., & Zheng, Z. (2014). Digital innovation as a fundamental and powerful concept in the information systems curriculum. *MIS Quarterly*, 38(2), 329 – A15.

15 Willyerd, K., Grünwald, A., Brown, K., Welz, B., & Traylor, P. (2016, March). A new model for corporate learning. *Digitalit Magazine*. Retrieved June 2, 2020, from www.digitalistmag.com/executive-research/a-new-model-for-corporate-learning

16 Willyerd, K., Grünwald, A., Brown, K., Welz, B., & Traylor, P. (2016, March). A new model for corporate learning. *Digitalit Magazine*. Retrieved June 2, 2020, from www.digitalistmag.com/executive-research/a-new-model-for-corporate-learning

17 Willyerd, K., Grünwald, A., Brown, K., Welz, B., & Traylor, P. (2016, March). A new model for corporate learning. *Digitalit Magazine*. Retrieved June 2, 2020, from www.digitalistmag.com/executive-research/a-new-model-for-corporate-learning

18 Sousa, M. J., & Rocha, Á. (2019). Digital learning: Developing skills for digital transformation of organizations. *Future Generation Computer Systems*, 91, 327–334; Sousa, M. J., & Rocha, Á. (2019). Digital learning: Developing skills for digital transformation of organizations. *Future Generation Computer Systems*, 91, 327–334.

19 Sousa, M. J., Cruz, R., & Martins, J. M. (2017). Digital learning methodologies and tools – A literature review. *EDULEARN17 Proceedings*, 5185–5192; Sousa, M. J., & Rocha, Á. (2019). Digital learning: Developing skills for digital transformation of organizations. *Future Generation Computer Systems*, 91, 327–334.

20 Sousa, M. J., Cruz, R., & Martins, J. M. (2017). Digital learning methodologies and tools – A literature review. *EDULEARN17 Proceedings*, 5185–5192; Sousa, M. J., & Rocha, Á. (2019). Digital learning: Developing skills for digital transformation of organizations. *Future Generation Computer Systems*, 91, 327–334.

21 Sousa, M. J., Cruz, R., & Martins, J. M. (2017). Digital learning methodologies and tools – A literature review. *EDULEARN17 Proceedings*, 5185–5192; Sousa, M. J., & Rocha, Á. (2019). Digital learning: Developing skills for digital transformation of organizations. *Future Generation Computer Systems*, 91, 327–334.

22 Sousa, M. J., Cruz, R., & Martins, J. M. (2017). Digital learning methodologies and tools – A literature review. *EDULEARN17 Proceedings*, 5185–5192; Sousa, M. J., & Rocha, Á. (2019). Digital learning: Developing skills for digital transformation of organizations. *Future Generation Computer Systems*, 91, 327–334.

23 Sousa, M. J., Cruz, R., & Martins, J. M. (2017). Digital learning methodologies and tools – A literature review. *EDULEARN17 Proceedings*, 5185–5192; Sousa, M. J., & Rocha, Á. (2019). Digital learning: Developing skills for digital transformation of organizations. *Future Generation Computer Systems*, 91, 327–334.

24 Warner, K. S., & Wäger, M. (2019). Building dynamic capabilities for digital transformation: An ongoing process of strategic renewal. *Long Range Planning*, 52(3), 326–349.

25 Busulwa, R., Tice, M., & Gurd, B. (2018). *Strategy execution and complexity: Thriving in the era of disruption*. Routledge.

26 Busulwa, R., Tice, M., & Gurd, B. (2018). *Strategy execution and complexity: Thriving in the era of disruption*. Routledge.

27 Busulwa, R., Tice, M., & Gurd, B. (2018). *Strategy execution and complexity: Thriving in the era of disruption*. Routledge.

28 Busulwa, R., Tice, M., & Gurd, B. (2018). *Strategy execution and complexity: Thriving in the era of disruption*. Routledge.

# CHAPTER 12

# Digital Customer Experience, Digital Customer Engagement, and Digital Stakeholder Engagement Capabilities

DOI: 10.4324/9781003254614-16

# INTRODUCTION

Digital technology advancements have disrupted customer and other stakeholder expectations and behaviors. Owing to this disruption, customers increasingly expect dramatically higher personalization of experiences and interactions, anytime/anywhere responsiveness, any device/any channel service availability, respect for the value of their time in interactions with organizations, feeling valued at all times, and feeling like they are part of a community when they use the product/service or engage with the organization. Living up to these expectations requires fundamental changes in the nature of customer engagement, stakeholder engagement, and customer experience practices. These transformed practices are respectively referred to as digital customer engagement, digital stakeholder engagement, and digital customer experience capabilities. They offer the promise of organizations not only being able to live up to changed and rapidly changing customer/stakeholder expectations but also having important bases for building strategic differentiation, adaptability, and agility from state-of-the-art practice of the capabilities. This chapter unpacks each capability and discuss what it means, how it differs from its traditional counterpart, and its value to organization performance and longevity. The chapter then identify the key roles leaders/managers/supporting professional can play in building and maintaining these organization capabilities and what competencies they require to perform those roles. As with earlier capabilities, each of these capabilities can be a complex area of practice with significant depth, interdisciplinary knowledge, slippery terms and concepts to make sense of, and practical practice challenges. Our aim was to provide a meaningful introduction to each digital capability, the required roles, and the required competencies, so leaders/managers/professionals can have a starting point and a contextual framework to support further and lifelong learning/competency development in these important capability areas.

---

**LEARNING OBJECTIVES**

- Develop knowledge of the key definitions and concepts related to digital customer experience, digital customer engagement, and digital stakeholder engagement capabilities
- Understand the meaning and role of these capabilities in the digital transformation strategy and digital business strategy of organizations
- Understand the roles leaders/managers/supporting professionals can play in these digital capabilities
- Understand the competencies required by leaders/managers/supporting professionals to maximize their roles in these digital capabilities
- Analyze and evaluate the implications of these capabilities, as well as related leadership/management/supporting professional roles and competencies, for organizations' digital transformation strategy and digital business strategy
- Apply knowledge and understanding to participate in, support, or lead workstreams or initiatives related to the building and optimization of these capabilities

---

# DIGITAL CUSTOMER ENGAGEMENT AND DIGITAL STAKEHOLDER ENGAGEMENT

## DIGITAL CUSTOMER ENGAGEMENT

Customer engagement refers to both the process and effect of organizations or brands creating deep connections with customers that drive purchase decisions, interaction, participation, and brand advocacy.[1] Its value to profitability and competitiveness is well established and includes benefits such as improved customer experience (e.g., through more empathetic service), improved customer relations/retention (e.g., greater trust/forgiveness of organization mistakes), improved brand/product awareness and image (e.g., through word of mouth), improved product innovation (e.g., through customers providing ideas for new products or for existing product improvements), improved competitor intelligence (e.g., getting information on competitor activities from customers), and improved risk mitigation (e.g., discovering information on fatal product flaws and customer grievances from customers). Given these benefits, competitive organizations have long been interested in building and continuously upgrading their customer engagement capability (i.e., the efficiency and effectiveness of the capability).[2]

In previous chapters, it was noted how digital technology advancements disrupt consumer expectations and behaviors, the competitive field and the bases of competition, and data availability. From a consumer engagement perspective, these disruptions have manifested themselves as, for example, dramatically higher expectations of personalization, dramatically higher expectations of anytime/anywhere responsiveness, dramatically higher expectations of any device/any channel availability, and dramatically higher expectations of experiencing a sense of community in purchasing or brand interactions. To deliver on these dramatically higher expectations, organizations succeeding at it have transformed the nature of their customer engagement processes and practices.

The new or transformed processes and practices are collectively referred to as digital customer engagement. Digital customer engagement is the use of digital technologies and tools in the processes/practices and effect of creating deep connections with customers that drive purchase decisions, interaction, participation, and advocacy (see Figure 12.1 for a juxtaposition of digital customer engagement versus traditional customer engagement). Digital customer engagement deals with all the ways current and prospective customers can and do interact in relation to an organization, brand, or product across digital channels, platforms, devices, and connected or smart things.[4] Digital customer engagement has rapidly evolved to include a rich repertoire of engagement strategies/approaches and specific engagement practices.[5] Examples

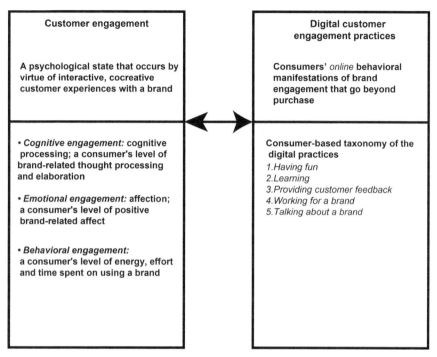

**Figure 12.1** *Traditional customer engagement vs digital customer engagement*[3]

of these include digitally managed loyalty programs (e.g., web-based or mobile app frequent flyer programs), online brand communities (discussion board/chat-style interactions with other customers/ prospective customers or with the organization, consumers solving other consumers' problems, consumers giving other consumers advice/ tips), digital customer engagement platforms (e.g., Zendesk, Freshdesk, HubSpot, Salesforce, Mailchimp), customer co-creation (product co-creation, product improvement feedback, product testing), brand websites, consumer-generated brand stories, consumer engagement on social media (e.g., liking, commenting, sharing, posting, calling up product photographs, hash-tagging), consumer reviews (e.g., search engine reviews, review platform reviews, social media reviews), brand-consumer interactions (e.g., liking a brand on Facebook, following a brand on Twitter), purchase funnel practices, brand fan pages, mobile interactions (e.g., SMS interactions), LiveChat platforms,

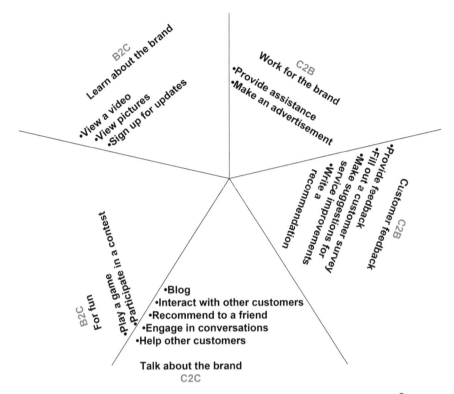

**Figure 12.2** *A research-derived taxonomy of digital customer engagement practices*[7]

mobile marketing, consumer-generated advertising (e.g., consumer-generated brand videos), consumer buzz (e.g., generate content by sharing personal experiences, providing online feedback, expressing sentiments), email marketing, customers' online brand related activities (COBRAs), consumption community participation, consumer initiated mobile marketing, and consumer advocates (remote voluntary work for the organization, act as multiplier of brand messages, accept invitations to company-related events, speak up for the brand at events).[6] Figure 12.2 provides a taxonomy of business to consumer (B2C), consumer to business (C2B), and consumer to consumer (C2C) engagement types, aims, and example activities.

Effectively done, digital customer engagement provides organizations with a range of other opportunities including being able to harness all their customer interactions across channels and platforms to inform decision making, develop breakthrough and market-validated products (e.g., from spotting new problems to solve for customers, liaising with customers about possible solutions, and receiving product test feedback from customers), involve more customers in digital innovation, get granular in their understanding of customer behaviors across market segments, and offer significantly improved customer service and customer experience (e.g., service that leverages interaction data to anticipate and solve customer issues in real time).

## DIGITAL STAKEHOLDER ENGAGEMENT

In addition to customers, a range of other stakeholders are critical to an organization's performance and well-being. These include employees, suppliers and partners, government and regulatory institutions, competitors, and different local and international communities. The organization must engage effectively with these different stakeholders in order to safeguard its existence, its legitimacy, and the opportunities available to it. For example, organizations must assure governments and regulatory institutions that they are complying with relevant laws or have acceptable reasons for not doing so; they must assure competitors that they are competing fairly; and they must ensure different communities that they are not violating their social, environmental, and ethical obligations or license to operate in those communities and environments. To effectively do this, they must communicate and transact with these stakeholders in such a way as to build positive, trusting relationships. This is the focus of stakeholder engagement. And like digital customer engagement, digital stakeholder engagement leverages digital technologies and tools to maximize the practice and outputs of stakeholder engagement. Digital technologies and tools can dramatically improve the cost, speed, scale/reach, transparency, measurability, and effectiveness of stakeholder engagement efforts. In turn, this translates into organizations enjoying greater trust, empathy, inclusion, growth, profitability, and other benefits from stakeholders.

## IMPLICATIONS FOR LEADERS, MANAGERS, AND SUPPORTING PROFESSIONALS

While organizations may leverage digital technologies and tools to dramatically improve customer engagement and stakeholder engagement, this is not enough. They must also do so more effectively and efficiently than competitors that leverage the same or similar digital technologies and tools. Leaders/managers/supporting professionals can play an important role in building and continuously upgrading digital engagement capabilities. For example, they set or clarify the organization's digital engagement vision and strategic objectives; they can help select the right combination of digital technologies and tools to maximize engagement of different customers and stakeholders (e.g., right technologies/platforms/tools, right configuration and integration of technologies/platforms/tools); they can promote and institute the right supporting mindsets/attitudes/behaviors to support effective digital engagement (e.g., that it's not just marketing's job); they can encourage their direct reports to participate in different digital channels in order to better empathize with stakeholders; they can ensure analytics dashboards are built that leverage and integrate interaction data from all channels; they can hire/develop in-house experts across channels and forms of engagement; and much more. To play such roles, leaders/managers/ supporting professionals need to have sufficient working knowledge of digital engagement objectives, processes, and practices. They need to have working knowledge of different digital channels and of how multichannel works. They also need to understand how to capture value for the organization from its digital engagement efforts. Finally, they need the digital leadership skills to enable them to develop, continuously upgrade, and realize value from digital engagement efforts.

# DIGITAL CUSTOMER EXPERIENCE

Customer experience refers to the quality of all of a customer's encounters with an organization's products, services, and brand.[8] Improvements in the quality of these encounters is linked to benefits such as improved customer acquisition, improved customer loyalty, improved revenue growth, and improved profitability. Perhaps it is for this reason that optimizing customer experience has been a strategic priority for organizations from as far back as the nineteenth century; and today, leading brands such as Ritz-Carlton, Apple, Netflix, and Singapore Airlines revolve their management strategies around customer experience optimization.[9] As with transformations of customer engagement and stakeholder engagement, digital technology advancements are changing the nature of effective customer experience management. The drivers of this change include more and more customer encounters with an organization's products/services/brand shifting to digital channels, a proliferation in digital channels (e.g., different search engines, different social media platforms, different payment platforms, different website management platforms, different computing and mobile devices, different mobile apps, different virtual/augmented/mixed reality platforms, different IoT platforms, different online video platforms, different television platforms), and significant differences in customer interaction requirements across channels. Irrespective of the digital channels they choose or their location and timing, customers want access to organizations' services and products in the most convenient way possible.[10] They are put off by having to repeat themselves from one channel to another or from one customer representative to another. They hate process and visual inconsistency across channels, as well as having to perform actions that waste their time. And they are far less patient on digital channels than they are in traditional channels (e.g., a study found that waiting 10 seconds for a page to load can result in half of customers terminating their encounter).[11]

Digital customer experience is the quality of all of a customer's encounters with an organization's products, services, and brand across all digital channels, touchpoints, and contact moments.[12] It also refers to the process of optimizing these encounters (e.g., having the right technology/platform/application infrastructure, having the right process and people, and having the right policies). By having the right supporting technologies, the right platforms/applications, the right management processes, and the right people, organizations can ensure they are available and can effectively serve customers in their preferred channels, at their preferred times, in their preferred locations, and in ways that respect their time (i.e., save them all possible effort rather than externalizing more effort to them due to the organization's shortcomings). Digital customer experience optimization strategies typically focus on enhancing reachability (e.g., customers being able to use preferred channels to interact with or about the organization, customers being aware of all of the organization's available channels), digital channel flexibility (e.g., switching between channels without losing context, having consistent information across channels, and not having to repeat themselves across channels), service convenience (e.g., access to clear, up-to-date information, access to quick/live support, ability to receive end-to-end support rather than being bounced across channels), purchase convenience (e.g., ability to conduct end-to-end transactions, broad payment options, ability to subscribe to new products/services, clear and up-to-date information), simplicity and ease of use (e.g., intuitive interface design, simple and guided journeys, simple and intuitive navigation), and personalization (e.g., recognition as a unique individual, having personal preferences automatically met, experiences suited to the customers' unique context).[13] Organizations can leverage a range of digital technology platforms and tools that exist to achieve these digital customer experience optimization objectives. For example, using omnichannel support platforms (e.g., Pega CRM, Five9), organizations can track, centralize, and tie together/orchestrate all interactions across channels (e.g., face-to-face, email, phone, social media, live chat), so that a customer's digital experience is integrated and smooth rather than fragmented and conflicting.

## IMPLICATIONS FOR LEADERS, MANAGERS, AND SUPPORTING PROFESSIONALS

To effectively lead or participate in digital customer experience optimization efforts, leaders/managers/supporting professionals can play roles such as setting/clarifying/communicating the organization's digital customer experience vision and strategic objectives, championing availability of the organization's offerings and support services across as many channels as possible, helping select the right combination of digital technologies/platforms/tools to maximize digital customer experience across customer preferred channels (e.g., right technologies/platforms/tools, right configuration and integration of technologies/platforms/tools), promoting and instituting the right supporting mindsets/attitudes/behaviors to maximize digital customer experience, encouraging their direct reports to participate in different digital channels in order to better empathize with customers' experiences and needs in those channels, ensuring analytics dashboards are built that leverage and integrate digital customer experience data from all channels, hiring/developing in-house experts across channels, and more. To play such roles, leaders/managers/supporting professionals need to have sufficient working knowledge of digital customer experience objectives, strategies, processes, and practices. They need to have strong working knowledge of customer journey mapping, customer journeys, and the key moments of truth in journeys across platforms. They need to have working knowledge of different digital channels and how multichannel works. Finally, they need the digital leadership skills to enable them to develop, continuously upgrade, and realize value from digital customer experience optimization efforts.

## GOOGLE AND REFLECT

| Digital capability | Common terminology |
|---|---|
| Digital customer engagement | Customer engagement, digital customer engagement, digital loyalty program, online brand community, digital customer engagement platform, customer co-creation, brand fan page, LiveChat platform, consumer-generated advertising, consumer buzz, customers' online brand related activities (COBRAs) |
| Digital stakeholder engagement | Stakeholder management, stakeholder engagement, digital stakeholder engagement, organizational legitimacy, social license to operate (SLO), corporate social responsibility (CSR) |

| Digital capability | Common terminology |
|---|---|
| Digital customer experience | Customer experience (CX), digital customer experience (DCX or Digital CX), customer experience management (CEM or CXM), customer experience program, customer sentiment, customer satisfaction score (CSAT), customer effort score (CES), customer delight, brand advocacy, customer lifetime value (CLV), voice of the customer (VoC), Net Promoter Score (NPS), Customer Effort Score (CES), customer experience design (CXD), customer journey mapping, digital touchpoint, digital customer experience moment of truth (MoT), omnichannel strategy, digital customer experience platform |

# DISCUSSION QUESTIONS

1   How is digital customer engagement different from traditional customer engagement?

2   Which leadership/managerial/supporting professional role in digital customer engagement is the most critical to building and maintaining that capability? Why?

3   Which digital customer engagement related competency is likely to have the greatest positive impact on a leader's or manager's career?

4   How is digital stakeholder engagement different from traditional stakeholder engagement?

5   Which leadership/managerial/supporting professional role in digital stakeholder engagement is the most critical to building and maintaining that capability? Why?

6   How is digital customer experience different from traditional customer experience?

7   Which leadership/managerial/supporting professional role in digital customer experience is the most critical to building and maintaining that capability? Why?

8  Which digital customer leadership/managerial/supporting professional competency is likely to have the greatest positive impact on a leader's or manager's career?

9  Which of the capabilities discussed in this chapter is the most important to succeeding at digital transformation and digital business?

# NOTES

1  Sashi, C. M. (2012). Customer engagement, buyer-seller relationships, and social media. *Management Decision*, 50(2), 253–272. https://doi.org/10.1108/00251741211203551

2  Hueffner, E. (2020). How digital customer engagement can boost your business. Retrieved June 3, 2020, from Zendesk website: www.zendesk.com/blog/digital-customer-engagement/; Sashi, C. M. (2012). Customer engagement, buyer-seller relationships, and social media. *Management Decision*, 50(2), 253–272. https://doi.org/10.1108/00251741211203551; Klein Wassink, B. J., & Santenac, I. (2019, February 11). How a new digital engagement model attracts and educates customers. Retrieved June 3, 2020, from Ey.com website: www.ey.com/en_gl/insurance/new-digital-customer-engagement-model; Ebrahim, S., Rabbani, U., & Rosenberg, R. (2015). Making digital customer engagement a reality. Retrieved June 3, 2020, from McKinsey & Company website: www.mckinsey.com/business-functions/marketing-and-sales/our-insights/making-digital-customer-engagement-a-reality; Ebrahim, S., Rabbani, U., & Rosenberg, R. (2015). Making digital customer engagement a reality. Retrieved June 3, 2020, from McKinsey & Company website: www.mckinsey.com/business-functions/marketing-and-sales/our-insights/making-digital-customer-engagement-a-reality; Hueffner, E. (2020). How digital customer engagement can boost your business. Retrieved June 3, 2020, from Zendesk website: www.zendesk.com/blog/digital-customer-engagement/

3  Eigenraam, A. W., Eelen, J., Van Lin, A., & Verlegh, P. W. (2018). A consumer-based taxonomy of digital customer engagement practices. *Journal of Interactive Marketing*, 44, 102–121.

4  Hueffner, E. (2020). How digital customer engagement can boost your business. Retrieved June 3, 2020, from Zendesk website: www.zendesk.com/blog/digital-customer-engagement/

5 Eigenraam, A. W., Eelen, J., Van Lin, A., & Verlegh, P. W. (2018). A consumer-based taxonomy of digital customer engagement practices. *Journal of Interactive Marketing*, 44, 102–121.

6 Eigenraam, A. W., Eelen, J., Van Lin, A., & Verlegh, P. W. (2018). A consumer-based taxonomy of digital customer engagement practices. *Journal of Interactive Marketing*, 44, 102–121.

7 Eigenraam, A. W., Eelen, J., Van Lin, A., & Verlegh, P. W. (2018). A consumer-based taxonomy of digital customer engagement practices. *Journal of Interactive Marketing*, 44, 102–121.

8 Borowski, C. (2015). What a great digital customer experience actually looks like. *Harvard Business Review*. Retrieved June 4, 2020, from Harvard Business Review website: https://hbr.org/2015/11/what-a-great-digital-customer-experience-actually-looks-like; Meyer, C., & Schwager, A. (2007). Understanding customer experience. *Harvard Business Review*, 85(2), 116.

9 Klaus, P. (2014). Towards practical relevance – delivering superior firm performance through digital customer experience strategies. *Journal of Direct, Data and Digital Marketing Practice*, 15(4), 306–316. https://doi.org/10.1057/dddmp.2014.20

10 Hyken, S. (2018). Customer experience is the new brand. *Forbes*. Retrieved from www.forbes.com/sites/shephyken/2018/07/15/customer-experience-is-the-new-brand/#1e586acf7f52

11 Borowski, C. (2015). What a great digital customer experience actually looks like. *Harvard Business Review*. Retrieved June 4, 2020, from Harvard Business Review website: https://hbr.org/2015/11/what-a-great-digital-customer-experience-actually-looks-like

12 Borowski, C. (2015). What a great digital customer experience actually looks like. *Harvard Business Review*. Retrieved June 4, 2020, from Harvard Business Review website: https://hbr.org/2015/11/what-a-great-digital-customer-experience-actually-looks-like

13 TTEC. (2020). Digital customer experience strategy: Six key areas to focus your efforts. Retrieved June 5, 2020, from TTEC website: www.ttec.com/articles/digital-customer-experience-strategy-six-key-areas-focus-your-efforts#:~:text=A%20digital%20experience%20strategy%20requires,service%20interactions%20is%20not%20sufficient.

# CHAPTER 13

# Enterprise Architecture Management, DT Adoption and Use, and Data Management/ Data Analytics/Data Science Capabilities

DOI: 10.4324/9781003254614-17

# INTRODUCTION

This primer puts a spotlight on three capabilities that, besides people, are probably the most important building blocks to effectively operating and competing as a digital business. The first, enterprise architecture management, relates to the organization routines/activities, structures, and/or processes that work together to configure the organization's technology infrastructure, information/data, and business processes as they should be configured. The second, digital technology (DT) adoption and use, refers to the routines/activities, structures, and/or processes that an organization has for effectively finding, choosing, procuring, adopting, and optimally using the technologies it should be using to optimize its digital business competitiveness. And the third, data management and data analytics, relates to an organization's ability to collect, validate, store, and leverage internal and external data to spur optimal data driven decision making. Taken together, the organization's ability to effectively build, maintain, and optimize these capabilities can drive or constrain its efficiency, differentiation, adaptability, and agility. This effect can be supercharged through the capacity of these particular capabilities to catalyze all other digital transformation and digital business capabilities. Leaders, managers, and supporting professionals need to play important roles in ensuring effective organization-wide involvement in these capabilities. Effectively establishing and continuously upgrading the competitiveness of these capabilities requires organization-wide involvement and cascades as an important part of leaders', managers', and supporting professionals' roles at all levels (i.e., vertically across the hierarchy and horizontally across functions). The roles leaders/managers/supporting professionals can play in each capability and the types of competencies required to effectively play such roles are discussed.

## LEARNING OBJECTIVES

- Develop knowledge of the key definitions and concepts related to enterprise architecture management, DT adoption and use, and data management/data analytics/data science capabilities

- Understand the meaning and role of these capabilities in the digital transformation strategy and digital business strategy of organizations
- Understand the roles leaders, managers, and support professionals can play in these digital capabilities
- Understand the competencies required by leaders, managers, and support professionals to maximize their roles in these digital capabilities
- Analyze and evaluate the implications of these capabilities, as well as related leadership or management roles and competencies, for organizations' digital transformation strategy and digital business strategy
- Apply knowledge and understanding to participate in, support, or lead workstreams or initiatives related to the building and optimization of these capabilities

# ENTERPRISE ARCHITECTURE AND ENTERPRISE ARCHITECTURE MANAGEMENT

## ENTERPRISE ARCHITECTURE

Enterprise architecture (EA) refers to the design or configuration of the different elements/assets of an organization (e.g., hardware, software, networks, business processes, information systems, information, data, etc.) and the resultant levels of efficiency, effectiveness, and longevity they enable an organization to have in the pursuit of its mission within its external environment. For example, one particular design or configuration may lead to mediocre levels of efficiency and effectiveness in the pursuit of the organization's mission (e.g., perhaps due to having a random collection of disparate hardware, software, networks, business processes, and information/data that don't work together – thus constraining connectivity, communication, collaboration, and customer experience). For an organization like the Ritz-Carlton Hotel, for example, such enterprise architecture would severely limit its mission of providing guests with the finest personalized service and experience;[1] and, in turn, limit its longevity. Another type of design or configuration might be suited maximizing connectivity, integrability, communication, collaboration, automation, adaptability, and customer experience – resulting in very high levels of efficiency and effectiveness. It is proposed that the latter is the type of enterprise architecture that leading digital businesses like Microsoft, Amazon, Google, and Netflix have. Enterprise architecture has had simpler, although perhaps less complete, definitions including that it is the process of aligning an organization's strategic vision with its information technology;[2] that it is how information/ business/technology flow together;[3] and that it is the organizing logic for how business processes and IT infrastructure should work together to meet operational requirements.[4]

Enterprise architecture is described as being layered (i.e., having business architecture, information architecture, information systems architecture, data architecture, and delivery architecture layers), spanning the entire organization (i.e., vertically across the hierarchy and horizontally across business functions), being both conceptual and physical (i.e., being a visual or written logical representations or the actual elements/ assets), being iterative (i.e., built or evolving over time through iterative additions/improvements), and being both current and forward looking (i.e., designs or configurations deal with both current and future business needs). According to practitioners and researchers, good enterprise architecture should enable both current and future strategy (e.g., operational effectiveness, business transformation),[5] be proactive (i.e., anticipate and prepare for the future needs of the business),[6] speed up processes (e.g., digitize, integrate, and automate key processes), enable adaptability (e.g., through plug and play digital assets that can be adapted to different internal and external systems/technologies/processes), ensure availability and accessibility of high quality data across the enterprise to drive decision making (e.g., cleaning, standardizing, sharing, presenting data), and instantiate the organization's digital business model.[7]

# ENTERPRISE ARCHITECTURE MANAGEMENT

Enterprise architecture management refers to the processes and practices of planning, implementing, maintaining, and continuously improving an organization's enterprise architecture. At a high level, it involves continuous and iterative activities of identifying EA stakeholders and their concerns, understanding the existing EA and the value it creates, designing the target EA, planning the implementation, transitioning to the target EA, and ensuring effective EA governance.[8] See Table 13.1[9] providing example EA activities and tasks, as well as the resultant artifacts (leaders, managers, and supporting professionals may be presented with and have to interpret these artifacts by EA leaders and/or consultants). The benefits from effective EA management are broad and include the capacity for reduced complexity and improved communication, collaboration, decision making, functional and external partner alignment, customer satisfaction, and more. EA researchers identify more than 40 benefits of effective enterprise architecture (see Table 13.2 listing 40 such benefits). Given the digital business transformation and digital business imperatives, the most important benefit, and the one integrating all 40 listed benefits into a single benefit, is successful digital business transformation and capacity to effectively compete as a digital business. Enterprise architecture leaders can ensure the design or configuration of, and transition to, architectures that simultaneously deliver efficiency, differentiation, adaptability, and agility capabilities. Although previously seen as being "either/or" choices, simultaneously having these capabilities has been shown to be essential in increasingly complex business environments.[10]

# IMPLICATIONS FOR LEADERS, MANAGERS, AND SUPPORTING PROFESSIONALS

Leaders, managers, and supporting professionals can play a range of roles to optimize enterprise architecture management. First, the top enterprise architecture management role can be filled by someone from the IT/IS/technology function but with deep operational process and industry knowledge, and/or it can be filled by someone from operations with

Table 13.1 Example enterprise architecture management activities, tasks, and artifacts

| EA management activities | EA management tasks | Resultant EA management artifacts |
| --- | --- | --- |
| Identifying EA stakeholders and their concerns | Identification of stakeholders and their concerns | List of stakeholders |
| | Identification of project motivation | Project goals and objectives |
| Understanding the existing EA and the enterprise value it creates | General view of the enterprise | Business model canvas "as is" |
| | Identification of company goals, objectives, and indicators for their measurement | Strategy map (or goal tree) |
| | | Balanced scorecard |
| | Identification of value proposition (VP) | Tree of products/services, value curve |
| | Identification of the value configuration "as is" | Value creation model |
| | Identification of the operations architecture "as is" | Function decomposition model |
| | | Processes landscape |
| | | Business process models (if necessary) |
| | Organizational structure and responsibility matrix "as is" | Organization chart |
| | | Responsibility matrix (or RACI-matrix) |
| | IT architecture "as is" (existing information systems and technological infrastructure) | Model of application/IS usage |
| | | Description of the application/IS landscape |
| | | Infrastructure use model |
| | General idea of EA "as is" | High-level (overview) EA model |

| | | |
|---|---|---|
| Designing the target EA (several alternative scenarios may be developed at this stage) | Development of target EA vision | Business model canvas "to be" |
| | Development of target EA with detailing of representations by layers | High-level (overview) model "to be" |
| | | Particular EA models, which will be affected by changes (composition of models as in the description of the current state) "to be" |
| Planning and effecting the implementation and transitioning to the target EA | Planning of the transition between the EA states (current, target, transitional) | Transition planning model (linking EA changes/gaps with work packages) |
| | Formation of development projects portfolio | Transformation and development program cards (proposed initiatives) |
| | Planning for implementation and transition (see project management) | Schedule of transformation projects (for example, in MS Project) |
| Ensuring effective EA governance | Establishing and maintaining effective EA organization structure with clear roles and responsibilities | EA Organization Chart, EA function job descriptions, KPIs |
| | Establishing and maintaining effective EA governance practices | EA governance model |
| | Establishing and maintaining effective EA standards and guidelines | EA framework |
| | Establishing and maintaining effective EA management tools | Architecture repository |

*Table 13.2 Benefits of effective enterprise architecture management*

| EA management benefits | |
| --- | --- |
| Document knowledge on the enterprise | Improve resource quality |
| Identify resource dependencies | Improve return on investments |
| Identify resource synergies | Improve situational awareness |
| Identify suboptimal resource use | Improve solution development |
| Improve alignment with partners | Improve stability |
| Improve change management | Increase agility |
| Improve compliance | Increase economies of scale |
| Improve customer satisfaction | Increase efficiency |
| Improve decision making | Increase growth |
| Improve employee satisfaction | Increase innovation |
| Improve enterprise-wide goal attainment | Increase market share |
| Improve information quality | Increase resource flexibility |
| Improve investment management | Increase resource reuse |
| Improve measurement | Increase resource standardization |
| Improve organizational alignment | Increase revenue |
| Improve organizational collaboration | Provide a high-level overview |
| Improve organizational communication | Provide directions for improvement |
| Improve resource alignment | Provide standards |
| Improve resource consolidation | Reduce costs |
| Improve resource integration | Reduce complexity |

sufficient IT/IS/technology competencies.[11] Both individuals are likely to be challenging to find and to keep for long. An alternative option is strong collaboration between someone from the IT/IS/technology function and someone from the operations function with deep industry and operational process knowledge. Thus, one role leaders, managers, and supporting professionals can play is to directly manage the EA function or sharing responsibility for it.

Outside of direct or shared management of EA, leaders, managers, and supporting professionals can play other important roles. For example, they can be involved in hiring the person to directly manage the EA function; they can be involved in setting or approving the EA vision and high-level objectives; they can be involved in interpreting and using EA artifacts; they can be involved in identifying and/or selecting among different technology/network/hardware/software/process options; they can participate in EA related discussions; they can be involved in choosing between different EA target state options; they can participate in EA governance or oversight of EA governance; or they can lead the changing of business processes to align with chosen EA target state options (see Figure 13.1 for example EA governance roles and responsibilities at different hierarchical levels). To effectively play one or more of these roles, leaders, managers, and supporting professionals need a working understanding of enterprise architecture and enterprise architecture management (e.g., what are their aims, how do they work, what are the opportunities and challenges), a working knowledge of EA artifacts (e.g., being able to read EA plans), a working knowledge of different digital technologies and the strategic opportunities and risks associated with those different digital technologies.

# DT ADOPTION AND USE

This capability refers to the organization routines/activities, structures, and/or processes that determine the extent and effectiveness with which firms leverage digital technologies in their strategic and operational activities.[12] This capability can be thought of as comprising of two sub-capabilities. The first sub-capability is digital technology sourcing, which refers to the effectiveness of an organization's processes/practices for finding, choosing, and procuring technology resources required for its current and desired enterprise architectures. Digital technology advancements and digital disruption have expanded the focus of technology sourcing from cost minimization and risk mitigation to driving innovation, revenue growth, customer retention, speed, adaptability, and agility.[13] Through finding, choosing, and partnering with the right vendors, as well as getting contracts right and managing the relationships appropriately, organizations can reap benefits such as having superior

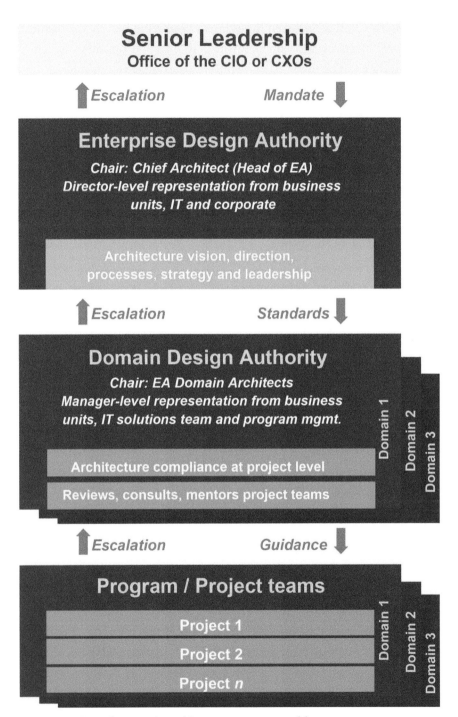

**Figure 13.1** *Example enterprise architecture governance model*

hardware/software/networks relative to competitors, product co-creation with vendors, vendor induced migration to state-of-the-art practices, introduction to new technologies and new customers, etc. Through finding, choosing, and adopting breakthrough technologies and products, an organization can speed up realization of their desired enterprise architectures or exceed what they thought possible from enterprise architecture. For example, imagine an organization being one of the first companies to discover, choose, and procure Amazon's Elastic Compute Cloud back in 2006. That organization would have been able to spin up a virtual desktop fully equipped with all of the organization's systems and data on any computer anywhere in the world from as far back as 2006. Depending on the nature of its core products, this could have given it unfair global portability and scalability advantages relative to competitors.

The second sub-capability relates to the adoption and use of sourced digital technologies. Although an organization may be able to be aware of, find, and procure a digital technology that may optimize its strategy and operations, actually testing and scaling the use of that digital technology into the wider organization can come with significant challenges. For one, some people within the organization may regard the potential benefits of the digital technology with skepticism, and others may see their existing ways of working and relevance within the organization threatened by the adoption and use of the new digital technology. Yet others may see the benefits of the digital technology and be able to shepherd its adoption and wide scale use but choose to suppress its adoption and wide scale use either consciously or unconsciously. In addition, wide scale adoption usually requires significant investment and sacrifices by many organization stakeholders. Thus, organizations need effective routines/activities, structures, and/or processes to enable and optimize the adoption and use of digital technologies.

## IMPLICATIONS FOR LEADERS, MANAGERS, AND SUPPORTING PROFESSIONALS

Leaders, managers, and supporting professionals can play critical roles in DT adoption and use including scouting for transformative technologies and vendors, building collaborative relationships with vendors, engaging in co-creation efforts with vendors,[14] sourcing informal advice from vendors, scouting for innovative business models that could be applied in their industry, scouting products/services used in the organization that are no longer needed/that need upgrading/or that have better or cheaper alternatives on the market, engaging their teams to be the organization's eyes and ears with regard to new technology breakthroughs or star vendors, and more. They can also fill formal roles such as procurement director, technology sourcing manager, vendor relationship manager, business engagement manager, contract manager, etc. In relation to the optimal adoption and use of new digital technologies, leaders, managers, and supporting professionals can become allies to those proposing or leading technology adoption initiatives; they can cultivate cultures amenable to technology adoption; and they can sacrifice key resources (such as key talent, budget, and organization attention) to enable the nurturing and scaling of digital technology adoption initiatives. To effectively undertake these roles, leaders and line managers need to build working knowledge of the role, functioning, strategies, and potential value of the technology procurement and sourcing function. They need working understanding of effective technology adoption and scaling approaches; different digital technologies, related products, and services; and the related vendor landscape. They also need to have an understanding of the organization's enterprise architecture and how to engage constructively with the enterprise architecture management team.

# DATA MANAGEMENT, DATA SCIENCE, AND DATA ANALYTICS

## DATA MANAGEMENT

Digital technology advancements have made and continue to make vast quantities of internal and external data available. For example, more than 500 million tweets, 294 billion emails, 5 billion search engine searches, and 4 petabytes of Facebook data are created each day – and it is estimated that there are up to 40 times more bytes of data than there are stars in the known universe.[15] The big challenge for organizations is how to leverage the vast quantities of internal and external data to improve their efficiency, differentiation, adaptability, and agility.[16] Effective data management and data analytics, which are covered in more detail in Chapter 18, play a critical role in addressing this challenge.

Data management capabilities refer to an organization's processes and practices for collecting, validating, storing, and using data most effectively.[17] This can be a challenge given the growing avalanche of internal and external data to manage and the growing sources of such data. For example, data can come from SaaS applications (software-as-a-service applications), ERP systems (enterprise resource planning systems), legacy systems, databases, data warehouses, and data lakes. Or it may come from the web, social media platforms, open data, and commercial data platforms. Alternatively, it may come from any number of devices including phones, computers, wearable devices, sensors, monitoring devices, etc. All this data has to be collected safely, validated, stored safely, and formatted and presented so that different parts of the organization can access the right information at the right time and in the right format to make the best decisions. This requires that organizations have the right technical leaders, the right technical specialists, the right technology platforms and the right policies, procedures, and practices. The data management function typically plays a leadership role in issues such as data governance (who has what decision rights and what accountability for data quality), data architecture (what rules, policies, standards, and models are in place to determine what data is collected, how it is stored, how it is integrated, and how it is used), data modeling and design (defining and analyzing data required to support business processes), database and storage management, and data security and privacy.

## DATA ANALYTICS AND DATA SCIENCE

Data analytics (also referred to just as analytics[18]) is an umbrella term referring to any form of analysis of data to uncover trends, patterns, anomalies, or simply to measure performance.[19] It also includes interpretation, presentation, and communication of discovered patterns to improve decision making. Analytics approaches or methods can include descriptive analytics (using historic or current data to determine "what" happened and "how it happened"), predictive analytics (understanding the "why" or cause-and-effect relationships within data in order to be able to make accurate predictions), and prescriptive analytics (using algorithms to suggest optimal decisions based on the results of descriptive and predictive analytics). Often going hand in hand with data analytics, data science is a method for drawing insights from large datasets of structured and unstructured data. It draws on approaches, methods, techniques, and theories from disciplines such as mathematics, statistics, computer science, and information science. For example, it may draw on machine learning and deep learning techniques from the computer science field to learn from past decisions in order to improve the quality of automatically prescribed decisions. Or it may draw on statistical methods such as regression analysis and structural equation modeling to improve the reliability of information used as a basis for prescribed decisions. The role of data scientists can include activities such as collecting data, cleaning data, organizing data, making statistical inferences, building/using machine learning or deep learning models, conducting online experiments, building customizable or personalized data products, visualizing data, communicating findings, and much more.[20] Collectively, data management, data analytics, and data science have the same aims: leveraging internal and external data to drive efficiency, differentiation, adaptability, and agility.

## IMPLICATIONS FOR LEADERS, MANAGERS, AND SUPPORTING PROFESSIONALS

Leaders, managers, and supporting professionals can play a range of roles in an organization's data management, data analytics, and data science efforts. For example, these include establishing a data management/ data analytics/data science function, establishing data and data analytics objectives, and ensuring use of data insights in decision making. They also include hiring/line managing data management/data analytics/ data science staff or service providers, sponsoring data management/ data analytics/data science leaders, and authorizing what systems to map and interconnect. Further roles include getting relevant parties on board with associated change efforts,[21] approving funding for data investment projects, approving what data to use from inside or outside the organization, releasing function specific data, approving procurement of particular data management technologies, ensuring the best data is used for decision making, and more. To effectively play one or more of these different roles, leaders, managers, and supporting professionals need to have a working understanding of data management, data analytics, and data science concepts, practices, and related artifacts (e.g., objectives, functioning, key terminology, methodologies/tools, challenges, and state-of-the-art practices). This is in addition to earlier enterprise architecture management and technology sourcing competencies.

# GOOGLE AND REFLECT

| Digital capability | Common terminology |
|---|---|
| Enterprise architecture management | Enterprise architecture, enterprise architectural planning (EAP), enterprise architecture management (EAM), enterprise architecture book of knowledge (EABOK), enterprise architect, enterprise architecture modelling (EAM), enterprise architecture framework, business architecture, information architecture, information systems architecture, data architecture, DevOps architecture, architecture repository, Service-Oriented Architecture (SOA), backward compatibility |
| Technology adoption and use | Procurement market intelligence, supplier co-creation, internal sourcing, partner-based sourcing, market-based sourcing, value chain sourcing, industry-university collaboration, technology scanning, technology transfer, technology licensing, technological alliance, technology acquisition, joint R&D, MVP, end-user adoption |

| Digital capability | Common terminology |
|---|---|
| Data analytics and data management | Database, data mart, data warehouse, data lake, data catalog, enterprise data hub, data fabric, operational data store, data governance, data architecture, open data, machine learning, deep learning, neural networks, data mining, data set, data democratization, natural language processing, data anonymization, behavioral analytics, citizen data scientist, data classification, decision trees, multidimensional database (MDB), online analytical processing (OLAP), outlier, predictive modelling, Python, R (programming language), random forest, validity, reliability, decision science, association analytics, sentiment analysis, time decomposition, cluster analysis |

# DISCUSSION QUESTIONS

1 What is the difference between enterprise architecture, IT architecture, and technology architecture?

2 What role does enterprise architecture play in digital business capabilities?

3 Which leadership and line management roles in enterprise architecture management are the most critical to building and maintaining that capability? Why?

4 Which enterprise architecture management competency is likely to have the greatest positive impact on building and optimizing that capability?

5 What is the difference between technology sourcing and technology procurement?

6 What leadership role in technology sourcing is the most critical to building and maintaining that capability? Why?

7 What is the difference between technology adoption and optimal technology use?

8 What is the difference between data management and data analytics?

9 Which is more important, data management or data analytics? Why?

10 What data management and data analytics leadership competency is likely to have the greatest positive impact on a line manager's career?

11 Which of the capabilities discussed in this chapter are the most important to succeeding at digital transformation and digital business competitiveness?

# NOTES

1 Ritz-Carlton. (2020). Gold standards. Retrieved June 6, 2020, from The Ritz-Carlton website: www.ritzcarlton.com/en/about/gold-standards

2 Daniel, D. (2007, March 31). The rising importance of the enterprise architect. *CIO*. www.cio.com/article/2439397/the-rising-importance-of-the-enterprise-architect.html

3 White, S. K. (2018, October 16). What is enterprise architecture? A framework for transformation. *CIO*. www.cio.com/article/3313657/what-is-enterprise-architecture-a-framework-for-transformation.html

4 Ross, J. W., Weill, P., & Robertson, D. (2006). *Enterprise architecture as strategy: Creating a foundation for business execution.* Harvard Business Press.

5 Daniel, D. (2007, March 31). The rising importance of the enterprise architect. *CIO*. www.cio.com/article/2439397/the-rising-importance-of-the-enterprise-architect.html

6 Daniel, D. (2007, March 31). The rising importance of the enterprise architect. *CIO*. www.cio.com/article/2439397/the-rising-importance-of-the-enterprise-architect.html

7 Suer, M. F. (2018, June 26). Enterprise architects as digital transformers. *CIO*. www.cio.com/article/3284475/enterprise-architects-as-digital-transformers.html

8 Kudryavtsev, D., Zaramenskikh, E., & Arzumanyan, M. (2018). The simplified enterprise architecture management methodology for teaching purposes. *Lecture Notes in Business Information Processing*, 76–90. https://doi.org/10.1007/978-3-030-00787-4_6

9 Kudryavtsev, D., Zaramenskikh, E., & Arzumanyan, M. (2018). The simplified enterprise architecture management methodology for teaching purposes. *Lecture Notes in Business Information Processing*, 76–90. https://doi.org/10.1007/978-3-030-00787-4_6

10  Ovans, A. (2015). What is strategy, again. *Harvard Business Review*. Retrieved June 7, 2020, from Harvard Business Review website: https://hbr.org/2015/05/what-is-strategy-again; Busulwa, R., Tice, M., & Gurd, B. *Strategy execution and complexity: Thriving in the era of disruption.* Routledge.

11  Daniel, D. (2007, March 31). The rising importance of the enterprise architect. *CIO.* www.cio.com/article/2439397/the-rising-importance-of-the-enterprise-architect.html

12  Busulwa, R., Pickering, M., and Mao, Iris. (2022). Digital transformation and hospitality management competencies: Toward an integrative framework. *International Journal of Hospitality Management* 102, 103132.

13  Pettey, C. (2018, July 16). Top trends for the future of IT procurement. Retrieved June 7, 2020, from Gartner.com website: www.gartner.com/smarterwithgartner/top-trends-for-the-future-of-it-procurement/

14  Sinclair, S. (2020). What are the future skills of sourcing? – Aalto University. Retrieved June 8, 2020, from Aaltopro.fi website: www.aaltopro.fi/en/aalto-leaders-insight/2020/what-are-the-future-skills-of-sourcing

15  Desjardins, J. (2019, April 17). How much data is generated each day? Retrieved June 7, 2020, from World Economic Forum website: www.weforum.org/agenda/2019/04/how-much-data-is-generated-each-day-cf4bddf29f/

16  Brylad, M (2019). Data literacy: A critical skill for the 21st century. *Tableau Software.* Retrieved 17 December 2019, from www.tableau.com/about/blog/2018/9/data-literacy-critical-skill-21st-century-94221

17  "What Is Data Management?" (2019). Oracle.Com. Retrieved December 9, 2019. www.oracle.com/au/database/what-is-data-management/.

18  Analytics. (2019). Gartner. Retrieved 16 December 2019, from www.gartner.com/en/information-technology/glossary/analytics

19  Comparing Business Intelligence, Business Analytics and Data Analytics. (2019). Tableau Software. Retrieved 16 December 2019, from www.tableau.com/learn/articles/business-intelligence/bi-business-analytics; Business Analytics: Everything You Need to Know. (2019). MicroStrategy. Retrieved 16 December 2019, from www.microstrategy.com/us/resources/introductory-guides/business-analytics-everything-you-need-to-know; Boulton, C. (2019). Data analytics examples: An inside look at 6 success stories. *CIO.* Retrieved 17 December 2019, from www.cio.com/article/3221621/6-data-analytics-success-stories-an-inside-look.html

20  Bowne-Anderson, H. (2018). What data scientists really do, according to 35 data scientists. *Harvard Business Review*. Retrieved 17 December 2019,

from https://hbr.org/2018/08/what-data-scientists-really-do-according-to-35-data-scientists; What is Data Science? | Oracle. (2019). Oracle.com. Retrieved 17 December 2019, from www.oracle.com/data-science/what-is-data-science.html

21 Daniel, D. (2007, March 31). The rising importance of the enterprise architect. *CIO.* www.cio.com/article/2439397/the-rising-importance-of-the-enterprise-architect.html

# Cybersecurity Management, Digital Risk Management, and Digital Governance Capabilities

DOI: 10.4324/9781003254614-18

# INTRODUCTION

The use of new digital technologies and business models introduce new and/or significantly expanded risk exposures. These new and significantly expanded risk exposures demand sophisticated and fast cybersecurity, risk management, and governance practices. Fortunately, despite the new risks they create, digital technologies also enable much more sophisticated approaches, practices, and tools for supercharging cybersecurity management, digital risk management, and digital governance. The resultant transformed approach to risk management and governance is what is commonly referred to as digital risk management and digital governance. And, although not changed in name, new digital technologies and business models demand and enable significant changes in cybersecurity management and cybersecurity capability. This primer reintroduces leaders, managers, and supporting professionals to these capabilities (i.e., what are they, how do they differ from their traditional counterpart terms, what their value propositions are, and how leaders, managers, and supporting professionals can optimize their contribution to the capabilities). The primer then discusses the roles and competencies they require of leaders, managers, and supporting professionals.

---

### LEARNING OBJECTIVES

- Develop knowledge of definitions and concepts related to cybersecurity management, digital risk management, and digital governance capabilities
- Understand the meaning and role of these capabilities in the digital transformation strategy and digital business strategy of organizations
- Understand the roles leaders, managers, and supporting professionals can play in these digital capabilities
- Understand the competencies required by leaders, managers, and supporting professionals to maximize their roles in these digital capabilities

---

- Analyze and evaluate the implications of these capabilities, as well as related leadership or management roles and competencies, for organizations' digital transformation strategy and digital business strategy
- Apply knowledge and understanding to participate in, support, or lead workstreams or initiatives related to the building and optimization of these capabilities

# CYBERSECURITY MANAGEMENT

## CYBERSECURITY

At a very high level, cybersecurity refers to the state of, or processes for, protecting anything in the cyber realm (e.g., devices, software, things, networks, information) and recovering from cyberattacks.[1] The terms information security, IT security, ICT security, computer security, and network security are sometimes interchangeably used to refer to cybersecurity, even though there are differences in meaning.[2] Typically, these terms refer to specific subsets of cybersecurity. For example, information security is mainly focused on protecting physical and digital information from unauthorized access, use, disclosure, disruption, modification, or destruction in order to provide confidentiality, integrity, and availability.[3] And IT security, ICT security, and computer security tends to focus more narrowly on protecting computers, networks, and data – but what about the exploding diversity in "things" and ecosystems? Given some of the limitations and slipperiness of these terms, the term cybersecurity has emerged as a more flexible and all-encompassing term. But there have still been differences in the way practitioners and researchers have defined cybersecurity. Daniel Schatz, global head of cybersecurity at Qiagen and former director of threat and vulnerability management at Thomson Reuters, and Julie Wall, a senior researcher at the University of East London, reviewed and synthesized the various definitions to arrive at a more specific, more encompassing, and complete definition of cybersecurity. They proposed that cybersecurity is:[4]

The approach and actions associated with security risk management processes followed by organizations and states to protect confidentiality, integrity and availability of data and assets used in cyberspace. The concept includes guidelines, policies and collections of safeguards, technologies, tools and training to provide the best protection for the state of the cyber environment and its users.

Cybersecurity may not have historically been in your consciousness as a big deal for people outside the IT or IS function. And you may be wondering what has changed to make it an issue warranting much attention from leaders, managers, and supporting professionals. If so, consider this: How much of your organization's information was indefinitely online in the past? How many devices within and outside of your organization were "plugged" into that information? How many people around the world were online and able to hack into your information systems? How sophisticated was the computation available to hackers? How fast was the internet connectivity speed? How much integration was there? As you may be starting to see, the race to digitally transform and become a digital business has meant that almost all of an organization's resources are now online and potentially accessible by billions of people anywhere in the world. On top of this, the exponentially growing proliferation of "things," external networks, and ecosystems plugging into an organization's online resources almost creates the effect of having millions, even billions, of potential front doors to your house that you may or may not be aware of. And data flows from and to devices, from and to core systems with sensitive data, from and to external networks and devices, from and to different locations around the world, and from and to different digital ecosystems. At any point during that flow or while it resides in a particular storage location, digitized data and information can be intercepted by sophisticated cybercriminals anywhere in the world. For example, they may intercept login details; they may steal identification information for onselling to identity thieves; they may steal company trade secrets or key stakeholder intellectual property; they may alter company records for their own gain; they may steal sensitive key persons' information and hold it for ransom; they may steal and dump sensitive customer data online in order jeopardize the organization; and much more. Thus, the significantly expanded digitization, connectivity, integration, and ubiquity related to digital transformation and digital business means new and significantly expanded digital vulnerabilities. In fact, massive cybersecurity breaches have become almost commonplace now, with even prestige brands regularly in attention-grabbing and alarming breach headlines.[5] For example, in early 2020, Marriott International was in one such headline.[6] A cybercriminal had hacked the login details of two employees from a franchise property and used those login details to access customer information from the app's back-end systems.[7] This impacted 5.2 million customers and included access to personal information including name, address, phone number, date of birth, gender, travel history, and travel plans.[8] It followed another incident in 2018 in which 383 million guests' details were stolen, including names, addresses, passport numbers, and credit card numbers.[9] Imagine how you would feel as a customer; any one of these incidents may have undone any credibility or brand trust. And it could have been much worse: imagine if cybercriminals used guests' travel history and mobile information to track down key persons in remote locations and hold them hostage or sell them into human trafficking rings. In addition to ruining customers' lives, almost a century of brand building could have been brought down almost overnight, and thousands of people could have lost their jobs. Perhaps due to the growing breaches and the significant risks customers are exposed to, a number of governments around the world have started to introduce mandatory data breach reporting laws, requiring organizations to report data breaches where personal information they hold is subject to unauthorized access or disclosure.[10] This makes the naming and shaming through attention-grabbing headlines a certainty for organizations that fail to protect the data entrusted into their care. Finally, it goes without saying that the financial costs involved in a breach can be ruinous; these are typically exacerbated by the time it takes to discover the breach, respond to it, and recover from the associated disruption – to the extent this is actually possible.[11] Figure 14.1 shows the top ten messages for leaders synthesized from the World Economic Forum's annual meeting exploring critical and emerging cybersecurity issues.

## 10 Messages for Global Leaders from the Annual Meeting on Cybersecurity

**1** Cyberattacks are increasing in frequency and sophistication. It is hence the responsibility of public and corporate leaders to take ownership for ensuring global cybersecurity and digital trust.

**2** Board and C-Suite members need to gain a better understanding of the cyber risks to which their organization is exposed and of their cyber readiness.

**3** Both public and private organizations need to improve their crisis management, develop holistic response and recovery plans, including a crisis communication strategy.

**4** Leaders need to create a culture of cybersecurity from the entry level to the top leadership of an organization.

**5** Leaders may need to rethink organizational structures and governance to enable a more robust cybersecurity posture.

**6** Innovation in cybersecurity and rapidly evolving technologies call for greater investment to stay ahead of cybercriminals who are adopting such technologies even faster and to their advantage.

**7** Global cooperation across the public and the private sectors is vital. Information-sharing, business cooperation with law enforcement agencies as well as skills and capacity development to be prioritized.

**8** Maintaining an open and secure internet requires a collaborative effort between the public and private sector.

**9** Trusted and verified cybersecurity ratings are required for the improved assessment of an organization's cyber resilience and comparability across peers.

**10** The World Economic Forum provides a neutral, trusted and globally recognized platform to facilitate cooperation and deliver tangible impact on the systemic challenge of global cybersecurity.

**Figure 14.1** *Ten messages for global leaders from the 2019 World Economic Forum annual meeting on cybersecurity*[12]

## CYBERSECURITY CAPABILITY AND CYBERSECURITY MANAGEMENT CAPABILITY

Cybersecurity capability refers to the effectiveness of an organization at protecting itself and recovering from cyber threats (i.e., the effectiveness of its cybersecurity infrastructure, consisting of hardware, software, processes, and people). And cybersecurity management refers to the processes and practices of planning, implementing, maintaining, and continuously upgrading an organization's cybersecurity capability. However, while at times the term cybersecurity capability is used to refer to only the outcome or outputs of cybersecurity management activities, at other times both terms are interchangeably used to refer the organization routines/activities, structures, and/or processes that that work together to effectively protect an organization against and enable it to recover from cyberthreats. For the remainder of this chapter, the terms cybersecurity capability and cybersecurity management are interchangeably used to mean the same thing – notwithstanding that cybersecurity capability can also be just the output of cybersecurity practice.

According to the National Institute of Standards and Technology cybersecurity framework[13] (NIST CSF), cybersecurity capability consists of five core functions: (1) identify, (2) protect, (3) detect, (4) respond, and (5) recover (see Figure 14.2). The identify function involves developing a clear understanding of the business' processes and environment, its supporting systems/people/assets/data/capabilities, the cyberthreats faced by these systems/people/assets/data/capabilities (e.g., ransomware, hacking, data leakage, insider threat), and the potential impact of these threats on the organization. It includes asset management, business environment, governance, risk assessment, and risk management strategy practices. The protect function involves establishing and maintaining appropriate safeguards to prevent or limit the impact of a potential cybersecurity event. It includes practices such as identity management and access control, awareness training, data security, information protection processes and procedures, and use of protective technology. The detect function involves establishing and maintaining appropriate activities for the timely identification of cybersecurity events. It includes practice such as anomaly detection, security continuous monitoring, and detection processes. The respond function involves establishing and maintaining processes for containing the impact of a detected cybersecurity incident. It includes practices such as response planning, communication, analysis, migration, and improvement. Finally, the recover function involves establishing and maintaining resiliency and service/capability restoration plans (i.e., plans that can be effected for timely recovery from a disruptive cybersecurity incident). It includes practices such as recovery planning, communication, and continuous improvement. The cybersecurity capability maturity model (C2M2) is an example of an alternative cybersecurity capability framework.[14]

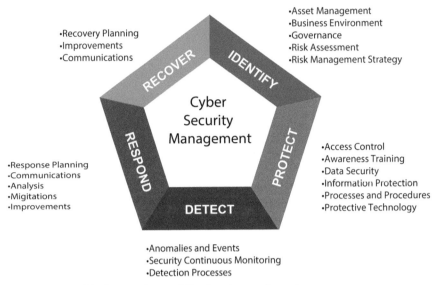

**Figure 14.2** *NIST cybersecurity capability functions and practices*

## IMPLICATIONS FOR LEADERS, MANAGERS, AND SUPPORTING PROFESSIONALS

Effective cybersecurity management and an effective cybersecurity capability require senior leadership ownership/engagement, a top-down strategy, and integration of cybersecurity policies/activities into operations to ensure cyber and privacy risks are managed effectively in every part of the organization.[15] It requires leaders to cultivate and drive the cultivation of a cyber risk management culture at all levels. A leader or manager may play the role of a senior leader with ownership for the organization's overall cybersecurity capability (e.g., hiring the right functional leader, building the credibility and influence of this leader, and establishing cybersecurity objectives and governance mechanisms), or they may play other roles such as ensuring employee understanding of, and compliance with, cybersecurity policies; ensuring employees report cybersecurity breach events; and ensuring employees have adequate knowledge of, and competency in, cybersecurity so that they are able to avoid cybersecurity compromising behaviors.[16] In either case, a working understanding of the cybersecurity function's objectives, functioning, and challenges is essential. Similarly, an understanding of cyber risks and threats, state-of-the-art cybersecurity practices, and cybersecurity terminology is essential. Having a cybersecurity event originate from, and be due to, lapses within a particular line manager's team can negatively impact that particular manager's career.

# DIGITAL RISK MANAGEMENT AND DIGITAL GOVERNANCE

## DIGITAL RISK MANAGEMENT AND DIGITAL GOVERNANCE VS TRADITIONAL RISK MANAGEMENT AND GOVERNANCE

Risk management is concerned with how effectively an organization detects, guards against, responds to, and recovers from risk exposures or events.[17] Governance is concerned with how effectively an organization is led, controlled, and the people operating it are held to account for the efficient, effective, and responsible pursuit of the organization's mission.[18] Effective risk management is a critical element of effective governance.[19] Digital risk management and digital governance refer to the management of the unique risk and governance issues associated with digital technologies/digital business, as well as the leveraging of digital technologies to maximize the efficiency and effectiveness of risk management and governance functions.

## NATURE OF DIGITAL RISK AND THE NEW RISK LANDSCAPE

Digital technology advancements, digital transformation, and digital business bring about new risks that haven't been encountered before and also add complexity to existing risks, thus significantly changing the risk landscape.[20] Examples of new risks and complexity introduced include inappropriate employee behaviors on social media, employees inadvertently clicking on suspect links in emails/online or divulging sensitive corporate information, and artificial intelligence product/tool algorithm-related risks (e.g., biased data, unsuitable modeling techniques, algorithmic bias). Further examples include an expanded number of cyberattack points due to expansion of IoT devices/platforms/networks integrating with an organization's infrastructure, an expanded number of cybercriminals online and having more sophisticated attack tools, and misinformation risks (cybercriminals/nation states/competitors or other troublemakers using sophisticated digital editing and imitation technologies like machine learning, bots, and natural language generation to spread false information, incite adverse reactions, delegitimize leaders and influencers, and damage brands). Additional examples include data misuse (e.g., lack of transparency, control, accuracy, ethics, security, reliability, and privacy), ubiquitous connectivity (e.g., attack is able to happen any time, most likely when key security staff are offline), and digital technology advancements outpacing laws and regulations (e.g., risk of new and less legally bound competitors entering market or risk that new business models adopted may be rendered obsolete as laws and regulations catch up). Yet further examples include culture risk (e.g., pace of change exceeds cultural readiness resulting in destructive resistance to change, disengagement/disenfranchisement, vindictive employees/partners/contractors) and digital ethics risk (e.g., risk that digital technologies are used for and/or in a manner that current and/or future societies consider unethical).[21]

## ROLE OF DIGITAL TECHNOLOGIES IN DIGITAL RISK MANAGEMENT AND GOVERNANCE

As just illustrated, the breadth in risk exposure and the mortal nature of the risks faced makes effective risk management and governance critical in the digital era. Fortunately, leaders, managers, and supporting professionals at all levels can leverage the same sophisticated digital technologies that drive these risk exposures to effectively detect, guard against, respond to, and recover from the diverse risk exposures or events.[22] Examples of this include leveraging robotic process automation for accelerated identity and access management; leveraging natural language generation to automate regulatory reporting; leveraging chatbots to improve understanding of policies and compliance requirements; leveraging computer vision to spot anomalies; leveraging virtual/augmented/ mixed reality to simulate crisis management situations; leveraging machine learning to spot policy and ethics violations; leveraging algorithms for continuous monitoring of credit reports/court/ sanctions lists/search engines to limit third-party risk exposures; leveraging blockchain-enabled proof-of-provenance to ensure the verifying origin, safety, and authenticity of products; leveraging predictive analytics to anticipate and intervene in risky behaviors before the fact; and leveraging digital twins (virtual replicas of physical objects) to anticipate and mitigate risk impacts.[23]

## IMPLICATIONS FOR LEADERS, MANAGERS, AND SUPPORTING PROFESSIONALS

Leaders, managers, and supporting professionals at all levels have shared responsibility in effective digital risk management and governance. They can play important roles such as being establishers/maintainers/continuous improvers of risk management and governance practices, being sourcers/evaluators/ procurers/vendor managers of digital risk management and governance technologies, being monitors of state-of-the-art risk management and governance practices, being monitors and testers of risk management technologies, being risk management practice auditors, and being crisis managers. Each of these roles requires an understanding of digital risk management and governance and of the digital technologies and opportunities/threats associated with them.

# GOOGLE AND REFLECT

| Digital capability | Common terminology |
|---|---|
| Cybersecurity management | Cyber risk, cybersecurity, cybersecurity capability, cybersecurity management, cybersecurity framework, NIST CSF, cybersecurity event, cyber resilience, identity management, access control, anomaly detection, security continuous monitoring, cyber response planning, cyber recovery planning, DevSecOps, cyber insurance, ransomware |
| Digital ethics | Privacy, information privacy, information privacy threat, right to be left alone, right to be forgotten, digital ethics, privacy enhancing technologies, breach disclosure, data breach notification, privacy act, data breach reporting laws |
| Digital risk management and digital governance | Risk management, digital risk management, governance, digital governance, governance operating model, governance structure, governance infrastructure, governance roles and responsibilities, risk exposure, risk event, biased data, algorithmic bias, attack surface, misinformation, imitation technologies, natural language generation, culture risk, digital ethics risk |

# DISCUSSION QUESTIONS

1 What is the difference between cybersecurity, IT security, and ICT security?
2 What is the difference between cybersecurity management capability and cybersecurity capability?
3 What is more important to an organization: digital ethics capability or cybersecurity management capability?
4 What is the relationship between risk management and governance?
5 What is the difference between risk management and digital risk management?
6 What are the three most dangerous risk exposures for organizations at the moment?

7 If you were a hacker or cybercriminal, which risk surface or attack point would you be most likely to successfully attack and why?

8 What are three ways digital technologies are being leveraged to enhance digital risk management?

9 Which managerial role in digital risk management and governance is most important to an organization's risk management and governance effectiveness?

10 Which competency related to risk management and governance is likely to have the greatest positive impact on a leader's or manager's career?

11 Which of the capabilities discussed in this chapter is the most important to succeeding at digital transformation and digital business?

# NOTES

1 Cisco. (2020). What is information security (InfoSec)? Retrieved June 8, 2020, from Cisco website: www.cisco.com/c/en/us/products/security/what-is-information-security-infosec.html; Secureworks. (2017). Cybersecurity vs. Network security vs. Information security. Retrieved June 8, 2020, from Secureworks.com website: www.secureworks.com/blog/cybersecurity-vs-network-security-vs-information-security; Norton. (2020). Retrieved June 8, 2020, from Norton.com website: https://us.norton.com/internetsecurity-malware-what-is-cybersecurity-what-you-need-to-know.html

2 Schatz, D., Bashroush, R., & Wall, J. (2017). Towards a more representative definition of cyber security. *Journal of Digital Forensics, Security and Law,* 12(2), 53–74.

3 Cisco. (2020). What is information security (InfoSec)? Retrieved June 9, 2020, from Cisco website: www.cisco.com/c/en/us/products/security/what-is-information-security-infosec.html; Secureworks. (2017). Cybersecurity vs. Network security vs. Information security. Retrieved June 8, 2020, from Secureworks.com website: www.secureworks.com/blog/cybersecurity-vs-network-security-vs-information-security

4 Schatz, D., Bashroush, R., & Wall, J. (2017). Towards a more representative definition of cyber security. *Journal of Digital Forensics, Security and Law,* 12(2), 53–74.

5 Castelli, C., Gabriel, B., Yates, J., & Booth, P. (2017). Strengthening digital society against cyber shocks. *PricewaterhouseCoopers: PwC*. Retrieved June 8, 2020, from PwC website: www.pwc.com/us/en/services/consulting/cybersecurity/library/information-security-survey/strengthening-digital-society-against-cyber-shocks.html

6 Cimpanu, C. (2020, March 31). Marriott discloses new data breach impacting 5.2 million hotel guests. Retrieved June 8, 2020, from ZDNet website: www.zdnet.com/article/marriott-discloses-new-data-breach-impacting-5-2-million-hotel-guests/

7 Cimpanu, C. (2020, March 31). Marriott discloses new data breach impacting 5.2 million hotel guests. Retrieved June 8, 2020, from ZDNet website: www.zdnet.com/article/marriott-discloses-new-data-breach-impacting-5-2-million-hotel-guests/

8 Cimpanu, C. (2020, March 31). Marriott discloses new data breach impacting 5.2 million hotel guests. Retrieved June 8, 2020, from ZDNet website: www.zdnet.com/article/marriott-discloses-new-data-breach-impacting-5-2-million-hotel-guests/

9 Fruhlinger, J. (2020, February 12). Marriott data breach faq: how did it happen and what was the impact? Retrieved June 9, 2020, from CSO Online website: www.csoonline.com/article/3441220/marriott-data-breach-faq-how-did-it-happen-and-what-was-the-impact.html; Cimpanu, C. (2019, January 4). Marriott says less than 383 million guests impacted by breach, not 500 million. Retrieved June 9, 2020, from ZDNet website: www.zdnet.com/article/marriott-says-less-than-383-million-guests-impacted-by-breach-not-500-million/

10 Easton, S. (2019, May 20). Almost 1000 data breaches in a year, and citizens don't know who to trust with privacy. Retrieved June 8, 2020, from The Mandarin website: www.themandarin.com.au/108762-almost-1000-data-breaches-in-a-year-and-citizens-dont-know-who-to-trust-with-privacy/; Innes, K. (2019). One year of mandatory data breach reporting: insights and lessons. *Bradley Allen Love Lawyers*. Retrieved June 8, 2020, from Bradley Allen Love Lawyers website: https://ballawyers.com.au/2019/05/28/mandatory-data-breach-reporting/

11 Swinhoe, D. (2020, May 8). What is the cost of a data breach? Retrieved June 9, 2020, from CSO Online website: www.csoonline.com/article/3434601/what-is-the-cost-of-a-data-breach.html#tk.ciofsb

12 Müller, M. S., & Zwinggi, A. (2020, January 19). Global leaders must take responsibility for cybersecurity. Here's why. Retrieved June 19, 2020, from World Economic Forum website: www.weforum.org/agenda/2020/01/global-leaders-must-take-responsibility-for-cybersecurity-here-s-why-and-how/

13 Christopher, J. (2018, November 1). Council post: The cybersecurity maturity model: A means to measure and improve your cybersecurity program. *Forbes*. Retrieved from www.forbes.com/sites/forbestechcouncil/2018/11/01/the-cybersecurity-maturity-model-a-means-to-measure-and-improve-your-cybersecurity-program/#32e367a680bc

14 Christopher, J. (2018, November 1). Council post: The cybersecurity maturity model: A means to measure and improve your cybersecurity program. *Forbes*. Retrieved from www.forbes.com/sites/forbestechcouncil/2018/11/01/the-cybersecurity-maturity-model-a-means-to-measure-and-improve-your-cybersecurity-program/#32e367a680bc

15 Castelli, C., Gabriel, B., Yates, J., & Booth, P. (2017). Strengthening digital society against cyber shocks. *PricewaterhouseCoopers: PwC*. Retrieved June 8, 2020, from PwC website: www.pwc.com/us/en/services/consulting/cybersecurity/library/information-security-survey/strengthening-digital-society-against-cyber-shocks.html; Oltsik, J. (2019, February 19). Enterprises need to embrace top-down cybersecurity management. Retrieved June 9, 2020, from CSO Online website: www.csoonline.com/article/3342036/enterprises-need-to-embrace-top-down-cybersecurity-management.html; Dutta, A., & McCrohan, K. (2002). Management's role in information security in a cyber economy. *California Management Review*, 45(1), 67–87. https://doi.org/10.2307/41166154

16 Dutta, A., & McCrohan, K. (2002). Management's role in information security in a cyber economy. *California Management Review*, 45(1), 67–87. https://doi.org/10.2307/41166154

17 Iso.org. (2018). ISO 31000:2018 Risk management – Guidelines. Retrieved June 12, 2020, from Iso.org website: www.iso.org/obp/ui/#iso:std:iso:31000:ed-2:v1:en

18 Siems, M., & Alvarez-Macotela, O. S. (2017). The G20/OECD principles of corporate governance 2015: A critical assessment of their operation and impact. *Journal of Business Law*, 4, 310–328; Japan Exchange Group. (2009). Principles of corporate governance for listed companies. Retrieved from www.jpx.co.jp/english/equities/listing/cg/tvdivq0000008j6d-att/principles_200912.pdf; Governance Institute of Australia. (2020). What is governance?

Governanceinstitute.com.au. Retrieved from www.governanceinstitute.com. au/resources/what-is-governance/

19  Iso.org. (2018). ISO 31000:2018 Risk management – Guidelines. Retrieved June 12, 2020, from Iso.org website: www.iso.org/obp/ ui/#iso:std:iso:31000:ed-2:v1:en

20  Marsh, J., Bhachawat, K., Maheshwari, S., & Nagpal, A. (2019). Future of risk in the digital era. *Deloitte*. Retrieved June 12, 2020, from Deloitte Online website: www2.deloitte.com/content/dam/Deloitte/fi/Documents/risk/future-of-risk-in-the-digital-era.pdf

21  Marsh, J., Bhachawat, K., Maheshwari, S., & Nagpal, A. (2019). Future of risk in the digital era. *Deloitte*. Retrieved June 12, 2020, from Deloitte Online website: www2.deloitte.com/content/dam/Deloitte/fi/Documents/risk/future-of-risk-in-the-digital-era.pdf

22  Marsh, J., Bhachawat, K., Maheshwari, S., & Nagpal, A. (2019). Future of risk in the digital era. *Deloitte*. Retrieved June 12, 2020, from Deloitte Online website: www2.deloitte.com/content/dam/Deloitte/fi/Documents/risk/future-of-risk-in-the-digital-era.pdf

23  Marsh, J., Bhachawat, K., Maheshwari, S., & Nagpal, A. (2019). Future of risk in the digital era. *Deloitte*. Retrieved June 12, 2020, from Deloitte Online website: www2.deloitte.com/content/dam/Deloitte/fi/Documents/risk/future-of-risk-in-the-digital-era.pdf

# Workforce Digital Competence, Digital Culture, and Digital Ethics Capabilities

DOI: 10.4324/9781003254614-19

# INTRODUCTION

This primer puts a spotlight on three organization capabilities that shape workforce capacity, and therefore shape whether employees catalyze or hinder digital transformation and digital business strategy making. Workforce digital competence refers to the organization routines/activities, structures, and/or processes that that work together to dynamically shape the nature and pervasiveness of digital technology competencies across the workforce. Digital culture refers to the extent to which an organization's culture reflects the cultural characteristics commonly associated with the effective execution of digital transformation strategy and digital business strategy. And digital ethics refers to a workforce's ability to exercise ethical responsibility in all perceived or actual uses of digital technologies and their outputs or associations with particular uses of them. The primer discusses how these capabilities impact digital transformation and digital business strategy; their implications for the roles of leaders, managers, and supporting professionals; and the competencies leaders, managers, and supporting professionals require to play their roles in the building and optimization of these capabilities.

**LEARNING OBJECTIVES**

- Develop knowledge of definitions and concepts related to workforce digital competence, digital culture, and digital ethics capabilities
- Understand the meaning and role of these capabilities in the digital transformation strategy and digital business strategy of organizations
- Understand the roles leaders, managers, and supporting professionals can play in these digital capabilities
- Understand the competencies required by leaders, managers, and supporting professionals to maximize their roles in these digital capabilities

- Analyze and evaluate the implications of these capabilities, as well as related leadership or management roles and competencies, for organizations' digital transformation strategy and digital business strategy
- Apply knowledge and understanding to participate in, support, or lead workstreams or initiatives related to the building and optimization of these capabilities

# WORKFORCE DIGITAL COMPETENCE

Workforce digital competence (also interchangeably referred to as workforce digital competencies, workforce digital maturity, or workforce digital literacy) refers to the nature and pervasiveness of digital technology skills possessed by an organization's workforce relative to those it requires. These competencies can vary from organization to organization depending on the desired versus actual digital maturity of the organization, the desired versus actual nature of its product/ service offerings, its desired versus actual business models, and its desire versus actual strategic and operational processes. Assuming all else is the same for two organizations, a workforce with broader, deeper, and more pervasive digital technology competencies is likely to be much better at making and executing digital transformation and digital business strategy. However, it is rare for all else to be the same for two organizations. And strengths in particular technologies are likely to make a much bigger difference to the digital business competitiveness of some organizations while having minimal impact on the competitiveness of other organizations. For example, the digital technology competencies that are required and are most valuable to a software-as-a-service business are likely to be quite different to those of food processing business. Further, most organizations rarely have the luxury of having unlimited breadth, depth, and pervasiveness of digital technology competencies. Thus, organizations need to be strategic about what tradeoffs they make in the breadth, depth, and pervasiveness of workforce digital technology competencies they build. As a capability, workforce digital competence refers to the organization routines/activities, structures, and/or processes that that work together to enable an organization to repeatedly and reliably effect the optimal competence across digital technologies and their use (e.g., optimal breadth, optimal depth, optimal pervasiveness of workforce digital technology competencies).

## IMPLICATIONS FOR LEADERS, MANAGERS, AND SUPPORTING PROFESSIONALS

Leaders, managers, and supporting professionals can play significant roles in their organization's workforce digital competency. For example, they can identify the most critical digital technology competencies required by their workforce; they can encourage employees to be curious about strategically relevant and/or new digital technologies; and they can incentivize employees to learn relevant and/or new digital technology related competencies. Further, they can encourage employees to apply digital technology competencies and help develop those of others; they can incorporate development of relevant digital technology competencies in employee appraisals and development plans; and they can invest in workforce digital technology competency development resources. To maximize the roles they can play, leaders, managers, and supporting professionals need a working understanding of different digital technologies, their value propositions, and their use cases. They also need to have a working understanding of optimal ways to cultivate different types of digital technology competencies. Armed with such knowledge and understanding, they can optimally encourage, direct, and invest in employee competency development efforts.

# DIGITAL CULTURE

Digital culture, also referred to as digital organization culture or digital ready culture, refers to the extent to which an organization's culture reflects the cultural characteristics commonly associated with the effective execution of digital transformation strategy and digital business strategy.[1] Put another way, digital culture refers to the extent to which an organization's shared assumptions, attitudes, understandings, or ways of working align with those cultural characteristics identified as being critical to the effective execution of digital transformation and digital business strategy.[2] Highly digital cultures have been described as cultures having the following characteristics: highly collaborative, agile and responsive, flexible and adaptable, curious/exploratory/experimental, open/transparent, risk taking, innovative, continuously learning, and customer value centered or even obsessed.[3] The high collaboration characteristic enables employees to work in interconnected cross functional teams and to freely share knowledge and best practices to solve problems and optimize customer value. The agile and responsive characteristic enables employees to work faster, learn quickly, minimize risks, and continuously adapt to changes in strategy, processes, structure, technology, and customer needs. As a result, they are able to be more responsive to customer and/or stakeholder needs and more adaptive to external and internal changes – so as to maximize customer and/or stakeholder value. Agile and responsive cultures often embrace and institutionalize Agile and Lean startup principles, values, and ways of working to effect the agile and responsive cultural characteristic. The flexible and adaptable characteristic enables employees to rapidly and effectively respond to internal and external disruptions the organization may face. For example, cultures with this characteristic were likely better positioned to rapidly reconfigure ways of working and ways of serving customers during the COVID-19 pandemic, which required organizations to rapidly find ways to work remotely and serve customers remotely. The curious/exploratory/experimental characteristic optimally positions employees to be curious about new digital technologies and their uses and to explore and experiment with them as means of optimizing efficiency or offering enhanced customer value. The open and transparent characteristic enables employees to feel safe in candidly sharing problems and failures. Similarly, employees can trust that leaders are being open and transparent with them. The risk taking and innovative characteristic enables employees to attempt to solve difficult problems and introduce innovative new digital solutions, knowing that if they fail, they will not be punished. The continuous learning characteristic enables employees to keep up with changes in digital technologies, the applications of those technologies, and the resultant changes in customer needs and behaviors. Finally, the customer value centered or even obsessed characteristic helps organizations to have improved customer value as an overriding motivation and target output in everything they do. There are ample guides now on how to build digital culture. For example, MIT researchers George Westerman and Deborah Soule, in conjunction with Anand Eswaran, Microsoft corporate vice president of enterprise, provide one guide.[4] Researchers and consultants Daniel Rowles and Thomas Brown provide another with their book on digital culture.[5] And Booz & Company provides yet another via its research report undertaken by Booz & Company in 2013.[6]

## IMPLICATIONS FOR LEADERS, MANAGERS, AND SUPPORTING PROFESSIONALS

Managers and leaders can play a range of roles to cultivate the shared assumptions, attitudes, understandings, and ways of working that make for an effective digital culture. For example, they can encourage employees to continuously and rapidly experiment with the use of new digital technologies; they can encourage employees to fail fast and share learnings; and they can find ways to make it easier and faster for employees to adjust their experiments and initiatives to fit within organization guidelines. Further, managers and leaders can provide their employees with the autonomy to create their own cross functional and inter-organization teams; they can configure ways for employees to move with speed without contravening organization policies; they can model and encourage transparency and information sharing; and they can actively disincentivize people who use policies and procedures to stifle necessary actions and experiments. To play necessary roles in cultivating and optimizing digital culture capability, leaders, managers, and supporting professionals need to have working knowledge of digital culture – for example, its aims, key practices, levers, and different roles and activities managers and leaders can play in it.

# DIGITAL ETHICS

Digital ethics considers the ethicality of the existing and potential impacts of digital technologies on political, social, economic, environmental, and legal dynamics and entities. For example, it considers and builds discussion of issues such as ethics of surveillance; when and what information can be given to the state; digital monopolies (growing concentration of power in large technology companies); uses of, and regulation of, artificial intelligence; automation and robotics-driven unemployment; disparities between tech-savvy and non-tech-savvy people; transparency in how data is held/where it is held/who has access to it; discrimination embedded in algorithms and big data; environmental impacts of digital technology related waste; and more. Organizations not conscious of, or not reflecting, these broader digital ethics issues in their policies and conduct can quickly find themselves on the wrong side of an issue. For example, Cambridge Analytica,[7] Facebook,[8] Google,[9] Twitter,[10] and Amazon[11] have recently found themselves in the crossfire in relation to one or more of these ethics issues. Thus, when choosing which digital technologies to leverage and how to leverage them, in addition to security and privacy implications, organizations need to consider the broader digital ethics implications relating to use of those digital technologies.

Consumers, governments, and advocacy groups are increasingly conscious of, and concerned with, information privacy and other digital ethics practices of organizations. Besides the resultant ethical threats these practices can create, for some consumers the practices are also about respect – and they feel disrespected by organizations that disregard or don't take seriously their privacy and digital ethics concerns. Thus, through their particular action or nonaction, organizations can alleviate threat/disrespect concerns and enhance the trust customers have in them, or they can heighten concerns and erode this trust. Their action or nonaction, then, can have significant consequences for their brand image, profitability, and longevity.

## INFORMATION PRIVACY

Information privacy is a critical subset issue of digital ethics. It refers to an individual's interest and/or ability to control, or at least significantly influence, the handling of data about themselves.[12] Information privacy includes personal communication privacy, personal behavior privacy, and personal data privacy.[13] The handling of data refers to issues including what data is collected and how, the primary use (the purpose for which the data is originally collected), the secondary use (purposes other than the primary purpose), any unauthorized secondary use, what analysis is done on the data, what improper access is it exposed to, what errors are in it, and how long will the data be kept for (e.g., does this impinge on a person's "right to be forgotten").

Although the concept of privacy existed before the advent of digital technologies,[14] the use of digital technologies results in significant privacy threats. For example, consider the expanded access to information (e.g., using big data, data analytics, search engines, social networks, triangulation algorithms), ubiquity (digital technologies with us when we sleep, when we wake up, while we are working, while we are socializing, etc.), undetectability (cookies, location-based services, real-time video analytics, miniaturized devices, etc.), and invasiveness (e.g., implantable chips) of digital technologies. Also consider the permanency of the data they capture, the near real-time external accessibility to this data, and the ease with which it can be sold and used anywhere around the world. Unfortunately, although consumers desire privacy, they are often in a situation where they can't receive certain services without sharing personal information. Outside of leveraging privacy enhancing technologies in the purchasing process and avoiding consumption, consumers place their trust in particular brands and/or in regulators.

## IMPLICATIONS FOR LEADERS, MANAGERS, AND SUPPORTING PROFESSIONALS

As with other digital capabilities, leaders, managers, and supporting professionals can play a critical role in their organizations' digital ethics capabilities. For example, they can embed a culture of privacy that enables information privacy compliance (e.g., by ensuring staff understand their privacy responsibilities, assigning roles and responsibilities for information privacy and digital ethics management, instituting reporting processes to keep top management informed about evolving ethics issues and practices), and they can put in place effective information privacy and digital ethics practices/procedures/ systems (e.g., having an information privacy and digital ethics policy, establishing processes for receiving and responding to information privacy and digital ethics issues or complaints, integrating information privacy and digital ethics into induction and training processes). They can also evaluate and continuously improve information privacy and digital ethics practices (e.g., regularly review policies/processes/ events, monitor performance to plan, establish processes for staff and other stakeholders to provide feedback, establish processes for staying up to date with evolving expectations/best practices in relation to information privacy and digital ethics).[15] In addition to playing the aforementioned roles, leaders, managers, and supporting professionals at all levels can set the tone[16] for information privacy and digital ethics through what they say, how they behave, how they handle information privacy and digital ethics situations,[17] who they reward, and who they promote. To effectively play these different roles, leaders, managers, and supporting professionals need a working understanding of information privacy and digital ethics issues and best practices. They also need to ensure they keep up with rapid evolutions in these issues and best practices.

# GOOGLE AND REFLECT

| Digital capability | Common terminology |
|---|---|
| Workforce digital competence | Digital literacy, digital skills, workforce digital maturity, digital workplace, digital ready workforce, digital workforce, digital talent, digital IQ, digital workforce strategy |
| Digital ethics | Privacy, information privacy, information privacy threat, right to be left alone, right to be forgotten, digital ethics, privacy enhancing technologies, breach disclosure, data breach notification, Privacy Act, data breach reporting laws |
| Digital culture | Privacy, information privacy, information privacy threat, right to be left alone, right to be forgotten, digital ethics, privacy enhancing technologies, breach disclosure, data breach notification, privacy act, data breach reporting laws |

# DISCUSSION QUESTIONS

1  Why is workforce digital competence critical to digital transformation?
2  What competencies does a leader or manager require to cultivate workforce digital competencies?
3  What is the difference between privacy and information privacy?
4  What is the relationship between information privacy and digital ethics?
5  What is the relationship between cybersecurity, information privacy, and digital ethics?
6  What are the top three digital ethics issues at the moment?
7  Which is most important: cybersecurity, information privacy, or digital ethics?
8  What managerial role in information privacy and digital ethics is most important to an organization's information privacy and digital ethics capability?
9  How is digital culture different from traditional organization culture?

10 What are the implications of digital culture for existing organization culture?

11 Which of the capabilities discussed in this chapter is the most important to succeeding at digital transformation and digital business?

# NOTES

1 Bughin, Jacques. (2017). *Digital success requires a digital culture*. Mckinsey & Company; E. Martínez-Caro, J. G. Cegarra-Navarro, F., & Alfonso-Ruiz, J. (2020). Digital technologies and firm performance: The role of digital organisational culture. *Technological Forecasting and Social Change*, 154, Article 119962.

2 Bughin, J. (2017). *Digital success requires a digital culture*. Mckinsey & Company; E. Martínez-Caro, J. G. Cegarra-Navarro, F., & Alfonso-Ruiz, J. (2020). Digital technologies and firm performance: The role of digital organisational culture. *Technological Forecasting and Social Change*, 154, Article 119962.

3 Cortellazzo, L., Bruni, E., & Zampieri, R. (2019). The role of leadership in a digitalized world: A review. *Frontiers in Psychology*, 10, 1938.

4 Westerman, G., Soule, D. L., & Eswaran, A. (2019). Building digital-ready culture in traditional organizations. *MIT Sloan Management Review*, 60(4), 59–68.

5 Rowles, D., & Brown, T. (2017). *Building digital culture: A practical guide to successful digital transformation*. Kogan Page Publishers.

6 Harshak, A., Schmaus, B., & Dimitrova, D. (2013). Building a digital culture: How to meet the challenge of multichannel digitization. *Booz & Company, Strategy &, Pwc*, 1, 1–15.

7 Facebook and Cambridge Analytica: What You Need to Know as Fallout Widens. (2018, March 19). *The New York Times*. Retrieved from www. nytimes.com/2018/03/19/technology/facebook-cambridge-analytica-explained.html; Wong, J. C. (2019). The Cambridge analytica scandal changed the world – But it didn't change Facebook. Retrieved June 10, 2020, from the Guardian website: www.theguardian.com/technology/2019/mar/17/the-cambridge-analytica-scandal-changed-the-world-but-it-didnt-change-facebook

8 Foroohar, R. (2020). EU and US regulators scrutinise big tech and digital "monopoly." Retrieved June 10, 2020, from FinancialTimes website: www.ft.com/content/f7b13372-3797-11ea-a6d3-9a26f8c3cba4

9 Novet, J. (2019). Google cancels A.I. ethics panel after uproar. Retrieved June 10, 2020, from CNBC website: www.cnbc.com/2019/04/04/google-cancels-controversial-ai-ethics-panel.html

10 Scott, M. (2020). Twitter labels Trump Tweet as "glorifying violence." Retrieved June 10, 2020, from POLITICO website: www.politico.com/news/2020/05/29/twitter-labels-trump-tweet-as-glorifying-violence-288356

11 Biswas, S. (2020). Why India is greeting Amazon's Jeff Bezos with protests. *BBC News*. Retrieved from www.bbc.com/news/world-asia-india-51117315

12 Bélanger, F., & Crossler, R. E. (2011). Privacy in the digital age: A review of information privacy research in information systems. *MIS Quarterly*, 35(4), 1017–1042.

13 Bélanger, F., & Crossler, R. E. (2011). Privacy in the digital age: A review of information privacy research in information systems. *MIS Quarterly*, 35(4), 1017–1042.

14 Bélanger, F., & Crossler, R. E. (2011). Privacy in the digital age: A review of information privacy research in information systems. *MIS Quarterly*, 35(4), 1017–1042; Igo, S. E. (2018). *The known citizen: A history of privacy in modern America*. Harvard University Press; Holvast, J. (2007). History of privacy. In *The history of information security* (pp. 737–769). Elsevier Science BV.

15 Office of the Australian Information Commissioner. (2016). Privacy management plan template (for Organizations). Retrieved June 10, 2020, from OAIC website: www.oaic.gov.au/privacy/guidance-and-advice/privacy-management-plan-template-for-organizations/

16 Southeastern Oklahoma State University. (2016). Why ethics are still essential in management. Retrieved June 9, 2020, from Southeastern Oklahoma State University website: https://online.se.edu/articles/mba/why-ethics-are-still-essential-in-management.aspx

17 Southeastern Oklahoma State University. (2016). Why ethics are still essential in management. Retrieved June 9, 2020, from Southeastern Oklahoma State University website: https://online.se.edu/articles/mba/why-ethics-are-still-essential-in-management.aspx

# CHAPTER 16

# Digital Leadership and Accelerated Change/ Transformation Capabilities

DOI: 10.4324/9781003254614-20

# INTRODUCTION

Digital disruption, digital transformation, and digital business demand rapid shifts in an organization's culture and its execution speed. Effectively bringing about the required cultural shifts and execution speed requires change and transformation approaches designed for speed. It also requires new or adapted leadership roles and competencies that are conceptualized as "digital leadership" and juxtaposed against traditional leadership. This primer puts a spotlight on digital leadership and accelerated change and transformation capabilities, which are critical for safely and effectively executing at the speed demanded by digital technology advancements and digital business competition. The primer discusses what these digital capabilities mean, their role in digital transformation and digital business change efforts, and the roles leaders, managers, and supporting professionals can play in the building and optimization of these capabilities.

---

**LEARNING OBJECTIVES**

- Develop knowledge of definitions and concepts related to digital leadership and accelerated change and transformation capabilities
- Understand the meaning and role of these capabilities in the digital transformation strategy and digital business strategy of organizations
- Understand the roles leaders, managers, and supporting professionals can play in these digital capabilities
- Understand the competencies required by leaders, managers, and supporting professionals to maximize their roles in these digital capabilities
- Analyze and evaluate the implications of these capabilities, as well as related leadership or management roles and competencies, for organizations' digital transformation strategy and digital business strategy
- Apply knowledge and understanding to participate in, support, or lead workstreams or initiatives related to the building and optimization of these capabilities

---

# DIGITAL LEADERSHIP
## DIGITAL LEADERSHIP VS TRADITIONAL LEADERSHIP

Digital disruption, digital transformation, and digital business present unique leadership challenges (e.g., the need for fast decision making and execution; the need to make rapid shifts in organization culture; the need to transform the workforce into a flexible and distributed workplace; the need for significant efficiency breakthroughs; the need to manage virtual workforces). These unique challenges require new leadership roles and/or adaptations of traditional leadership roles and activities. The augmentation of traditional leadership roles and activities with new or adapted roles and activities is what is referred to as digital leadership (also referred to as e-leadership in academic research). Thus, digital leadership refers to the new or adapted roles/activities required of leaders to effectively lead digital transformation and digital business. And it refers to the augmentation of traditional leadership roles/activities with these new or adapted roles and activities. It also refers to the effect of carrying out these roles and activities to lead in a digital environment (e.g., Figure 16.1 identifies how a highly digital environment differs from a traditional or less digital one). Digital leadership can be considered from an individual leader level (e.g., the capacity of a leader to lead digital transformation and digital business) or from an organization capability perspective (the collective ability of an organization's leaders, at all levels, to lead digital transformation and digital business). Organization digital leadership capability, then, refers to the presence and collective effectiveness of digital leaders in every part of the organization. Or, to put another way, it is the effectiveness of the configuration of an organization's digital leaders at all levels of the organization and across all parts of the value chain.

## THE NEW OR ADAPTED LEADERSHIP ROLES OF DIGITAL LEADERSHIP

Several researchers and practitioners have discussed what new or adapted digital leadership roles/activities are required. Typically, these discussions focus on nine roles/activity groups. First, digital leaders have to set a digital

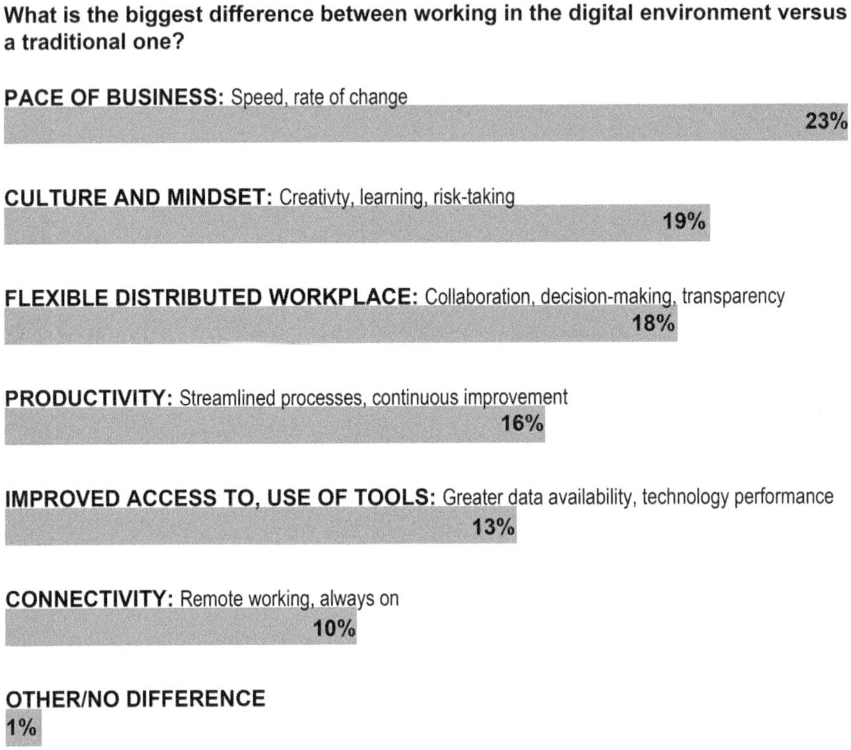

**What is the biggest difference between working in the digital environment versus a traditional one?**

**PACE OF BUSINESS:** Speed, rate of change

**23%**

**CULTURE AND MINDSET:** Creativty, learning, risk-taking

**19%**

**FLEXIBLE DISTRIBUTED WORKPLACE:** Collaboration, decision-making, transparency

**18%**

**PRODUCTIVITY:** Streamlined processes, continuous improvement

**16%**

**IMPROVED ACCESS TO, USE OF TOOLS:** Greater data availability, technology performance

**13%**

**CONNECTIVITY:** Remote working, always on

**10%**

**OTHER/NO DIFFERENCE**
**1%**

*Figure 16.1* *Results of a survey of 3,300* MIT Sloan Management Review *readers, "Deloitte Dbriefs" webcast subscribers, and other interested parties regarding what is different about working in a digital business environment*

transformation/digital business vision and direction. This is a critical and unique role in that it requires leaders to understand how digital technology advancements, digital disruption, and digital transformation may play out at the consumer, organization, industry, geographic, and societal levels[1] before they can set the digital transformation/digital business vision and direction. The role can be viewed as an augmentation of the traditional leadership role of vision/direction setting[2] with deep digital technology, digital disruption, digital transformation, and digital business strategy knowledge/skills. For example, it is symbolically represented by the visionary digital leadership capabilities of leaders like Bill Gates (Microsoft), the late Steve Jobs (Apple), Reed Hastings (Netflix), and the late Andy Grove (Intel). Digital transformation/digital business vision/ direction setting, and digital technology competency are viewed as being

**What is the most important skill organizational leaders should have to succeed in a digital workplace? (Only one skill accepted per response)**

**TRANSFORMATIVE VISION:** Knowledge of market and trends, business acumen, problem solver

**23%**

**FORWARD-LOOKING:** Clear vision, sound strategy, foresight

**20%**

**UNDERSTANDS TECHNOLOGY:** Prior experience, digital literacy

**18%**

**CHANGE ORIENTED:** Open-minded, adaptable, innovative

**18%**

**STRONG LEADERSHIP:** Pragmatic, focused, decisive

**11%**

**OTHER:** For example, collaborative, team builder

**11%**

*Figure 16.2* Results of a survey of 3,300 MIT Sloan Management Review readers, "Deloitte Dbriefs" webcast subscribers, and other interested parties regarding the most important skill leaders need to succeed in a digital workplace

among the top three leadership skills critical to success in digital workplaces (see Figure 16.2). Second, digital leaders have to be strong change agents and digital enablers who are able to push their organizations to seize the opportunities offered by digital technologies and digital disruption. These are typically fleeting opportunities with tight and closing time windows. Thus, they require organizations to change their capabilities quickly and then execute fast in order to seize them. For example, Netflix was able to change itself quickly to seize the opportunities offered by the internet and then by cloud computing, whereas the opportunity window closed on Blockbuster. Digital leaders play a critical role in effectively driving the necessary rapid capability change and subsequent execution. Third, digital transformation and digital business require leaders to use a more inclusive leadership style that involves employees in day-to-day decision processes (often in real time) and takes into account their ideas and concerns in strategic issues.[3] Fourth, digital leaders need to effectively lead virtual teams and facilitate virtual teamwork. For example, this can involve leveraging the right digital technology tools to facilitate communication, workflows, and resource sharing. It can also involve effectively supporting employees with virtual work issues. Owing to virtual, remote, and autonomous work, employees can be prone to peer alienation, weak social bonds, and challenges dealing with typically greater autonomy and increased job demands. So digital leaders need to unearth these issues and support employees with them.

The fifth discussed role is that digital leaders need to proactively build an enabling digital culture (e.g., digital cultures have been described as being agile and responsive, flexible and adaptive, curious/exploratory/ experimental, continuously learning, connected/networked, open, and highly collaborative).[4] Sixth, digital leaders need to build relationships with stakeholders across partner and competitor networks and ecosystems.[5] Both the way they do this and the extent to which they do it differ from networking and relationship roles/activities associated with traditional leadership. Seventh, digital leadership plays important roles in enabling and maximizing digital innovation effectiveness. In Chapter 11, the importance of digital innovation for effectively competing as a digital business was discussed. To drive digital innovation, digital leadership plays important roles such as creating or shaping virtual networks among internal and external communities of practice, breaking down silos, democratizing access to information, enabling the free flow of ideas, and thus enabling these communities to rapidly respond to change, solve business problems, and introduce new products/solutions.[6] Eighth, digital leaders determine how sourcing, assessment, and/or approval of the digital technologies, platforms, and tools used in the organization occurs. The choice of technologies, platforms, and tools can significantly impact the efficiency and effectiveness of internal processes (e.g., planning and monitoring, decision making, customer engagement, collaboration) and of organization adaptability and agility. For example, the use of sophisticated data tools has enabled hospitals to have real-time visibility of hospital capacity, patient flow, and patient conditions, thus dramatically improving the ability of healthcare leaders, managers, and supporting professionals to drive the efficiency and effectiveness of internal processes.[7] Ninth, digital leaders need to play an important role in building and continuously upgrading the effectiveness of their organizations' digital ethics practices. This requires a clear understanding of cybersecurity, information privacy, and other digital ethics issues to be able to identify and mitigate digital ethics risks.

## IMPLICATIONS FOR LEADERS, MANAGERS, AND SUPPORTING PROFESSIONALS

Researchers and practitioners have identified a range of digital leadership competencies including adaptability/flexibility (e.g., being able to effectively respond to new/surprising work demands and events), mastery of a variety of virtual communication platforms (e.g., understanding which platforms offer optimal or the best tradeoffs in richness, synchronicity, speed of feedback, ease of understanding by nonexperts, and reprocessing capability benefits), practices (e.g., how to set the right tone in virtual communication, how to communicate in a clear/organized/miscommunication free manner), and leadership/management of disruptive change (e.g., being able to guide teams to effectively respond to new/surprise consumer expectations and behaviors, competitors, technological obsolescence). Additional digital leadership competencies identified include management of connectivity (e.g., intra-organizational, inter-organizational, and extra-organizational connectivity), leadership/facilitation of virtual teams (e.g., managing the forming, storming, norming, performing stages of virtual teams), and possession of sufficiently deep technical knowledge of relevant digital technologies (e.g., IoT, blockchain, edge computing, robotics, cloud).

# ACCELERATED CHANGE AND TRANSFORMATION

One of the biggest challenges organizations face in their digital transformation and digital business efforts is the scale and speed with which the change and transformation are occurring externally

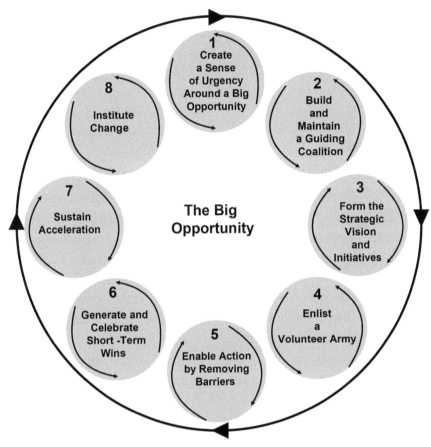

**Figure 16.3** *Having working knowledge of accelerated change and transformation methodologies like the Change Acceleration Process can be an invaluable tool in digital leaders' rapid change and transformation arsenal*

and need to occur internally. This scale and speed are incompatible with change and transformation approaches that were not designed for environments characterized by high dynamism, uncertainty, technological obsolescence, and disruption. Fortunately, organizations that have long existed in such environments, typically high technology firms, use a range of methodologies to effect rapid transformation and execution, enabling them to adapt and thrive in such environments. These methodologies are collectively referred to as accelerated change and transformation methodologies. Examples of these accelerated change and transformation methodologies include Agile innovation,[8] Lean thinking,[9] Lean startup,[10] change acceleration,[11] strategy as Simple Rules, design thinking,[12] seed accelerators/corporate accelerators,[13] blitz-scaling,[14] and hackathon methods or approaches.[15] To effectively leverage one or more of these methods or approaches (e.g., to use it to facilitate digital transformation initiatives or drive digital innovation, to encourage particular teams to use it, or to play an effective role in catalyzing its effectiveness), leaders, managers, and supporting professionals need to have a working understanding of how these different methodologies work, their key roles and responsibilities in each methodology, and the strengths and limitations of each methodology. Armed with such understanding (i.e., both knowledge and experience), they can leverage the right weapon for the right job in digital transformation efforts. Figure 16.3 provides an example of the key management roles/activities that are part of the Change Acceleration Process (an accelerated change and transformation method mentioned earlier).

# GOOGLE AND REFLECT

| Digital capability | Common terminology |
| --- | --- |
| Digital leadership | Leadership, digital leadership, e-leadership, digital leadership capability, digital leader, digital transformation vision, digital business vision, change agent, digital change agent, digital enabler, inclusive leadership, virtual team, virtual communication style, digital innovation |
| Accelerated change and transformation | Uncertainty, complexity, complicatedness, high velocity environment, fleeting opportunity, change management, organization transformation, Agile innovation, Lean thinking, Lean startup, change acceleration, design thinking, seed accelerator, corporate accelerator, blitz-scaling, hackathon |

# DISCUSSION QUESTIONS

1 What is the difference between traditional leadership, e-leadership, and digital leadership?

2 What is the difference between change and transformation? How does accelerated change and accelerated transformation differ?

3 What are the three most dangerous risk exposures for organizations at the moment?

4 What are Lean startup and Agile innovation approaches to strategy execution? What are their advantages for executing digital transformation and digital business strategy?

5 How are accelerators different from hackathons? Which is more useful to executing digital business strategy?

6 What are the Change Acceleration Process and Simple Rules processes and how do they differ from traditional strategy execution processes?

7 What competency related to risk management and governance is likely to have the greatest positive impact on a leader's or manager's career?

8 Which of the capabilities discussed in this chapter is the most important to succeeding at digital transformation and digital business?

# NOTES

1 Kane, G. C. (2019, March 12). How digital leadership Is(n't) different. *MIT Sloan Management Review*. Retrieved from https://sloanreview.mit.edu/article/how-digital-leadership-isnt-different/

2 Cortellazzo, L., Bruni, E., & Zampieri, R. (2019). The role of leadership in a digitalized world: A review. *Frontiers in Psychology*, 10, 1938.

3 Cortellazzo, L., Bruni, E., & Zampieri, R. (2019). The role of leadership in a digitalized world: A review. *Frontiers in Psychology*, 10, 1938; Schwarzmüller, T., Brosi, P., Duman, D., & Welpe, I. M. (2018). How does the digital transformation affect organizations? Key themes of change in work design and leadership. *MREV Management Revue*, 29(2), 114–138.

4 Cortellazzo, L., Bruni, E., & Zampieri, R. (2019). The role of leadership in a digitalized world: A review. *Frontiers in Psychology*, 10, 1938.

5 Cortellazzo, L., Bruni, E., & Zampieri, R. (2019). The role of leadership in a digitalized world: A review. *Frontiers in Psychology*, 10, 1938.

6 Cortellazzo, L., Bruni, E., & Zampieri, R. (2019). The role of leadership in a digitalized world: A review. *Frontiers in Psychology*, 10, 1938.

7 Cortellazzo, L., Bruni, E., & Zampieri, R. (2019). The role of leadership in a digitalized world: A review. *Frontiers in Psychology*, 10, 1938.

8 Gothelf, J. (2014). Bring agile to the whole organization. *Harvard Business Review*, 92(11); Busulwa, R., Tice, M., & Gurd, B. (2018). *Strategy execution and complexity: Thriving in the era of disruption*. Routledge; Rigby, D. K., Sutherland, J., & Takeuchi, H. (2016). The secret history of agile innovation. *Harvard Business Review*, 4; Morris, L., Ma, M., & Wu, P. C. (2014). *Agile innovation: The revolutionary approach to accelerate success, inspire engagement, and ignite creativity*. John Wiley & Sons.

9 Collins, D. (2016). Lean strategy. *Harvard Business Review*, 94(3), 63–68; Busulwa, R., Tice, M., & Gurd, B. (2018). *Strategy execution and complexity: Thriving in the era of disruption*. Routledge.

10 Ries, E. (2011). *The lean startup: How today's entrepreneurs use continuous innovation to create radically successful businesses*. Crown Books; Busulwa, R., Tice, M., & Gurd, B. (2018). *Strategy execution and complexity: Thriving in the era of disruption*. Routledge.

11 Kotter, J. P. (2014). *Accelerate: Building strategic agility for a faster-moving world*. Harvard Business Review Press; Kotter, J. (2012). How the most innovative companies capitalize on today's rapid-fire strategic challenges-and still make their numbers. *Harvard Business Review*, 90(11), 43–58; Busulwa, R., Tice, M., & Gurd, B. (2018). *Strategy execution and complexity: Thriving in the era of disruption*. Routledge.

12 Liedtka, J. (2018). Why design thinking works. *Harvard Business Review*, 96(5), 72–79.

13 Busulwa, R., Birdthistle, N., & Dunn, S. (2020). *Startup accelerators: A field guide*. John Wiley & Sons; Say, M. (2016, February 23). Corporate accelerators: What's in it for the big companies? *Forbes*. Retrieved from www.forbes.com/sites/groupthink/2016/02/23/corporate-accelerators-whats-in-it-for-the-big-companies/#7445a2d45f62; Hathaway, I. (2016). What startup accelerators really do. *Harvard Business Review*, 7.

14 Sullivan, T. (2016). Blitzscaling. *Harvard Business Review*, 94(4), 15; Kuratko, D. F., Holt, H. L., & Neubert, E. (2020). Blitzscaling: The good, the bad, and the ugly. *Business Horizons*, 63(1), 109–119; Hoffman, R., & Yeh, C. (2018).

*Blitzscaling: The lightning-fast path to building massively valuable businesses.* Broadway Business.

15 Spaulding, E., & Caimi, G. (2016). Hackathons aren't just for coders. *Harvard Business Review*. Retrieved from https://hbr.org/2016/04/hackathons-arent-just-for-coders; Rosell, B., Kumar, S., & Shepherd, J. (2014). Unleashing innovation through internal hackathons. *2014 IEEE Innovations in Technology Conference*. https://doi.org/10.1109/innotek.2014.6877369

# Part V

# Understanding Digital Technologies

## Primers for Leaders and Managers

CHAPTER 17

# Data, Big Data, and Data Management Primer

DOI: 10.4324/9781003254614-22

# INTRODUCTION

Data literacy and proficiency of leaders/managers refer to their ability to understand and effect leveraging of the vast quantities of internal and external data to improve an organization's efficiency, effectiveness, and agility.[1] During the last 30 years, the data available to businesses have increased exponentially, thereby causing information overload. Technology innovation resulted in even more information becoming available in a greater variety of formats (emails, spreadsheets, social media, wikis, apps, etc.). This information is accessible through a greater variety of media and communication channels resulting in an increasingly complex and rich information environment.[2] Gartner expects that 80% of organizations have either rolled out internal data literacy initiatives to upskill their workforce, or they intend to do so in the coming year. Reaping major rewards from data has become a critical organization issue, with data now being argued to be an even more important resource than oil.[3] Used effectively, the large volumes of internal and external data being created every minute provide organizations with great opportunities for breakthroughs in how they organize, operate, manage talent, create value, and scale their reach.[4] Effectively capturing, storing, organizing, integrating, protecting, analyzing, and making the most of their data requires an organization-wide team effort.[5] There are limited benefits to managing data in silos or restricting its management to a few experts in a technical function within the organization.[6] Given this, nontechnical stakeholders in every part of the organization also need to be literate and proficient with data.

It follows, then, that leaders and managers who lead, supervise, or oversee these stakeholders particularly need to be literate and proficient with data to ensure that data literacy and proficiency requirements are reflected in hiring, performance management/development, and employment termination decisions. But leaders and managers tend to avoid getting dragged into data issues, perhaps due to the technical terminology, the complex methodologies, the sheer scale and messiness of the data sets involved, and the lack of sufficient technical grounding in data management foundations.[7] This makes it tempting to "leave it to the experts".[8] But that is a major mistake, as data issues are now quintessential business issues for leaders and managers at all levels of the organization.[9] It is leaders and managers who advocate, set the objectives, and allocate resources for data management efforts. It is leaders and managers who have the domain expertise critical to the development of data products to optimize the parts of the business they lead or manage.[10] It is leaders and managers who are the ultimate users or nonusers of data products and insights. And it is leaders and managers who most need to understand what opportunities particular data, data sets, and data products offer – how to best develop them, how to remove barriers to their adoption, and how to make the most of them.[11]

This primer provides an introduction to data, data management, and data issues from a leadership managerial perspective. It is intended to be a starting point to enable leaders and managers to understand the value of data, the key data/data management concepts and terminologies, some of common data management platforms and vendors, and the manager's role in data management.

---

### LEARNING OBJECTIVES

- Develop knowledge of definitions and concepts related to data, big data, and data management technologies
- Understand how these technologies and their related methods/techniques can impact the efficiency, differentiation, adaptability, and agility of an organization
- Understand the roles leaders and managers can play in maximizing the leveraging of these technologies and their related methods/techniques
- Analyze and evaluate the implications of these technologies and their related methods/techniques, as well as related leadership or management roles in their optimal use for organizations' digital transformation strategy and digital business strategy
- Apply knowledge and understanding of these technologies and their related methods/techniques to participate in, support, or lead workstreams or initiatives related to the leveraging of these technologies to enhance organization performance and longevity

---

# DATA
## DATA AS THE NEW OIL

As it relates to digital technologies, the term data refers to a collection of the smallest units of information that can be stored, processed, or transmitted by a computer (datum is the singular form of data). What constitutes data can range from numbers and letters to pictures, sounds, and videos. Although we only see the video, for example, within digital technologies data are represented as a series of binary digits or bits. (To be more specific, we should talk about data that "are", not data that "is", since data is the plural of datum;[12] but data used as a singular is more common in speaking about data. A mixture of both approaches is used throughout the book to balance technical accuracy and ease of comprehension.) Also, the term "information assets" can be used instead of data, as it encompasses data, information, and knowledge. The term data is used throughout this book to improve understandability, but in using it the book is referring to data, information, and knowledge. Each binary digit is either a one or zero, so that at the most basic level, all data are a bunch of ones and zeros referred to as binary data. This enables it to be stored, processed, and transmitted by computers. Data can be stored on a physical or virtual computer (e.g., virtual machine) and can be transmitted between computers via a network connection. It can also be stored on a physical storage device (e.g., USB, hard drive) and manually transferred onto another storage device or computer.

In the early days of computing, usable data was limited to the few internal information systems or software applications within an organization (e.g., accounting systems, HR systems, procurement systems) and limited external statistical data. But over time, there has been a proliferation in the number of devices and software applications collecting data. These include millions of devices with sensors, cameras, and audio recording and the digitization and facilitation of more and more business processes and workflows through software applications. In addition to this, many of these devices, processes, and workflows are connected to the internet and therefore able to interact with each other, with physical or virtual computers, and with people. This results in vast amounts of data being created, stored, and available to use every second. The opportunities for organizations that are able to effectively manage this data are almost unlimited. For example, organizations can format, integrate, organize, analyze, and leverage insights from this data as a source of vast revenues (e.g., Google and Facebook), as a source of operational and strategic intelligence, to drive product innovation, to enhance customer experience, to form and better manage strategic partnerships, to disrupt industry offerings, and much more. Given this proliferation in available data and vast power possible from effectively leveraging it, some experts have contended that "data is the new oil" (i.e., that data may be an even greater source of global power and prosperity than oil).[13] Unverified data refers to data that data managers are not sure is true or untrue. Trusting such data and making decisions based on it can be highly dangerous. For example, imagine having unverified data about customer preferences and investing in capabilities to satisfy those preferences, only to discover after the investment that they were completely wrong.

## TYPES OF DATA

Not all data are the same. Some data are readily usable and of great value. Other data are of little value or can't be used without undergoing extensive formatting, organizing, integration, analysis, and presentation. Leaders and managers may come across a range of terminologies relating to data types including structured data, unstructured data, machine data, open data, dark data, real-time data, spatiotemporal data, unverified data, and outdated data. Structured data are usually preformatted and highly organized, making analysis easy (e.g., credit card numbers, first names, or annual revenue figures). In contrast, unstructured data are not preformatted or organized, making collection, processing, and analysis challenging (e.g., audio files or Twitter conversations about a brand). Machine data are data created by machines such as airplanes, elevators, and traffic lights and by devices such as mobile phones and fitness-monitoring devices. This data can provide a real-time record of the behavior and activities of customers or other stakeholders (e.g., delays, difficulties, frustrations, hesitations, delights while using a service) and the performance or effectiveness of machines and devices such as servers, networks, heating systems, and mobile devices. Open data refers to data that is free for anyone to use, without the usual copyright, privacy, or other legal restrictions. For example, government and international agencies may make available some of the data they collect as open data. Organizations may then be able to combine this open data with other external and internal data to optimize operational and strategic decisions. Dark data are data that is collected, processed, and stored through the normal course of business but not actually used;[14] making use of such data may open up great new opportunities for an organization. Real-time data can be used immediately, as it is created. For example, real-time customer experience data may reveal when a customer is getting frustrated, enabling a manager to intervene and override routine procedures that may have resulted in loss of repeat business from that customer. Information based on outdated data can be equally bad, if not worse. For example, imagine tourism service operators basing destination package information on customer experience satisfaction data from the 1970s. People will most likely want different things out of their holiday package today than they did in the 1970s.

This is not an exhaustive list of data types. Rather, it touches on some of common ones to illustrate that when making decisions based on data, understanding the type of data that has been used is important. Similarly, understanding the nature of data and data issues is invaluable to managers when making decisions about whether to hire data specialists, who to hire in data roles, or whether to invest resources into data formatting, organizing, integration, analysis, and presentation projects. Figure 17.1 provides a visualization of some of the different types of data leaders and managers may be commonly faced with.

## DATA RISKS AND OTHER ISSUES

The growing value and power in data also brings with it great and ever-growing risks. Dark organizations, groups, and individuals obtaining both authorized and unauthorized access to organizations' data can

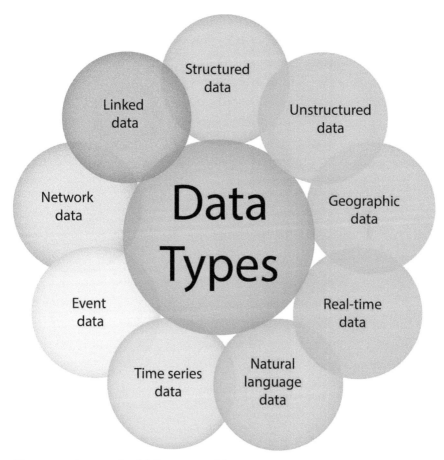

**Figure 17.1** *An example of different types of data*

use it for dark purposes ranging from using customers' data to stealing their identity and their property,[15] selling customer data to criminal organizations, using customer data to interfere in elections [16] and stir up social unrest,[17] using customer data to take customers hostage, and much more. Early on, data-related risks were largely limited to storage, risk of loss, and data recovery challenges. But now, with almost all data being transmitted or stored online, the most important data-related risks include data security, user privacy, ethical collection, and ethical use of data. These issues have grown in prominence, as the only barrier between an organization's data and reckless, dark, or criminal entities are the measures that employees at all levels take to safeguard their organization's data. In their leadership, policy setting, hiring, and performance management decisions, leaders and managers play a crucial role in determining employees' attitude to, actions with, and responsible use of data. Other data-related issues typically focus on how to make the most of the mounting data organizations are collecting and have access to in order to enhance strategy and operations. Such issues involve addressing questions such as how to format, organize, integrate, analyze, and present data to maximize the value derived from that data.

# BIG DATA

Big data is a term that refers to data sets that are so voluminous and complex and are being created so fast that traditional data processing software and approaches cannot handle them. This data can include text, video, images, sounds, sensor data, and more (Figure 17.2 provides some examples of sources of big data). Six characteristics or dimensions of big

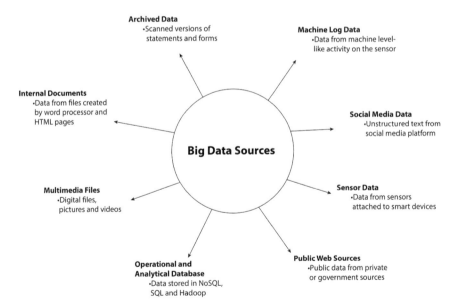

*Figure 17.2* *Examples of sources of big data*

data are often discussed: volume, velocity, variety, variability, veracity, and value. Volume simply refers to there being massive amounts of data to capture, organize, store, manage, and/or use. For example, there are more than 500 million tweets per day,[18] and it will be challenging for organizations to analyze a year's worth of Twitter data (e.g., in order to understand what is being said about their brand in tweets). Velocity refers to the fast rate at which data are received, processed, and need to be acted upon. For example, more than half a million comments and nearly 300,000 status updates are received, analyzed, and stored in Facebook's databases every minute. Acting on the analyzed data, Facebook can respond to inappropriate comments in near real time. Variety refers to the many types of data sets. For example, there is traditional structured data, such as numbers and characters in a database, and unstructured data, such as text documents, images, videos, sounds, and emails. Variability refers to data whose meaning is constantly changing and also changing rapidly. For example, in our earlier example of a brand analyzing tweets, the exact same tweets can have different meanings depending on the context (e.g., one tweet saying "Great, I love this brand!" may mean that person loves the brand, while another tweet saying "Great, I love this brand!" may be from someone being sarcastic who actually hates the brand). Veracity refers to the quality of the data. Not all the voluminous data sets that an organization has access to will be accurate. Also, those that are accurate are not likely to be in a format that can be used without significant effort to validate them, separate out what is useful and what is not, reformat them, integrate them with other data, and make them available in systems where they can be used for decision making. Some data sets are more reliable and easier to work with than others, making them of better quality. Finally, value is concerned with what benefits it is possible to derive from data sets (e.g., monetization, customer experience optimization, improved performance management).

In summary, the term big data relates to massive and rapidly expanding data sets from lots of different sources and in lots of different formats. The data are typically noisy, messy, and ever changing. The conversation about big data can be thought of as made up of two parts. One part is a conversation about the different voluminous data sets organizations can access, the quality of these data sets, and the potential value or riches that can be discovered in them. The other part is about approaches, practices, and methodologies to unlocking and leveraging that value (e.g., methodologies and practices for capturing, storing, analyzing, transferring, presenting, and updating big data).

# DATA MANAGEMENT

Given the value, power, and risks associated with data, it may not be surprising that a formal practice has evolved to ensure value derived from data is maximized while risks and costs are minimized. This practice is known as data management and is concerned with how to collect, validate, store, and use data most effectively.[19] Effective data management is a significant challenge for organizations given the avalanche of internal and external data to manage and the growing sources of such data. For example, data can come from SaaS applications, ERP systems, legacy systems, databases, data warehouses, and data lakes. The data may also come from the web, social media platforms, open data, and commercial data platforms. Alternatively, it may come from any number of devices including phones, computers, wearable devices, sensors, and monitoring devices. All this data must be collected safely, validated, stored safely, and formatted and presented so that different parts of the organization can access the right information at the right time and in the right format to make the best decisions. This requires that organizations have good technical leaders, capable technical specialists, the right technology platforms, and clear and enforced policies, procedures, and practices. The data management function typically plays a leadership role in issues such as data governance (who has what decision rights and accountability for data quality), data architecture (what rules, policies, standards, and models are in place to determine what data are collected, how it is stored, how it is integrated, and how it is used), data modeling and design (defining and analyzing data required to support business processes), database and storage management, and data security and privacy. By having a working understanding of data management practices, leaders and managers will be better positioned to hire the right leaders for the data management function, hire the right operational staff to collaborate with the data management function, support investment in the right data management technologies, encourage the development of the right competencies to enable effective data management, and not inadvertently undermine change efforts intended to deliver effective data management.

# GOOGLE AND REFLECT

| Technology concept | Common terminology |
| --- | --- |
| Data | Raw data, clean data, metadata, structured data, unstructured data, semi-structured data, data quality |
| Big data | Database, data mart, data warehouse, data lake, data catalog, enterprise data hub, data fabric, operational data store, SaaS application, ERP system, legacy system, deployment platform, edge computing, data governance, data architecture, open data |
| Data management | Online analytical processing (OLAP), data mining, process mining, complex event processing, business performance management, benchmarking, text mining, descriptive analytics, prescriptive analytics, business analytics, business analyst, data analyst |

# EXAMPLE TOOLS AND VENDORS

| Technology concept | Example tools and vendors |
| --- | --- |
| Data | GoSpotCheck, IBM Datacap, Mozenda, Octoparse, OnBase by Hyland, OpenRefine, Data Ladder, Cloudingo, IBM Infosphere Quality Stage |

| Technology concept | Example tools and vendors |
|---|---|
| Big data | Amazon Redshift, Ataccama ONE, Cloudera, EnterWorks, Google BigQuery, Hortonworks Data Platform, IBM Db2 Hybrid Data Management Hadoop, Quoble, HPCC, Cassandra, MongoDB, Apache Storm, Rapidminer, Talend, Teradata, Apache Spark, Apache SAMOA, DataCleaner, Oracle Big Data Cloud, Oracle Big Data Cloud Service, Oracle Big Data SQL Cloud Service, Oracle NoSQL Database, SAP master data management software, SAS Data Management |
| Data management | Microsoft (Power BI), Google (e.g., Google Data Studio), Tableau, Qlik, ThoughtSpot, Sisense, Salesforce (e.g., Einstein Analytics), TIBCO Software, SAS BI, SAP (e.g., SAP business intelligence, SAP NetWeaver BW, SAP Business Objects), Oracle (e.g., Oracle BI, Oracle Enterprise BI Server, Oracle Hyperion System), IBM (e.g., IBM Cognos Intelligence), Birst, Yellowfin BI, Domo, Locker, MicroStrategy, GoodData, BOARD International, Logi Analytics, Information Builders, Pyramid Analytics |

# DISCUSSION QUESTIONS

## DATA

1 Do you agree that data is the new oil? Provide three arguments for and three arguments against the view that data can be regarded as the new oil.

2 What is the most high-profile data breach to have occurred to an organization recently that compromised the security and privacy of customer data? What customer information was accessed, and how many customers were affected?

3 What personal data are you emitting each day (via social media, search engines, mobile devices, etc.)?

4 What are some practical strategies for protecting your privacy?

5 What can leaders and managers do to minimize the risks to their employers' data?

6   Imagine you are a senior leader or manager and you have the choice between two candidates to fill a vacant management position. One candidate has 5 years more experience, including time working for a well-respected competitor, but has zero data literacy. Another candidate has 5 years less experience and has not worked at an organization as respected as your top competitor, but this candidate is very data literate (e.g., did a Master of Data Science with their MBA degree and spent 3 years working in the data management team at a leading bank). Which candidate would you hire and why?

## BIG DATA

1   What is the difference between raw data, unstructured data, and structured data?
2   What is clean data, and what does the data cleansing process involve?
3   What is the difference between a database, a data warehouse, and a data lake?
4   If an organization has a data lake, can it do without a data warehouse?
5   What are five free open data sources that could be useful in your industry, and how could they be useful?
6   What are three open data use cases in your industry?
7   Briefly describe three ways you can use big data to improve your performance as a leader or manager.

## DATA MANAGEMENT

1   Why is data management a significant and growing challenge?
2   What roles can leaders and managers play in effective data management?

# NOTES

1   Brylad, M. (2019). Data literacy: A critical skill for the 21st century. *Tableau Software.* Retrieved December 17, 2019, from www.tableau.com/about/blog/2018/9/data-literacy-critical-skill-21st-century-94221

2  Mariani, M., Baggio, R., Fuchs, M., & Höepken, A. W. (2017). Business intelligence and big data in hospitality and tourism: A systematic literature review. *International Journal of Contemporary Hospitality Management*, 30(12), 3514–3554.

3  Vanian, J. (2016). Why data is the new oil. *Fortune*. Retrieved December 9, 2019, from https://fortune.com/2016/07/11/data-oil-brainstorm-tech/; Parkins, D. (2017). The world's most valuable resource is no longer oil, but data. *Economist*. Retrieved December 9, 2019, from www.economist.com/leaders/2017/05/06/the-worlds-most-valuable-resource-is-no-longer-oil-but-data

4  Mayhew, H., Saleh, T., & Williams, S. (2019). *Making data analytics work for you – instead of the other way around*. McKinsey & Company. Retrieved December 17, 2019, from www.mckinsey.com/business-functions/mckinsey-digital/our-insights/making-data-analytics-work-for-you-instead-of-the-other-way-around

5  Mayhew, H., Saleh, T., & Williams, S. (2019). *Making data analytics work for you – instead of the other way around*. McKinsey & Company. Retrieved December 17, 2019, from www.mckinsey.com/business-functions/mckinsey-digital/our-insights/making-data-analytics-work-for-you-instead-of-the-other-way-around

6  Mayhew, H., Saleh, T., & Williams, S. (2019). *Making data analytics work for you – instead of the other way around*. McKinsey & Company. Retrieved December 17, 2019, from www.mckinsey.com/business-functions/mckinsey-digital/our-insights/making-data-analytics-work-for-you-instead-of-the-other-way-around

7  Mayhew, H., Saleh, T., & Williams, S. (2019). *Making data analytics work for you – instead of the other way around*. McKinsey & Company. Retrieved December 17, 2019, from www.mckinsey.com/business-functions/mckinsey-digital/our-insights/making-data-analytics-work-for-you-instead-of-the-other-way-around

8  Mayhew, H., Saleh, T., & Williams, S. (2019). *Making data analytics work for you – instead of the other way around*. McKinsey & Company. Retrieved December 17, 2019, from www.mckinsey.com/business-functions/mckinsey-digital/our-insights/making-data-analytics-work-for-you-instead-of-the-other-way-around

9  Mayhew, H., Saleh, T., & Williams, S. (2019). *Making data analytics work for you – instead of the other way around*. McKinsey &

Company. Retrieved December 17, 2019, from www.mckinsey. com/business-functions/mckinsey-digital/our-insights/ making-data-analytics-work-for-you-instead-of-the-other-way-around

10 Oracle BrandVoice: How to Extract Business Value from Data Science: It's All About the Teamwork. (2019). Forbes.com. Retrieved December 17, 2019, from www.forbes.com/sites/oracle/2018/12/05/how-to-extract-business-value-from-data-science-its-all-about-the-teamwork/#4134870c651c

11 Oracle BrandVoice: How to Extract Business Value from Data Science: It's All About the Teamwork. (2019). Forbes.com. Retrieved December 17, 2019, from www.forbes.com/sites/oracle/2018/12/05/how-to-extract-business-value-from-data-science-its-all-about-the-teamwork/#4134870c651c

12 Bridgwater, A. (2018). The 13 types of data. *Forbes*. Retrieved from www.forbes.com/sites/adrianbridgwater/2018/07/05/ the-13-types-of-data/#5a94baad3362

13 Parkins, D. (2017). The world's most valuable resource is no longer oil, but data. *Economist*. Retrieved December 9, 2019, from www.economist.com/ leaders/2017/05/06/the-worlds-most-valuable-resource-is-no-longer-oil-but-data; Vanian, J. (2016, July). Why Data is the New Oil. *Fortune*.

14 Dark Data. (2019). Gartner. Retrieved December 6, 2019, from www.gartner. com/en/information-technology/glossary/dark-data

15 Winder, D. (2018). Hack of Marriott Starwood hotels hits 500 million guests. *ABC News*. Retrieved December 7, 2019, from www.abc.net.au/news/2018-12-01/massive-data-breach-at-marriott-starwood-hotels/10573562; Winder, D. (2018). Hack of Marriott Starwood hotels hits 500 million guests. *ABC News*. Retrieved December 7, 2019, from www.abc.net.au/news/2018-12-01/ massive-data-breach-at-marriott-starwood-hotels/10573562

16 Cadwalladr, C., & Graham-Harrison, E. (2018). Revealed: 50 million Facebook profiles harvested for Cambridge analytica in major data breach. *The Guardian*, 17, 22; Rafter, D. (2018). Cyberthreat trends: 15 cybersecurity threats for 2020. *Norton.Com*. Retrieved September 20, 2020, from Norton.com website: https://us.norton.com/internetsecurity-emerging-threats-cyberthreat-trends-cybersecurity-threat-review.html; Cambridge Analytica Shuts All Operations After Facebook Scandal. (2018). Fortune. Retrieved December 7, 2019, from https://fortune.com/2018/05/02/ cambridge-analytica-shutting-down/

17 Anderson, J. (2018). "Fake News" and unrest in Nicaragua. *The New Yorker*. Retrieved December 7, 2019, from www.newyorker.com/

magazine/2018/09/03/fake-news-and-unrest-in-nicaragua; Nast, C. (2018). The co-opting of french unrest to spread disinformation. *Wired*. Retrieved December 7, 2019, from www.wired.com/story/ co-opting-french-unrest-spread-disinformation/

18  58 Incredible and Interesting Twitter Stats and Statistics. (2019). Brandwatch. Retrieved December 10, 2019, from www.brandwatch.com/blog/ twitter-stats-and-statistics/

19  "What is Data Management?" (2019). Oracle.Com. Retrieved December 9, 2019, from www.oracle.com/au/database/what-is-data-management/

# CHAPTER 18

# Business Intelligence, Data Analytics, and Data Science Primer

DOI: 10.4324/9781003254614-23

# INTRODUCTION

The use of business intelligence, data analytics, and data science technologies and related practices/tools/methods/techniques is no longer optional for organizations needing to become and compete as digital businesses. These technologies and their related practices and tools can be a game changer for organizations that properly use them – driving breakthroughs in operational efficiency and effectiveness, enabling product and business model innovations, and enabling data driven strategic decisions. This primer provides leaders, managers, and supporting professionals with an overview of the relevant technologies, their related practices/tools/methods/techniques, and the roles leaders, managers, and supporting professionals can play in their proper use.

---

**LEARNING OBJECTIVES**

- Develop knowledge of definitions and concepts related to business intelligence, data analytics, and data science technologies
- Understand how these technologies and their related practices/tools/methods/techniques can impact the efficiency, differentiation, adaptability, and agility of an organization
- Understand the roles leaders, managers, and supporting professionals can play in maximizing the leveraging of these technologies and their related practices/tools/methods/techniques
- Analyze and evaluate the implications of these technologies and their related practices/tools/methods/techniques, as well as related leadership or management roles in their optimal use, for organizations' digital transformation strategy and digital business strategy
- Apply knowledge and understanding of these technologies and their related methods/techniques to participate in, support, or lead workstreams or initiatives related to the leveraging of these technologies to enhance organization digital transformation and digital business strategy

---

# BUSINESS INTELLIGENCE AND BUSINESS ANALYTICS

## BUSINESS INTELLIGENCE

The vast amounts of data emanating from business operations are of little value if they are not used to improve operational and strategic decisions. Business intelligence (BI) is a term that refers to the collection, storing, and analyzing of this operational data in order to use it to improve operational and strategic decisions;[1] it can also refer to the methods and tools used to do so. BI focuses on descriptive analytics, showing "what" has happened in the past or what is currently happening and "how" it is happening.[2] So, for example, a BI dashboard may show us that food and beverage sales have spiked to four times normal levels during the April–June quarter last year. As a result, we need to decide whether to ramp up stock and staffing by three to four times normal levels for this period. Thus, BI answers "what" and "how" questions to help us decide whether we should continue doing what we are doing, do more/less of what we are doing, or completely change what we are doing.[3] BI was once seen as an added utility, but this is no longer so. In the new data driven environment, BI is critical to both competitiveness and survival.[4] The terms big data and business intelligence are closely related. Data are the underlying resource for BI, and the relationships existing between the two are often so close that it is difficult to separate them.[5]

## BUSINESS ANALYTICS

Business analytics (BA) is a subset of business intelligence that focuses on predictive analytics.[6] That is, it focuses on the discovery, interpretation, and communication of meaningful patterns in data sets. Business analytics answers "why" questions or cause-and-effect determination questions.[7] Armed with answers about cause and effect, we can predict the outcomes of certain actions or failures to act. Whereas BI dashboards might indicate that food and beverage sales previously spiked in the April–June quarter, through BA we may discover that the spike happened because a big festival was relocated to our town for the next 3 years, bringing an influx of young and hip guests; we may get this from mining website traffic data and discovering that the increased traffic was the result of a favorable influential blog post relating to the festival. Armed with this "why" information, we may decide not only to ramp up our stock and staffing levels during that period but also to send a thank-you gift to the influential blogger and a free hotel experience invitation to other influential bloggers.

# DATA ANALYTICS AND DATA SCIENCE

## DATA ANALYTICS

The term data analytics (also referred to just as analytics)[8] is an umbrella term referring to any form of analysis of data to uncover trends, patterns, or anomalies or to simply measure performance.[9] It also includes interpretation, presentation, and communication of discovered patterns to improve decision making. Data analytics or analytics can also refer to one or more approaches, methodologies, and tools used to achieve the objectives of data analytics. Analytics approaches or methods include:

- Descriptive analytics – using historic or current data to determine "what" happened and "how" it happened
- Diagnostic analytics – using historic data to understand "why" it happened
- Predictive analytics – using descriptive and diagnostic analytics to "predict" or "forecast" what will happen in future
- Prescriptive analytics – algorithms that use descriptive, diagnostic, and predictive analytics to prescribe or suggest optimal decisions or choices that decision makers should choose
- Cognitive analytics – analytics tools that combine data analytics and artificial intelligence algorithms to learn and act on data analysis like humans (e.g., cognitive analytics tools may continuously go through an organization's emails or contracts, identify emerging fraud or risk events, and alert/incentivize relevant leaders to ensure the events are prevented).

Specialty applications of data analytics include value chain activities (e.g., marketing analytics, HR analytics, supply chain analytics), sectors (e.g., retail analytics, healthcare analytics), workflows (e.g., call analytics), data sources (e.g., video analytics, web analytics, speech analytics), and more.

## DATA SCIENCE

Data science is a method for drawing insights from large data sets of structured and unstructured data.[10] It is a multidisciplinary field, meaning it draws on approaches, methods, techniques, and theories from varied disciplines such as mathematics, statistics, computer science, and information science. For example, it may draw on machine learning and deep learning techniques from the computer science field to learn from past decisions in order to improve the quality of automatically prescribed decisions, or it can draw on statistical methods such as regression analysis and structural equation modeling to improve the reliability of information used as a basis for prescribed decisions. The role of data scientists can include activities such as collecting data, cleaning data, organizing data, making statistical inferences, building/using machine learning or deep learning models, conducting online experiments, building customizable or personalized data products, visualizing data, communicating findings, and much more.[11] The value of data science to leaders/managers includes revenue growth (e.g., leveraging patterns in data to maximize sales opportunities), cost reduction (e.g., leveraging data insights to eliminate waste), improved customer experience (e.g., from combining customer analytics and big data insights), product innovation/new product development (e.g., discovering product shortcomings or unmet customer needs in big data), and improved agility and adaptability (e.g., sensing and preparing for effective adaptation to, or benefiting from, pending industry disruptions). Figure 18.1 shows that data science brings together operations and business function knowledge, math or statistics knowledge, and data management knowledge.

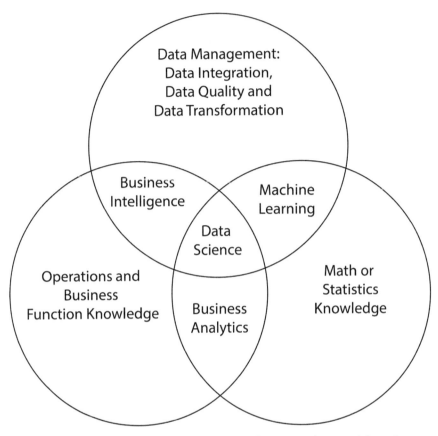

**Figure 18.1** *Data management, business intelligence, business analytics, and data science overlaps*[12]

# DATA VISUALIZATION

Data visualization refers to the communication of insights from data through visual representation.[13] The format of visual representation can vary from dashboards, infographics, and interactive charts to heat maps, network diagrams, cartograms, word clouds, videos, and more.[14] The insights discovered in data need to be communicated effectively and efficiently in order for potential users to make the most of them. This can be a challenging task when the interrelationships in data and the related insights are extensive, complex, or scenario dependent. Data visualization expands the repertoire of approaches and tools for communicating insights in the most efficient and impactful way. So, rather than a boring 30-minute PowerPoint slide presentation, a well-designed and interactive infographic may get the same information across much faster and with much greater impact. It is not just data specialists who can benefit from the use of data visualization methods, techniques, and tools; leaders/managers also spend much of their time communicating data insights to their direct reports, stakeholders within the broader organization, and up the hierarchy. Data visualization proficiency can improve the efficiency and impact of their communications.

# IMPLICATIONS FOR LEADERS, MANAGERS, AND SUPPORTING PROFESSIONALS

Leaders, managers, and supporting professionals may play BI and analytics roles such as data driven decision makers, functional data analysts, analytics team managers/leaders, analytics investment or capability optimization decision makers, and decision support service providers or advisors. Either way, they will typically need to work with data systems architects and developers and with data analysts and data scientists within or outside the organization. They may also be involved in hiring and line managing data analytics and data management leaders and specialists. In either situation, their ability to work with data and collaborate with data analytics specialists will be critical to their leadership or managerial effectiveness. Figure 18.2 provides examples of data analytics and data science related roles and the common job or position titles of employees performing those roles.

| DSA Framework Category | Functional Role | Sample Occupations |
|---|---|---|
| Data Scientists & Advanced Analytics | Create sophisticated analytical models used to build new datasets and derive new insights from data | Data Scientist / Economist |
| Data Analysts | Leverage data analysis and modeling techniques to solve problems and glean insight across functional domains | Data Analyst / Business Intelligence Analyst |
| Data Systems Developers | Design, build and maintain organization's data and analytical infrastructure | Systems Analyst / Database Administrator |
| Analytics Managers | Oversee analytical operations and communicate insights to executives | Chief Analytics Officer / Marketing Analytics Manager |
| Functional Analysts | Utilize data and analytical models to inform specific functions and business decisions | Business Analyst / Financial Analyst |
| Data-Driven Decision Makers | Leverage data to inform strategic and operational decisions | IT Project Manager / Marketing Manager |

*Analytical Rigor* (vertical axis label, arrow pointing upward)

**Figure 18.2** *Data-related roles and type of expertise*[15]

# GOOGLE AND REFLECT

| Technology concept | Common terminology |
| --- | --- |
| Business intelligence | Online analytical processing (OLAP), data mining, process mining, complex event processing, business performance management, benchmarking, text mining, descriptive analytics, prescriptive analytics, business analytics, business analyst, data analyst |
| Data analytics and data science | Machine learning, deep learning, neural networks, data mining, data set, data democratization, algorithm, natural language processing, machine vision, data anonymization, artificial intelligence, behavioral analytics, citizen data scientist, data classification, decision trees, multidimensional database (MDB), online analytical processing (OLAP), outlier, predictive modeling, Python, R (programming language), random forest, validity, reliability, decision science,[16] association analytics, sentiment analysis, time decomposition, cluster analysis |
| Data visualization | Charts, geospatial visualization, interactive visualization, climate change art, data art, data profiling, infographic, information visualization, interaction design, interaction techniques, scientific visualization, software visualization, statistical graphics, visual analytics, visual journalism, warming stripes, table or crosstab, distribution, flow, spatial, change over time, part to whole,[17] brainstorm, bubble chart, bubble map, circle packing, connection map, density plot, flow chart, flow map, heatmap, network diagram, population pyramid, radar chart, scatterplot, span chart, spiral plot, stacked area graph, stacked bar graph, stem and leaf plot, stream graph, sunburst diagram, tally chart, timeline, timetable, tree diagram, tree map, Venn diagram, violin plot, word cloud |

# EXAMPLE TOOLS AND VENDORS

| Technology concept | Example tools and vendors |
|---|---|
| Business intelligence and business analytics | Microsoft (Power BI), Google (e.g., Google Data Studio), Tableau, Qlik, ThoughtSpot, Sisense, Salesforce (e.g., Einstein Analytics), TIBCO Software, SAS BI, SAP (e.g., SAP business intelligence, SAP NetWeaver BW, SAP Business Objects), Oracle (e.g., Oracle BI, Oracle Enterprise BI Server, Oracle Hyperion System), IBM (e.g., IBM Cognos Intelligence), Birst, Yellowfin BI, Domo, Locker, MicroStrategy, GoodData, BOARD International, Logi Analytics, Information Builders, Pyramid Analytics |
| Data analytics and data science | R, Python, C/C++, SQL, GoSpotCheck, IBM Datacap, Mozenda, Paxata, Trifacta, DataRobot, Feature Labs, Anaconda, Tableau, SAS, Alteryx, KNIME, RapidMiner, IBM Cognos, Hadoop, Hive, Pig, Spark,[18] Octoparse, OnBase by Hyland, Domino Data Lab, Informatica, KNIME Analytics Platform, Informatica, Anaconda Enterprise, Databricks, H20.ai |
| Data visualization | Tableau, Google Fusion Tables, JReport by Jinfonet, Google Charts, Microsoft Power BI, Infogram, Qlik, SAS, Cluvio, Visme |

# DISCUSSION QUESTIONS
## BUSINESS INTELLIGENCE AND BUSINESS ANALYTICS

1  What is the difference between business intelligence and business analytics?
2  Which of the business intelligence tools under "Example Tools and Vendors" are open-source tools?
3  Which of the business intelligence tools under "Example Tools and Vendors" are suited to enterprise-level customers, and which are suited to small/medium-sized business customers?

## DATA ANALYTICS AND DATA SCIENCE

1 What is the difference between data science and data analytics?
2 What is the difference between the roles of data analyst, business analyst, and data scientist?
3 As a leader or manager, who would be more valuable to you: a data analyst, a business analyst, or a data scientist?
4 Is it better to have a data scientist report to you as an operating manager or to report to someone in the IT team?
5 Given a choice between hiring a data scientist with very strong statistical skills and knowledge of external data sets but with no knowledge of your industry and a data analyst who has been working in the industry for 10 years, who would you rather hire and why?
6 What are the top five benefits to a leader or manager understanding data analytics and data science terminology, tools, methods, and approaches?

## DATA VISUALIZATION

1 As a leader or manager, how could you benefit from being proficient in one or more data visualization tools?
2 As a leader or manager, what can you do to benefit from data visualization tools if you are not proficient in them yourself?
3 Which of the data visualization tools in "Example Tools and Vendors" are open-source tools?
4 Which of the data visualization tools in "Example Tools and Vendors" would be best suited for use in an enterprise-level organization, and which would be more suitable for use in a small to medium-sized business?

# NOTES

1 Pratt, M., & Fruhlinger, J. (2019). What is business intelligence? Turning data into business insights. *CIO*. Retrieved December 17, 2019, from www.cio.com/article/2439504/business-intelligence-definition-and-solutions.html; Comparing Business Intelligence, Business Analytics and Data Analytics.

(2019). Tableau Software. Retrieved December 17, 2019, from www.tableau.
com/learn/articles/business-intelligence/bi-business-analytics

2 Pratt, M., & Fruhlinger, J. (2019). What is business intelligence? Turning data
into business insights. *CIO*. Retrieved December 17, 2019, from www.cio.
com/article/2439504/business-intelligence-definition-and-solutions.html;
Comparing Business Intelligence, Business Analytics and Data Analytics.
(2019). Tableau Software. Retrieved December 17, 2019, from www.tableau.
com/learn/articles/business-intelligence/bi-business-analytics

3 Comparing Business Intelligence, Business Analytics and Data Analytics.
(2019). Tableau Software. Retrieved December 17, 2019, from www.tableau.
com/learn/articles/business-intelligence/bi-business-analytics

4 Mariani, M., Baggio, R., Fuchs, M., & Höepken, A. W. (2017). Business
intelligence and big data in hospitality and tourism: A systematic literature
review. *International Journal of Contemporary Hospitality Management*,
30(12), 3514–3554.

5 Mariani, M., Baggio, R., Fuchs, M., & Höepken, A. W. (2017). Business
intelligence and big data in hospitality and tourism: A systematic literature
review. *International Journal of Contemporary Hospitality Management*,
30(12), 3514–3554.

6 Business Intelligence vs. Business Analytics. (2018). Analytics.hbs.edu.
Retrieved December 16, 2019, from https://analytics.hbs.edu/blog/business-
intelligence-vs-business-analytics/; Ofori-Boateng, C. (2019). Data analytics
versus business intelligence – and the race to replace decision making
with software. Forbes.com. Retrieved December 17, 2019, from www.
forbes.com/sites/forbestechcouncil/2019/06/21/data-analytics-versus-
business-intelligence-and-the-race-to-replace-decision-making-with-
software/#29cab372612b

7 Comparing Business Intelligence, Business Analytics and Data Analytics.
(2019). Tableau Software. Retrieved December 17, 2019, from www.tableau.
com/learn/articles/business-intelligence/bi-business-analytics

8 Analytics. (2019). Gartner. Retrieved December 16, 2019, from www.gartner.
com/en/information-technology/glossary/analytics

9 Comparing Business Intelligence, Business Analytics and Data Analytics.
(2019). Tableau Software. Retrieved December 16, 2019, from www.
tableau.com/learn/articles/business-intelligence/bi-business-analytics;
Business Analytics: Everything You Need to Know. (2019). MicroStrategy.
Retrieved December 16, 2019, from www.microstrategy.com/us/resources/

introductory-guides/business-analytics-everything-you-need-to-know; Boulton, C. (2019). Data analytics examples: An inside look at 6 success stories. *CIO*. Retrieved December 17, 2019, from www.cio.com/article/3221621/6-data-analytics-success-stories-an-inside-look.html

10  Olavsrud, T. (2019). What is data science? Transforming data into value. *CIO*. Retrieved December 16, 2019, from www.cio.com/article/3285108/what-is-data-science-a-method-for-turning-data-into-value.html

11  Bowne-Anderson, H. (2018). What data scientists really do, According to 35 data scientists. *Harvard Business Review*. Retrieved December 17, 2019, from https://hbr.org/2018/08/what-data-scientists-really-do-according-to-35-data-scientists; What is Data Science? | Oracle. (2019). Oracle.com. Retrieved December 17, 2019, from www.oracle.com/data-science/what-is-data-science.html

12  Gao Institute of Management. (2020). Retrieved June 17, 2020, from www.gim.ac.in/content.php?name=ABOUT-PGDM-(BDA)&id=134

13  MicroStrategy. (2019). Data visualization: What it is and why we use it. Retrieved December 17, 2019, from www.microstrategy.com/us/resources/introductory-guides/data-visualization-what-it-is-and-why-we-use-it; Sas.com (n.d.). Data visualization: What it is and why it matters. Sas.com. Retrieved December 17, 2019, from www.sas.com/en_au/insights/big-data/data-visualization.html

14  Data Visualization Beginner's Guide: A Definition, Examples, and Learning Resources. (2019). Tableau Software. Retrieved December 17, 2019, from www.tableau.com/learn/articles/data-visualization; Data Visualization: What It is and Why We Use It. (2019). MicroStrategy. Retrieved December 17, 2019, from www.microstrategy.com/us/resources/introductory-guides/data-visualization-what-it-is-and-why-we-use-it

15  Gao Institute of Management. (2020). Retrieved June 17, 2020, from www.gim.ac.in/content.php?name=ABOUT-PGDM-(BDA)&id=134

16  Data Science Terminology: 26 Key Definitions Everyone Should Understand. (2019). Bernard Marr. Retrieved December 17, 2019, from www.bernardmarr.com/default.asp?contentID=1446

17  Glossary of Data Visualizations. (2019). Tableau Software. Retrieved December 17, 2019, from www.tableau.com/learn/articles/data-visualization/glossary

18  "Top Data Science Tools." (2019). James Cook University. Retrieved December 17, 2019. https://online.jcu.edu.au/canada/blog/top-data-science-tools

# Internet of Things (IoT), Industry 4.0, Smart Things, and Edge Computing Primer

DOI: 10.4324/9781003254614-24

# INTRODUCTION

At the heart of the Internet of Things and related technologies or concepts is the use of connected sensors and algorithms to make things "smart." These things can range from devices, equipment, and buildings to factories, biological processes, systems, and business processes. Long established, sensor technology has advanced to the point where there are sensors able to detect almost anything – from motion, voice, proximity, and touch to temperature, light, smoke, and much more. Although sensors have been capable of many of these things for a long time, what has changed is the ability to connect them to each other and to the internet. This enables them to share collected information with each other and with any other devices or things or people connected to the internet. Through the use of connected sensors, all manner of things can be connected to the internet. This connection enables these things to communicate the data they collect through built-in embedded sensors with each other. And through the use of software algorithms the things can analyze collected information, use it to make decisions, and issue or follow instructions to and from each other or to and from people. The ability of things to do all this makes them smart.

The sensing, connectivity, and smartness of things is set to profoundly alter how organizations create and deliver value. The ability of all things involved in organization workflows capable of being smart offers significant opportunities for novel new products/services and enhanced product/service offerings (e.g., while hotel staff may not be in a room with a guest at all times, certain smart devices are that may be able to take guest service to new levels); it also offers vastly improved opportunities for efficiency (the vast array of data collected from all the different devices can be integrated and used to pinpoint wasted effort, bottlenecks, activities that could be automated, or costs that could be minimized), effectiveness (concepts like smart workplaces and smart buildings can be leveraged to improve staff effectiveness), and agility (through leveraging data on the things of strategic partners, government, and the community, organizations may be able to better anticipate and adapt to crisis events, disruptions, and other changes). Leaders, managers, and supporting professionals play a critical role in ensuring their organizations recognize and seize the opportunities offered by the Internet of Things and related technologies and concepts. In order to play this role, they must understand the foundations, functioning, opportunities and threats, and use cases of the Internet of Things and related technologies and concepts.

## LEARNING OBJECTIVES

- Develop knowledge of definitions and concepts related to the Internet of Things, Industry 4.0, smart things, and edge computing
- Understand how these technologies and their related applications/practices/tools/methods/techniques can impact the efficiency, differentiation, adaptability, and agility of an organization
- Understand the roles leaders, managers, and supporting professionals can play in maximizing the leveraging of these technologies and their related applications/practices/tools/methods/techniques
- Analyze and evaluate the implications of these technologies and their related applications/practices/tools/methods/techniques, as well as the related leadership/management/supporting professional roles in their optimal use, for organizations' digital transformation strategy and digital business strategy
- Apply knowledge and understanding of these technologies and their related applications/practices/tools/methods/techniques to participate in, support, or lead workstreams or initiatives related to the leveraging of these technologies to enhance organization digital transformation and digital business strategy

# INTERNET OF THINGS (IoT) AND INTERNET OF EVERYTHING (IoE)

## INTERNET OF THINGS

The Internet of Things is a collection of connected or linked things (e.g., computers, devices, cars, industrial equipment, buildings) that are able to transfer data or communicate with each other, usually without requiring the input or intervention of a human being.[1] The things are usually connected, transfer information, and communicate with each other via a network (e.g., a small private network or a much bigger national or global network). At a global network level, you can think of it as the internet but with many more devices or things being connected than just computers (e.g., cars, phones, printers, traffic lights, bridges, planes, pillows, dust), and these devices or things are able to communicate and transfer data and instructions to each other. For example, this could be as simple as your fridge sending instructions to your phone for it to create a reminder for you to pick up some milk on the way home. On a more involved level, your fridge could go online to find a same-day milk delivery supermarket, order the milk, and notify your door lock to expect the delivery at a certain time and be ready to open the door once the milk arrives. If you have a robot in the home, the fridge or the lock could instruct the robot to pick up the milk from the front door and put it on a particular shelf in the fridge so it is ready for you when you arrive home. The network connection between devices or things enables them to communicate and send data and instructions to each other (e.g., order information, payment information, instructions for actions to take or places to go). These things also need to be able to read or sense themselves and/or their environment (e.g., the fridge has to be able to sense that the milk is running out and when the milk has been replaced). Because of this, the devices or things are usually fitted with or have built-in or embedded sensors (e.g., touch sensors, proximity sensors, motion sensors, voice sensors, temperature sensors, liquid sensors, light sensors, heartbeat sensors, infrared sensors, gas sensors, smoke sensors, chemical sensors).[2] The job of the sensors is to collect information that things can communicate or use. In addition, the things are usually also equipped with software systems or algorithms that can then analyze the sensed information and use it to issue corresponding instructions. For example, a sensor in a car may sense that a truck is coming at a particular speed toward a car; the built-in software system may analyze this data and determine the truck is about to collide with the car. The software system may issue instructions for the steering wheel and the brakes to perform actions that will prevent the accident. This is not so different from our eyes seeing that that the truck is speeding toward the car, our brain working out that an accident is going to eventuate, and our brain issuing our body parts instructions for actions to take (e.g., signal with our hands for the truck to stop or for the driver to get out of the way). Taken together, the combination of sensors and software algorithms equip the things with significant ability to emulate or even transcend human ability in some activities. For example, it is more likely that your fridge can reliably ensure that you never run out of milk than you may be able to (you may get distracted, forget, or be too tired, whereas this will not happen to the fridge). With the right combination of sensors and software algorithms, almost all things can now be connected to the internet and become "smart" things with expanding potential for action; that is, things able to act on instructions from anywhere around the world or act independently to serve us, protect us, enhance our performance, and much more.

## INTERNET OF EVERYTHING

The Internet of Everything extends the Internet of Things by connecting people, processes, data, and things (see visualization in Figure 19.1).[3] These are often referred to as the four pillars of the Internet of Everything. The IoE's expanded power is derived from the vastly expanded possibilities of everything coming online to share data, communicate, and interact in almost unlimited ways.[4] This differs from the Internet of Things, which is limited to the connection of physical things.[5] The people pillar refers to people's identity, interests and preferences, interaction, healthcare, work, address, payment, and other information being

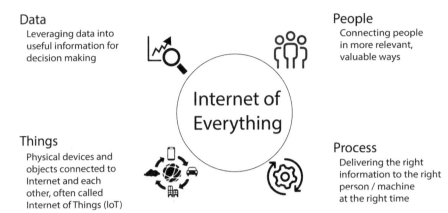

**Data**
Leveraging data into useful information for decision making

**People**
Connecting people in more relevant, valuable ways

**Internet of Everything**

**Things**
Physical devices and objects connected to Internet and each other, often called Internet of Things (IoT)

**Process**
Delivering the right information to the right person / machine at the right time

**Figure 19.1** *The Internet of Everything extends the Internet of Things by connecting people, processes, data, and things*

digitized and online and able to be interacted with. Once online, our virtual selves can interact with other people or their virtual selves, with businesses, business processes that are online, and with the things that are online (e.g., machines, devices). For example, they can customize products to suit us, they can intervene in activities we are undertaking if we are at risk (e.g., your car could sense, unbeknownst to you, that you are about to be hit by another car and either warn you to avoid it or take over the steering to avoid it – if legally authorized to do so). The process pillar refers to processes or aspects of processes being able to be done online, inputting into other online processes, or requiring outputs from other online processes. For instance, a connected car may send data to the car manufacturer about the condition of each part in your car, enabling the manufacturer to know when critical parts will be in poor condition and book you in for a change of brake pads at a service center that is walking distance from your workplace. In this case, information from you and your car has fed into and triggered the manufacturer's vehicle monitoring and servicing processes. The data pillar relates to the collection, analysis, and use of data to facilitate and optimize processes. For example, in the case of our booking for a change of brake pads, it is the collection, analysis, and use of data from people (you) and things (the car) that has enabled that process to occur and to occur at the optimal time. Finally, the things pillar is about the different physical things that are connected to each other and to everything else online (e.g., machines, devices, buildings, traffic lights, car parks). Bringing these pillars together, the IoE offers greater integration, automation, and "smarts" than has ever been possible. It is set to revolutionize value creation and delivery.[6]

## CONNECTED VS SMART VS AUTONOMOUS

The terms connected, smart, and autonomous often come up in IoT-related topics. In addition to capturing and storing data (e.g., through the use of sensors), IoT devices are "connected" if they can send and receive information. This enables them to, for example, send sensor data they've collected and receive instructions. For example, your monitoring system may sense that someone is at the door and send you live video of that person. You may decide to send it instructions not to activate the alarm and, instead, to unlock the door because it is one of your relatives at the door dropping off something you forgot at their place. Without the connectivity (which may be via a mobile network such as 5G, some other Wi-Fi network, or Bluetooth), the transfer of sensor data and corresponding instructions may be difficult. IoT devices are "smart" if, in addition to being connected, they can gather information about their environment, process it (e.g., perform computations), and respond to that information. So, for instance, an air conditioner is smart if it can sense the room temperature and adjust its output to ensure the room can remain at a comfortable temperature. An IoT device is autonomous to the extent that it can sense, understand, and appropriately respond to sensing, understanding, adapting, and reacting to its environment – minimizing the need for human intervention. So, for instance, a smart fridge would be highly autonomous if it can sense (hear) that you are planning to have a large number of guests over, work out that you won't have enough milk to offer them all tea, and order the right amount of extra milk to be delivered in time so you don't run out of milk. Even the smart air conditioner described earlier is autonomous if it works out on its own how to keep the temperature at a comfortable level for you. Sometimes these terms are interchangeably used through misunderstanding or through the boundaries between connection, intelligence, and autonomy having some overlaps. There can be degrees to a device's connectivity, smartness, and autonomy such that one device may be smarter and more autonomous than another.

# EDGE COMPUTING AND THE IoT EDGE

While cloud architecture or the cloud offers almost unlimited storage and computation, a major shortcoming for some IoT-related uses is the time delay involved in sending sensor data to the cloud and awaiting computation results or other data to be sent back prior to other actions being able to occur. Sean Bryson, vice president of Microsoft technology at Hitachi Consulting, gives the example of an autonomous vehicle traveling down a busy road. He points out that if that car has to stop immediately to prevent an accident, sending sensor data to the cloud and awaiting computation and sending back of the results is not viable – it will just take too long.[7] Edge computing provides a solution to this issue for IoT devices. It is a form of distributed computing that brings cloud computing capabilities (i.e., computation and storage capabilities) to local devices.[8] These devices can then collect data via sensors, process it, and use the results for subsequent decisions and actions instead of having to send sensor data to the cloud and awaiting the results of cloud computation. In the case of the autonomous vehicle needing to stop immediately to stop an accident, Sean notes that the thousands of sensors within the vehicle can collect necessary data, assess the status of every piece of equipment, and respond in fractions of a second.[9] Subsequent or nonurgent data can still be sent to the cloud for storage and computation (see visualization in Figure 19.2). Thus, IoT edge refers to technologies or platforms that bring cloud capabilities locally to IoT devices, enabling them to sense, analyze, and respond in near real time. IoT edge technologies can minimize delays in processing, prevent delay-related product quality issues, and minimize financial risks and even fatality risks.

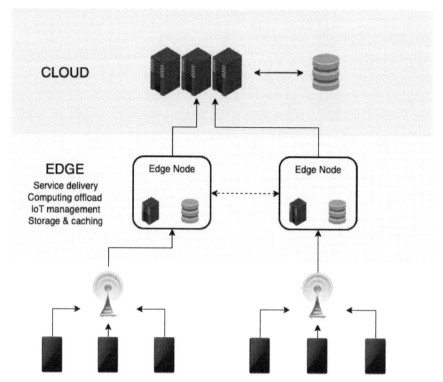

**Figure 19.2** *Edge computing brings computation and data storage to the locations where they are needed instead of requiring sensor data to be sent to the cloud and waiting for the cloud to send the results of computation back to the location*

# INDUSTRIAL INTERNET OF THINGS (IIoT)

The Industrial Internet of Things (IIoT), also known as the industrial internet, is essentially the extension and use of the Internet of Things in industrial sectors and applications (e.g., in equipment/machine/device intensive industries such as oil and gas, power generation, manufacturing, aviation, logistics, food and beverage, and healthcare).[10] The ability of machines and devices to communicate with each other (also known as machine to machine or M2M), with people, and with processes, combined with big data and sophisticated analytics algorithms, offers the opportunity for industrial sector organizations to make unprecedented breakthroughs in reliability, efficiency, effectiveness, and agility.[11] Industrial machinery and operational processes can be monitored and optimized in ways that have not been possible before. For example, systems can monitor, collect, exchange, analyze, and deliver information on the condition of machines and equipment (e.g., detecting or predicting corrosion inside a refinery pipe), on the interaction of machines with each other and with people (e.g., detecting when one machine is limiting the productivity others), and on the status, efficiency, and effectiveness of processes (e.g., detecting errors and inefficiencies in the supply chain). Sophisticated algorithms can use the information being collected and analyzed to optimize processes and workflows (e.g., automatically scheduling on-call staff, laying off those who aren't improving, recommending who should receive bonuses, booking machine maintenance calls, recommending which vendors to continue buying equipment from). These things and more are made possible by real-time data from sensors and the ability for data to be collected, analyzed, and routed between machines, people, and processes anywhere around the world in near real time. Leaders, managers, and supporting professionals may work in industrial or technology sectors, in which case IIoT use cases and innovations will likely directly apply to them. If not, they may deal with industrial sector companies who may be vendors, strategic partners, or competitors. In either case, a good understanding of IIoT dynamics, use cases, and innovations can be invaluable. For example, such knowledge may enable a leader or manager to go with a vendor who will have the best quality, safest, cheapest, most reliably delivered, and most integrable offering. Without such knowledge, the benefits of advances in the particular vendor's IIoT use may not receive the attention they ought to.

# CYBER-PHYSICAL SYSTEMS, THE FOURTH INDUSTRIAL REVOLUTION, AND INDUSTRY 4.0

## CYBER-PHYSICAL SYSTEMS

Cyber-physical systems (CPS) are systems in which integrations of digital and physical things and processes enable the digital management of physical processes and environments (e.g., digital includes software and network connectivity, while physical includes hardware/species/ biological/chemical elements). CPS are able to dynamically sense, adapt to, and manage changes in a physical process and in process settings in real time.[12] They do this by collecting data from different sensors, combining it with data from a range of different systems, analyzing/ interpreting this data, using the analysis/interpretations to make decisions (e.g., about how physical processes or environments need to change), and creating and relaying instructions for things and people to perform (e.g., turn up the temperature switch, activate the nurse call alarm, prepare a patient management plan).[13]

Examples of CPS are abundant in a range of industries. In healthcare, CPS can be used to remotely monitor and manage a patient's health in real time.[14] For example, patient condition data can be collected via sensors in wearable healthcare technologies; this data can be analyzed/interpreted and combined with healthcare information system data to enable the right paramedics team to be called, for the patient to be taken to an emergency department with available capacity, and for the patient's general practitioner to preserve a booking spot to see that patient as soon as possible after they are discharged. This whole process is capable of occurring automatically, with only critical activities being performed by doctors, nurses, and paramedics. In manufacturing, CPS can be used to digitally manage particular manufacturing workflows at a plant, entire plants or groups of plants, or the entire manufacturing process across plants.[15] For manufacturing, Roberto Sabella, head of the Ericsson Research branch in Italy, invites people wanting to understand the power of CPS to imagine a situation in which robots, automated guided vehicles (AGVs), sensors, controllers, raw materials, products, and databases can communicate with one another and where they can all be automatically orchestrated through a central intelligent system.[16] For an industry such as shipping/logistics, he invites people to imagine a port where cranes, vessels, AGVs, trucks, and containers can communicate with each other while being orchestrated by a central system aiming to optimize waiting time, damage rates, maintenance costs, environmental impact, safety, and so forth.[17]

CPS and their elements can leverage technologies such as artificial intelligence, machine learning, and data analytics to be intelligent (or smart) and autonomous. For example, an "intelligent" cyber-physical system (or iCPS) may orchestrate all the activities of a "smart factory," automating and distributing different activity groups among different intelligent agents (e.g., intelligent sub-systems, intelligent things, intelligent processes, human beings).[18] CPS leverage the vastly expanded sensing, communication, analytics, automation, intelligence, autonomy, and other possibilities of digital-physical integration for breakthroughs in organization value creation, efficiency, agility, and adaptability.

## THE FOURTH INDUSTRIAL REVOLUTION OR INDUSTRY 4.0

The term "Fourth Industrial Revolution", sometimes interchangeably referred to as "Industry 4.0", refers to the ushering in of cyber-physical systems and related technologies that are set to drastically change how organizations create and deliver value and, in turn, how societies function and how individuals live their lives.[19] This change is anticipated to be similar to, but of an even greater scale, than earlier industrial revolutions that drastically changed the functioning of businesses and societies.[20] For example,[21] the First Industrial Revolution ushered in the use of water and steam power to enable the creation of mechanical production facilities. The Second Industrial Revolution ushered in the use of electricity and enabled the division of labor, use of assembly lines, and the mass production of products. The Third Industrial Revolution ushered in IT systems to automate and better control production lines.

In each revolution, the change in how organizations created value transformed the nature of work significantly. In turn, each revolution significantly transformed the functioning of cities and nation states and of how individuals lived their lives. For example, in the main, we are no longer subsistence farmers, factory laborers, or machine operators. We do more knowledge-oriented and creative work, earn much more, have much more free time, and live in cities and nation states that are very different from those in preceding industrial revolutions. In each revolution, the power and fortunes of individuals, organizations, and nation states leading or keeping up with the revolutions were drastically transformed.[22] For example, the First and Second Industrial Revolutions elevated the wealth and power of nation states like the United States and Japan.[23] It also elevated the fortunes of industrialists like Andrew Carnegie[24] and John Rockefeller.[25] And the Third Industrial Revolution has elevated nations like India and Japan and modern-day industrialists like Masayoshi Son, Jack Ma, N. R. Narayana Murthy, Bill Gates, and Sergey Brin. For individuals, organizations, and nation states that have not made sufficient effort to keep up with industrial revolutions, the revolutions have often diminished their wealth and power – if not marginalized them altogether.

Although the term Industry 4.0 (or Industrie 4.0) is sometimes used interchangeably with the Fourth Industrial Revolution, it was originally more specifically used to refer to the digital transformation of the manufacturing industry. Viewed this way, it is a subset of the Fourth Industrial Revolution. Whereas the Fourth Industrial Revolution is an all-encompassing term (i.e., referring to changes in how businesses produce products, in how cities/societies function, and in how individuals live), Industry 4.0 is limited to digital transformation of the manufacturing industry, manufacturing organizations, and manufacturing processes (e.g., exploring how manufacturing industries, organizations, and processes can be transformed to make the most of the Fourth Industrial Revolution). Industry 4.0 considers issues such as what "smart manufacturing" and "smart factories" are, how they ought to work, and how to transform manufacturing and factories to be smart.

# SMART BUILDINGS, SMART WORKSPACES, AND SMART HOMES
## SMART BUILDINGS

In a nutshell, smart buildings are buildings that leverage the Internet of Things, cyber-physical systems, artificial intelligence, and other technologies to optimize the functioning, usability, and externalities of buildings. The functioning of buildings can be optimized through reduced energy costs, improved temperature and ventilation control, reduced maintenance costs, improved access control, improved useful life, improved safety, improved building condition/value, and more. Externalities, or impacts on communities and the environment, can be optimized through minimization of negative externalities (e.g., carbon emissions, energy consumption, hazardous waste) and maximization of positive externalities (e.g., negative emissions, positive impacts on community well-being). Usability can be optimized through improvements in the efficiency and effectiveness of the activities the building is being used for. Optimizations such as these are logical if we imagine, as an example, every component of a building being fitted with sensors, being online, being able to communicate with all other physical and digital components (e.g., devices, systems, processes), and being able to leverage artificial and data science to make autonomous smart decisions. As a result of all of this, a building would be able to know on its own who is in a building, where they are, what their comfort requirements are and how to meet them, what devices to activate and when, what video footage to analyze, who to notify if security anomalies are detected, what the conditions of a building's external environmental are, when there are likely to be issues with electrical grids and how to avoid the impact of those grids, and much more. Through integrations with workflow management systems, smart buildings may be able to drastically improve process efficiency and effectiveness. For example, a smart building may be able to check which people entering the building have an appointment, automatically register them in the visitor management system, send them an email or SMS confirmation sign-off upon arrival, direct them to skip the security cue and scan their QR code, and notify the person they are meeting to go down the elevator at the right time to greet them.

## SMART WORKPLACES

Smart workplaces combine concepts like smart buildings, the Internet of Things, cyber-physical systems, artificial intelligence, and other technologies with design and workflow management concepts to optimize the efficiency, effectiveness, and attraction of work settings. For example, smart buildings can be leveraged to ensure lighting, airflow, sunlight, and heating and air conditioning that anticipates and caters to worker's needs so as to enable them to do their best work efficiently and effectively (e.g., in regard to lighting, circadian rhythm lighting can optimize alertness, energy, and focus). IoT, data science, and artificial intelligence can be leveraged to ensure that workplace conditions, equipment, tools, and resources automatically turn on and shut down in time to optimize accessibility and energy efficiency. The right data can be made available to the right devices and people, in the right format, in the right places, and at the right time – the first time, every time.

Smart buildings can communicate with other smart buildings, draw data from the external environment, pull in live traffic and public transportation data to ensure employees arrive and leave at the best times, maximize their breaks (e.g., best times to get lunch at their favorite cafes), avoid getting caught in the rain, and avoid areas most often associated with getting sick. Many more smart workplace use cases and best practices are emerging. Smart workplaces can be a potent attraction tool in the war for talent – for instance, consider the word of mouth and pulling power of Apple's and Google's work settings.

## SMART HOMES

Smart homes are essentially like smart workplaces, except the focus is on maximizing efficiency, effectiveness, safety, security, livability, and comfort of a home's occupants. For example, smart solar systems, smart meters, and smart devices may ensure that power costs are kept at a minimum or that a household actually generates more electricity than it uses. Smart fridges, smart washing machines, smart air conditioners, and smart locks may autonomously take care of household tasks like food shopping, washing, climate control, and home access. Through Google's and Apple's connected or smart home platforms, home occupants can interact with devices at their home in real time from anywhere around the world. These devices can in turn interact with each other and with external systems and platforms. For example, a home monitoring system may automatically call police or an ambulance if it senses a security or safety threat within or outside the home.

# SMART INFRASTRUCTURE, SMART CITIES, AND SMART GOVERNMENT
## SMART INFRASTRUCTURE

Infrastructure refers to the physical structures and facilities needed for the effective functioning of society (e.g., roads, bridges, power lines, public buildings) and, sometimes, enterprise. Like other IoT things, infrastructure can also be connected, smart, and autonomous through leveraging concepts like smart buildings, the Internet of Things, cyber-physical systems, artificial intelligence, and other technologies.[26] Through leveraging these concepts and technologies, infrastructure can sense what is happening within itself and in the external environment. It can share the sensed information with other infrastructure (e.g., roads, traffic systems, streetlights), machines and devices (e.g., cars, smartphones, parking meters), institutions (e.g., the fire department, the local emergency department, policing and intelligence agencies), and information systems and workflows (e.g., government procurement systems, government healthcare systems, government emergency management systems, tender documents, ambulance diversion workflows). Infrastructure can also receive information from external systems and leverage artificial intelligence and data science, for example, to be self-aware and self-managing (e.g., sense the need for and coordinate its own maintenance depending on external weather conditions and government budget performance, anticipate and prevent public safety issues, coordinate with other infrastructure to limit traffic congestion, suggest/request changes to other infrastructure that may be creating bottlenecks or be the point of bottlenecks, prevent infrastructure abuse, limit the impact of public disorder events). The use cases for smart infrastructure are only limited by imagination and political/legal/

social constraints. Diverse use cases can include letting swimmers know where it is safe to swim in real time in order to avoid shark attacks and drowning, anticipating wastewater overflow due to rain and coordinating preemptive action (e.g., to remove existing and emerging blockages), eliminating congestion from road networks by analyzing real-time data on the whereabouts of cars and redirecting them to alternate routes, recognizing criminals and stolen cars and directing police to their anticipated getaway routes, automatically analyzing video footage and alerting policing and public safety institutions to current and anticipated risks, optimizing infrastructure performance by pinpointing performance issues and limitations, and enabling real-time changing of public signage (e.g., street signs could automatically change speed limits and street accessibility). Governments that make smart infrastructure data publicly available enable businesses and consumers to leverage that data to improve available products/services and to improve the functioning of cities and regions. For example, when Transport for London shared public transportation data (e.g., what pickup spots and at what times), businesses and individuals used this data to create mobile apps or integrate the data into existing apps to improve public transport accessibility.[27] Optimizing the performance and capacity of assets can help meet challenges related to population growth, rising consumer/society expectations, and national productivity.

## SMART CITIES

Smart cities are cities that enable and leverage smart infrastructure and the integration of smart infrastructure data with data collected from other things, individuals, and institutions to better govern and serve communities. For example, they can automatically source and integrate data from roads, bridges, buildings, transportation systems, water supply networks, drainage networks, police departments, citizens, schools, libraries, hospitals, social media platforms and other public services, assets, information systems, and platforms. They then leverage data analytics, data science, and artificial intelligence to better manage public service quality (e.g., availability of services, accessibility of services, timeliness, efficiency, safety, security), reduce costs (e.g., city capital and operating costs), reduce resource consumption (e.g., water, energy, labor), improve community engagement, and improve the quality-of-life satisfaction of citizens. As with smart infrastructure use cases and examples, smart city technology use cases and examples are abundant. For example, on its continuing journey to becoming a smart city, the city of Barcelona implemented a network of optics throughout the city, enabling it to support IoT and to provide free high-speed Wi-Fi. This then enabled smart water, smart lighting, and smart parking management, saving the city over $98 million and creating 47,000 new jobs. In its continuing journey, the city of Boston implemented smart trash cans that automatically determine when they need collection and the most efficient routes for sanitation workers. The city of Amsterdam has migrated to real-time monitoring of traffic flow, energy usage, and public safety data to enable immediate adjustments to be made about their management.[28] Figure 19.3 shows where a range of cities around the world are on the smart city maturity journey.

## SMART GOVERNMENT

Smart government extends the concepts of smart infrastructure and smart cities to optimize governance of democratic processes, the management of public service institutions, and the delivery of public services. Given

| City Name | Roadmap Designed | Smart City Department | Smart City Application Domains | | | |
|---|---|---|---|---|---|---|
| | | | Business | Citizen | Environment | Government |
| Bilbao | No | No | Yes | Yes | Yes | Yes |
| Birmingham | Yes | Yes | No | Yes | No | Yes |
| Bristol | Yes | Yes | Yes | Yes | Yes | Yes |
| Cape Town | No | No | No | Yes | Yes | Yes |
| Cleveland | Yes | No | No | Yes | Yes | Yes |
| Copenhagen | Yes | Yes | Yes | Yes | Yes | Yes |
| Fujisawa | Yes | Yes | Yes | Yes | Yes | Yes |
| Melbourne | No | No | No | Yes | No | Yes |
| Ottawa | Yes | Yes | Yes | Yes | Yes | Yes |
| Santander | No | No | No | Yes | No | Yes |
| Seattle | Yes | Yes | Yes | Yes | Yes | Yes |
| Seoul | Yes | Yes | No | Yes | No | Yes |
| Singapore | Yes | No | Yes | Yes | No | Yes |
| Stockholm | Yes | Yes | Yes | Yes | Yes | Yes |
| Toronto | Yes | No | No | Yes | Yes | Yes |

**Figure 19.3** *Cities around the world and their smart city (SC) maturity (e.g., if they have a smart city roadmap or a smart city department and have effected key smart city domains or application areas)*[29]

their experiences with the business world, citizens expect responsive, efficient, and accountable government services and institutions. As their expectations grow, they are becoming more intolerant of bureaucratic delays, lack of service availability, lack of service access, siloed government departments that don't talk to each other, and infrastructure that is not digitally enabled or able to interface with consumer devices. Examples of smart government initiatives include mobile apps that enable citizens to be community guardians (e.g., to capture and report incidents, to suggest improvements), single point sign-on to access all government services, leveraging business and consumer data to warn consumers about organizations misleading them,[30] leveraging big data to anticipating security threats (e.g., leveraging travel/aviation data, traffic data, social media data, search engine, and other data), ensuring security and privacy of government information, enabling the use of digital IDs and digital government workflows, and enabling the secure integration of business and consumer systems and devices with government systems and devices.

# IMPLICATIONS FOR LEADERS, MANAGERS, AND SUPPORTING PROFESSIONALS

As with many other digital technologies, key risks and issues of IoT-related technologies include privacy, security, ethics, and constantly changing technology standards. Examples of privacy-related issues include increased risks of unauthorized exposure of customer, citizen, or organization data. Examples of security risks include increased points of access to sensitive information for almost anyone around the world; whereas earlier, a hacker was limited by lower availability of internet connectivity, slower internet speeds, lower availability of hacking targets, only computers as an access/breach point – as opposed to an array of smart phones and IoT devices, and minimal online information to use. Today all these things are almost pervasive, unlimited in their availability, or their capacity/speed growing almost exponentially. This creates a very big security challenge for organizations needing to manage risk exposures from all their people, things, systems, and processes.[31] Organizations and governments are expected to be ethically responsible in how they use the vast treasure troves of data available to them. This becomes a much bigger challenge with so many connected, smart, and autonomous devices. For example, it can be easy for artificial intelligence algorithms to create new information (by integrating and analyzing integrated data) but for it not to be acceptable for an organization to use or even access that data (e.g., it wouldn't be difficult for Google to create digital profiles of citizens and use artificial intelligence algorithms to comb the internet and internet-connected devices for extensive personal data about citizens, but this would likely be met with community outrage that could even lead to communities taking away Google's license to operate in particular communities). Finally, constantly changing technology standards mean that IoT-related technology users must always keep in mind that technology standards could change rapidly (e.g., from NFC to Bluetooth to 5G), and they ought to have platforms and devices that can accommodate new standards (e.g., able to adapt to new standards or are cheap to replace).

## GOOGLE AND REFLECT

IoT-enabled product-as-a-service, things as customers, IoT-enabled applications, managed IoT services, IoT cloud platform, mobile IoT (MIoT), IoT protocol, narrowband IoT (NBIoT), IoT security, IoT services, IoT platform, intelligent building automation systems, managed machine-to-machine services, IT/OT alignment, asset performance management, IoT integration, smart lighting, cloud MOM services (momPaaS), MDM of product data, MDM of "thing" data, internet of meat, edge AI, IoT edge analytics

## EXAMPLE TOOLS AND VENDORS

Google Home voice-controlled speaker, Amazon Echo Plus, August Doorbell Cam, Nest Smoke Alarm, NETGEAR Orbi Ultra-Performance Whole Home Mesh Wi-Fi System, Kuri Mobile Robot, August Smart

Lock, Arm Pelion, Bosch IoT Suite, Bosch Sensors, Cambium Networks cnReach Narrowband Wireless Solution, Cisco Intent-Based Networking (IBN) Solutions, Dell IoT Connected Bundles, Eaton PredictPulse, HP Enterprise Edgeline OT Link Platform, Intel OpenVINO, Intel IoT Market Ready Solutions, Lenovo ThinkSystem SE350, Particle IoT Rules Engine, Qualcomm Vision Intelligence Platform, Qualcomm 9205 LTE modem, Rigado Cascade Edge-as-a-Service, Roambee sensors and beacons, Roambee Honeycomb IoT API platform, Siemens/Alibaba MindSphere, Software AG Cumulocity IoT platform, Hitachi Lumada, PTC Thingworx, Nexiot Globehopper smart sensors, Huawei NBIoT platform, SAP Leonardo, GE Predix, Ingenu RPMA device management platform, AWS IoT Core, Google Cloud IoT Core, Microsoft Azure IoT, Arundo Analytics, Bright Machines, Dragos, FogHorn, Iguazio, Preferred Networks, READY Robotics, SparkCognition, Element Analytics[32]

# DISCUSSION QUESTIONS

1 What is the best metaphor you can think of to explain how the Internet of Things works?

2 Is it possible for every single thing (living or nonliving) to be connected to the internet? For example, could dust, water, bacteria, diseases, plates, trees, and volcanoes be connected to the internet?

3 What do we mean when we say "things" can communicate with each other? What types of communication can they do?

4 What is a sensor? How is a connected sensor different?

5 What are ten different types of sensors?

6 What sensors could you attach to a chair to give it human-like senses?

7 What is the difference between the Internet of Things (IoT), the Internet of Everything (IoE), and the Industrial Internet of Things (IIoT)?

8 What is the difference between a connected IoT device, a smart IoT device, and an autonomous IoT device?

9 What is edge computing? What is the IoT edge?

10 What is a cyber-physical system (CPS)? Are there different types of cyber-physical systems?

11 What is the difference between Industry 4.0, Industrie 4.0, and the Fourth Industrial Revolution?

12 Are Industry 4.0 and the Fourth Industrial Revolution possible without cyber-physical systems?

13 What is the difference between a smart building, a smart workplace, and a smart home?

14 Can you have smart workplaces and smart homes without smart buildings?

15 Which comes first: smart infrastructure, smart cities, or smart government?

16 What are five ways IoT and IoT-related technologies can compromise a person's privacy, security, and health?

# NOTES

1 Frangoul, A. (2017). The internet of things: why it matters. *CNBC*. Retrieved December 23, 2019, from www.cnbc.com/2017/10/23/the-internet-of-things-why-it-matters.html

2 What is a Sensor? Different Types of Sensors, Applications. (2017). Electronics Hub. Retrieved December 20, 2019, from www.electronicshub.org/different-types-sensors/

3 The Internet of Everything. (2019). Cisco.com. Retrieved December 20, 2019, from www.cisco.com/c/dam/en_us/about/business-insights/docs/ioe-value-at-stake-public-sector-analysis-faq.pdf

4 The Internet of Everything. (2019). Cisco.com. Retrieved December 20, 2019, from www.cisco.com/c/dam/en_us/about/business-insights/docs/ioe-value-at-stake-public-sector-analysis-faq.pdf

5 The Internet of Everything. (2019). Cisco.com. Retrieved December 20, 2019, from www.cisco.com/c/dam/en_us/about/business-insights/docs/ioe-value-at-stake-public-sector-analysis-faq.pdf

6 Seven Things You Need to Know about IIoT in Manufacturing. (2019). Forbes.com. Retrieved December 23, 2019, from www.forbes.com/sites/louiscolumbus/2019/06/02/seven-things-you-need-to-know-about-iiot-in-manufacturing_updated/#7de9c6095f56

7 Bryson, S. (2019). Internet of things (IoT) – five components of IoT edge devices. *Cisco*. Retrieved December 30, 2019, from www.cisco.com/c/en/us/solutions/internet-of-things/iot-edge-devices.html

8 Bryson, S. (2019). Internet of things (IoT) – five components of iot edge devices. *Cisco*. Retrieved December 30, 2019, from www.cisco.com/c/en/us/solutions/internet-of-things/iot-edge-devices.html

9 Bryson, S. (2019). Internet of things (IoT) – five components of iot edge devices.

10 Everything You Need to Know about IIoT | GE Digital. (2019). Ge.com. Retrieved December 23, 2019, from www.ge.com/digital/blog/everything-you-need-know-about-industrial-internet-things

11 Industrial Internet of Things (IIoT) – Definition – Trend Micro USA. (2019). Trendmicro.com. Retrieved December 23, 2019, from www.trendmicro.com/vinfo/us/security/definition/industrial-internet-of-things-iiot; Everything You Need to Know about IIoT | GE Digital. (2019). Ge.com. Retrieved December 23, 2019, from www.ge.com/digital/blog/everything-you-need-know-about-industrial-internet-things

12 Sabella, R. (2018). Cyber physical systems for industry 4.0. *Ericsson.com*. Retrieved December 30, 2019, from www.ericsson.com/en/blog/2018/10/cyber-physical-systems-for-industry-4.0

13 Sabella, R. (2018). Cyber physical systems for industry 4.0.

14 Sabella, R. (2018). Cyber physical systems for industry 4.0.

15 King, A. (2019). What are cyber-physical systems? RMIT university. *Rmit.edu.au*. Retrieved December 30, 2019, from www.rmit.edu.au/industry/develop-your-workforce/tailored-workforce-solutions/c4de/articles/what-are-cyber-physical-systems

16 Sabella, R. (2018). Cyber physical systems for industry 4.0. *Ericsson.com*. Retrieved December 30, 2019, from www.ericsson.com/en/blog/2018/10/cyber-physical-systems-for-industry-4.0

17 Sabella, R. (2018). Cyber physical systems for industry 4.0. *Ericsson.com*. Retrieved December 30, 2019, from www.ericsson.com/en/blog/2018/10/cyber-physical-systems-for-industry-4.0

18 Sabella, R. (2018). Cyber physical systems for industry 4.0. *Ericsson.com*. Retrieved December 30, 2019, from www.ericsson.com/en/blog/2018/10/cyber-physical-systems-for-industry-4.0

19 Wilson, B. (2016). What is the fourth industrial revolution & how will it affect you? *Blogs.oracle.com*. Retrieved December 30, 2019, from https://blogs.oracle.com/oracleuniversity/what-is-the-fourth-industrial-revolution-how-will-it-affect-you; Schulze, E. (2019). Everything you need to know about the fourth industrial revolution. *CNBC*. Retrieved December 30, 2019,

from www.cnbc.com/2019/01/16/fourth-industrial-revolution-explained-davos-2019.html

20 Sabella, R. (2018). Cyber physical systems for industry 4.0. *Ericsson.com.* Retrieved December 30, 2019, from www.ericsson.com/en/blog/2018/10/cyber-physical-systems-for-industry-4.0

21 Wilson, B. (2016). What is the fourth industrial revolution & how will it affect you? Blogs.oracle.com. Retrieved December 30, 2019, from https://blogs.oracle.com/oracleuniversity/what-is-the-fourth-industrial-revolution-how-will-it-affect-you

22 Diamond, J. M. (1998). *Guns, germs and steel: A short history of everybody for the last 13,000 years.* Random House.

23 Porter, M. E. (2011). *Competitive advantage of nations: Creating and sustaining superior performance.* Simon and Schuster.

24 Nasaw, D. (2007). *Andrew carnegie.* Penguin.

25 Rockefeller, J. D., & Chernow, R. (1998). *Titan: The life of John D. Rockefeller, Sr.* Random House

26 Siemens. (2020). Intelligent infrastructure: How to make a smart building more profitable. Retrieved January 3, 2020, from https://assets.new.siemens.com/siemens/assets/api/uuid:396710f1-ea9e-4089-ae2f-8408528094c7/version:1560771253/cc-us-bt-cpp-intel-infrstrctr-wp.pdf

27 Macaulay, T. (2019). How startups aim to transform cycling with enormous new TfL dataset. techworld. Retrieved January 3, 2020, from www.techworld.com/data/startups-aim-transform-urban-cycling-with-enormous-new-tfl-dataset-3701170/; Financial Times. (2020). Uber integrates transport for london info into app. *Ft.com.* Retrieved January 3, 2020, from www.ft.com/content/d557d9ec-6a8e-11e9-80c7-60ee53e6681d

28 Ellsmoor, J. (2019). Smart cities: The future of urban development. *Forbes.com.* Retrieved January 3, 2020, from www.forbes.com/sites/jamesellsmoor/2019/05/19/smart-cities-the-future-of-urban-development/#8ee0ae72f900

29 Sánchez-Corcuera, R., Nuñez-Marcos, A., Sesma-Solance, J., Bilbao-Jayo, A., Mulero, R., Zulaika, U., . . . & Almeida, A. (2019). Smart cities survey: Technologies, application domains and challenges for the cities of the future. *International Journal of Distributed Sensor Networks*, 15(6). https://doi.org/10.1177/1550147719853984.

30 Grieve, C. (2019). Worst performing superannuation funds exposed by APRA "heatmap." *The Sydney Morning Herald.* Retrieved January 3, 2020, from www.smh.com.au/business/banking-and-finance/

worst-performing-superannuation-funds-exposed-by-apra-heatmap-20191210-p53ihq.html

31 Trendmicro. (2019). IIoT security risk mitigation in the industry 4.0 era. *trendmicro.com*. Retrieved January 3, 2020, from https://documents.trendmicro.com/assets/rpt/IIoTsecurity-risk-mitigation-in-the-industry-4-era.pdf; Wood, E. (2019). It's time to secure the internet of everything: Regulations rise as the IoT continues to expand. *Forbes.com*. Retrieved January 3, 2020, from www.forbes.com/sites/forbestechcouncil/2019/09/30/its-time-to-secure-the-internet-of-everything-regulations-rise-as-the-iot-continues-to-expand/#711b22f7fa44

32 Martin, D. (2019). 2019 internet of things 50: 15 coolest IoT hardware companies. CRN. Retrieved January 5, 2020, from www.crn.com/slide-shows/internet-of-things/2019-internet-of-things-50–15-coolest-iot-hardware-companies/1; Staff, C. (2020). The most powerful IoT companies in the world. *Computerworld*. Retrieved January 5, 2020, from www.computerworld.com/article/3412287/the-most-powerful-internet-of-things-iot-companies-to-watch.html#slide16

CHAPTER 20

# Artificial Intelligence Primer

DOI: 10.4324/9781003254614-25

# INTRODUCTION

The overarching theme of the digital technologies and concepts covered in this chapter is the design, use, and optimization of information systems and applications that can sense, comprehend, and recommend or take action. The design and use of such digital technologies and concepts are collectively referred to as artificial intelligence (AI). Artificial intelligence includes but extends far beyond familiar AI technologies like robots, smart devices, chatbots, and virtual assistants. AI is set to fundamentally transform how products and services are delivered and how the organizations delivering these products and services operate. Andrew Ng, co-founder of Coursera, AI Fund, Landing.AI, and Google Brain uses the metaphor of the disruptive and transformative power of the internet to explain the disruptive and transformative power of AI.[1] The advent of the internet saw some companies aspire to become internet-enabled companies and others aspire to become true internet companies. While those aspiring to be internet-enabled companies focused on building and operating a website, those aspiring to be true internet companies focused on architecting the whole company to fully leverage the new capabilities of the internet.[2] Many companies focusing on being internet enabled missed the point (the disruptive and transformative power of the internet) and were leapfrogged by true internet companies (e.g., Blockbuster vs Netflix, Borders vs Amazon). In the same way, today many companies may be aspiring to become AI-enabled companies when they really ought to be aspiring to become true AI companies (rearchitecting the whole organization to fully leverage the new capabilities of AI).

AI technologies and related concepts offer organizations significant efficiency opportunities (e.g., using AI to perform routine tasks that can be automated through "if this-then-that" rules), effectiveness opportunities (using AI to augment human decision making and thus make better value delivery decisions), product and business model innovation opportunities (using AI to create new AI-based products and services such as automated analysts, digital assistants, robots, AI-augmented services, data management services), scalability opportunities (being able to offer automated AI-based services 24/7 worldwide), and adaptability and agility opportunities (leveraging AI's sensing and intelligence capabilities to anticipate disruptions and opportunities, better adapt to disruptions, or seize opportunities first).

Enabling the transformation into an AI company is the responsibility of leaders, managers, and supporting professionals at all levels from top management strategic leaders and supporting professionals to frontline managers and supporting professionals. Leaders, managers, and supporting professionals can play a critical role in shaping workforce attitudes toward AI, workforce AI capabilities, organization adoption of AI, and the scale and state of AI practice within an organization. To effectively play this role, they have to at least understand and keep up with AI terminologies and concepts. Although this is an iterative process of learning to keep up with digital technologies, this chapter provides a basic starting point. The chapter begins by introducing high-level AI and machine learning concepts. It then goes on to introduce interpretation, modeling, and learning and prediction tools and concepts that underpin the "intelligence" in artificial intelligence (e.g., natural language processing, speech recognition, computer vision, knowledge graphs, artificial neural networks, deep learning, expert systems). Finally, the chapter identifies some of the key AI-related issues and risks. Taken together, readers should get a high-level understanding of AI and machine learning and of the interpretation, modeling, and learning and prediction tools and concepts underpinning AI. This will enable them to pursue self-directed follow-on learning with confidence so they can keep up with evolving AI developments and applications.

## LEARNING OBJECTIVES

- Develop knowledge of definitions and concepts related to artificial intelligence technologies
- Understand how these technologies and their related applications/practices/tools/methods/techniques can impact the efficiency, differentiation, adaptability, and agility of an organization

- Understand the roles leaders, managers, and supporting professionals can play in maximizing the leveraging of these technologies and their related applications/practices/tools/methods/techniques
- Analyze and evaluate the implications of these technologies and their related applications/practices/tools/methods/techniques, as well as related leadership/management/supporting professional roles in their optimal use, for organizations' digital transformation strategy and digital business strategy
- Apply knowledge and understanding of these technologies and their related applications/practices/tools/methods/techniques to participate in, support, or lead workstreams or initiatives related to the leveraging of these technologies to enhance organization digital transformation and digital business strategy

# ARTIFICIAL INTELLIGENCE

Artificial intelligence (also referred to as machine intelligence, computational intelligence, or cognitive computing) is intelligence demonstrated by machines (e.g., computers, computer-based or computer-like machines). As a branch of computer science, it is the study of how intelligent agents (e.g., computer programs or computer-based machines) can best sense and adapt to changes in their environment to achieve their goals (e.g., winning a chess game, driving a car on a busy road, completing an obstacle course, dealing with a customer inquiry, or even taking out a military threat during a war). Artificial intelligence is often a foundational building block, enabler, catalyst, and/or extender of many other digital technologies and related concepts such as predictive and prescriptive data analytics, IoT smart devices, robotics, drones, and cyber-physical systems. The term artificial is used in contrast to natural human intelligence to signify that artificial intelligence (AI) attempts to mimic human intelligence or cognitive functions and behaviors such as attention, memory, learning, thinking, problem solving, decision making, natural language literacy, motor coordination, planning, manipulation, social intelligence, and creativity. When used, the term artificial intelligence (or its abbreviation AI) can be referring to the definition of AI (discussed earlier) or to the set of AI-based technologies and applications.

## GENERAL AI VS NARROW AI

There are two broad types of AI: general AI and narrow AI. General AI (also referred to as artificial general intelligence [AGI], strong AI, full AI, or general intelligent action) is the type of adaptable and adaptive intelligence that humans are capable of, which enables them to autonomously perform a diverse range of actions by leveraging all human cognitive functions. This is the type of AI in Hollywood depictions of AI like *The Terminator*. Such depictions usually refer to general AI or to super-intelligence (i.e., artificial intelligence that exceeds human cognitive capabilities). New York University professor Meredith Broussard, who researches the role of artificial intelligence in journalism, proposes that general AI can be thought of as the equivalent of putting a human brain inside machines, thus enabling them to learn or be taught the full range of human capabilities (e.g., from empathizing and falling in love, to building a spreadsheet or a computer program, to raising children or leading a nation state).[3] Meredith contends that we are very far from achieving this type of AI, which is mostly fantasy. Although some artificial intelligence researchers contend it may be possible to achieve general AI at some point, others contend it is not possible for us to ever achieve it. Figure 20.1 shows the different types of AI, what they are capable of, and the performance implications resulting from their capability.

Narrow AI (also known as weak AI or applied AI) is actually what is a commercial reality today. Narrow AI refers to programs or machines that can be taught or can learn to perform specific and well-defined tasks without explicitly being programmed to do so (e.g., analyze a data set of past winning and losing moves in chess, learn from them, and determine the optimal move to make in order to beat a chess

| Types of AI | Artificial Narrow Intelligence (ANI) | Artificial General Intelligence (AGI) | Artificial Super Intelligence (ASI) |
|---|---|---|---|
| **What is it capable of?** | Executive specific tasks without ability to self-expand functionality | Perform broad tasks, reason, and improve capabilities in a way that is comparable to humans. | Demonstrate intelligence beyond human capabilities. |
| **What are the implications?** | Outperform humans in specific repetitive functions like driving, medical diagnosis, games, etc. | Compete with humans on all fronts, such as earning university degrees, and convincing humans that it is human (Turing Test). | Outperform humans, helping to achieve societal objectives or threatening the human race. |

**Figure 20.1** *Types of AI, their capabilities, and implications for human beings*

grandmaster). Narrow AI can be thought of as AI that can perform a single activity or a narrow set of related activities that would typically require a human brain to be done. This is the type of AI in virtual assistants like Siri and Google Assistant, which can learn to decipher and respond to human speech in limited ways. It is also the type of AI used in purchase recommendation engines that suggest what other products you might like to buy based on your past behavior or that of others. Professor Broussard contends that narrow AI is really just beautiful mathematics, or computational statistics on steroids. That is, it is largely about machines being taught or learning to find patterns in data sets and then using these patterns as the basis for optimal recommendations, decisions, instructions, or actions. This type of AI is very different from the Hollywood stereotypes of machines like *The Terminator* with broad human-like intelligence and capabilities. While narrow AI is limited to specific tasks, the number and range of specific tasks it can perform are almost limitless. Additionally, different types of tasks can be combined and build on each other to expand what is possible, so that narrow AI is not so narrow. For example, a range of specific tasks can be integrated and sequenced in such a way as to manage a smart home, a smart workplace, a smart factory, or even a smart city.

## BOTS

Bots are an application of narrow AI. A bot is a software application or program that runs/performs an automated task (or a script). Bots usually operate over the internet and are hence sometimes referred to as internet robots or web robots. Bots can be taught or can learn to perform a vast array of processes, activities, and routines using business data sets and publicly available online data sets or search engines. For example, chatbots are programs that interact with people in written or voice format to answer their questions, provide them services, or entertain them. Applications like Siri and Google Assistant are examples of voice-based chatbots. The range of bots available on the market is extensive and includes friend bots, digital assistants (like Siri), meeting planners, bot writers, language tutoring bots, legal bots (e.g., querying and refuting parking tickets), Q&A bots (e.g., customer service), therapy bots, survey bots, sales bots, and insurance claim bots. Although they can't solve all customer service/support issues, bots enable 24/7 availability of a limited level of service/support.

# MACHINE LEARNING

Machine learning (ML) is a subset of artificial intelligence. As a subset, it is artificial intelligence that focuses on algorithms for equipping machines with the ability to analyze and automatically learn from data sets and then use this learning as the basis for recommendations, decisions, instructions, or actions. This is not so different from the way a human being analyzes or reflects on their past experiences, learns from them, and uses this learning to guide future actions. Typically, machine learning involves machines being fed large amounts of historical data, and the ML algorithms using this data as "training data" (e.g., data from which to identify cause-and-effect patterns and make inferences based on statistical methods and mathematical optimization). Bots and recommendation engines are an example of a machine learning application. It is machine learning algorithms in GPS maps that anticipate upcoming traffic and offer optimal routes to take, and it is machine learning that enables clinicians to be alerted by a wearable healthcare device that a patient is about to have a heart attack if there isn't an immediate intervention. In commercial uses, machine learning can also be referred to as predictive analytics.

# KNOWLEDGE GRAPHS, NEURAL NETWORKS, AND DEEP LEARNING

## KNOWLEDGE GRAPHS

A knowledge graph is a graphical representation of the links between data and their meaning.[4] The links can be between different types of data in a data set (e.g., text, images, video), between data subgroups (e.g., homes in a particular country as a subgroup of homes in a data set), and/or between different data sets (e.g., databases, data stores, data lakes, external knowledge graphs, and other information). The links and meaning are represented in a natural language-like format. The "graph" is usually in a network-like format, making it one of the most flexible formal data structures. This makes it easy to add on other data links or to modify a data link. Figure 20.2 shows part of a knowledge graph representing information about an aspect of the US election at a point in time. Knowledge graphs are data and thus require graph databases and related components (e.g., taxonomy and ontology editors, entity extractors, graph mappers, validation, visualization, and search tools).[5] While technical specialists maintain knowledge graphs, nontechnical specialists can contribute their domain expertise to improve the quality and meaningfulness of the connections. There is huge power in having meaningful links between information that are constantly evolving as new data sets are added or as patterns are found in existing data sets. Both human beings and artificial intelligence algorithms can query this data using natural language or using graph-computing techniques and algorithms, like shortest-path computations or network analysis. Knowledge graphs bring together disparate data silos to provide an integrated view of the available information for problem solving, link structured and unstructured data to illuminate relationships between them, and provide a structured way to

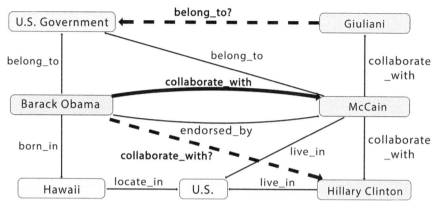

**Figure 20.2** *Part of a knowledge graph showing information about key figures in US politics at a point in time*[67]

capture and store the insights of nontechnical domain experts (e.g., with regard to the links and meaning of links between a company's different data and information). In doing so, they enable better and faster decisions to be made and be made at scale (i.e., able to be made quickly 24/7 by people and machines anywhere in the world).

## NEURAL NETWORKS AND DEEP LEARNING

Neural networks are a branch of machine learning. A neural network (also referred to as a neural net [NN] or artificial neural network [ANN]) is an algorithm or set of algorithms that mathematically model the relationship between inputs and their outputs to enable accurate prediction to occur. The "neural" part of the term is derived from the neural networks approach having been inspired by, and attempting to mimic, the biological functioning of brains (e.g., brain neural pathways comprising connected neurons that communicate with each other and with other cells via a process called "neuronal firing"). The "network" part of the term is derived from the network-like connections. Although mimicking biological brain functioning in problem solving was the original inspiration, neural networks have deviated away from this somewhat and moved more toward mathematical modeling. Still, artificial neural networks are made up of neurons as the basic computational unit that receives data, processes it, and sends signals

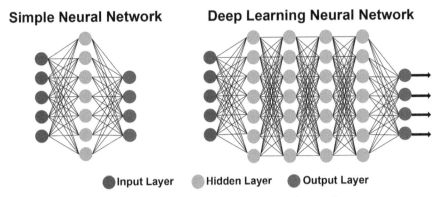

*Figure 20.3* *A simple neural network vs a deep learning neural network*

to other neurons connected to it within the neural network structure. In this way, they still emulate a simplified form of brain functioning. Nevertheless, neural networks are still able to automatically learn from data and adapt signals and predictions to changing inputs. Business applications of neural networks are extensive and include evaluating loan applications (in banking), customer behavior modeling, facial recognition (in security and law enforcement), and medical image/scan analysis (in healthcare). Extending neural networks, deep learning (also referred to as deep structured learning, hierarchical learning, deep neural learning, or deep neural networks) is a machine learning method that uses multi-layer neural networks to solve complex problems. Figure 20.3 contrasts a simple neural network with a simple deep learning neural network.

# NATURAL LANGUAGE PROCESSING, SPEECH RECOGNITION, AND COMPUTER VISION

## NATURAL LANGUAGE PROCESSING AND SPEECH RECOGNITION

Natural language processing (NLP), speech recognition, and computer vision are important subfields of artificial intelligence. NLP is concerned with how to get machines to understand and process natural human language (e.g., English, Chinese, Spanish). Advances in natural language processing are enabling machines to understand instructions from us and to converse with us in our natural language. Natural language processing applications usually focus on enabling machines to understand and process speech and text (i.e., spoken language and written language). Applications of NLP include Google Assistant and Siri. Speech recognition is concerned with finding the best way to get machines to understand speech and translate it into machine readable format. Applications of speech recognition include call routing (e.g., when you call a bank or a phone company and are directed to sales service based on you saying you want a new product), voice dialing (e.g., "call Jonathan"), and voice search (e.g., "OK, Siri, what is the weather tomorrow"?). Speech recognition and NLP are often used together in applications like Google Assistant and Siri. For example, speech recognition may hear what is being said and convert it to text, but then NLP is needed for machines to understand what the text actually means or what commands the person is actually issuing.

## COMPUTER VISION

Finally, computer vision (and its subset, machine vision) are concerned with enabling machines to "see" through capturing, analyzing, and understanding captured images and video. Through image and video analysis, computer vision algorithms can detect faces of specific people or groups of people, shapes of objects, writing, movement, poses, motion, emotion, changes in objects, and environments. Combined with additional information that a whole range of different sensors can detect, it is not hard to imagine how computer vision and machine vision can be very powerful. For example, they can provide machines such as robots and drones with vastly expanded possibilities (e.g., to fly through a dense and obstacle-filled rain forest at high speed, to recognize a suspect walking in a crowd and immediately call the police, to give robots human-like movement and body control). Figure 22.3, in Chapter 22, shows how computer vision can enable self-driving cars to "see" better than humans (e.g., simultaneous 360-degree sight, undistractable, better multi-tasking, faster processing/computation).[8]

# EXPERT SYSTEMS

Expert systems were one of the early successful applications of AI. Essentially, they are systems that emulate the decision-making ability of human experts to solve complex problems. Expert systems have built-in "if this-then-that" rules that enable them to make decisions based on a large number of inputs.[9] Expert systems are usually made up of an inference engine and a knowledge base. The inference engine applies the rules to the knowledge base (the knowledge base represents both the facts and the rules). Expert systems are used in healthcare for medical diagnosis (e.g., early diagnosis of cancer),[10] in banking to assess mortgage applications, and in engineering to diagnose the condition of infrastructure (e.g., infrastructure such as water dams).

# IMPLICATIONS FOR LEADERS, MANAGERS, AND SUPPORTING PROFESSIONALS

Although AI has been around for a long time, it has gone through phases where it has been overhyped and subsequently under-delivered. In addition, it has often received negative media attention and warnings regarding its associated risks to society (e.g., potential loss of jobs, potential unintended consequences such as machines taking unethical actions or their intelligence outpacing the ability of humans to control them).[11] Because of background issues such as this, proposed AI ideas, projects, or strategies in organizations are sometimes met with disregard, skepticism, trivialization, passive-aggressiveness, or even hostility. Other AI-related issues or risks include data management issues (e.g., ingesting, sorting, linking, and properly using the vast amounts of data from sensors, devices, machines, people, media, and digital platforms; not managing this data properly limits the reliability of AI algorithms), technology and process issues (e.g., technical issues or process breakdowns resulting in AI malfunction such as oversights or incorrect decisions), privacy and security issues (e.g., hackers and fraudsters breaching stored data or data in transit resulting in violations in customer privacy and related legal issues), misguided AI models (e.g., incomplete or biased AI models making blatantly sexist or racist decisions), and interaction issues (e.g., empathy and social skill limitations of AI can ruin customer experience and brand credibility).[12]

Most organizations have large volumes of data available on existing and prospective customers, current and past employees, current and past suppliers, current and past products/services, and current and past events. In the past, human and financial resources limited the ability to leverage this information as a powerful competitive weapon. Artificial intelligence technologies remove both the human and financial constraints. They provide powerful intelligence, automation, availability, scalability, efficiency, and effectiveness across digital and physical service channels. In the digital era, it is the critical role of leaders, managers, and supporting professionals to understand these digital technologies and their potential and to be able to leverage them to redesign their organizations for game changing breakthroughs in efficiency, differentiation, adaptability, and agility.

# GOOGLE AND REFLECT

Algorithm, heuristic programming, inductive reasoning, reinforcement learning, backpropagation, convolutional neural network (CNN), forward chaining, generative adversarial networks (GAN), unsupervised machine learning, Turing test,[13] bots/chatbots, cluster, cognitive science, image recognition, semantic analysis, supervised learning,[14] autonomous artificial intelligence, black box, transfer learning,[15] bias, semi-supervised learning, autonomic computing, classification algorithm, cognitive computing, game AI, genetic algorithm, logic programming, machine intelligence, recurrent neural network (RNN), swarm behavior,[16] AlphaGo, neuromorphic computing, spiking neural networks (SNN)

# EXAMPLE TOOLS AND VENDORS

Apple HomePod, Apple FaceID, Apple Siri, IBM Project Debater, Microsoft Cortana, Google Assistant, Amazon Alexa, Baidu Deep Voice, Facebook DeepFace, Alibaba City Brain, Google DeepMind, Waymo self-driving technology, Google Duplex, Amazon Go, Microsoft AIaaS, MATLAB, IBM Watson Machine Learning, IBM Watson Studio, Google Cloud AI Platform, Microsoft Azure Machine Learning Studio, Salesforce Einstein, Pega Platform, Amazon SageMaker, Microsoft Azure Machine Learning, TensorFlow, Box Skills, DataRobot, Deep Cognition, Anaconda Enterprise, Oracle Data Science Cloud Service, Azure Batch AI, IBM Watson Machine Learning Accelerator, Infosys Nia, H2O Driverless AI, Infor Coleman, Microsoft Cognitive Toolkit (CNTK), NVIDIA AI Platform for Developers, Apple Core ML 3, Apple Create ML, Apple A-series chips, Apple Neural Engine, Intel's OpenVINO Toolkit, CyberInt, HEALTH[at]SCALE Technologies, Algolux, Brodmann17, Dynamic Yield, SoundHound, AntWorks, Zimperium, Sensory TrulySecure, Awake Security, Security Knowledge Graph, Stardog enterprise knowledge graph platform, Franz Semantic Graph Database technology, Pilot.ai, Shazura, Nyris, 20 Billion Neurons, EVK, SpiNNaker, Intel Loihi

# DISCUSSION QUESTIONS

1 What is the difference between artificial intelligence, machine learning, and deep learning?
2 What is the difference between general AI and narrow AI?
3 Are there more applications of general AI or of narrow AI in general?
4 What is the difference between an artificial neural network and a deep neural network?
5 What is the difference between an AI-enabled company and a true AI company?
6 What are the top seven AI use cases in your industry?
7 What is the difference between a bot, a chatbot, and a robot?
8 What types of things can you do with a neural network that you can't do with a knowledge graph?

9 What is the difference between computer vision and machine vision?

10 What is an example of an expert system use case in your industry?

11 Rank the top six biggest risks and issues in relation to using artificial intelligence.

12 What organization capabilities do organizations need in order to become true AI companies?

# NOTES

1 Ng, A., & Chui, M. (2018). *How artificial intelligence and data add value to businesses.* McKinsey & Company. Retrieved January 13, 2020, from www.mckinsey.com/featured-insights/artificial-intelligence/ how-artificial-intelligence-and-data-add-value-to-businesses

2 Ng, A., & Chui, M. (2018). *How artificial intelligence and data add value to businesses.* McKinsey & Company. Retrieved January 13, 2020, from www.mckinsey.com/featured-insights/artificial-intelligence/ how-artificial-intelligence-and-data-add-value-to-businesses

3 Broussard, M., Lowe, L. (2019) Author discussion on technology series: Artificial unintelligence. *C-SPAN.* Retrieved September 20, 2020, from C-SPAN.org website: www.c-span.org/video/?457638-2/ artificial-unintelligence

4 Stichbury, J. (2017). WTF is a knowledge graph? *Hackernoon. com.* Retrieved January 9, 2020, from https://hackernoon.com/ wtf-is-a-knowledge-graph-a16603a1a25f

5 Semantic Web Company. (2020). What is a knowledge graph – Transforming data into knowledge. *PoolParty Semantic Suite.* Retrieved January 9, 2020, from www.poolparty.biz/what-is-a-knowledge-graph

6 Anadiotis, G. (2019, March 18). Salesforce research: Knowledge graphs and machine learning to power einstein. Retrieved June 21, 2020, from ZDNet website: www.zdnet.com/article/salesforce-research-knowledge-graphs-and-machine-learning-to-power-einstein/

7 Lin, Y., Liu, Z., Luan, H., Sun, M., Rao, S., & Liu, S. (2015). Modeling relation paths for representation learning of knowledge bases 1506:00379. arXiv preprint arXiv. https://arxiv.org/abs/1506.00379

8 Tara, R. (2018). Technology vs. Humans. Engineers seek answers in uber's fatal self driving car accident. Retrieved June 21, 2020, from Engineering. com website: www.engineering.com/Hardware/ArticleID/16756/

Technology-vs-Humans-Engineers-Seek-Answers-in-Ubers-Fatal-Self-Driving-Car-Accident.aspx; Burke, K. (2019). How does a self-driving car see? *Nvidia*. Retrieved June 22, 2020, from https://blogs.nvidia.com/blog/2019/04/15/how-does-a-self-driving-car-see

9 Leonard-Barton, D., & Sviokla, J. (1988). Putting Expert systems to work. *Harvard Business Review*. Retrieved January 12, 2020, from https://hbr.org/1988/03/putting-expert-systems-to-work

10 Başçiftçi, F., & Avuçlu, E. (2018). An expert system design to diagnose cancer by using a new method reduced rule base. *Computer Methods and Programs in Biomedicine*, 157, 113–120.

11 Clifford, C. (2018). Elon Musk: "Mark my words – A.I. is far more dangerous than nukes." *CNBC*. Retrieved January 8, 2020, from www.cnbc.com/2018/03/13/elon-musk-at-sxsw-a-i-is-more-dangerous-than-nuclear-weapons.html; Marr, B. (2018). Is artificial intelligence dangerous? 6 AI risks everyone should know about. *Forbes.com*. Retrieved January 8, 2020, from www.forbes.com/sites/bernardmarr/2018/11/19/is-artificial-intelligence-dangerous-6-ai-risks-everyone-should-know-about/#3c5d4a942404

12 Cheatham, B., Javanmardian, K., & Samandari, H. (2020). *Confronting the risks of artificial intelligence*. McKinsey & Company. Retrieved January 13, 2020, from www.mckinsey.com/business-functions/mckinsey-analytics/our-insights/confronting-the-risks-of-artificial-intelligence

13 Rosso, C. (2018). Defining artificial intelligence: A glossary of key AI Terms. *Psychology Today*. Retrieved January 13, 2020, from www.psychologytoday.com/au/blog/the-future-brain/201810/defining-artificial-intelligence-glossary-key-ai-terms

14 Kniahynyckyj, R. Artificial intelligence: Terms marketers need to know. *Business.twitter.com*. Retrieved January 13, 2020, from https://business.twitter.com/en/blog/artificial-intelligence-terms-marketers-need-to-know.html

15 Greene, T. (2017). A glossary of basic artificial intelligence terms and concepts. *The Next Web*. Retrieved January 13, 2020, from https://thenextweb.com/artificial-intelligence/2017/09/10/glossary-basic-artificial-intelligence-terms-concepts/

16 Davis, S. (2017). Artificial intelligence terms you need to know. *DZone AI. dzone.com*. Retrieved January 13, 2020, from https://dzone.com/articles/ai-glossary

# CHAPTER 21

# Blockchain and Other Distributed Ledger Technologies Primer

DOI: 10.4324/9781003254614-26

# INTRODUCTION

Blockchain and other distributed ledger technologies offer new tamper-proof ways to verify identity and ownership, make near-instant payments without the need for the involvement of third parties, store value (e.g., through cryptocurrency), facilitate peer-to-peer fundraising and lending (e.g., ICOs and STOs), automate the execution of contractual agreements and related workflows (e.g., via smart contracts), improve auditability, distribute data storage, and do all of this more securely.[1] The transformative impact of blockchain technologies has been equated to the advent of the internet. As with early applications of the internet, the applications of blockchain technologies are just in their infancy and have much more potential for growth in breadth and impact on business and society. The business value of these expanding blockchain applications includes expanded opportunities for product innovation (companies offering new or enhanced products and services enabled by use of blockchain technologies), business model innovation (finding more efficient, effective, and profitable ways to serve existing and/or new customers), operational efficiency (automating workflows, removing third parties and related costs, reducing downtime and errors), customer access (being able to remotely serve billions of customers in developing economies who previously couldn't be served due to lack of bank accounts identity verification mechanisms and high third-party costs), risk mitigation (enhanced security, privacy, and auditability from blockchain's sophisticated cryptography, distributed consensus, immutability, and ability to shard data so it does not exist in complete form on any one node), and social change (enhanced transparency may lead to changes in customer behaviors that businesses can capitalize on or may need to adapt to).[2] It is the responsibility of leaders, managers, and supporting professionals to understand the business value and use cases of blockchain technology, safely explore and experiment with its adoption at their organizations, and lead the investment and implementation of tested and proven blockchain adoption decisions. Abdicating this responsibility may result in their organizations being outdone by competitors who might have first mover advantage or being disrupted by a technology that seemed far-fetched or not relevant to them (e.g., in the same way Borders got disrupted by the internet and internet companies).

---

**LEARNING OBJECTIVES**

- Develop knowledge of definitions and concepts related to blockchain and other distributed ledger technologies
- Understand how these technologies and their related applications/practices/tools/methods/techniques can impact the efficiency, differentiation, adaptability, and agility of an organization
- Understand the roles leaders, managers, and supporting professionals can play in maximizing the leveraging of these technologies and their related applications/practices/tools/methods/techniques
- Analyze and evaluate the implications of these technologies and their related applications/practices/tools/methods/techniques, as well as related the related leadership/management/supporting professional roles in their optimal use, for organizations' digital transformation strategy and digital business strategy
- Apply knowledge and understanding of these technologies and their related applications/practices/tools/methods/techniques to participate in, support, or lead workstreams or initiatives related to the leveraging of these technologies to enhance organization digital transformation and digital business strategy

---

# DISTRIBUTED LEDGER TECHNOLOGY (DLT)

In contrast to an accounting ledger (such as a general ledger, purchase ledger, or sales ledger), a digital ledger is a digital file, collection of files or a database (a database is an organized collection of data or files).

In contrast to a centralized database (a database that exists in a fixed location, like a particular computer or a cloud location), a distributed ledger (also referred to as a shared ledger or distributed ledger technology [DLT]) is a database that exists in several locations and among several participants (e.g., sites, institutions, geographies, computers, devices).[3] The term distributed (also referred to as decentralized) refers to this existence across several locations. Being distributed, any additions or updates to the ledger (the collection of files or the database) are synchronized or copied to all participants' version of the ledger almost instantly (in seconds or minutes). But before any additions or updates can occur, they have to be agreed on and accepted by other participants (i.e., authorized, validated, and accepted). The process of agreeing is referred to as distributed ledger consensus or a consensus mechanism. It is facilitated by sophisticated algorithms. Because of this consensus mechanism, no centralized agent (e.g., a bank, a government, a corporation, a person) is needed to authorize, validate, and accept proposed updates.[4] A peer-to-peer network is required in order for the distributed ledger to exist in several locations and among several participants; this peer-to-peer network could be as simple as two computers being connected via USB or as complex as several computers being connected by a network infrastructure. Distributed ledgers are immutable, meaning that once ledger records are created, they cannot be deleted or altered – instead, other records are added to correct errors, omissions, or improvements (e.g., if the record was a transaction where a $100 purchase was made, but it was meant to be $80, then a $20 refund transaction is added rather than altering the original transaction). All records or files in a distributed ledger are date/time stamped and have a unique cryptographic signature. This provides a verifiable and auditable history of record creation and any subsequent updates.

Brought together, all these features of distributed ledgers (i.e., existing in several locations via a peer-to-peer network, consensus mechanism algorithms to facilitate updates, record immutability, date/time stamping, and cryptographic signature) offer new levels of efficiency (e.g., minimizing or eliminating the need for centralized monitoring, authorization, and updating activities and related infrastructure) and security (e.g., due to the decentralized nature, immutability, cryptographic signatures, and auditability).[5] For example, regarding security, distributed ledgers ensure that the record of a financial transaction is near impossible to fake, create without permission, delete, modify, or hide. Not only would this be near impossible to achieve on every computer (or node) on the peer-to-peer network, but an incriminating auditable trail would likely catch up with the instigator.

# BLOCKCHAIN
## WHAT IT IS, AND HOW IT WORKS

Blockchain is one type of distributed ledger that consists of blocks of data linked or "chained" together using high-end cryptography (cryptography is concerned with how to best convert information into unintelligible codes to prevent it being decoded and accessed by unauthorized people or entities).[6] Each block in a blockchain stores information or data (e.g., transaction information like date, purchaser, seller, or payment amount). Each block also has a code called a "hash" that is unique to the information stored in that block. Figure 21.1 shows the elements of a block.

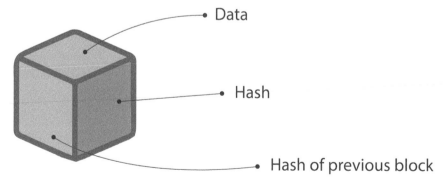

**Figure 21.1** *Each blockchain block contains some data, the hash of the block, and the hash of the previous block*

If the information stored in a block is modified in any way, the block's hash also changes to a different code that is unique to the modified or changed information. In addition to the information or data stored in it, a block also contains a time stamp of when that information was created or edited. Each block also stores the hash (or unique code) of its previous block. Before a new block can be added to the blockchain, it must correctly refer to the hash of the previous block; this cannot happen if the previous block has been modified, because its hash is different from what it should be. Storing the hash of its preceding block is how a block is linked or "chained" to preceding blocks. This link or chain between blocks is what makes blockchain so secure. Besides making tampering or modification of blocks nearly impossible (e.g., each must refer to the correct previous hash, which is copied across many nodes in the peer-to-peer network), blockchain provides a perfect audit trail or log of every change that occurred on the blockchain. Figure 21.2 shows a chain of blocks within a blockchain, including the genesis block.

In addition to its linked block structure, blockchain functions with all the features of distributed ledgers (since it is a type of distributed ledger). That is, it operates over a peer-to-peer network, uses consensus mechanism algorithms to facilitate blockchain updates, uses date/time stamping and cryptographic signatures, and has immutable records). Blockchain technology platforms enable people to transact without the

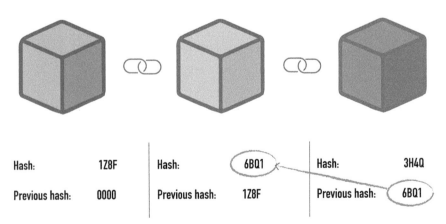

| Hash: | 1Z8F | Hash: | 6BQ1 | Hash: | 3H4Q |
| Previous hash: | 0000 | Previous hash: | 1Z8F | Previous hash: | 6BQ1 |

**Figure 21.2** *A chain of blocks, with each block other than the genesis block having the hash of the previous block*

need for a central third party to assess and approve the authorization, validity, or security of the transaction (no need to pay, wait for, or trust the third party, no need to disclose personal information to a third party or be exposed to third-party risks), meaning cheap, instant, secure, anonymous, and risk minimized transactions.

## COMMON BLOCKCHAIN TERMINOLOGY

In addition to the distributed ledger and blockchain terminology discussed earlier, it is often difficult to discuss or read about blockchain without one or more of the following terminologies coming up.

## APPEND-ONLY DATA STRUCTURE

This refers to the fact that you can only add new blocks to the blockchain, which then get chained to previous blocks; you can't alter or delete blocks once they've been added. This is one of the reasons blockchain is considered tamper proof and has an auditable history of record creation.

## PERMISSIONLESS VS PERMISSIONED BLOCKCHAIN

A permissionless blockchain is one where anyone can join the network and perform certain actions on the network without requiring permission from anyone else on the network. In contrast, a permissioned network is one in which the network owner decides who can join a network and who can verify blocks. The consensus can be the same, or it can be tailored to the owner's preferences (e.g., it could be authority or credibility based).

## MINING VS MINERS

Mining is the process of verifying transactions to enable new blocks to be added to the blockchain network. Miners are blockchain nodes or participants that use their computers/computing power to perform this process. The process usually involves participants using mining programs for performing complex mathematical calculations to verify transactions and enable the creation of new blocks. In return, miners are usually paid a reward (e.g., on the Bitcoin blockchain, the reward is an amount of Bitcoin). Miners may compete to be the first to perform the mathematical calculations and verify the transaction, as only the first person to verify is paid the reward. It can cost miners money (e.g., cost of computing power or loss of deposit money they may pay to verify transactions in accordance with the rules). Some miners build a massive infrastructure (e.g., buildings or computing hardware and software) and hire large numbers of people to mine or verify blockchain transactions as a key source of income.

## PROOF OF WORK

This is a widely used type of consensus algorithm for verifying transactions and adding new blocks to the blockchain. It involves miners competing with each other to be the first to solve the mathematical calculations required to verify transactions. Once the first miner solves the mathematical puzzle, it is broadcast to the network so other miners can confirm the solution is correct and so the block can be added to the blockchain. The first miner then receives a reward for being first to solve the mathematical puzzle and thus enable appending of the new block.

## PUBLIC KEY VS PRIVATE KEY

To read or add data to the blockchain, you need a public key and a private key. A public key is like the address or location where the information is stored, and everyone knows its address. But although they may know where it is stored, it is encrypted (or locked) and can only be unlocked or decrypted with a private (or personal) key that authorizes reading or updating of the information stored in that location. A private key is what prevents other people from reading or updating your information and thus keeping it secure.

## GENESIS BLOCK

Also referred to as block zero, a genesis block is the first block created on a blockchain.

## SMART CONTRACT

Smart contracts are legal contracts that self-execute on the blockchain once the terms and conditions of the contract have been satisfied. This is possible because the contract details (e.g., parties, terms, and conditions) have already been agreed to and converted into self-executing code (e.g., if prospective purchasers meet the seller's criteria for sale of land plus the government's criteria for purchase of land and the seller pays the specified amount, then approve the transaction to title ownership over the land to the purchaser). This self-executing code sits on the blockchain, ready to be run or executed on the blockchain once triggered (by the satisfaction of the contract terms and condition). Once on the blockchain, a smart contract cannot be changed; it automatically happens without a third party once the triggering criteria are met. Being on the blockchain, the transaction can occur anonymously; it can occur without corruption; and it can occur without one or more of the parties coming back to muddy the meaning or interpretation of the contract terms.

# TYPES OF BLOCKCHAINS

There are four common types of blockchains, the types being differentiated by who can join, what type of access they can have, and how consensus is achieved. A brief summary of each is provided below.

## PUBLIC BLOCKCHAINS

A public blockchain is a permissionless blockchain. It is public in that anyone can join this blockchain network with read and write permission; they do not need authorization from anyone else on the network. This is the main type of blockchain that has been discussed so far, with features and advantages such as openness (anyone can join and view/add to it), distributed consensus, immutability (once a block is added, it can't be deleted or altered), scalability (existing on a large and ever-expanding network of nodes), and transparency. Disadvantages of public blockchains include difficulty changing the rules governing them and the risk that the blockchain can be compromised if the rules are not strictly enforced.

## PRIVATE BLOCKCHAINS

A private blockchain is a permissioned blockchain, which is owned by an entity (e.g., a person, an organization, or other group). That entity or its delegate decides who can access the blockchain, what type of access they can have (e.g., read, write, or audit), and how consensus will be achieved (e.g., who can mine and what rules apply). Private blockchains bring together some of the benefits of central control and some of the benefits of distributed ledgers, usually with aims such as reduced transaction cost, transaction efficiency, improved security, improved audit ability, and the flexibility to change blockchain read, write, and audit rules. An example of a private or permissioned blockchain includes Hyperledger (a blockchain funded to enable industry collaboration for advancing blockchain-based distributed ledgers).

## CONSORTIUM OR FEDERATED BLOCKCHAINS

This type of blockchain is like a private blockchain, but instead of a single individual or company making all the decisions, a group of companies or their representative individuals make decisions collectively for the benefit of the whole blockchain network (e.g., decisions about who can access the blockchain, who can read/write to it, and what operating rules apply). Benefits of consortium or federated blockchains include pooling together of resources to establish and operate the blockchain network, better quality decisions from broader expertise of consortium members and representatives, and better security from curation of blockchain participants and their access rights. Examples of consortium blockchains include the R3 blockchain consortium (established as an invitation-only blockchain consortium for major banks like JP Morgan and Santander) and Energy Web Foundation (EWF; an enterprise-grade blockchain for organizations in the energy industry including Mercados Electricos, FlexiDAO, Scytale Horizon, and Wirepas).

## HYBRID BLOCKCHAINS

As their name indicates, hybrid blockchains aim to leverage the benefits of both public and private blockchains. Aspects of the network can be made private, so transactions with some types of stakeholders or things are permissioned, whereas other aspects of the network are public or open to anyone. For example, Facebook's proposed cryptocurrency Libra may need a hybrid blockchain composed of an open consumer-facing network and a private blockchain network for banks backing the currency.

# BLOCKCHAIN APPLICATIONS AND USE CASES

Although many blockchain and other distributed ledger technology applications are still in their early stages, the applications are broadening rapidly and more and more applications are maturing.[7] For example, applications of blockchain technologies to cryptocurrency, smart contracts, bank settlement systems, and data storage are creating real customer and business value today.[8]

## CRYPTOCURRENCY

Cryptocurrency is a type of digital currency or electronic money. Although it only exists in digital form, it can be converted into physical or government-issued currency via cryptocurrency exchanges (e.g., at the time of writing this paragraph, the cryptocurrencies Bitcoin and Ethereum were trading at \$8,671 and \$166, respectively). There are thousands of cryptocurrencies in existence, and with almost any organization or individual able to create their own currency, this number is likely to keep growing. Each cryptocurrency has unique features and benefits that influence its value, which is not too different from the unique features and benefits of different nations' currencies influencing their values. Examples of these features and benefits include supply limitations (e.g., there was a limited number of Bitcoins created, and this cannot be increased), transaction acceptability (e.g., Bitcoin has been the most widely accepted cryptocurrency for ordinary transactions like buying a home or buying food), public interest (e.g., part of the reason behind Bitcoin's stellar price is that it is the most well-known and talked-about cryptocurrency), stability (e.g., the value of Bitcoin is generally seen as being more stable than lesser-known cryptocurrencies), and risk (e.g., during the boom and bust cycles of cryptocurrencies, some rose to price levels thousands of times their initial purchase price, only for prices to subsequently fall way below the initial purchase price and remain there; this was especially the case for lesser-known cryptocurrencies). Typically, anyone can purchase cryptocurrencies on a cryptocurrency exchange using real money, and they can exchange one cryptocurrency owned for another at the prevailing exchange rate. Although some fees are involved, these are minuscule compared to ordinary currency exchange rates, and transaction fees are usually negligible.

The benefits of cryptocurrencies over government-issued currencies include the ability to transact directly without third parties and third-party fees (e.g., banks, brokers, agents, legal representatives), the clear and permanent audit trail of each transaction, confidentiality (nobody needs to know who you are, where you come from, who you bank with, where you live, where you work, what your credit card number is, etc.), reduced privacy risks (if personal information isn't collected, it can't be accidentally accessed), faster transactions (a cryptocurrency transaction can happen almost instantly, while a similar bank transaction can take days), stronger security (the risk of someone discovering and using your private key is very low), and the ability to transact with people who previously couldn't be reached (e.g., people in some developing countries who previously had no access to a bank account).

Disadvantages of cryptocurrency include complexity (although it is improving, a high level of technical expertise is still needed to purchase and use cryptocurrency), risk of loss (cryptocurrency exchanges have been breached resulting in cryptocurrency losses, and scammers have posed as cryptocurrency platform agents to steal money intended to purchase cryptocurrencies), price volatility (in 1 year the Bitcoin price rose to $22,000 and then crashed to $6,000 – and it is one of the less volatile cryptocurrencies), lack of regulation (there is as yet very little regulation of cryptocurrencies relative to government currencies). This often results in unwitting users being scammed: criminal enterprises have used cryptocurrency as a money laundering and criminal activity payment vehicle; people have lost large amounts of money speculating on future cryptocurrency price growth; and people have bought cryptocurrencies that are worthless.

Some organizations have had great success using cryptocurrency for fundraising purposes. Such organizations have used initial coin offerings (ICOs) as fundraising mechanisms, in which they create and sell their own coins or tokens in much the same way that another company may sell its shares on a stock exchange to investors. For example, Block.one raised $4 billion via its 2018 ICO despite its blockchain development product not being fully launched and investors not being clear on exactly how the funds would be spent.[9] Government interventions in ICOs have reduced the number and size of ICOs, but they remain viable fundraising vehicles that can result in higher fundraising success (e.g., speed, amount, and cost of fundraising) than traditional fundraising channels (e.g., banks, professional investors, stock exchange listings). ICOs are increasingly being replaced by STOs (security token offerings), which are essentially the same thing but, thanks to government intervention, offer better protection against fraud, are based on real registered assets, comply with consumer financial safeguard laws, and are incorporated into the established securities market.

## SMART CONTRACTS

Smart contracts were defined earlier as contracts whose terms and conditions exist on the blockchain as self-executing algorithms.[10] Smart contracts have been applied to numerous types of contracts in different industries.[11] In trade finance, smart contracts can be used to automate approval workflows and clearing calculations; in healthcare, smart contracts can be used to authorize access to patient records; in real estate, smart contracts can be used to automate property leasing and purchase agreements as related workflows (e.g., paying bond, holding bond, releasing bond, cooling off, title search, settlement, rent payment reconciliation);[12] in insurance, smart contracts can be used to automate claims processing; in government, smart contracts can be used to record election votes and announce the winner in a tamper-proof way; and obviously smart contracts can be used in peer-to-peer transactions.[13]

## BANKING

Banks are using or exploring using blockchain for clearing and settlement activities (e.g., the Australian stock exchange is exploring shifting its post-trade clearing and settlement onto a blockchain system to improve the efficiency and effectiveness of these activities), for payments (creating their own cryptocurrencies or utility tokens, such as UBS' utility settlement coin for financial markets, which works like other cryptocurrencies but is convertible into cash on deposit at central banks), to facilitate trade finance processes and authorization documents (e.g., bill of lading or letter of credit), to facilitate identity verification, and to facilitate syndicated loans.[14] Figure 21.3 shows the traditional funds transfer process versus a blockchain-based one (adapted from Kean Wu, Manlu Liu, and Jennifer Xu in 2019 issue of *Current Issues in Auditing*).

## DATA STORAGE

The application of blockchain technology to data storage is anticipated to disrupt cloud data storage.[16] Proponents of this application of blockchain technology (e.g., proponents such as FileStorm, Sia, Storj, and Maidsafe)

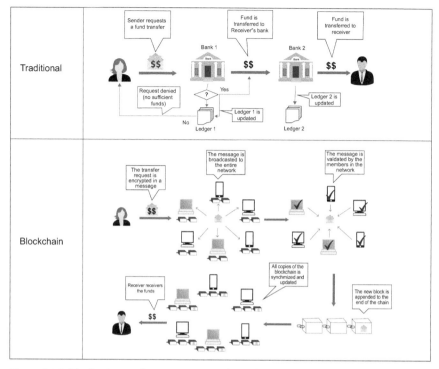

**Figure 21.3** *The funds transfer process in a traditional digital ledger vs in a blockchain network*[15]

propose that decentralized data storage (distributing data files across a large peer-to-peer node network) is much more secure, makes it harder to lose data, and will be cheaper than the current centralized cloud infrastructure approach.[17] In addition, blockchain-based data files can be split up and spread piecemeal across nodes all over the world, thus restricting who can see the full integrated file.[18]

## OTHER APPLICATIONS

Other blockchain applications include verification of the authenticity of goods through blockchain-enabled supply chains, notarization to ensure proof of existence, validity of intellectual property origins, and more. Blockchain use cases are rapidly expanding in diversity and realization of the business benefits they promise.[19]

# IMPLICATIONS FOR LEADERS, MANAGERS, AND SUPPORTING PROFESSIONALS

Early adopters of blockchain technology will have significant advantages for locking in key partnerships (consider Hilton and its partnership with IBM or the way Microsoft locked in key distributors in the PC business), locking in valuable customer segments (consider how Microsoft locked in enterprise customers or how Bitcoin is better known/trusted and has a much higher market capitalization than other cryptocurrencies), setting industry case standards, and enjoying superior profits. But such firms have to take care not to overinvest or attempt to scale too early (before customers are ready or before the technology is ready for certain types of use cases).[20] Other blockchain issues include lack of regulation (unsuspecting customers may fall for scammer platforms pretending to be the real platform or people pretending to be representatives of your organization), significant power consumption and related environmental implications (the sophisticated blockchain calculations require significant power), complexity (the benefits of blockchain products and services can be obscured by complex processes required to identify users and for users to use them), slow and cumbersome nature (e.g., due to their complexity and sophisticated calculations), and resistance from entrenched entities (wide scale adoption of blockchain will disrupt the existing order in much the same way that the internet disrupted business). As a result, entrenched entities may be incentivized to discredit or fight blockchain adoption. Early adopters must tread with care, as the aforementioned issues result in risks that could derail their efforts or bring harm to their organizations.

# GOOGLE AND REFLECT

Blockchain node, blockchain address, P2P network, blockchain block, block explorer, block height, chain linking, hash, hashing, hash rate, satoshi, altcoin, blockchain wallet, hot wallet, cold wallet, blockchain forking, hard fork, soft fork, dApp, nonce, proof-of-stake, proof-of-authority, lightning network, stale block, orphan block, uncle block, multi-signature, blockchain oracle, whitepaper, Byzantine fault-tolerance, cryptographic hash function (CHF), Merkle tree, cryptography, double spending problem, hashcash, computational trust, public key cryptography, Ripple currency (XRP), Litecoin currency, Libra currency, Monero currency, cryptocurrency exchange, blockchain sharding

## EXAMPLE TOOLS AND VENDORS

IBM Blockchain, Ripple, Etherium, Hyperledger Fabric, Microsoft Azure Blockchain, Stellar, Quorum, Blockstream, NEO, Oracle Blockchain Cloud Service, Hyperledger Iroha, MultiChain, Tendermint, ConsenSys,[21] PixelPlex, Accubits, SoluLab, PATRON, Celsius Network, Hyperledger Sawtooth, R3 Corda, Menlo One, Gameflip, DACC, Goldilock, FCoin[22]

## DISCUSSION QUESTIONS

1 What is the difference between blockchain and a distributed ledger?
2 What are three different metaphors you could use to explain to your grandmother how blockchain works?
3 Is blockchain trustworthy? Why?
4 What is the difference between blockchain, Bitcoin, Ethereum, and Ripple (XRP)?
5 What is the difference between a public key and a private key?
6 What are the four main components of a blockchain ecosystem?
7 What are the different types of blockchain, and what is the value of each?
8 Identify and explain the six top features or properties of blockchains.
9 What is a blockchain block, and how is it created?
10 Can blockchain blocks be modified?
11 What type of data can be stored in a blockchain?

12 What is the double spending problem, and how does blockchain overcome it?

13 What is a consensus algorithm?

14 Identify and explain ten different types of consensus algorithm.

15 What are the top five platforms for developing blockchain applications?

16 How is a smart contract different from a normal contract?

17 How is a dApp different from a normal app?

18 Explain how cryptocurrency mining works.

19 What problems does blockchain sharding solve?

20 What are the top five blockchain applications or types of use cases?

21 What organizations in your industry are successfully leveraging blockchain technology, and how are they using it?

22 What is the business value of blockchain? What six areas of business value have been identified in this chapter?

23 Of all the blockchain use cases, which offers the biggest opportunity for cost reduction in your industry?

24 Of all the blockchain use cases, which offers the best opportunity for business model innovation in your industry?

25 Of all the blockchain use cases, which offers the best opportunity for product innovation in your industry?

26 Of all the blockchain use cases, which offers the best opportunity for safeguarding the security and privacy of customer data in your industry?

27 Of all the blockchain use cases, which offers the best opportunity to enhance the adaptability and agility of organizations in your industry?

# NOTES

1 Finley, K., & Barber, G. (2019). Blockchain: The complete guide. *Wired*. Retrieved January 22, 2020, from www.wired.com/story/guide-blockchain/; Mearian, L. (2020). What is blockchain? The complete guide. *Computerworld*. Retrieved January 22, 2020, from www.computerworld.com/article/3191077/ what-is-blockchain-the-complete-guide.html?page=2

2 Bender, J. P., Burchardi, K., & Shepherd, N. (2019). Capturing the value of blockchain. *Bcg.com*. Retrieved January 22, 2020, from www.bcg.com/en-au/publications/2019/capturing-blockchain-value.aspx; Bender, J. P., Burchardi, K., & Shepherd, N. (2019). Capturing the value of blockchain. *Bcg.com*. Retrieved January 22, 2020, from www.bcg.com/en-au/publications/2019/capturing-blockchain-value.aspx; Panetta, K. (2019). The CIO's guide to blockchain. *Gartner.com*. Retrieved January 22, 2020, from www.gartner.com/smarterwithgartner/the-cios-guide-to-blockchain/; Carson, B., Romanelli, G., Walsh, P., & Zhumaev, A. (2018). *Open interactive popup blockchain beyond the hype: What is the strategic business value?* McKinsey & Company. Retrieved January 22, 2020, from www.mckinsey.com/business-functions/mckinsey-digital/our-insights/blockchain-beyond-the-hype-what-is-the-strategic-business-value; Scribani, J. (2018). This is the value of blockchain to different industries. *World Economic Forum*. Retrieved January 22, 2020, from www.weforum.org/agenda/2018/12/the-business-value-of-the-blockchain/; Plansky, J., O'Donnell, T., & Richards, K. (2016). A strategist's guide to blockchain. *strategy+business*. Retrieved January 22, 2020, from www.strategy-business.com/article/A-Strategists-Guide-to-Blockchain?gko=9d4ef

3 Finley, K., & Barber, G. (2019). Blockchain: The complete guide. *Wired*. Retrieved January 22, 2020, from www.wired.com/story/guide-blockchain/; Mearian, L. (2020). What is blockchain? The complete guide. *Computerworld*. Retrieved January 22, 2020, from www.computerworld.com/article/3191077/what-is-blockchain-the-complete-guide.html?page=2

4 Finley, K., & Barber, G. (2019). Blockchain: The complete guide. *Wired*. Retrieved January 22, 2020, from www.wired.com/story/guide-blockchain/; Mearian, L. (2020). What is blockchain? The complete guide. *Computerworld*. Retrieved January 22, 2020, from www.computerworld.com/article/3191077/what-is-blockchain-the-complete-guide.html?page=2

5 Mearian, L. (2020). What is blockchain? The complete guide. *Computerworld*. Retrieved January 22, 2020, from www.computerworld.com/article/3191077/what-is-blockchain-the-complete-guide.html?page=2

6 Mearian, L. (2020). What is blockchain? The complete guide. *Computerworld*. Retrieved January 22, 2020, from www.computerworld.com/article/3191077/what-is-blockchain-the-complete-guide.html?page=2; CompTIA. (2018). Harnessing the blockchain revolution – CompTIA's practical guide for the public sector. *Default*. Retrieved January 22, 2020, from www.comptia.org/content/research/

harnessing-the-blockchain-revolution-comptia-s-practical-guide-for-the-public-sector

7 Blockchain-council.org. (2019). Top 10 promising blockchain use cases. Retrieved January 22, 2020, from www.blockchain-council.org/blockchain/top-10-promising-blockchain-use-cases/

8 Carson, B., Romanelli, G., Walsh, P., & Zhumaev, A. (2018). *Open interactive popup blockchain beyond the hype: What is the strategic business value?* McKinsey & Company. Retrieved January 22, 2020, from www.mckinsey.com/business-functions/mckinsey-digital/our-insights/blockchain-beyond-the-hype-what-is-the-strategic-business-value; Bender, J. P., Burchardi, K., & Shepherd, N. (2019). Capturing the value of blockchain. *Bcg.com*. Retrieved January 22, 2020, from www.bcg.com/en-au/publications/2019/capturing-blockchain-value.aspx

9 Silva, M. (2019). Crypto companies are settling with the SEC, but that's not stopping them. *Quartz*. Retrieved January 20, 2020, from https://qz.com/1720295/after-4b-ico-block-ones-24m-sec-settlement-lets-it-keep-building/ Rooney, K. (2018). A blockchain start-up just raised $4 billion without a live product. *CNBC*. Retrieved January 20, 2020, from www.cnbc.com/2018/05/31/a-blockchain-start-up-just-raised-4-billion-without-a-live-product.html

10 Deloitte CFO Insights. (2016). Getting smart about smart contracts. Retrieved January 22, 2020, from www2.deloitte.com/tr/en/pages/finance/articles/cfo-insights-getting-smart-contracts.html

11 Cheng-Shorland, C. (2018). Moving beyond smart contracts: What are the next generations of blockchain use cases? Retrieved January 22, 2020, from www.forbes.com/sites/forbestechcouncil/2018/12/05/moving-beyond-smart-contracts-what-are-the-next-generations-of-blockchain-use-cases/#259adfdb13e5; Ream, J., Chu, Y., & Schatsky, D. (2016). Upgrading blockchains. *Deloitte Insights*. Retrieved January 22, 2020, from www2.deloitte.com/us/en/insights/focus/signals-for-strategists/using-blockchain-for-smart-contracts.html

12 Cheng-Shorland, C. (2018). How technology is changing the real estate market. *Forbes.com*. Retrieved January 22, 2020, from www.forbes.com/sites/forbestechcouncil/2018/07/31/how-technology-is-changing-the-real-estate-market/#40ff325b6d06; Deloitte. (2018). Blockchain and smart contracts could transform property transactions. Retrieved

January 20, 2020, from https://deloitte.wsj.com/cfo/2018/01/03/
blockchain-and-smart-contracts-could-transform-property-transactions/

13 Ream, J., Chu, Y., & Schatsky, D. (2016). Upgrading blockchains. *Deloitte Insights*. Retrieved January 22, 2020, from www2.deloitte.com/us/en/insights/
focus/signals-for-strategists/using-blockchain-for-smart-contracts.html

14 Arnold, M. (2017). Five ways banks are using blockchain. *Financial Times*. Ft.com. Retrieved January 20, 2020, from www.ft.com/
content/615b3bd8-97a9-11e7-a652-cde3f882dd7b

15 Liu, M., Wu, K., & Xu, J. J. (2019). How will blockchain technology impact auditing and accounting: Permissionless versus permissioned blockchain. *Current Issues in Auditing*, 13(2), A19–A29.

16 Nelson, P. (2019). How data storage will shift to blockchain. *Network World*. Retrieved January 22, 2020, from www.networkworld.com/article/3390722/
how-data-storage-will-shift-to-blockchain.html

17 Nelson, P. (2019). How data storage will shift to blockchain. *Network World*. Retrieved January 22, 2020, from www.networkworld.com/article/3390722/
how-data-storage-will-shift-to-blockchain.html

18 Nelson, P. (2019). How data storage will shift to blockchain. *Network World*. Retrieved January 22, 2020, from www.networkworld.com/article/3390722/
how-data-storage-will-shift-to-blockchain.html

19 CompTIA. (2018). Harnessing the blockchain revolution – CompTIA's practical guide for the public sector. *Default*. Retrieved January 22, 2020, from www.comptia.org/content/research/harnessing-the-blockchain-revolution-comptia-s-practical-guide-for-the-public-sector; Scribani, J. (2018). This is the value of blockchain to different industries. *World Economic Forum*. Retrieved January 22, 2020, from www.weforum.org/agenda/2018/12/
the-business-value-of-the-blockchain/

20 Gartner. (2019). Gartner 2019 hype cycle for blockchain business shows blockchain will have a transformational impact across industries in five to 10 years. Retrieved January 22, 2020, from www.gartner.com/en/newsroom/
press-releases/2019-09-12-gartner-2019-hype-cycle-for-blockchain-business-shows; Panetta, K. (2019). The CIO's guide to blockchain. *Gartner.com*. Retrieved January 22, 2020, from www.gartner.com/smarterwithgartner/
the-cios-guide-to-blockchain/; Raconteur. (2016). The future of blockchain in 8 charts. Retrieved January 22, 2020, from www.raconteur.net/
business-innovation/the-future-of-blockchain-in-8-charts

21 Gartner Peer Insights. (2020). Blockchain platforms reviews. Retrieved January 22, 2020, from www.gartner.com/reviews/market/blockchain-platforms

22 Rossow, A. (2020). 10 new blockchain companies to watch for in 2018. *Forbes.com*. Retrieved January 22, 2020, from www.forbes.com/sites/andrewrossow/2018/07/10/top-10-new-blockchain-companies-to-watch-for-in-2018/#40d089705600

# CHAPTER 22

# Video Content Analytics, Computer Vision, and Machine Vision Primer

DOI: 10.4324/9781003254614-27

# INTRODUCTION

The digital technologies discussed in this chapter enable organizations to leverage the growing troves of video data captured from a range of devices and stakeholders (e.g., CCTV, smartphones, online uploads) to offer new or enhanced products/services, and to make new operational efficiency and effectiveness breakthroughs (e.g., drastically improving quality assurance through automated identification of defects). They also enable the leveraging of machines or algorithms that can "see" their environment, understand it, and recommend or take optimal actions in response to eventuating or non-eventuating environmental events or stimuli. To realize the business value of these digital technologies requires leaders, managers, and supporting professionals to have a working understanding of how the technologies work, understand the current and potential use cases for these technologies, and understand how organizations can leverage these technologies to enhance efficiency, differentiation, adaptability, and agility. This primer provides an introductory overview of the technologies, how they work, their business value, example use cases, common terminologies, and example vendors and platforms.

---

**LEARNING OBJECTIVES**

- Develop knowledge of definitions and concepts related to video content analytics, computer vision, and machine vision technologies
- Understand how these technologies and their related applications/practices/tools/methods/techniques can impact the efficiency, differentiation, adaptability, and agility of an organization
- Understand the roles leaders, managers, and supporting professionals can play in maximizing the leveraging of these technologies and their related applications/practices/tools/methods/techniques

---

- Analyze and evaluate the implications of these technologies and their related applications/practices/tools/methods/ techniques, as well as related leadership or management roles in their optimal use, for organizations' digital transformation strategy and digital business strategy
- Apply knowledge and understanding of these technologies and their related applications/practices/tools/methods/techniques to participate in, support, or lead workstreams or initiatives related to the leveraging of these technologies to enhance organization digital transformation and digital business strategy

# VIDEO ANALYTICS OR VIDEO CONTENT ANALYTICS (VCA)

## WHAT IS VIDEO ANALYTICS OR VIDEO CONTENT ANALYTICS (VCA)?

Video analytics (also referred to as video content analysis, intelligent video analytics, video content analytics, or VCA) involves the use of software algorithms to analyze or check video data (e.g., recorded video footage or live streaming video) for particular objects, events, patterns, people, or issues. Once one or more particular issues, events, patterns, objects, or people are identified, the software can report it or generate automatic alerts, prescribe action, or take follow-on actions in response to what has been identified. For example, if the software recognizes a known criminal walking down the street, it can immediately alert police or request a police squad and direct it to the specific spot the criminal is about to walk to. The software may identify that vandalism occurred or that it routinely occurs at particular times of the day. Based on analysis of historical video footage, VCA software may even identify that theft is about to occur in a particular location and alert security or request police attendance (e.g., raising an urgent call request via the company's workflow management systems). VCA software may notice a confused or lost guest and request someone from

*Figure 22.1* *An example of VCA/computer vision software developed by Voxel51[1]*

guest services to check in on them. Alternatively, it might notice people entering a restricted area or that a guest room has not been made up in time for a guest's arrival. In either case, it can alert or request the right people to take action and even prescribe the optimal actions to take. Although lacking the benefit of different colors, Figure 22.1 shows VCA/computer vision software identifying different people, different cars, different cross walks, road conditions, traffic conditions, and more.

## HOW VIDEO CONTENT ANALYTICS WORKS

Video analytics is a subset of computer vision, which in turn is a subset of artificial intelligence. Thus, VCA works by leveraging image processing/image enhancement technologies and techniques like image sensors, image pixilation, image compression, image stabilization (reducing blurring associated with an imaging device), unsharp masking (sharpening an image or making it clearer), super resolution (improving the resolution of an image), and other AI learning and prediction algorithms. A video is essentially just a series of image frames,[2] so analyzing video requires extracting and interpreting what is in image frames. An algorithm (e.g., a recurrent neural network algorithm) can be trained to do this. This involves providing it with lots of data that it can compare against what it is seeing in video image frames. In this case, the data would consist of a sequence of image frame descriptions. For example, we can provide an algorithm with a sequence of image frames for taking cleaning equipment to a room door and label this sequence "room cleaning preparation". We can then provide it with a sequence of image frames for opening the room door for cleaning and label it "room cleaning start". We can also provide it with a series of images for packing up cleaning equipment, and label it "room cleaning completion". We can then collectively label the three groups of images as "room cleaning". The algorithm is able to learn from these images and labels so that when new video data is fed into it, the algorithm can go through the video's image frames and identify any image, sequence of image frames, or group of sequences of image frames that it already knows. For example, it might notice a sequence of image frames corresponding to the existing sequence of image frames for "room cleaning completion" and, triangulating this with other data available to it, work out that a room has been cleaned or that cleaning is about to start and will be completed in time for a guest's arrival. The algorithm can learn from its calculations, conclusions, decisions, and mistakes and become more accurate over time. Video analytics can be used to detect faces of particular people or groups of people in videos, shapes of objects, writing, movement, poses, motion, emotion, particular events, changes in objects and environments, and much more. Figure 22.2 shows VCA/computer vision software recognizing people, their actions, and occurring events. The exponentially growing number of devices capturing or able to capture video, the exponentially growing availability of images and video footage available online, and the growing sophistication of VCA algorithms, make video footage a potently powerful source of value right now. Organizations are capturing some video data, but they can capture much more; they can access vast troves of video data on the internet to train their VCA algorithms (e.g., YouTube video and associated chat history, Facebook video and associated chat history, LinkedIn video and associated chat

**Figure 22.2** *An example of VCA/computer vision software recognizing both people and actions/events[3]*

history), and they can access sophisticated VCA platforms to make the most of all the internal and publicly available video data.

# COMPUTER VISION (CV) AND MACHINE VISION (MV)

Computer vision (also known as machine vision [MV]), is essentially the real-time recording of video/audio/other data and the leveraging of video content analytics and sophisticated pattern recognition algorithms to sense or understand the makeup of an environment (e.g., what objects are there, where are they, how are they moving).[4] Video content analysis is a subset of computer vision, which is a subset of artificial intelligence. And the terms machine vision and computer vision are often interchangeably used to refer to the real-time recording of video/audio/other data and the leveraging of video content analytics and/or sophisticated pattern recognition algorithms to sense and/or understand the makeup of an environment (e.g., what objects are there, where are they, how are they moving).[5] Thus, computer vision and machine vision enable machines to "see" by capturing, analyzing, and understanding captured images and video. Through image and video analysis, computer vision algorithms can detect faces of specific people or groups of people, shapes of objects, writing, movement, poses, motion, emotion, changes in objects, and environments. Combined with additional information that a whole range of different sensors can detect (e.g., motion, sound, proximity, touch, temperature, light, smoke, air), it is not hard to imagine how computer vision and machine vision can be very powerful. For example, they can provide machines such as robots and drones with vastly expanded possibilities (e.g., to fly through a dense and obstacle-filled rain forest at high speed, to recognize a suspect walking in a crowd and immediately call the police, to give robots human-like movement and body control). Figure 22.3 shows how computer vision can enable self-driving cars to "see" better than humans (e.g., simultaneous 360-degree sight, undistractable, better multi-tasking, faster processing/computation). Although the terms machine vision and computer vision are often used interchangeably, machine vision is also often conceptualized as a subset

Side and rear facing cameras work in collaboration to construct a continuous view of the vehicle's surroundings

Top mounted lidar units provide a 360 degree 3-D scan of the environment

Forward facing camera array focuses both close and far fields, watching for braking vehicles, crossing pedestrians, traffic lights, and signage

360 degree radar coverage

Custom designed compute and storage allow for real-time processing of data while a fully integrated cooling solution keeps components running optimally

Roof mounted antennae provide GPS positioning and wireless data capabilities

**Figure 22.3** *Computer vision can enable self-driving cars to "see" better than humans*[6,7]

of computer vision. As a subset of computer vision, machine vision often focuses more on industrial or industry applications of computer vision (e.g., applications of computer vision in manufacturing to identify and prevent product defects or other quality/workflow issues).

## BUSINESS VALUE OF VCA/ COMPUTER VISION/MACHINE VISION

The business value of VCA/computer vision/machine vision includes product innovation opportunities (offering new VCA/computer vision/machine vision-related products and services, like an industry-specific VCA/computer vision/machine vision platform), product/ service enhancement opportunities (e.g., using VCA/computer vision/ machine vision to anticipate and respond to guest issues before they occur, thus optimizing customer experience), business model innovation opportunities (e.g., video-based service delivery models), operational efficiency opportunities (e.g., using VCA/computer vision/machine vision to anticipate, prevent, or minimize disruptive events such as vandalism or theft that may slow down operational processes or result in higher costs), and risk mitigation opportunities (e.g., learning from VCA/computer vision/machine vision when or how particular security and other threats occur and taking action to prevent or minimize them). This business value can be expanded and significantly enhanced with real-time VCA/computer vision/machine vision that is combined with smart things[8] (e.g., devices, robots, bionics) to provide real-time, human-like sensing and responding.

## EXAMPLE VCA/COMPUTER VISION/ MACHINE VISION USE CASES

Example VCA/computer vision/machine vision use cases included enhanced site or asset security through incident detection (e.g., identifying unattended objects in crowded or high people traffic spots, identifying disruptive individuals, identifying camera tampering or minimizing footage tampering, identifying suspicious activity), intrusion management (e.g., detecting unauthorized people in secure zones), and people/crowd counting (e.g., counting foot traffic and attendance to analyze patronage and conversion). They further include automatic number plate recognition (e.g., detecting unauthorized tailgating in secure car entrances), facial recognition (e.g., monitoring faces as they enter premises and high-risk areas, searching through faces for an investigation, searching for the location of particular individuals across a large facility), and demand management (using heat maps to understand people traffic density and traffic choke points by time of day, understand people's traffic movement in areas of interest). Additional use cases include demographic analytics (identifying the demographic profile of people entering particular areas, where they stay, how long they stay, where they go, what their mood is)[9] and quality assurance on production lines in manufacturing. Some hospitality and tourism organizations are integrating VCA/computer vision/machine vision with guest service and guest loyalty data to provide even better value for their most valuable guests. For example, the Hawaii Tourism Authority's "Discover Your Aloha" campaign analyzed the expressions of travelers' faces in video captured via webcams to determine what custom offers to push to them; it used facial recognition in videos and predictive analytics to identify the best offer for a traveler and to push it to them along with a booking link.[10] Similarly, Cherokee Nation Entertainment (CNE) used VCA across its ten casinos in Oklahoma to relieve its security team of the need to review video footage manually. As a result, they could focus on more proactive and preventative tasks. VCA analyzed camera footage from entrances and exits, gaming machines, and other areas, enabling CNE to have real-time visibility and alerts of traffic patterns, people counts, and any risky events or situations unfolding.[11] VCA/computer vision/machine vision offer a lot of possibilities for understanding customers and for optimizing customer experiences, enhanced operational insights, and operations management.

# GOOGLE AND REFLECT

CCTV, OpenCV, rule-based analytics, area of interest (AOI), region-of-interest, region-of-uninterest, smart surveillance engine, video management system, view group, dynamic masking, motion detection, shape recognition, object detection, tamper detection, video tracking, video error level analysis (VELA), object co-segmentation

# EXAMPLE TOOLS AND VENDORS

Google Cloud Vision, Cloud Vision Intelligence, Agent Vi savVi, Agent Vi innoVi, NVIDIA DeepStream SDK, NVIDIA Jetson, NVIDIA Tesla, NVIDIA GPU Cloud (NGC),[12] Python Imaging Library (PIL), Open-Source Computer Vision (OpenCV), Cognex IN-SIGHT 2000 VISION SENSOR, Datalogic A30 Series smart camera, Omron FH Series Vision System

# DISCUSSION QUESTIONS

1 What are the similarities and differences between VCA and other forms of data analytics?

2 What is a recurrent neural network? How is it different from other neural networks?

3 Where can organizations obtain the vast quantities of data required to train recurrent neural network algorithms to understand what they are seeing in video data?

4 Can VCA be applied to virtual reality, augmented reality, and mixed reality?

5 How can a hotel use VCA to improve its operational efficiency?

6 What is an example of an innovative new product leveraging VCA that a tourism operator could offer?

7 What are the top three enterprise-grade VCA platforms, and which is the best?

8 What are the top three SME-grade VCA platforms?

9 How can VCA be used to improve product/service quality within your industry?

10 Would adding real-world objects to a virtual reality setting fit the definition of augmented reality?

11 Within the example tools and vendors provided, identify three leading vendors and products in each of these product categories: consumer, small business, enterprise.

# NOTES

1 NIST. (2019). Enhancing public safety video analytics with computer vision and artificial intelligence. Retrieved June 21, 2020, from NIST website: www.nist.gov/news-events/news/2019/11/enhancing-public-safety-video-analytics-computer-vision-and-artificial

2 Robinson, S. (2018). How computer vision works. *YouTube*. Retrieved January 27, 2020, from www.youtube.com/watch?v=OcycT1Jwsns

3 NIST. (2019). Enhancing public safety video analytics with computer vision and artificial intelligence. Retrieved June 21, 2020, from NIST website: www.nist.gov/news-events/news/2019/11/enhancing-public-safety-video-analytics-computer-vision-and-artificial

4 PCMag. (2020). Definition of computer vision. PCMag. Retrieved June 17, 2020, from www.pcmag.com/encyclopedia/term/computer-vision; Schmelzer, R. (2020). Understanding the recognition pattern of AI. *Forbes*. www.forbes.com/sites/cognitiveworld/2020/05/09/understanding-the-recognition-pattern-of-ai/#3d30130621c7

5 PCMag. (2020). Definition of computer vision. *PCMag*. Retrieved June 17, 2020, from www.pcmag.com/encyclopedia/term/computer-vision; Schmelzer, R. (2020). Understanding the recognition pattern of AI. *Forbes*. www.forbes.com/sites/cognitiveworld/2020/05/09/understanding-the-recognition-pattern-of-ai/#3d30130621c7

6 Tara, R. (2018). Technology vs. Humans. *Engineers Seek Answers in Uber's Fatal Self Driving Car Accident*. Retrieved June 21, 2020, from Engineering.com website: www.engineering.com/Hardware/ArticleID/16756/Technology-vs-Humans-Engineers-Seek-Answers-in-Ubers-Fatal-Self-Driving-Car-Accident.aspx

7  Burke, K. (2019). How does a self-driving car see? *Nvidia*. Retrieved June 22, 2020, from https://blogs.nvidia.com/blog/2019/04/15/how-does-a-self-driving-car-see

8  Ganesan, V., Ji, Y., & Patel, M. (2020). *Video meets the internet of things*. McKinsey & Company. www.mckinsey.com/industries/technology-media-and-telecommunications/our-insights/video-meets-the-internet-of-things

9  Hughes Systique Corp. (2019). The role of video analytics in tourism, travel & hospitality industry. Retrieved January 27, 2020, from https://hsc.com/Blog/The-Role-of-Video-Analytics-in-Tourism-Travel-Hospitality-Industry; Agent Vi. (2020). Entertainment and hospitality solutions. *Agentvi.com*. Retrieved January 27, 2020, from www.agentvi.com/portfolio-items/entertainment-hospitality/?portfolioCats=19; Security Magazine. (2017). Securitymagazine. com. Retrieved January 27, 2020, from www.securitymagazine.com/articles/89083-using-video-analytics-to-create-efficiencies; UBAC Group. Face recognition & video analytics for campus & retail hospitality – UBAC Pte Ltd. *Ubacgroup.com*. Retrieved January 27, 2020, from https://ubacgroup. com/face-recognition-data-analytics/intelligent-surveillance-face-detection/

10  Bhattacharjee, D., Seeley, J., & Seitzman, N. (2017). *Advanced analytics in hospitality*. McKinsey & Company. Retrieved January 27, 2020, from www.mckinsey.com/business-functions/mckinsey-digital/our-insights/advanced-analytics-in-hospitality

11  Agentvi.com. Retrieved January 27, 2020, from https://agentvi.com/wp-content/uploads/2018/10/Agent_Vi_Solutions_Entertainment_Hospitality-1.pdf

12  MSV, J. (2019). Microsoft and NVIDIA deliver intelligent video analytics at the edge. *Forbes.com*. Retrieved January 27, 2020, from www.forbes.com/sites/janakirammsv/2019/03/23/microsoft-and-nvidia-deliver-intelligent-video-analytics-at-the-edge/#16eba1927623

# CHAPTER 23

# Virtual Reality (VR), Augmented Reality (AR), and Mixed Reality (MR) Primer

DOI: 10.4324/9781003254614-28

# INTRODUCTION

Virtual reality (VR), augmented reality (AR), and mixed reality (MR) technologies represent continuing blurring of the boundary between the real world and the virtual world that enable enhanced or new experiences and enhanced or new business opportunities.[2] These digital technologies can be leveraged to offer new virtual products and services (e.g., virtual-world products and experiences or enhanced real-world products and experiences), make new operational efficiency breakthroughs (e.g., drastically improving staff training and enhancing technology-based support for staff through the use of augmented and mixed reality), craft novel marketing campaigns (e.g., novel virtual, augmented, or mixed reality marketing campaigns), approach after-sales support differently (e.g., virtual, augmented, or mixed reality guided repairs performed by customers), and much more. To realize the business value of these digital technologies, leaders, managers, and supporting professionals need to have a working understanding of how these technologies work, understand the current and potential use cases for these technologies, and understand how they can be leveraged to enhance organization efficiency, differentiation, adaptability, and agility. This chapter provides an introductory overview of the technologies, how they work, their business value, example use cases, common terminologies, and example vendors and platforms. The aim of the primer is to provide a base-level overview of the technologies in order to enable leaders, managers, and supporting professionals to undertake their own self-directed and more in-depth learning so as to keep up with rapid developments in these technologies and their applications.

## LEARNING OBJECTIVES

- Develop knowledge of definitions and concepts related to virtual reality, augmented reality, and mixed reality technologies
- Understand how these technologies and their related applications/practices/tools/methods/techniques can impact

the efficiency, differentiation, adaptability, and agility of an organization

- Understand the roles leaders, managers, and supporting professionals can play in maximizing the leveraging of these technologies and their related applications/practices/tools/ methods/techniques

- Analyze and evaluate the implications of these technologies and their related applications/practices/tools/methods/ techniques, as well as related leadership or management roles in their optimal use, for organizations' digital transformation strategy and digital business strategy

- Apply knowledge and understanding of these technologies and their related applications/practices/tools/methods/techniques to participate in, support, or lead workstreams or initiatives related to the leveraging of these technologies to enhance organization digital transformation and digital business strategy

# VIRTUAL REALITY (VR)

Virtual reality (VR) has been around since the 1930s as a technology for enabling users to experience a fully computer generated or digital environment.[3] Once in the digital environment, users can see, hear, and interact with the digital environment. Although other senses can be incorporated to make the digital world experience more immersive, VR is not yet at the fully immersive, nerve-connected experiences depicted in movies like *The Matrix*. Still, VR can provide highly immersive experiences through great graphics, 360-degree visuals, binaural sound (3D stereo sound sensation that emulates actually being there to hear the full rich sound), and tapping into other human senses.[4] Virtual worlds or environments can be unique digital creations that don't exist in the real world, recreations or emulations of the real world, or somewhere in between. For example, virtual reality games can be played in fantasy digital worlds completely detached from reality, or they can be played in emulations of real-world conditions and rules such as a World War II setting. In contrast to games, tourism operators may replicate the experience of navigating protected environments to enable tourists to "see" them without putting those environments and species at risk. Virtual reality experiences typically require specialized hardware such as VR headsets.[5] Depending on how immersive VR experience needs to be, other sensory optimization hardware like noise-cancelling headphones, cameras to track room space and boundaries, and motion capture technology may also be required.[6] VR is characterized by three elements: visualization, immersion, and interactivity. Information can be retrieved in multi-sensory modalities by the users in a VR environment.[7]

# AUGMENTED REALITY (AR)

To augment means to make something greater by adding to it. Thus augmented reality (AR) refers to adding or superimposing digital data and/or images and animations on real-world elements to enhance them.[8] That is, it involves enhancing the real world with digital details that can, for example, improve understandability of the digital world or engagement with the real world.[9] Augmented reality devices and applications can place digital objects in the real world; for example, Pokémon Go game creators enabled overlaying of the game's buildings and characters on real-world areas like streets and buildings in a town so players could play the game by navigating real-world streets and buildings. They can also overlay animations, information, or a combination of objects, animations, and information.[10] AR-capable hardware includes mobile phones (e.g., AR apps available in most app stores), smart tablet devices (e.g., iPad), wearable AR devices (e.g., AR glasses like Epson Moverio or AR headsets like Oculus Go), and custom enterprise AR equipment.

# MIXED REALITY (MR)

Drawing on next-generation sensing and imaging technologies, mixed reality "mixes" the real and virtual worlds and allows users to see, immerse themselves in, and interact with both worlds.[11] Users can manipulate the virtual world using their own hands, or they can make changes to the real world guided by virtual objects or by making changes to virtual objects.[12] For example, surgeons at Imperial College London use Microsoft's HoloLens mixed reality devices to enable them to see "inside" a patient's body during an operation:[13] bones, blood vessels, and other body parts revealed in scans can be reconceptualized, animated, and superimposed on the patient's body so that surgeons can move them around as in a real surgery and see exactly where cut or implant a device without obstructing the functioning of other body parts. Perhaps less complex, a patient's blood vessels can be superimposed on their arm so that nursing staff can see exactly where the best spot to inject a needle is and trial the injection virtually in that spot before actually doing it. Figure 23.1 shows architecture students interacting with their building designs using a Microsoft HoloLens 2 headset.

# BUSINESS VALUE OF VR, AR, AND MR

Although VR, AR, and MR technologies are of value to all areas of business, they hold stand-out value in areas like product innovation, operational efficiency and effectiveness, marketing, HR, and after-sales support. In the product innovation area, they offer the opportunity to provide customers new or improved products (e.g., to create and offer virtual versions of any real-world environment or experience, to augment existing products and services with digital data and virtual objects, to create new products and services leveraging mixed reality). In the operational efficiency area, these technologies offer businesses the opportunity to provide their staff with the ability to see through opaque things and interact with them (e.g., underground infrastructure, cabling in walls, vessels in the brain, arteries in the body). This can result in faster repair times, minimization of costly errors, avoidance of equipment damaging actions, and more. And what is seen through this X-ray like vision and interacted with is an increasingly more exact representation of the real thing thanks to connected IoT sensors and

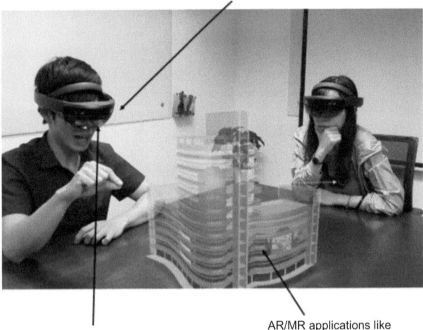

HoloLens 2 has improved field of view, easier ways to control holograms

HoloLens 2 resolution minimizes eye fatigue, so you can read text and see intricate details on 3D assets

AR/MR applications like HoloLens enable professionals to interact with holographic objects–not just look at them in 3D

**Figure 23.1** *Using a HoloLens 2 headset*

AI algorithms. For example, the superimposed blood vessel can expand or contract or burst in sync with, and to the same degree as, the real thing, enabling whoever is interacting with it to see, for example, the implications of shifting it one way or applying a little bit more pressure to it. AR and MR can also enable remote or automatic interaction with things, thanks to IoT and AI. For example, virtual versions of things can be linked to real versions so that a change in the virtual-world version automatically results in a change in the real-world version. Taken together, these abilities provide organizations with opportunities to redesign their workflows for greater efficiency and effectiveness (e.g., greater possibilities for automation, greater possibilities for remote supervision and management).

From an HR perspective, VR, AR, and MR can enable provision of real-time, on-site, interactive step-by-step training, guidance, or coaching that is superior to any manual or video. It could be used for better assessing aptitude prior to giving someone the responsibility for a task; that is, before undertaking a high-risk task in the real world, an employee may be required to first competently perform that task in the virtual world. Using analytics, employee's performance of such tasks in the virtual world could be contrasted to their performance in the real world to improve VR-based training. From a marketing perspective, VR, AR, and MR can be powerful marketing tools (e.g., enabling virtual experiences of products and services to drive sales, enabling customers to see how a product fits into their home setting, enabling gamification of marketing campaigns drawing on viral games like Pokémon Go). From an after-sales perspective, VR, AR, and MR can be used to enable customers to effectively make their own repairs, assemble items quicker, or coach customers through the repair process (e.g., imagine VR or AR-guided assembly of IKEA furniture). Together, these different value propositions can transform how employees learn, the quality of the decisions they make, how they interact with customers, how they buy and who they buy from, how customers interact with a business' products, and much more.

Example VR, AR, and MR industry use cases include virtual experiences, virtual purchasing processes, interactive facilities, Pokémon Go style gamified entertainment, and augmented environments.[14] An example of virtual experiences in action is the Atlantis Dubai, which provides a very inviting virtual tour of its premises. An example of virtual booking processes in action is Amadeus, which set up a virtual booking process that enables customers to enter a virtual world where they can look for flights, walk on the plane to inspect it and find the perfect seat, then compare hotel prices and look inside the hotel room before finally making a booking. On completion, they exit the virtual world but have made real-world bookings which they don't need to be anxious about – since they have experienced most aspects of the bookings.[15] An example of interactive hotel rooms is The Hub Hotel from Premier Inn in the United Kingdom, which used a combination of maps on hotel room walls and AR to enable guests to point their phones at different map locations to see additional information and places of interest in those locations – thus enhancing customer experience).[16] An example of gamification is organizations incorporating their sites or services in established AR games or creating their own VR or AR gaming apps for promotional purposes. For example, hospitality and leisure organization Best Western Kelowna set up an Augmented Reality Quest for kids staying at the hotel to play alone or with other kids or with their parents.[17] Most early use cases have focused on VR and AR applications for entertainment and consumer engagement, providing X-ray like vision, or delivering training or simulating situations. But there are great possibilities for VR, AR, and MR.

# GOOGLE AND REFLECT

CCTV, OpenCV, rule-based analytics, area of interest (AOI), region-of-interest, region-of-uninterest, smart surveillance engine, video management system, view group, dynamic masking, motion detection, shape recognition, object detection, tamper detection, video tracking, video error level analysis (VELA), object co-segmentation, Immersive VR, virtual space, AR space, head-mounted display (HMD), haptics, VR head tracking, VR eye tracking, VR position tracking, VR field of view, VR blind spot, VR headset latency, VR headset interpupillary distance (or IPD), VR judder, VR headset refresh rate, 360 video, VR video stitching, VR sickness, low persistence, VR 1 to 1 movement, asynchronous time warp, spatial desync, VR ride, Social VR platform, cinematic VR, fish tank VR, virtual theater, directional sound, motion platform/omnidirectional treadmill, discrete graphics processor, computer-aided design (CAD), extended reality (XR), GL transmission format (gITF), hologram, simultaneous localization and mapping (SLAM), six degrees of freedom (6DoF) tracking, visual-inertial odometry (VIO), waveguide displays, augmented face mesh, simulation-based learning, blended space, lifelike experience, multimodal interaction, simulated reality, supranet, telexistence, multiexperience development platform (MXDP), Google ARCore, PTC Vuforia, Augmentir, Amazon Sumerian, HP Reveal, SmartReality

## EXAMPLE TOOLS AND VENDORS

Oculus Rift, HTC Vive, and PlayStation VR, Google Cardboard, iStaging LiveTour, Cupix, Viar360, BRIOVR, Scanta, Fishermen Labs, Groove Jones, Program-Ace, Xtrematic, Niantic Real World Platform, Windows Mixed Reality platform, Zappar ZapWorks platform, Lucyd Lab AR, Qualcomm Snapdragon platforms, Apple ARKit 3, Apple Reality Composer, Apple RealityKit, Magic Leap 1, PlayStation VR, FOVE Eye Tracking Virtual Reality Headset, Samsung Gear VR, Epson Drone Soar augmented reality app, Epson Moverio AR glasses, DAQRI Worksense, Bosch Common Augmented Reality Platform (CAP)

## DISCUSSION QUESTIONS

1 Would adding real-world objects to a virtual reality setting fit the definition of augmented reality?
2 Would adding real-world objects to a virtual reality setting fit the definition of mixed reality?
3 How could augmented reality be used to improve product/service delivery in your industry?
4 How could marketing functions use mixed reality to attract more customers?
5 What are the top five challenges of adopting and using VR, AR, and MR?
6 What are the top five risks associated with using VR, AR, and MR in your industry?
7 What are the top three risks of not adopting or at least experimenting with VR, AR, and MR?

8 Within the example tools and vendors provided, identify three leading vendors and products in each of these product categories: virtual reality, immersive VR, augmented reality, mixed reality.

9 Within the example tools and vendors provided, identify three leading vendors and products in each of these product categories: consumer, small business, enterprise.

10 Within the example tools and vendors provided, identify three leading vendors and products in each of these product categories: gaming, marketing, healthcare, hospitality/tourism.

11 Group the example tools and vendors provided into the following categories: hardware products, software products, VR/AR/MR development platforms.

# NOTES

1 Intel. (2019). Virtual reality vs. augmented reality vs. mixed reality. Retrieved January 30, 2020, from Intel website: www.intel.com.au/content/www/au/en/tech-tips-and-tricks/virtual-reality-vs-augmented-reality.html

2 Intel. (2019). Virtual reality vs. augmented reality vs. mixed reality. Retrieved January 30, 2020, from Intel website: www.intel.com.au/content/www/au/en/tech-tips-and-tricks/virtual-reality-vs-augmented-reality.html

3 Intel. (2019). Virtual reality vs. augmented reality vs. mixed reality. Retrieved January 30, 2020, from Intel website: www.intel.com.au/content/www/au/en/tech-tips-and-tricks/virtual-reality-vs-augmented-reality.html

4 Intel. (2019). Virtual reality vs. augmented reality vs. mixed reality. Retrieved January 30, 2020, from Intel website: www.intel.com.au/content/www/au/en/tech-tips-and-tricks/virtual-reality-vs-augmented-reality.html; Hackernoon.com. (2019). Augmented reality vs. mixed reality vs. virtual reality. Retrieved January 30, 2020, from Hackernoon.com website: https://hackernoon.com/augmented-reality-vs-mixed-reality-vs-virtual-reality-ik8730gv

5 Tussyadiah, I.P., Wang, D., Jung, T.H., & Dieck, M.C.T. (2018). Virtual reality, presence, and attitude change: Empirical evidence from tourism. *Tourism Management*, 66, 140–154; Mofokeng, N.E.M., & Matima, T.K. (2018). Future tourism trends: virtual reality based tourism utilizing distributed ledger technologies. *African Journal of Hospitality, Tourism and Leisure*, 7(3), 1–14;

Huang, Y. C., Backman, K. F., Backman, S. J., & Chang, L. L. (2016). Exploring the implications of virtual reality technology in tourism marketing: An integrated research framework. *International Journal of Tourism Research*, 18(2), 116–128.

6  Ambalina, L. (2019). Augmented reality vs. mixed reality vs. virtual reality. Retrieved January 28, 2020, from Hackernoon.com website: https://hackernoon.com/augmented-reality-vs-mixed-reality-vs-virtual-reality-ik8730gv

7  Tussyadiah, I. P., Wang, D., Jung, T. H., & Dieck, M.C.T. (2018). Virtual reality, presence, and attitude change: Empirical evidence from tourism. *Tourism Management*, 66, 140–154; Yung, R., & Khoo-Lattimore, C. (2019). New realities: a systematic literature review on virtual reality and augmented reality in tourism research. *Current Issues in Tourism*, 22(17), 2056–2081.

8  Intel. (2019). Virtual reality vs. augmented reality vs. mixed reality. Retrieved January 30, 2020, from Intel website: www.intel.com.au/content/www/au/en/tech-tips-and-tricks/virtual-reality-vs-augmented-reality.html

9  Lau, C.K.H., Chui, C.F.R., & Au, N. (2019). Examination of the adoption of augmented reality: A VAM approach. *Asia Pacific Journal of Tourism Research*, 24(10), 1005–1020; Yung, R., & Khoo-Lattimore, C. (2019). New realities: A systematic literature review on virtual reality and augmented reality in tourism research. *Current Issues in Tourism*, 22(17), 2056–2081; Hackernoon.com. (2019). Augmented reality vs. mixed reality vs. virtual reality. Retrieved January 30, 2020, from Hackernoon.com website: https://hackernoon.com/augmented-reality-vs-mixed-reality-vs-virtual-reality-ik8730gv

10  Hackernoon.com. (2019). Augmented reality vs. mixed reality vs. virtual reality. Retrieved January 30, 2020, from Hackernoon.com website: https://hackernoon.com/augmented-reality-vs-mixed-reality-vs-virtual-reality-ik8730gv

11  Intel. (2019). Virtual reality vs. augmented reality vs. mixed reality. Retrieved January 30, 2020, from Intel website: www.intel.com.au/content/www/au/en/tech-tips-and-tricks/virtual-reality-vs-augmented-reality.html; Marr, B. (2019). The important difference between augmented reality and mixed reality. Retrieved January 30, 2020, from Bernard Marr website: https://bernardmarr.com/default.asp?contentID=1912

12  Hackernoon.com. (2019). Augmented reality vs. mixed reality vs. virtual reality. Retrieved January 30, 2020, from Hackernoon.com website: https://hackernoon.com/augmented-reality-vs-mixed-reality-vs-virtual-reality-ik8730gv

13 Microsoft News Centre UK. (2018, February 8). Surgeons are using hololens to "see inside" patients before they operate on them. Retrieved from https://news.microsoft.com/en-gb/2018/02/08/surgeons-use-microsoft-hololens-to-see-inside-patients-before-they-operate-on-them/

14 Revfine.com. (2019). How Virtual Reality (VR) can enrich the hospitality industry. Retrieved January 30, 2020, from Revfine.com website: www.revfine.com/virtual-reality-hospitality-industry/; Revfine.com. (2019, August 8). How augmented reality is transforming the hospitality industry. Retrieved January 30, 2020, from Revfine.com website: www.revfine.com/augmented-reality-hospitality-industry/

15 Revfine.com. (2019). How Virtual Reality (VR) can enrich the hospitality industry. Retrieved January 30, 2020, from Revfine.com website: www.revfine.com/virtual-reality-hospitality-industry/

16 Revfine.com. (2019). How Virtual Reality (VR) can enrich the hospitality industry. Retrieved January 30, 2020, from Revfine.com website: www.revfine.com/virtual-reality-hospitality-industry/; Revfine.com. (2019, August 8). How augmented reality is transforming the hospitality industry. Retrieved January 30, 2020, from Revfine.com website: www.revfine.com/augmented-reality-hospitality-industry/

17 Revfine.com. (2019). How Virtual Reality (VR) can enrich the hospitality industry. Retrieved January 30, 2020, from Revfine.com website: www.revfine.com/virtual-reality-hospitality-industry/

# CHAPTER 24

# Robots and Robotics Primer

DOI: 10.4324/9781003254614-29

# INTRODUCTION

R obots and robotics have come a long way since early perception as hulk-like goliaths on manufacturing assembly lines and the domain of sci-fi imagination.[1] Today, contemporary robots are capable of highly autonomous and sophisticated abilities to understand sense and understand their surroundings and to take physical response actions or activities as well as, or even better than, humans can.[2] These continuously and rapidly advancing capabilities of robots represent significant product innovation, cost saving/productivity improvement, operational effectiveness, risk mitigation, customer experience enhancement, staff engagement, and organization adaptability/agility opportunities. Commercial applications of robotics are growing rapidly, and they are expected to impact almost every sector and industry.[3] This primer reintroduces leaders, managers, and supporting professionals to key concepts and issues relating to robots and robotics, the use cases and growing business value of robots, and the implications of accelerating advancements in robotics for organizations.

---

**LEARNING OBJECTIVES**

- Develop knowledge of essential definitions and concepts relating to robots and robotics technologies
- Understand how these technologies and their related applications/ practices/tools/methods/techniques can impact the efficiency, differentiation, adaptability, and agility of an organization
- Understand the roles leaders, managers, and supporting professionals can play in maximizing the leveraging of these technologies and their related applications/practices/tools/ methods/techniques
- Analyze and evaluate the implications of these technologies and their related applications/practices/tools/methods/ techniques, as well as related leadership or management roles in their optimal use, for organizations' digital transformation strategy and digital business strategy

---

- Apply knowledge and understanding of these technologies and their related applications/practices/tools/methods/techniques to participate in, support, or lead workstreams or initiatives related to the leveraging of these technologies to enhance organization digital transformation and digital business strategy

# ROBOTS AND ROBOTICS

Robotics is the field of study concerned with how to best design, build, operate, and use many different types of robots. The field deals with all subfields or disciplines that that are involved in the design, building, operation, and optimal use of robots (e.g., electrical engineering, electronics engineering, mechanical engineering, and software engineering, and design). Robots are machines that can be programmed to physically interact with the world around them and automatically carry out a series of actions/motions or a range of actions with varying levels of autonomy and intelligence.[4] Put differently, contemporary and more sophisticated robots are artificially intelligent agents existing in a physical form that can take actions to affect the physical world.[5] Robots can be designed to carry out an astounding variety of tasks, particularly when they leverage sophisticated artificial intelligence algorithms. For example, robots can manufacture product parts, assemble cars, fill prescriptions, play with kids, provide customer service, fight wars, spy on others, and much more.

## BUILDING BLOCKS OF ROBOTS

Robots can differ greatly in their design, capabilities, and uses. For example, a robot for customer service is quite different from a robot for fighting wars or a robot for assembling cars. Despite this, they usually share common building blocks. At a very high level, they all have mechanical, electrical, and computer program elements. The mechanical element is the physical form, frame, or construct of the robot. The design of the mechanical element is usually based on the specific tasks or actions the robot will be performing; this could be a human-like form for a customer service robot, or it could just be a mechanical arm for welding car parts together. The electrical element is all the electrical and electronic components that operate in concert to power the robot, collect information via sensors from the robot's environment, enable controlled movement of the robot, and enable it to perform its task. The electrical element incorporates sub-elements like power supplies (batteries, solar, AC), motors/actuators (to convert electrical energy into movement), driving mechanisms (gears, chains, pulleys, belts, and gearboxes to enable movement in different directions and at different speeds), electronic controls (to control mechanical systems like brakes and suspension through switches), sensors (to sense things like proximity, sound, and light), and effectors (to effect a change on an object or the environment or to do the task the robot is meant to do, such as pick up a box or push an item in place). The computer program element is the embedded computer hardware and software code that either enables the robot to be instructed on what to do (e.g., through an internet-based software program) or to autonomously work out what to do (e.g., via artificial intelligence algorithms). As with other computer programs, there are specific programming languages used to write the software code or programs for robots to understand and act on. Examples of these languages include Variable Assembly Language (VAL), Robotic Markup Language (Robo ML), and Extensible Robot Control Language (XRCL).

## HOW ROBOTS WORK

In a nutshell, you can think of the functioning of a robot in terms of an input, processing, and output system. The input could involve the robot's sensors gathering information from its environment (e.g., images, object proximity, temperature, smoke, pressure, light, color, light and color intensity, touch), or it could be human-originated data entered via a keyboard, microphone, and/or a user interface. The collected sensor data is passed on to the embedded computer program, which interprets it, determines what specific objects are in front of the robot, anticipates the actions and risks of those objects, determines how to best respond to them, and creates a set of response action instructions for the robot to take. The instructions are translated into electrical signals that are sent directly to the robot's hardware: switches might be turned on to activate particular wheels and move the robot into a particular position; then signals might be sent to move arms into a particular position so as to grab and then throw the object. The effect of the robot on the physical world (e.g., spinning wheels to move, picking up an object) is the output. During this whole input/processing/output process, the robot's sensors can still be picking up real-time information and passing it back to the computer program to do near real-time processing, thus enabling response instructions (and therefore the actions the robot takes) to be adapted as necessary.

## TYPES OF ROBOTS

There are many different types of robots. The different types are commonly classified by the environment in which they operate or by their application field. Other typologies focus on their level of autonomy or human resemblance. Classified by environment, there are fixed robots (operating in fixed and therefore well-defined environments, such as a robotic assembly line arm mounted on the ground) and mobile robots (operating in changing environments and therefore presenting additional challenges in accurately interpreting and operating in those different environments, such as mobile vacuum cleaners and self-driving cars). Mobile robots operate in diverse environments including underwater, in the air, in a dense jungle, or on the surface of the moon. These different environments may require robots to have one or more features such as wheels, legs, propellers, wings, or parachutes to enable them to navigate. Classified by field of application, there are industrial robots (large mounted robotic arms for assembling cars or mobile robots for moving inventory around in a warehouse) and service robots (robots that assist people to carry out tasks, especially dull, repetitive, and/ or dangerous aspects of work). Service robots can be further classified into specific service areas or industries, such as healthcare/medical robots (e.g., surgical robots that perform surgeries requiring a very high degree of precision), home robots (e.g., robot vacuum cleaners, mobile webcam robots, robotic lawn mowers), defense or military robots (e.g., armed robotic vehicles or military drones), and educational robots (e.g., educational robokits such as the mBot-STEM Educational Robot Kit). Other types of robots include agricultural robots (robots that can perform agricultural activities such as fruit picking or farming activities like herding livestock or wildlife),[6] collaborative robots (robots designed to work safely with humans in a shared space), nanorobots (robots operating at the atomic or molecular level), swarm robots (the coordination of multiple robots to interact with each other and their environment so as to collectively achieve a particular task, similar to schools of fish or flocks of birds), and telepresence robots (robots that double as a person, are controlled remotely, and provide an alternative to physically being at a particular event or location).[7]

## BUSINESS VALUE AND USE CASES OF ROBOTS AND ROBOTICS

The business value of robotics includes cost savings, enhanced productivity, reduced risk, overcoming skill shortages, improved staff engagement, new or enhanced products, operational effectiveness, and more.[8] Robotics-related cost savings can come from robots performing activities previously performed by humans. Such activities can include repetitive but low-skill activities, high safety risk activities, or low error tolerance activities; for example, fast-food outlets like Wendy's and McDonalds have implemented automated order kiosks/robots to reduce staffing levels at particular outlets, and mining companies like Rio Tinto are leveraging robotics to remotely manage mining operations for autonomous drilling and autonomous haulage.[9] A robot replacement can work 24 hours a day, seven days a week without needing to take a break or experiencing stress and strain. It does not need line management to maximize its productivity once programmed appropriately, does not require privacy from monitoring, does not require leave, and does not get involved in costly political conflicts. In addition to the benefits just discussed, robotics-related productivity improvements can come from improved output per employee if organizations augment employees' work with the strengths of robots[10] (e.g., the da Vinci Surgical System improves the productivity of surgeons by enabling them to perform surgery using surgical robots and 3D vision systems).[11] In industries like manufacturing and logistics, companies such as beer and beverage maker Carlsberg use collaborative robots (or "cobots") in tandem with employees; robots do the heavy lifting or the unsafe work, leaving employees to do the tasks that necessitate human intelligence or input.[12]

Robots can be used in many different ways to reduce risks. For example, robots can perform tasks that are unsafe for humans (e.g., lifting back-straining loads, deactivating bombs, entering infectious areas to enforce infection control measures, welding intricate components at very high temperatures, entering terrorist zones). Robots can also mitigate or reduce risk by anticipating or spotting risks and either taking mitigating action or alerting people to take mitigating action; for example, in aged care robots are being used to anticipate and/or prevent patient falls.[13] Robots can be used to overcome skill shortages; for example, robots are being used to provide nursing and patient support services either in aged care facilities or in patients' own homes.[14] Robots can be used to provide companionship, ensure patients take their medications, facilitate patient exercise, and manage patient's daily routines,[15] thereby overcoming skill shortages in aged care. Robots can also be used to improve staff engagement and reduce absenteeism by taking over less desirable parts of a job and freeing employees to focus on the more desirable aspects. For example, robots can take over manual, repetitive, and time consuming tasks and thus enable employees to do more creative or strategic work. This may even result in employees having more work/life balance flexibility, no longer bogged down with repetitive tasks that have to routinely occur at a set time in a set location.

Robotics can be leveraged for product innovation and/or business model innovation. On the product innovation front, robotics can be used to create new products/services or to enhance existing products/services. Disruptive new consumer, SME, and enterprise robotics products or services that leverage the capabilities of robotics are possible. Examples of robotics-driven product innovations in action are numerous across industries. In education, institutions are leveraging robots to innovate teaching delivery; for example, some educators are using Sphero's app-enabled robotic ball in classrooms to teach through play. In healthcare, companies are designing intelligent robots for hospitals and other care facilities; for example, Diligent Robotics designed Moxi, an autonomous robot that can independently navigate hospital hallways and tight spaces, find relevant medical equipment, set up patient rooms, and restock supply rooms. In agriculture and farming, specialty robots are being designed to perform or assist in the management of agricultural and farming processes. The increased use of robots in business operations and in homes creates a need for new software platforms, robotics support, and other services. Thus, product innovation is possible from offering new robot forms, leveraging robots to carry out new forms of service delivery, leveraging robots to augment existing product or service offerings, and offering new services for robot users or owners. Robotics can also be leveraged to create entirely new business models or to enhance existing business models.[16] For example, some companies servicing the agricultural industry are shifting to a "robot-as-a-service" (RaaS) business model (e.g., to provide robot-based weeding services that limit the need for their agricultural customers to purchase and manage robots for so many different farming activities). Other industries have started to develop similar RaaS offerings such as delivery RaaS, security RaaS, and cleaning RaaS.[17] For example, RaaS startup Robomart is trialing a driverless grocery-on-wheels service enabling people in the Boston area to grocery shop from their doorstep.[18] Finally, robotics can be leveraged to improve operational effectiveness. The combination of enhanced employee capability and the speed, precision, and 24/7 capabilities of robots can be leveraged to deliver better quality products and customer experiences.

# GOOGLE AND REFLECT

| Digital technology | Common terminology |
|---|---|
| Robotics | Robot axis/degrees of freedom, robot hand guiding, robot reach, robot repeatability, exoskeleton robot, social robots, robot payload, robot grip force, force limited robot, actuator, bionics, robot CPU, cloud robotics, cobots, cyborg, robot end effector, humanoid robot, gynoid robot, android robot, industrial robot, nanobot, RPA, robot uptime, adaptive motion control, robot path simulation, aerobot, combat robot, cruise missile, delta robot, forward chaining, haptic, robot hydraulics, service robot |

# EXAMPLE TOOLS AND VENDORS

| Digital technology | Tools and vendors |
|---|---|
| Robotics | iRobot Roomba 960, iRobot Braava 380T, GreyOrange Butler, GreyOrange Flexo, Arduino, Epson SCARA robots, Boston Dynamics, Boston Dynamics' ATLAS, Boston Dynamics' SPOT, Locus Robotics, SCHUNK, SCHUNK SVH, SCHUNK PGN-plus-E, ASI robots, ASI Chaos High Mobility Robot, ASI Forge Robotic Platform, Honda ASIMO, Softbank Robotics, Softbank's Pepper, Samsung Bot Retail, SamsungBot Care, SamsungBot Air, Sanbot by Qihan technology, Romeo by Softbank Robotics, by Blue Frog Robotics, Aibo by Sony, PIAGGIO "GITA" Cargo Bot, HRP-5P by AIST, Sphero, Diligent Robotics, Picknik Robotics, Sarcos, Bluefin Robotics, Petronics, AMP Robotics, Left Hand Robotics, Harvest Automation, Intuitive Surgical, Myomo, MakerBot Industries, Autodesk Fusion 360, ABB Robotics, Kuka industrial robots |

# DISCUSSION QUESTIONS

1 What is the difference between robots and robotics?
2 What is the difference between robotics and artificial intelligence?

3 What is the difference between a humanoid, an android, and a gynoid robot?

4 What is the most important part of a robot, and why?

5 What is the most common robotic programming language?

6 What is the best way to classify robots, and why?

7 What is the most important business value of robots?

8 How can using robots improve work satisfaction and engagement?

9 How can human beings best compete with robots in the workplace?

10 What five types of sensors can have the greatest impact on the capability of a robot, and how can a robot use the information from each type of sensor?

11 What is the most important ethical issue in relation to using robots?

12 How can robots be used to reduce business risk?

13 What are three examples of product innovation using robots?

14 What are three examples of business model innovation using robots?

# NOTES

1 Nichols, G. (2018). Robotics in business: Everything humans need to know. Retrieved February 3, 2020, from ZDNet website: www.zdnet.com/article/ robotics-in-business-everything-humans-need-to-know/

2 Nichols, G. (2018). Robotics in business: Everything humans need to know. Retrieved February 3, 2020, from ZDNet website: www.zdnet.com/article/ robotics-in-business-everything-humans-need-to-know/; Simon, M. (2017, August 24). What is a robot? Retrieved February 3, 2020, from Wired website: www.wired.com/story/what-is-a-robot/

3 Nichols, G. (2018). Robotics in business: Everything humans need to know. Retrieved February 3, 2020, from ZDNet website: www.zdnet.com/article/ robotics-in-business-everything-humans-need-to-know/

4 Nichols, G. (2018). Robotics in business: Everything humans need to know. Retrieved February 3, 2020, from ZDNet website: www.zdnet.com/article/ robotics-in-business-everything-humans-need-to-know/

5 Simon, M. (2017, August 24). What is a robot? Retrieved February 3, 2020, from Wired website: www.wired.com/story/what-is-a-robot/

6   Holley, P. (2019). New Zealand farmers have a new tool for herding sheep: Drones that bark like dogs. *The Washington Post*. Retrieved from www. washingtonpost.com/technology/2019/03/07/new-zealand-farmers-have-new-tool-herding-sheep-drones-that-bark-like-dogs/; Christian, J. (2019). This drone is a sheepdog. Retrieved February 11, 2020, from World Economic Forum website: www.weforum.org/agenda/2019/03/new-zealand-farmers-are-using-drones-to-herd-sheep/; Paranjape, A. A., Chung, S. J., Kim, K., & Shim, D. H. (2018). Robotic herding of a flock of birds using an unmanned aerial vehicle. *IEEE Transactions on Robotics*, 34(4), 901–915.

7   Double Robotics – Telepresence Robot for Telecommuters. (2020). Doublerobotics.Com. Retrieved from www.doublerobotics.com/

8   Wolfgang, M., Vladimir, L., Sander, A., Martin, J., & Küpper, D. (2017). Gaining robotics advantage. *www.Bcg.Com*. Retrieved from www.bcg.com/en-au/publications/2017/strategy-technology-digital-gaining-robotics-advantage.aspx

9   Crozier, R. (2018). Rio Tinto to build new "intelligent" mines. *ITnews*. Retrieved from www.itnews.com.au/news/rio-tinto-to-build-new-intelligent-mines-494651; Mining Global. (2014). Rio Tinto: Mine of the future. *Miningglobal.Com*; Admin. Retrieved from www.miningglobal.com/operations/rio-tinto-mine-future

10  Wilson, H. J., & Daugherty, P. R. (2018). How Humans and ai are working together in 1,500 companies. *Harvard Business Review*. Retrieved from https://hbr.org/2018/07/collaborative-intelligence-humans-and-ai-are-joining-forces

11  Siegel, E. R., McFadden, C., Monahan, K., Lehren, A. W., & Siniauer, P. (2018). The da Vinci surgical robot: A medical breakthrough with risks for patients. Retrieved February 4, 2020, from NBC News website: www.nbcnews.com/health/health-news/da-vinci-surgical-robot-medical-breakthrough-risks-patients-n949341; Wolfgang, M., Vladimir, L., Sander, A., Martin, J., & Küpper, D. (2017). Gaining robotics advantage. Www.Bcg.Com. Retrieved from www.bcg.com/en-au/publications/2017/strategy-technology-digital-gaining-robotics-advantage.aspx

12  Francis, S. (2020). Carlsberg reduces risk of accidents with universal robots. Retrieved February 4, 2020, from Robotics & Automation News website: https://roboticsandautomationnews.com/2020/01/06/carlsberg-reduces-risk-of-accidents-with-universal-robots/28215/

13  Maneeprom, N., Taneepanichskul, S., Panza, A., & Suputtitada, A. (2019). Effectiveness of robotics fall prevention program among elderly in senior

housings, Bangkok, Thailand: A quasi-experimental study. *Clinical Interventions in Aging*, 14, 335–346. https://doi.org/10.2147/cia.s182336

14 Fischinger, D., Einramhof, P., Papoutsakis, K., Wohlkinger, W., Mayer, P., Panek, P., . . . & Vincze, M. (2016). Hobbit, a care robot supporting independent living at home: First prototype and lessons learned. *Robotics and Autonomous Systems*, 75, 60–78. https://doi.org/10.1016/j.robot.2014.09.029

15 Bemelmans, R., Gelderblom, G. J., Jonker, P., & de Witte, L. (2012). Socially assistive robots in elderly care: A systematic review into effects and effectiveness. *Journal of the American Medical Directors Association*, 13(2), 114–120.e1. https://doi.org/10.1016/j.jamda.2010.10.002; DPS Publishing. (2016). The future is here – robots in aged care. Retrieved February 5, 2020, from Aged Care Guide website: www.agedcareguide.com.au/talking-aged-care/the-future-is-here-robots-in-aged-care

16 PricewaterhouseCoopers. (2015). CEO pulse: Pulse on robotics: PwC. Retrieved February 14, 2020, from PwC website: www.pwc.com/gx/en/ceo-agenda/pulse/robotics.html; Accenture. (2018). Foster innovation with enterprise robotics. Retrieved from www.accenture.com/_acnmedia/pdf-71/accenture-robotics-pov-web.pdf; AMFG. (2019). 5 Examples of how 3D printing is creating new business models. Retrieved February 14, 2020, from AMFG website: https://amfg.ai/2019/11/29/5-examples-of-how-3d-printing-is-creating-new-business-models/

17 PR Newswire. (2019). New robotics: Shifting business models. Retrieved February 5, 2020, from Prnewswire.com website: www.prnewswire.com/news-releases/new-robotics-shifting-business-models-300818816.html

18 Dumont, J. (2019, January 17). Stop & shop will pilot driverless delivery in Boston. Retrieved February 5, 2020, from Grocery Dive website: www.grocerydive.com/news/stop-shop-will-pilot-driverless-delivery-in-boston/546223/

# CHAPTER 25

# Drones Primer

DOI: 10.4324/9781003254614-30

# INTRODUCTION

While they may have initially been seen as merely fads or playthings, commercial applications of drones have grown and continue to grow rapidly. Their use cases across industries now range from delivery or transportation, inspection or monitoring, and video data collection to providing expanded internet connectivity, firefighting/disaster response, inventory tracking, policing, and much more.[1] The varied and growing drone use cases represent opportunities to leverage this technology products and services, reduce costs and risks, enhance operational efficiency and effectiveness, create strategic differentiation, and enhance organization adaptability and agility. However, along with these opportunities come risks – such as regulatory and ethical risks. This primer provides a friendly introduction to key concepts and issues relating to drones, the use cases and growing business value of drones, and the implications of accelerating advancements in drone technology for organizations.

---

**LEARNING OBJECTIVES**

- Develop knowledge of essential definitions and concepts relating drone technologies
- Understand how these technologies and their related applications/practices/tools/methods/techniques can impact the efficiency, differentiation, adaptability, and agility of an organization
- Understand the roles leaders, managers, and supporting professionals can play in maximizing the leveraging of these technologies and their related applications/practices/tools/methods/techniques
- Analyze and evaluate the implications of these technologies and their related applications/practices/tools/methods/techniques, as well as related leadership or management roles in their optimal use, for organizations' digital transformation strategy and digital business strategy

---

- Apply knowledge and understanding of these technologies and their related applications/practices/tools/methods/techniques to participate in, support, or lead workstreams or initiatives related to the leveraging of these technologies to enhance organization digital transformation and digital business strategy

# KEY DRONE CONCEPTS AND BUILDING BLOCKS
## WHAT IS A DRONE?

Drones, also known as unmanned/uncrewed aerial vehicles or systems (UAV or UAS), are aerial vehicles or aircraft that are remotely or autonomously piloted (i.e., not piloted by a human on board).[2] Their counterparts are unmanned or uncrewed ground vehicles (UGVs), which are also remotely or autonomously driven with no human on board. Drones and UGVs can come in many sizes and have many different designs, depending on the task or activities they are designed to carry out.[3] For example, military-style drones and UGVs can be up to the size of commercial airplanes or bigger, whereas hobby-style drones are typically much smaller. In addition to having flight capability, drones can be fitted with a wide variety of sensors to gather information about their environment and robotic capabilities to take actions in that environment.[4] For example, drones for military purposes may be equipped with both computer vision and machine guns; drones for agricultural purposes may be equipped with different sensors and with crop spraying or crop harvesting mechanics; and drones for zoological purposes may have a combination of sensors and robotic features that enable them to enter species' territories, pretend to be one of the species, and fit into a species' social hierarchy[5] (e.g., for recording video footage of the social dynamics of species).[6]

## BUILDING BLOCKS AND FUNCTIONING OF DRONES

Like robots, drones can differ greatly in their design, capabilities, and uses,[7] but they all share some common high-level building blocks (see Figure 25.1 for a visualization of the common building blocks of a drone). All drones usually have a body or frame that is suited to the desired flight approach (e.g., fixed wing or rotary) and the types of tasks or activities the drone is to perform (e.g., surveillance, aerial photography, transporting people).[8] Fixed wing drones fly similar to, or emulate, the flight of normal planes. Therefore, they have a body very similar to normal planes, with rigid wings to generate lift and engines to generate thrust (e.g., to move the drone along the ground fast enough so air pressure can be generated below the wings for lift off). Rotary drones, on the other hand, have two or more rotor blades that not only turn on fixed masts and generate lift but also shape flight direction and speed as the blades rotate through the air.

Drone body size, shape, and internal/external configuration are dependent on the task the drone is to do.[9] For example, a drone to spy on birds or bees

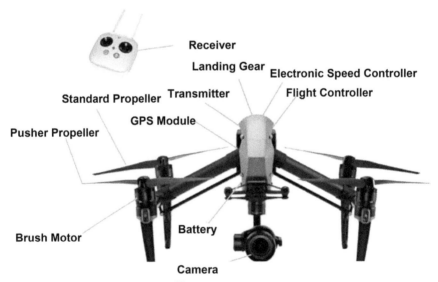

**Figure 25.1** *Components of a drone*[12]

may emulate the shape and appearance of the birds or bees being spied on,[10] whereas a drone to transport people may be designed to prioritize the safety and comfort of passengers and the aesthetics of the drone.[11] Drones usually have some sort of landing gear (e.g., helicopter-style gear for rotary drones and airplane-style gear for fixed wing drones). This landing gear may be an obvious part of the drone's body/frame, or it may require activation. The design of the landing gear depends on the nature of the task to be performed by the drone and the constraints of the environment (e.g., landing on a stark ocean cliff face versus a flat football field or a still river).

Drones usually have propellers, motors, and some form of power supply.[13] For fixed wing drones, propellers propel or provide the forward propulsion to enable the rigid wings to generate lift. For rotary drones, the propellers provide lift and enable speed and steering (e.g., a rotary drone with four propellers may have two standard propellers for lift and two pusher propellers for forward and backward thrust).[14] Motors spin the propellers to enable flight (typically a brushless motor,[15] but it could be other types of motors or even a miniature engine).[16] A rotary drone with four propellers typically has a motor for each propeller, each of which draws on the drone's power supply (e.g., batteries, solar cells, hydro fuel cell, combustion engine, AC cable tethering, laser transmitter).[17] The power supply is usually encased in the body of the drone. Without the power supply, it would be difficult to activate all the onboard components (e.g., motors, sensors, cameras, computers, robot-like mechanics).

Drones also have a flight controller and electronic speed controllers (ESC). A flight controller is an onboard computer that receives control information from the pilot on the ground (instructions such as: more lift, more speed, change direction), from onboard sensors (objects in the way, wind speed and direction), and from the GPS module (specifying location in longitude, latitude, and elevation).[18] The flight controller combines this information to send instructions to the propellers (spin the forward propellers this direction, create this much lift). The electronic speed controllers connect the flight controller to the motors, so a four-propeller drone or quadcopter would need an ESC for each propeller motor.[19]

The ESCs take instructions from the flight controller and power from the drone's power supply to make propeller motors spin a particular way.[20]

Drones usually have a transmitter and receiver to enable communication with the drone. The transmitter is a remote-control device that the pilot on the ground or drone operator uses to send instructions (e.g., radio signals) to the receiver on the drone.[21] The job of the receiver is to receive the instructions or signals and pass them on to the flight controller.[22] The receiver may also pass data back to the transmitter for the pilot or operator on the ground to use. Drones usually have one or more onboard sensors, which can vary from drone to drone depending on what the drone will be used for.[23] Examples of onboard drone sensors include gyroscopes, barometers, accelerometers, GPS, magnetometers, range finders, obstacle sensors, distance sensors, thermal sensors, chemical sensors, and orientation sensors.

The components discussed thus far are found on most drones. Cameras, onboard computers, smartphone-like capabilities, and robotic capabilities are other less common components. Although less common, these components can significantly enhance the capabilities of drones and their business value. For example, sophisticated cameras and computation can enable sophisticated surveying and computer vision based remote monitoring. Robotic capabilities and onboard computers can enable remote action (e.g., picking up and moving objects, taking out a terrorist, cleaning skyscraper windows). Adding sophisticated artificial intelligence algorithms can empower drones to take autonomous action (e.g., search and chase a person of interest while deploying and directing nearby police squads to capture them, rescue people from burning buildings, map a neighborhood or construction site, herd livestock, identify and remove dangerous obstacles, fight fires, find and destroy other drones).[24] Smartphone-like capabilities can enable remote voice-based instructions, the building of apps to expand the drone's capabilities, and more.[25] An important issue for many geographies is ensuring drones operate in an aerial space in which there they don't interfere with aircraft space, suburban infrastructure, and dwelling spaces (e.g., see Figure 25.2 for NASA's proposed space for drone operation).

*Figure 25.2* *NASA's proposed space for drone operation: below aircraft space and above suburban infrastructure and dwellings*[26]

# BUSINESS VALUE AND USE CASES OF DRONES

Drone use cases to date have included 3D mapping, delivery or transportation, inspection or monitoring, infrastructure maintenance, expanded internet connectivity, video data collection, search and rescue, firefighting/disaster response, filmmaking, lighting, inventory tracking, insurance, policing, and more.[27] For 3D mapping, drones have been used in industries such as agriculture, construction, and mining to survey sites, take photos, and create accurate contour maps that would otherwise be impossible or much less efficient to produce.[28] For delivery and transportation, drones have been used to deliver parcels; for example, Zipline is a US-based company that uses drones to deliver blood and vaccines to regions in developing countries still lacking infrastructure) and even hot food much more efficiently than a driver.[29] And in some regions of the world, drone-based taxi or Uber services are being offered.[30]

For inspection and monitoring, drones have been used to inspect site, building, and other infrastructure conditions.[31] For infrastructure maintenance, companies such as Aerones produce industrial drones that can remove ice buildup on wind turbines, clean skyscraper windows, stitch or fill cracks, clean drainage areas, and sand and paint.[32] For expanded internet connectivity, drones are being used to establish or amplify wireless internet connectivity during large-scale events or in regions where this previously was not possible without expensive infrastructure.[33] For video data collection, drones can be used to capture video footage in remote or hard to access locations and sensitive settings (e.g., silently and inconspicuously capturing wildlife interactions up close).[34] For search and rescue, drones have been used in a variety of challenges including monitoring beaches and dropping life buoys to swimmers in trouble, spotting shark threats and alerting swimmers, finding lost hikers, locating people in burning buildings, and assessing the status or impact of disaster events.[35]

Filmmaking drones like the DJI Inspire 2 put cinema quality filming capabilities in the hands of the average person and provide film professionals with the opportunity to film using angles, stability, and focus types not possible with normal film cameras.[36] For lighting, drones can be used to create completely new spectacles at concerts, fireworks, and sporting events. For inventory tracking, drones with time-of-flight (ToF) sensors are used in industries like mining, agriculture, and forestry to measure amounts of soil, timber, stones, waste, and so forth.[37] For insurance, drones can fly over natural event or accident sites to assess damage severity and causes, which can help with claim applications.[38] Drones can be applied for a wide variety of policing uses such as helicopter replacements, self-directing monitoring devices, and crowd or population control devices (e.g., a drone could be used to inconspicuously follow a fugitive, leading police right to him without the commotion of a car or helicopter chase).[39]

These example use cases are just the beginning; many more exist and even more will emerge each year as drone technologies impact every industry.

Drones are not a fad; in fact, some observers have equated the evolution and impact of drones to that of personal computers and mobile phones – while their potential value was clear, the eventual pace, scale, and pervasiveness of their impact was hard to imagine.

## GOOGLE AND REFLECT

| Digital technology | Common terminology |
| --- | --- |
| Drones | Ready-to-fly (RTF) drone, almost-ready-to-fly (ARTF) drone, bind-and-fly (BNF) drone, quadcopter, octocopter, multicopter, drone flight time, gimbal, drone collision/obstacle avoidance, drone pitch, drone roll, drone yaw, UAS (unmanned aircraft system), drone frequency, drone S mode, drone P mode, A mode, dronie, field of view (FOV), drone firmware, FPV (first-person view) drone, geofencing, GLONASS, gyroscope, inertial measurement unit (IMU), infrared drone/UAV, photogrammetry, PIC (pilot in command), racing drone, drone return to home (RTH), target drone, decoy drone, reconnaissance drone, combat drone |

## EXAMPLE TOOLS AND VENDORS

| Digital technology | Tools and vendors |
| --- | --- |
| Drones | DJI drones, GoPro Karma Drone, 3D Robotics IRIS+, Hubsan Zino, Lockheed Martin RQ-170 Sentinel, Parrot AR.Drone 2.0, Yuneec Typhoon Q500 quadcopter, EVO by Autel Robotics, ambulance drone by Delft Technical University, Plan Bee drone, Volocopter, Flirtey Eagle drone, SureFly, GimBall, PD-100 Black Hornet, Aerix Aerius, RoboBee X-Wing, DJI MG-1P Agricultural Spraying Drone, Neurala, Skycatch software, Alive software platform, Skydio drone |

# DISCUSSION QUESTIONS

1  What is the difference between a helicopter-sized drone, a helicopter, and a flying robot?
2  What is the most important sensor on a drone?
3  What is the smartest part of a drone?
4  What is the minimum and maximum number of propellers a drone can have?
5  How could artificial intelligence be used in a drone?
6  Could a drone be used to autonomously hedge trim a hedge? How could it work?
7  What is the biggest public concern about drones?
8  What is the biggest legal issue in relation to drones?
9  What is the most important business value of drones?

# NOTES

1  McKinsey & Company. (2017). Commercial drones are here: The future of unmanned aerial systems. Retrieved from www.mckinsey.com/industries/capital-projects-and-infrastructure/our-insights/commercial-drones-are-here-the-future-of-unmanned-aerial-systems; Taking flight. (2016). *The Economist*. Retrieved from www.economist.com/technology-quarterly/2017-06-08/civilian-drones; Corrigan, F. (2019). What are drones used for from business to critical missions. *DroneZon*. Retrieved from www.dronezon.com/drones-for-good/what-are-drones-used-for-and-best-drone-uses/

2  Taking flight. (2016). *The Economist*. Retrieved from www.economist.com/technology-quarterly/2017-06-08/civilian-drones; Corrigan, F. (2019). How do drones work and what is drone technology. *DroneZon*. Retrieved from www.dronezon.com/learn-about-drones-quadcopters/what-is-drone-technology-or-how-does-drone-technology-work/; Pierce, D. (2018). Drones: The Complete Guide. Retrieved February 11, 2020, from Wired website: www.wired.com/story/guide-drones/

3  Taking flight. (2016). *The Economist*. Retrieved from www.economist.com/technology-quarterly/2017-06-08/civilian-drones; Corrigan, F. (2019). How do drones work and what is drone technology. *DroneZon*.

Retrieved from www.dronezon.com/learn-about-drones-quadcopters/
what-is-drone-technology-or-how-does-drone-technology-work/

4  Corrigan, F. (2019). How do drones work and what is drone technology.
   *DroneZon*. Retrieved from www.dronezon.com/learn-about-drones-quadcopters/
   what-is-drone-technology-or-how-does-drone-technology-work/

5  Baggaley, K. (2019). Forget Props and fixed wings. *New Bio-Inspired Drones
   Mimic birds, Bats and Bugs*. Retrieved February 6, 2020, from NBC News
   website: www.nbcnews.com/mach/science/forget-props-fixed-wings-new-
   bio-inspired-drones-mimic-birds-ncna1033061

6  Mingle, J. (2019). Saving the planet one drone at a time. *Department of
   Zoology*. Retrieved February 6, 2020, from Ox.ac.uk website: www.zoo.ox.ac.
   uk/article/saving-planet-one-drone-time

7  Corrigan, F. (2019). How do drones work and what is drone technology.
   *DroneZon*. Retrieved from www.dronezon.com/learn-about-drones-quadcopters/
   what-is-drone-technology-or-how-does-drone-technology-work/

8  Corrigan, F. (2019). How do drones work and what is drone technology.
   *DroneZon*. Retrieved from www.dronezon.com/learn-about-drones-quadcopters/
   what-is-drone-technology-or-how-does-drone-technology-work/

9  Corrigan, F. (2019). How do drones work and what is drone technology.
   *DroneZon*. Retrieved from www.dronezon.com/learn-about-drones-quadcopters/
   what-is-drone-technology-or-how-does-drone-technology-work/

10 Baggaley, K. (2019). Forget props and fixed wings. *New Bio-Inspired
   Drones Mimic birds, Bats and Bugs*. Retrieved February 11, 2020, from
   NBC News website: www.nbcnews.com/mach/science/forget-props-fixed-
   wings-new-bio-inspired-drones-mimic-birds-ncna1033061; New Scientist.
   (2005). Airborne robotic spycraft inspired by seagulls. Retrieved February 11,
   2020, from New Scientist website: https://institutions.newscientist.com/
   article/mg18725155-900-airborne-robotic-spycraft-inspired-by-seagulls/

11 Flanagan, B. (2019, September 9). The maker of Dubai's flying taxi aims to set
   flight within the next three years. Retrieved February 6, 2020, from WIRED
   Middle East website: https://wired.me/science/transportation/dubai-drone-
   flying-taxis-volocopter/; Blanchard, S., & Randall, I. (2019). Self-driving flying
   taxi with 18 drone-like propellers is tested in the skies of Singapore. Retrieved
   February 6, 2020, from Mail Online website: www.dailymail.co.uk/sciencetech/
   article-7599343/Hover-taxi-whizzes-Singapore-firm-eyes-Asian-push.html

12 Grind Drone. (2017). Drone components and what they do. Retrieved from
   http://grinddrone.com/drone-features/drone-components

13 Corrigan, F. (2019). How do drones work and what is drone technology. *DroneZon*. Retrieved from www.dronezon.com/learn-about-drones-quadcopters/what-is-drone-technology-or-how-does-drone-technology-work/

14 Corrigan, F. (2019). How do drones work and what is drone technology. *DroneZon*. Retrieved from www.dronezon.com/learn-about-drones-quadcopters/what-is-drone-technology-or-how-does-drone-technology-work/

15 Renesas Electronics. (2020). What are brushless DC motors. Retrieved February 11, 2020, from www.renesas.com/us/cn/support/technical-resources/engineer-school/brushless-dc-motor-01-overview.html

16 Nichols, G. (2019). Why don't drones use small versions of commercial aircraft engines? *ZDNet*. Retrieved from www.zdnet.com/article/why-dont-drones-use-small-versions-of-commercial-aircraft-engines/

17 Arriansyah, A. (2016). The 6 known ways to power a drone. *Techinasia.Com*. Retrieved from www.techinasia.com/talk/6-known-ways-power-a-drone

18 Corrigan, F. (2019). How do drones work and what is drone technology. *DroneZon*. Retrieved from www.dronezon.com/learn-about-drones-quadcopters/what-is-drone-technology-or-how-does-drone-technology-work/

19 Corrigan, F. (2019). How do drones work and what is drone technology. *DroneZon*. Retrieved from www.dronezon.com/learn-about-drones-quadcopters/what-is-drone-technology-or-how-does-drone-technology-work/

20 Corrigan, F. (2019). How do drones work and what is drone technology. *DroneZon*. Retrieved from www.dronezon.com/learn-about-drones-quadcopters/what-is-drone-technology-or-how-does-drone-technology-work/

21 Corrigan, F. (2019). How do drones work and what is drone technology. *DroneZon*. Retrieved from www.dronezon.com/learn-about-drones-quadcopters/what-is-drone-technology-or-how-does-drone-technology-work/

22 Corrigan, F. (2019). How do drones work and what is drone technology. *DroneZon*. Retrieved from www.dronezon.com/learn-about-drones-quadcopters/what-is-drone-technology-or-how-does-drone-technology-work/

23 Corrigan, F. (2019). How do drones work and what is drone technology. *DroneZon*. Retrieved from www.dronezon.com/learn-about-drones-quadcopters/what-is-drone-technology-or-how-does-drone-technology-work/

24 Wyder, P. M., Chen, Y. S., Lasrado, A. J., Pelles, R. J., Kwiatkowski, R., Comas, E. O., . . . & Xiong, Z. (2019). Autonomous drone hunter operating by deep learning and all-onboard computations in GPS-denied environments. *PLoS ONE*, 14(11).

25 Daley, S. (2018). Fighting fires and saving elephants: How 12 companies are using the AI drone to solve big problems. Retrieved February 10, 2020, from Built In website: https://builtin.com/artificial-intelligence/drones-ai-companies; Leswing, K. (2015). DJI's powerful new computer will lead to better drone apps. Retrieved February 11, 2020, from Fortune website: https://fortune.com/2015/11/02/dji-manifold-computer/

26 McLellan, C. (2018, May 15). The new commute: How driverless cars, hyperloop, and drones will change our travel plans. Retrieved June 21, 2020, from TechRepublic website: www.techrepublic.com/article/the-new-commute-how-driverless-cars-hyperloop-and-drones-will-change-our-travel-plans/

27 McKinsey & Company. (2017). Commercial drones are here: The future of unmanned aerial systems. Retrieved from www.mckinsey.com/industries/capital-projects-and-infrastructure/our-insights/commercial-drones-are-here-the-future-of-unmanned-aerial-systems; Taking flight. (2016). *The Economist*. Retrieved from www.economist.com/technology-quarterly/2017-06-08/civilian-drones; Corrigan, F. (2019). What are drones used for from business to critical missions. *DroneZon*. Retrieved from www.dronezon.com/drones-for-good/what-are-drones-used-for-and-best-drone-uses/

28 Taking flight. (2016). *The Economist*. Retrieved from www.economist.com/technology-quarterly/2017-06-08/civilian-drones; Corrigan, F. (2019). What are drones used for from business to critical missions. *DroneZon*. Retrieved from www.dronezon.com/drones-for-good/what-are-drones-used-for-and-best-drone-uses/

29 Taking flight. (2016). *The Economist*. Retrieved from www.economist.com/technology-quarterly/2017-06-08/civilian-drones; Corrigan, F. (2019). What are drones used for from business to critical missions. *DroneZon*. Retrieved from www.dronezon.com/drones-for-good/what-are-drones-used-for-and-best-drone-uses/; Amazon. (2019). Amazon.com: Prime Air. *Amazon.Com*. Retrieved from www.amazon.com/Amazon-Prime-Air/b?node=8037720011

30 Flanagan, B. (2019). The maker of Dubai's flying taxi aims to set flight within the next three years. Retrieved February 11, 2020, from WIRED Middle East website: https://wired.me/science/transportation/dubai-drone-flying-taxis-volocopter/

31 Taking flight. (2016). *The Economist*. Retrieved from www.economist.com/
technology-quarterly/2017-06-08/civilian-drones; Corrigan, F. (2019). What
are drones used for from business to critical missions. *DroneZon*. Retrieved
from www.dronezon.com/drones-for-good/what-are-drones-used-for-and-
best-drone-uses/

32 Heater, B. (2018). Aerones makes really big drones for cleaning turbines and
saving lives. *TechCrunch*. Retrieved from https://techcrunch.com/2018/03/17/
aerones-makes-really-big-drones-for-cleaning-turbines-and-saving-
lives/; Aerones. (2018). Aerones. Retrieved from www.aerones.com/eng/
wind_turbine_maintenance_drone/

33 Etherington, D. (2014). Google acquires titan aerospace, the drone company
pursued by Facebook. *TechCrunch*. Retrieved from https://techcrunch.
com/2014/04/14/google-acquires-titan-aerospace-the-drone-company-
pursued-by-facebook/; Taking flight. (2016). *The Economist*. Retrieved from
www.economist.com/technology-quarterly/2017-06-08/civilian-drones;
Russell, J. (2019). Facebook is reportedly testing solar-powered internet
drones again – this time with airbus. *TechCrunch*. Retrieved from https://
techcrunch.com/2019/01/21/facebook-airbus-solar-drones-internet-
program/; Hickey, M. (2016). Report: Google working on awesome solar-
powered broadband drones for 5g wireless internet. *Forbes*. Retrieved
February 10, 2020, from www.forbes.com/sites/matthickey/2016/01/31/
report-google-working-on-awesome-solar-powered-broadband-drones-
for-5g-wireless-internet/#23e6c2f96a43; Hickey, M. (2016). Report:
Google working on awesome solar-powered broadband drones for
5g wireless internet. *Forbes*. Retrieved from www.forbes.com/sites/
matthickey/2016/01/31/report-google-working-on-awesome-solar-powered-
broadband-drones-for-5g-wireless-internet/#1524f1ff6a43

34 Taking flight. (2016). *The Economist*. Retrieved from www.economist.com/
technology-quarterly/2017-06-08/civilian-drones; Corrigan, F. (2019). What
are drones used for from business to critical missions. *DroneZon*. Retrieved
from www.dronezon.com/drones-for-good/what-are-drones-used-for-and-
best-drone-uses/; Baggaley, K. (2019). Forget props and fixed wings. *New
Bio-Inspired Drones Mimic Birds, Bats and Bugs*. Retrieved February 11,
2020, from NBC News website: www.nbcnews.com/mach/science/
forget-props-fixed-wings-new-bio-inspired-drones-mimic-birds-ncna1033061

35 Taking flight. (2016). *The Economist*. Retrieved from www.economist.
com/technology-quarterly/2017-06-08/civilian-drones; Corrigan, F.

(2019). What are drones used for from business to critical missions. *DroneZon*. Retrieved from www.dronezon.com/drones-for-good/what-are-drones-used-for-and-best-drone-uses/

36 Corrigan, F. (2019). What are drones used for from business to critical missions. *DroneZon*. Retrieved from www.dronezon.com/drones-for-good/what-are-drones-used-for-and-best-drone-uses/

37 Corrigan, F. (2019). What are drones used for from business to critical missions. *DroneZon*. Retrieved from www.dronezon.com/drones-for-good/what-are-drones-used-for-and-best-drone-uses/

38 Corrigan, F. (2019). What are drones used for from business to critical missions. *DroneZon*. Retrieved from www.dronezon.com/drones-for-good/what-are-drones-used-for-and-best-drone-uses/; Taking flight. (2016). *The Economist*. Retrieved from www.economist.com/technology-quarterly/2017-06-08/civilian-drones

39 Corrigan, F. (2019). What are drones used for from business to critical missions. *DroneZon*. Retrieved from www.dronezon.com/drones-for-good/what-are-drones-used-for-and-best-drone-uses/

# CHAPTER 26

# 3D and 4D Printing Primer

DOI: 10.4324/9781003254614-31

# INTRODUCTION

3D and 4D printers use computer-generated blueprints and "inks" made from an almost unlimited variety materials to create or "print" required objects. Sometimes this is through depositing the "inks" layer by layer and other times producing the objects instantly through exposure of printing materials to light, for example. For businesses that do or can design, use, and sell physical goods, 3D and 4D printers present opportunities to democratize production or present new ways to produce or source such goods much more cost effectively, often with less supply or usage limitations, less storage issues, and less obsolescence issues. For example, imagine a seller producing the goods needed for sale on demand at the push of a button, at significantly reduced cost, and absent the ordering, shipping, inventory management, and obsolescence risks typically associated with inventory businesses. Or imagine a designer circumventing the traditional manufacturing challenges by 3D/4D printing their designs themselves or by just selling their designs direct to consumers who have access to 3D printers. 3D/4D printing technology has extensive and growing use cases across industries that offer product innovation, business model innovation, efficiency, effectiveness, product/service differentiation, and improved customer experience opportunities. As of 2020, the global 3D printing market was valued at $12.6 billion and forecast to grow at an annual compound rate of 21–24% over the next 7 years. It is likely that these forecasts are too conservative. This primer provides a friendly introduction to the key concepts and issues relating to 3D/4D printers, their use cases and growing business value, and the implications of accelerating advancements in 3D/4D printing technology for organizations.

## LEARNING OBJECTIVES

- Develop knowledge of essential definitions and concepts relating to 3D/4D printing technologies
- Understand how these technologies and their related applications/practices/tools/methods/techniques can impact

the efficiency, differentiation, adaptability, and agility of an organization

- Understand the roles leaders, managers, and supporting professionals can play in maximizing the leveraging of these technologies and their related applications/practices/tools/methods/techniques

- Analyze and evaluate the implications of these technologies and their related applications/practices/tools/methods/techniques, as well as related leadership or management roles in their optimal use, for organizations' digital transformation strategy and digital business strategy

- Apply knowledge and understanding of these technologies and their related applications/practices/tools/methods/techniques to participate in, support, or lead workstreams or initiatives related to the leveraging of these technologies to enhance organization digital transformation and digital business strategy

# KEY 3D/4D PRINTING CONCEPTS AND BUILDING BLOCKS

## WHAT IS 3D AND 4D PRINTING?

The term 3D printing (also known as additive manufacturing or desktop fabrication) refers to the use of commercial or consumer equipment (a printer) that, under computational control, deposits material layer by layer until a three-dimensional object is created in accordance with the specifications of a computer-aided design (CAD) model.[1] Originally, the printed object may have been scanned with 3D object scanners or designed with CAD software. These 3D printers can recreate the object with superior precision, accuracy, and efficiency.[2] A 4D printer also builds 3D objects layer by layer but, unlike 3D printing, smart materials are used that enable an object to change its shape over time if exposed to water, heat, light, current, or magnetic fields – this change in shape is the "fourth dimension" that gives 4D printing its name. So 4D printing brings together 3D printing, smart materials (e.g., photo-polymeric liquid that hardens when exposed to light or photoresist material that decompose already solid polymers into liquids), and shape-changing design.

## BUILDING BLOCKS AND FUNCTIONING OF 3D AND 4D PRINTING

Although what they do is sophisticated, the common elements of 3D printers are straightforward (see Figure 26.1 for common elements of a basic 3D printer). 3D printers usually have a frame, power supply, and motion components. The frame houses all the components of the 3D printer. The frame design affects stability and durability of the machine and the size of what can be printed (assuming what is printed does not later expand). Some 3D printers have an open frame and others have a semi-closed or completely enclosed frame. The benefits of an enclosed frame include temperature stability and protection from dust and other things that could get stuck in the 3D printer. The power supply powers everything in the 3D printer. It is commonly encased together with the user interface and mounted on the frame. The power supply influences the temperature or heat the 3D printer can generate and thus the type of layering material (or filament) that it uses to print. The motion components are the combination of motors, belts, and other parts that ensure the nozzle depositing the layering material and/or the object being worked on are continuously moved into the right position along the three dimensions (e.g., the right combination of left and right, up and down, and forward and backward). The motion components basically translate computational instructions into the right physical movement or positioning of the nozzle and object being worked on.

The 3D printer has a controller board and some form of user interface. The controller board (sometimes referred to as the motherboard, mainboard, or brain of the 3D printer) sends motion instructions to the motion components based on commands it receives from a computer and on information it gets from sensors (e.g., heat and motion sensors). The user

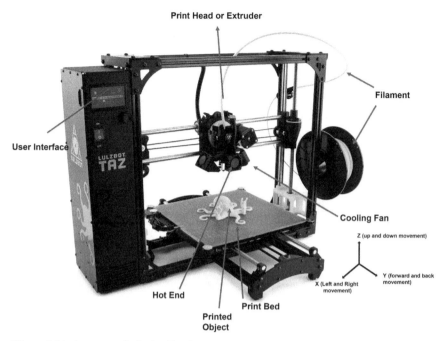

**Figure 26.1** *Anatomy of a basic 3D printer*

interface is a screen that enables a user to receive status information and make adjustments (e.g., pause layering, reload layering material). The user interface is usually already built into the frame but can also be a separate unit. Either way, the user interface can be a basic LCD screen controlled with knobs, dials, and buttons or it could be a high-end touch screen.

For the layering process, 3D printers have filaments, print heads (or extruders), and a print bed. The filament is the material deposited in the layering process, or what the 3D printed objects are made out of. It is similar to ink for a normal 2D printer. There are many different types of filaments (e.g., made of different materials, different colors, different sizes/ diameters). Filaments usually come on a spool (like those used to coil wire around), which is loaded on the 3D printer's spool holder. One end of the filament is inserted into the print head (or extruder) and gradually feeds into the print head at the rate the depositing is occurring. The print head is made up of cold end and hot end sections. The cold end clamps the filament and pushes it into the hot end. The hot end then melts the filament and deposits it or layers it (via the print head nozzle) as per the CAD model specifications of the object being printed. The sections of the print head have various drives, fans, and sensors to ensure that the filament is kept at the right temperature as it is fed from the spool and out the print head nozzle. Nozzles are interchangeable and come in different sizes depending on what is being printed and the desired print speed. A 3D printer can have a print head with more than one nozzle, or it can have more than one print head. In turn, the different print heads or nozzles can use different filaments at the same time, to enable printing of an object with more than one material. The print bed on 3D printers is the surface on which the layered printing of the object occurs. In Figure 26.1 you can see that the print bed moves the object being printed forward and back to have it in the required position for depositing. The print bed surface can be made of various materials that can influence how flat the surface is kept, how easy it is to remove the printed object, how easy it is to clean the surface, and more. A 3D printer may be connected to a network to enable remote control or monitoring of the printing process, and it may have one or more file transfer options (e.g., USB or SD card) so users can upload files for printing and initiate the print job using the available user interface.

## TYPES OF 3D PRINTERS

There are different types of 3D printers depending on their approach to 3D printing. Commonly, the types include fused deposition modeling (FDM) printers, stereolithography (SLA) printers and laser sintering (SLS) printers. For FDM printers, the approach is as just described (i.e., filament is fed into a print head, melted, and extruded through the print head nozzle for layering). These types of printers are inexpensive (starting at a few hundred dollars), are widely used, and therefore have a wide variety of parts and materials available. In contrast, SLA printers start out with a liquid resin that is then hardened by a beam of UV light (i.e., instead of starting out with filament that needs to be melted). This type of printer is ideal for printing objects that contain great detail and require a smooth finish. Starting prices for this type of printer can be two to five times those of FDM printers. Finally, SLS printers work like SLA printers except that they start off with a powder instead of a liquid (e.g., nylon). This type of printer spreads a layer of the powder and then uses laser beams to sinter, or raise the temperature, of specific parts of the powder layer so as to trace out and solidify a layer of the model. This process is repeated layer by layer until the physical object is fully printed. This type of printing enables printing using aluminum, nylon, sandstone, silver, and steel. It also enables very finely detailed objects to be made. Pricing for these types of printers start at around 40,000 to 50,000 times the price of SLA printers.

# 3D AND 4D PRINTING BUSINESS VALUE AND USE CASES

Early value from 3D printing includes product innovation, business model innovation, efficiency, effectiveness, product/service differentiation, and improved customer experience. The emphasized value and use cases have varied from industry to industry.[3] For product innovation, a number of organizations in different industries are using 3D printing for cost effective and faster prototyping of product designs. Yet other organizations are using 3D printers to create add-on components that significantly expand the usability of existing products used in day-to-day operations. For business model innovation, some organizations are offering completely new 3D printing-based business models that include licensing of 3D printing designs and 3D printing-as-a-service (e.g., HP Inc. established HP 3D Printing Solutions as a new business that offers 3D printers, care services, lifecycle management, training, and optimization advisory services).[4] For efficiency, organizations in a range of industries are using 3D printing for low volume manufacturing of custom products and parts, thereby saving on costly engagement of high volume manufacturers (e.g., creating and using highly customized products that improve the efficiency of value chain processes or recreating a version of existing products/components that are too expensive via existing sourcing channels).[5] Some organizations are creating novel components to fit existing equipment, thus greatly expanding the usability of that equipment and therefore the efficiency of processes using it. For effectiveness, 3D printers are being used to plug component/part accessibility gaps for parts/components that are out of production but still required for a particular business' operations (e.g., it may be that the sole manufacturer has shut down or ceased making the part). In healthcare, this includes custom organs or other body parts for which there may not be enough human donors.[6] For product differentiation, some organizations are using 3D printers to create unique branded accessories and art that enhance brand awareness and value and enhance consumer experiences of particular settings. Products and parts that are 3D printed eliminate shipping costs, minimize inventory costs (e.g., by enabling 3D designs to be "stored in the cloud" so physical versions can be printed on demand),[7] eliminate product portability issues (e.g., the design can simply be emailed and printed, rather than needing to package and send to different locations), and more. As with other digital technologies covered so far, these use cases are just the beginning.[8]

# 3D AND 4D PRINTING ISSUES AND RISKS

While 3D and 4D printing continue to evolve quickly and to create expanding efficiency, effectiveness, differentiation, and adaptability opportunities for organizations, they come with inherent risks. These include ambiguous and underdeveloped regulation, security and privacy, societal attitudes toward them, dependability and reliability issues, and availability of assurance and support services. Regarding regulations, it is easy for staff using 3D/4D printers to be unaware of and breach copyrighted 3D/4D designs. It is also easy for staff to use these digital technologies for activities for which there is no restricting regulation as yet but that may be frowned on by society (e.g., robots or drones may capture and use sensitive video footage, causing community outrage). Regarding security and privacy, early versions of digital technologies are typically made by startup companies that may not yet have fully addressed possible social/environmental impacts (e.g., energy consumption, waste, environmental pollution impacts that might arise from use of 3D/4D printers). If organizations don't consider such concerns, they may find any gains from technology use being undone by communities boycotting their services. Finally, digital technologies go through hype and disillusionment cycles, and organizations have to ensure they don't get carried away with the hype (thus pushing the implementation of technologies that aren't quite dependable/reliable yet) or carried away with the disillusionment (thus denying, ignoring, or undertaking technology adoption so glacially that they become another Kodak or Blockbuster).

# GOOGLE AND REFLECT

| Digital technology | Common terminology |
|---|---|
| 3D/4D Printing | Acrylonitrile butadiene styrene (ABS), 3D printing G-code, polylactic acid (PLA), RepRap, 3D printer slicer, STL file format, 3D model slicer, heated print bed, Kapton tape, subtractive manufacturing, 3D print shell, 3D print raft, 3D print infill, 3D print curing, 3D sculpting, 3D printing overhang |

# EXAMPLE TOOLS AND VENDORS

| Digital technology | Tools and vendors |
|---|---|
| 3D/4D Printing | Lulzbot Mini, Prusa i3 MK2, Formlabs Form 2, Anycubic Photon, Monoprice Maker Select Plus, Stratasys Fortus 250mc, MakerBot Replicator Z18, HP Jet Fusion 3D 4200 Printer, ProJet MJP 3600, Tronxy X5ST-500, BigRep ONE v3, Erectorbot EB 2076 LX, Builder Extreme 2000, BLB Industries THE BOX, Sciaky EBAM 110, AutoDesk Inventor, Autodesk 123D, Google SketchUp Make, Slic3r, Skeinforge, KISSlicer, HP 3D printing, Proto Labs, 3D Systems, Materialise 3D printing, Arcam AB, Autodesk, Stratasys Ltd, The ExOne Company, Hoganas AB, Optomec, Inc., Organovo Holdings, Inc., Ponoko Limited, Voxeljet AG, Formlabs 3D printers, Revolution 3D Printers, Airwolf 3D Printers |

# DISCUSSION QUESTIONS

1 How is a 3D printer different from a 2D printer?
2 Can a 3D printer be used for 4D printing?
3 Which is the more important technology: 3D printing or additive manufacturing?
4 If you had an old machine for which there were no longer any repair parts being made, how would you go about using a 3D printer to solve that problem?
5 What is the cheapest type of 3D printing technology? What is the most expensive type?
6 Which 3D printing technology is best for making products out of metal?
7 Which 3D printing technology is best for making decorative glass products?
8 Are 3D-printed products as good as those manufactured traditionally?
9 Will 3D printing be bigger than the internet? Why?
10 What is the best 3D printer for consumer use, and why?
11 What is the best 3D printer for industrial use, and why?
12 What types of services are provided for 3D printing-as-a-service (3daaS)?
13 What is the most serious strategic risk for businesses in relation to adopting 3D printing?

# NOTES

1 Gewirtz, D. (2020). Everything You need to know about 3D printing and its impact on your business. Retrieved February 14, 2020, from ZDNet website: www.zdnet.com/article/everything-you-need-to-know-about-3d-printing-and-its-impact-on-your-business/
2 Gewirtz, D. (2020). Everything You need to know about 3D printing and its impact on your business. Retrieved February 14, 2020, from ZDNet website: www.zdnet.com/article/everything-you-need-to-know-about-3d-printing-and-its-impact-on-your-business/

3   Conlin, B. (2018). More than prototypes: A look at the 3D printing industry. Retrieved February 14, 2020, from Business News Daily website: www.businessnewsdaily.com/9297-3d-printing-for-business.html

4   Hewlett Packard Inc. (2017). HP 3DaaS – 3D Printer services, supplies and support | HP® official site. Retrieved February 12, 2020, from Hp.com website: www8.hp.com/us/en/printers/3d-printers/services/3daaS.html; Rayna, T., & Striukova, L. (2016). From rapid prototyping to home fabrication: How 3D printing is changing business model innovation. *Technological Forecasting and Social Change*, 102, 214–224. https://doi.org/10.1016/j.techfore.2015.07.023

5   Graphic Display World. (2019). The new business case for 3D printing. Retrieved February 14, 2020, from Graphicdisplayworld.com website: www.graphicdisplayworld.com/features/the-new-business-case-for-3d-printing

6   Starr, M. (2015). Cancer patient receives 3D-Printed sternum and ribs. Retrieved February 14, 2020, from CNET website: www.cnet.com/news/cancer-patient-receives-3d-printed-sternum-ribs/

7   Gannes, L. (2013). With KeyMe, an iPhone Pic now means you can always print more house keys later. *AllThingsD*. Retrieved from http://allthingsd.com/20130808/with-keyme-an-iphone-pic-now-means-you-can-always-print-more-housekeys-later/

8   Columbus, L. (2018). The state of 3D printing, 2018. *Forbes*. Retrieved from www.forbes.com/sites/louiscolumbus/2018/05/30/the-state-of-3d-printing-2018/#423edb287b0a

# CHAPTER 27

# 6G, 5G, 4G, LTE, and Other Cellular Networks Primer

DOI: 10.4324/9781003254614-32

# INTRODUCTION

This primer on cellular networks is the first of four primers that have an overarching focus on connectivity technologies. That is, technologies that enable people, systems, devices, and other things to pass and receive information from each other. It is the passing and receiving of this information, in combination with computation and storage, that is at the heart of and extends the power of other digital technologies like cloud computing, the Internet of Things, artificial intelligence, and robotics/drones. The primer introduces cellular standards, data transmission speed, transmission range, the amount of data that can be sent, connectivity reliability, connection security, connection availability, and connection portability. It also discusses issues such as power consumption, infrastructure setup and maintenance costs, and connectivity equipment availability/reliability. The range of available connectivity technologies/standards require leaders, managers, and supporting professionals to understand how different technologies/ standards work and what their strengths and shortcomings are. It also requires them to make important choices about which standards to go with for what purposes and when to experiment with a particular technology/standard, when to cut the cord on an existing connectivity technology/standard, and when to undertake large-scale adoption of a new standard.

---

**LEARNING OBJECTIVES**

- Develop knowledge of essential definitions and concepts relating cellular network technologies
- Understand how these technologies and their related applications/practices/tools/methods/techniques can impact the efficiency, differentiation, adaptability, and agility of an organization
- Understand the roles leaders, managers, and supporting professionals can play in maximizing the leveraging of these

---

technologies and their related applications/practices/tools/
methods/techniques

- Analyze and evaluate the implications of these technologies
  and their related applications/practices/tools/methods/
  techniques, as well as related leadership or management roles
  in their optimal use, for organizations' digital transformation
  strategy and digital business strategy
- Apply knowledge and understanding of these technologies and
  their related applications/practices/tools/methods/techniques to
  participate in, support, or lead workstreams or initiatives related
  to the leveraging of these technologies to enhance organization
  digital transformation and digital business strategy

# CELLULAR NETWORKS AND HOW THEY WORK

If you look in the top corner of your phone, you are likely to see a 5G, 4G, or 3G symbol (or, in the worst case, a 2G symbol). These symbols indicate the type of cellular or mobile network you are using to send and receive data to and from other devices and equipment. Cellular networks use land-based towers (also referred to as cell towers, cell sites, cellular base stations, or base transceiver stations) for sending and receiving data. Essentially, a cellular network divides up geographic areas into transmission areas called "cells." The cell towers or transceiver stations have all the necessary components to serve that cell (e.g., antennas, transceivers, control electronics, backup power, sheltering). The transceiver stations provide the network coverage that devices or equipment then use to send or receive different types of data. The bigger the geographic area requiring network coverage, the more transceiver stations need to be built and operated. There can be set up and maintenance costs, demand, environmental degradation, and other issues that limit the size and types of areas that can or cannot be covered. This is why you might suddenly lose the ability to send or receive data on your device in particular locations; you may be out of

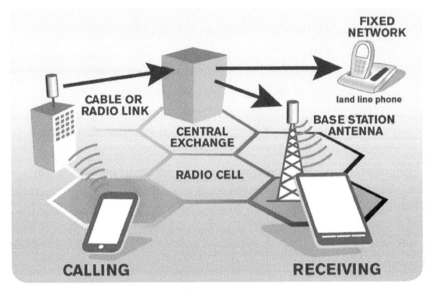

**Figure 27.1** *How cellular phones work*[1]

range of a transceiver station for your cellular network, or the signal may be unable to reach you. Cellular networks can be contrasted with satellite networks, which transmit data through satellites orbiting the Earth. Unlike the relatively short range of transceiver stations and the large number of transceiver stations required to create a large cellular network, satellites can beam coverage to very large and even hard to reach areas, but satellites have traditionally still been much more costly to build, put in orbit, and maintain. Figure 27.1 provides a visualization of a cellular network and how they work together to enable connectivity/data exchange.

# 4G, LTE, AND OTHER CELLULAR NETWORKS

The "G" in cellular network symbols stands for "generation"; subsequent generations (or increments) of the "G" symbol (e.g., from 1G and 2G to 3G and 4G to 5G and 6G) represent breakthroughs or expansions in the minimum speed, connectivity, and reliability of cellular networks as set by the International Telecommunication Union Radiocommunication (or ITU-R) Sector. For example, while 1G enabled us to be able to talk to each other over a cellular network, 2G expanded the functionality to include the ability to send text messages and limited MMS (i.e., multimedia messages); 3G further expanded this functionality to include web pages, music, and videos. However, speeds were very slow relative to, say, a broadband internet connection; 4G and LTE extended cellular network speeds to more closely resemble the speed of a broadband internet connection. This enabled users to enjoy rich experiences on their mobile devices including streaming video, high-quality music, and multimedia apps – and all almost instantaneously, without long buffering times. The ITU-R set standards for 4G in early 2008, requiring any cellular service referred to as 4G to have peak speeds of at least 100 megabits per second for high-mobility communication (e.g., moving cars and trains) and 1,000 megabits per second (or 1 gigabit per second) for stationary or low-motion communication (e.g., walking or not moving). These standards represented a significant leap over existing speeds; despite significant investments, the cellular industry could not reach 4G standards. However, a new technology standard known as LTE (Long Term Evolution), first proposed in Japan in 2004, had evolved from proposal to successful trials to adoption in 2010. LTE became an international standard by 2011–2012. Although quite short of 4G standards, LTE offered significant improvements on 3G speeds.[2] Due to the significant improvements on 3G and perhaps to the challenges attaining 4G standards, the ITU-R allowed LTE to be called 4G. Cellular networks varied in whether they labeled their LTE offerings 4G LTE or just 4G. But in either case, it wasn't true 4G as it wasn't up to the original ITU-R standards. Over time, improvements in LTE technology resulted in LTE-Advanced (LTE-A) and LTE-Advanced Pro, reaching and even surpassing the true 4G standards.

# 5G AND 6G CELLULAR NETWORKS

As good as 4G technology has been, advancements in IoT technologies and exponential growth in the number of connected things have pushed it to its limits (e.g., as of 2020 there were an estimated 20 billion connected devices). Fortunately, 5G technology has been in development and, as early as 2018 and 2019, most major economies had trialed or already started providing 5G network service. It is expected that 5G will have significantly greater capacity, with initial speeds of between 10 and 20 times faster than 4G, and potentially up to 100 times faster than 4G.[3] Among other things, it is expected to have greater latency (the time required for data to travel from one point to another) of 1 to 4 milliseconds, be more energy efficient, be able to support up to a million connected devices per square foot, and be able to work at greater speeds. It is expected to be a major step toward satisfying the connectivity requirements of advancements in technologies like the cloud, IoT, big data, artificial intelligence, augmented/mixed reality, and robotics/drones.[4] As 5G is being rolled out and improved, research on 6G has already begun to explore the types of use cases that won't be possible with 5G and that will require a 6G network. Such use cases identified to date include solving remaining accessibility problems (e.g., connecting all people, information, and things in ultra-real time irrespective of location), improving communication between humans and things (e.g., ultra-high definition VR/AR/MR, ultra-real-time communication with things), an expanded communication environment (high-rise buildings, remote geographic areas, the sky, underwater, and space will all become high activity/communication areas), and increasingly sophisticated cyber-physical fusion (e.g., greater integration of cyberspace with human bodily functions, human thought, and human action).[5]

# GOOGLE AND REFLECT

| Digital technology | Common terminology |
| --- | --- |
| Cellular networks | Hz/MHz/GHz, cellular bandwidth, cellular network latency, 4G LTE, 5G New Radio (5G NR), eMBB, mMTC, URLLC, 10-nanometer chip, 7-nanometer chip, cloud radio access network (cRAN), mmWave spectrum, 5G massive machine type communication (mMTC), cellular network capacity, MIMO, network slicing, small-cell densification, licensed spectrum, unlicensed spectrum, 3GGP, carrier aggregation, cell tower, evolved packet system |

# EXAMPLE TOOLS AND VENDORS

| Digital technology | Tools and vendors |
| --- | --- |
| Cellular networks | Verizon 4G LTE, T-Mobile HSPA+, AT&T 5G+, Telstra 5G, Optus 5G, Deutsche Telekom, EE, Vodafone, China Mobile, SK Telecom |

# DISCUSSION QUESTIONS

1 Explain in plain language how a cellular network works.
2 What could you do with 2G that was not possible with 1G?
3 What can you do with 5G that you cannot do with 4G?
4 What is an example of a product innovation opportunity for your industry presented by 5G and 6G?
5 What is an example of a business model innovation opportunity for your industry presented by 5G and 6G?
6 What are the potential financial costs and risks of adopting 5G too early? What are the risks of adopting it too late?
7 How can cellular network technology advancements be used to enhance the adaptability and agility of organizations?

# NOTES

1 Telstra. (2014). Mobile base stations and health – consumer advice. Retrieved June 21, 2020, from Telstra.com website: www.telstra.com.au/consumer-advice/eme/base-stations
2 Segan, S. (2015, February 10). 3G vs. 4G: What's the difference? *PCMag*. www.pcmag.com/news/3g-vs-4g-whats-the-difference
3 jameswhyte. (2018, March 14). What is the difference between 4G and . . . Just Ask Gemalto. Retrieved from www.justaskgemalto.com/en/difference-4g-5g/
4 BBC News. (2020). What is 5G and what will it mean for you? Retrieved from www.bbc.com/news/business-44871448
5 NTT DOCOMO, INC. (2020). 5G evolution and 6G. (n.d.). Retrieved March 2, 2020, from www.nttdocomo.co.jp/english/binary/pdf/corporate/technology/whitepaper_6g/DOCOMO_6G_White_PaperEN_20200124.pdf

# CHAPTER 28

# GPS III or GPS Block III and Low Earth Orbit Satellites Primer

DOI: 10.4324/9781003254614-33

# INTRODUCTION

This primer on global navigation satellite systems (e.g., those used by GPS devices) and low earth orbit satellites is the second of four primers that have an overarching focus on connectivity technologies. That is, technologies that enable people, systems, devices, and other things to pass and receive information from each other. It is the passing and receiving of this information, in combination with computation and storage, that is at the heart of, and extends, the power of other digital technologies like cloud computing, the Internet of Things, artificial intelligence, and robotics/drones. The primer provides an overview of global navigation satellite systems and low earth orbit satellite standards, data transmission speed, transmission range, the amount of data that can be sent, connectivity reliability, connection security, connection availability, and connection portability. It also discusses issues such as power consumption, infrastructure setup and maintenance costs, and connectivity equipment availability/reliability. The range of available connectivity technologies/standards require leaders, managers, and supporting professionals to understand how different technologies/standards work and what their strengths and shortcomings are. It also requires them to make important choices about which standards to go with for what purposes and when to experiment with a particular technology/standard, when to cut the cord on an existing connectivity technology/standard, and when to undertake large-scale adoption of a new standard.

**LEARNING OBJECTIVES**

- Develop knowledge of essential definitions and concepts relating global navigation satellite system and low earth orbit satellite technologies
- Understand how these technologies and their related applications/practices/tools/methods/techniques can impact the efficiency, differentiation, adaptability, and agility of an organization

- Understand the roles leaders, managers, and supporting professionals can play in maximizing the leveraging of these technologies and their related applications/practices/tools/methods/techniques
- Analyze and evaluate the implications of these technologies and their related applications/practices/tools/methods/techniques, as well as related leadership or management roles in their optimal use, for organizations' digital transformation strategy and digital business strategy
- Apply knowledge and understanding of these technologies and their related applications/practices/tools/methods/techniques to participate in, support, or lead workstreams or initiatives related to the leveraging of these technologies to enhance organization digital transformation and digital business strategy

# GPS AND GPS III AND OTHER GLOBAL NAVIGATION SATELLITE SYSTEMS (GNSS)

The Global Positioning System (GPS) is a constellation of space-based satellites that orbit the Earth at an altitude of about 20,000 km. At regular intervals, the satellites transmit information about their position and the current time. These signals travel at the speed of light and can be intercepted by GPS receivers. GPS receivers can use the intercepted signals to provide precise location, navigation, and timing information. How do GPS receivers do this? At any point or location on the Earth, there is line visibility to at least four GPS satellites.[1] A GPS receiver is able to intercept the signal from each of these four satellites and use it to calculate how far away each satellite is (based on how long it takes for the signal to travel from the satellite to the receiver at the speed of light).[2] Once it knows how far away at least three of the satellites are, the GPS receiver can use a process called trilateration to pinpoint its exact location (or your location).[3] We use GPS almost daily, sometimes without even realizing it. We use it for directions, to provide pilots with real-time positioning information, to survey, to track the movement of things, for live recording, for military purposes, to avoid collision in shipping, for self-driving cars, and much more.[4] The GPS system was originally developed and is owned by the US Department of Defense, although anyone with a receiver can use it. But it isn't the only system used around the world. Europe has a similar system known as Galileo; China's system is known as BeiDou; and Russia's system is known as GLONASS (*Globalnaya navigatsionnaya sputnikovaya sistema*). Even though the term GPS is often used to refer to all these systems, GPS is technically only the US system; the better name to refer to all systems is the global navigation satellite system (GNSS).[5]

GPS III refers to the next generation of GPS satellites designed and built by Lockheed Martin, with the first of these satellites launched in December 2018.[6] GPS III brings significant improvements in pinpointing location accuracy[7] (e.g., from within 3 m to within 1 m), significant improvements in signal strength (e.g., signals will be much easier to pick up even in obstructed areas like tree canopies and inside buildings), significantly improved security and reliability (e.g., GPS signals will be much harder to maliciously or accidentally jam/obstruct), and interoperability with other global navigation satellite systems. Advancements in GPS III hold a range of benefits for organizations including improved user experience, product innovation, and new market potential – as long as device makers have devices available to take full advantage of GPS III.[8] GPS III is anticipated to be fully capable by mid-2023 and to improve when another ten satellites go into orbit between 2026 and 2034.[9] Other global navigation satellite systems have also been working on upgrading their systems.

## LOW EARTH ORBIT (LEO) SATELLITES

Low Earth orbit satellites (or LEO) are satellites that orbit the Earth at a much lower altitude (about 400–2,000 km),[11] unlike conventional satellites that orbit at about 36,000 km and GNSS that orbit at about 20,000–26,000 km. There are several benefits to a low orbit, including better signal strength and less power to transmit the signal (as the

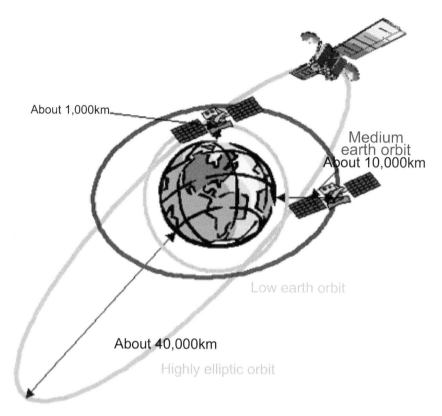

About 1,000km

Medium earth orbit
About 10,000km

Low earth orbit

About 40,000km

Highly elliptic orbit

**Figure 28.1** *Low Earth orbit (LEO), medium Earth orbit (MEO), and geostationary orbit (GEO)*[10]

satellite is near the Earth), lower propagation delay (good for applications requiring real-time data), and lower-priced satellite equipment. There are also disadvantages, including more satellites being needed to cover the Earth (as the lower a satellite is, the less area it can cover), regular maintenance requirement (due to having to continuously travel through the much denser atmosphere), and shorter life span. One aim of LEO satellites is to reach the more than 4 billion people who are without high-speed internet due to cellular infrastructure being too expensive.[12] Companies such as OneWeb are working on provision of Wi-Fi hotspots connected to their LEO satellites.[13] LEO satellites also offer new scientific exploration opportunities at significantly reduced cost (e.g., miniature satellite versions weighing between 1 g and 100 kg are now possible).[14]

| Type of Use | Type of Orbit / Type of Satellite |
|---|---|
| Astronomy | Several orbits |
| Climate, weather forecast | LEO, GEO |
| Communications | GEO(low latitude), Molniya(high latitude) |
| Earth observation | GEO, LEO, global coverage |
| Global positioning, navigation | LEO, MEO, global coverage |
| Military | Several LEO orbits |
| Space environment | Several, including sounding rockets |
| Space station | LEO |
| Technology development | Several orbits |

*Note*: Low Earth orbit(LEO), medium altitude Earth orbit(MEO), geostationary orbit(GEO).

**Figure 28.2** *Types of satellite or orbit, and what they are used for*[17]

On the IoT front, LEO satellites offer a way to connect "things" no matter where they are on Earth. Their lower orbits (therefore higher detail) also enhance remote sensing capabilities of smart devices. Companies such as Iridium and Globalstar recently launched LEO satellites (64 and 24, respectively); Amazon intends to launch 3,236 LEO satellites to provide internet to areas without it; and SpaceX has sought permission to launch more than 30,000 satellites.[15] LPWAN technology companies like Semtech, the owner of LoRa technology, are experimenting with LEO satellite LoRa connectivity that covers the whole planet. Iridium has been working with Amazon to develop a satellite cloud-based solution with global coverage for IoT applications.[16] Figure 28.2 shows the different types of orbits and their different uses.

# GOOGLE AND REFLECT

| Digital technology | Common terminology |
|---|---|
| GPS III and LEO satellites | GPS accuracy, GPS bearing, GPS coordinate systems, GPS navigation, NAVSTAR, Wide Area Augmentation System (WAAS), medium Earth orbit (MEO), geosynchronous equatorial orbit (GEO), picosatellite, microsatellite, minisatellite |

# EXAMPLE TOOLS AND VENDORS

| *Digital technology* | *Tools and vendors* |
|---|---|
| GPS III and LEO satellites | Else Astrocast LEO constellation for IoT communications, OneWeb satellites, Space Exploration Technologies Corp satellites, Iridium satellites, Virgin Orbit satellites, Amazon satellites, Eutelsat Communications SA satellites |

# DISCUSSION QUESTIONS

1 What is the difference between Global Positioning System (GPS) based connectivity and low earth orbit satellite-based connectivity?

2 What is an example of a product innovation opportunity presented by GPS III or LEO satellites in your industry?

3 What is an example of a business model innovation opportunity presented by GPS III or LEO satellites for your industry?

# NOTES

1 Physics.Org. (2020). How does GPS work? Retrieved from www.physics.org/article-questions.asp?id=55

2 Physics.Org. (2020). How does GPS work? Retrieved from www.physics.org/article-questions.asp?id=55; Dempster, A. (2013, March 7). Explainer: What is GPS? *The Conversation*. Retrieved from https://theconversation.com/explainer-what-is-gps-12248

3 Physics.Org. (2020). How does GPS work? Retrieved from www.physics.org/article-questions.asp?id=55

4 Dempster, A. (2013, March 7). Explainer: What is GPS? *The Conversation*. Retrieved from https://theconversation.com/explainer-what-is-gps-12248

5 Dempster, A. (2013, March 7). Explainer: What is GPS? *The Conversation*. Retrieved from https://theconversation.com/explainer-what-is-gps-12248

6 Pappalardo, J. (2018, December 26). USAF's next-gen GPS satellites will be a huge upgrade . . . eventually. *Popular Mechanics*. Retrieved from www.popularmechanics.com/space/satellites/a25683704/gps-iii/

7   Lockheed Martin. (2018). Unbelievable accuracy: GPS III. Retrieved from www.lockheedmartin.com/en-us/news/features/history/gps-iii.html

8   Cozzens, T. (2019, January 9). GPS III finally aloft, benefits on the way. *GPS World*. Retrieved from www.gpsworld.com/gps-iii-finally-aloft-benefits-on-the-way/

9   Cozzens, T. (2019, January 9). GPS III finally aloft, benefits on the way. *GPS World*. Retrieved from www.gpsworld.com/gps-iii-finally-aloft-benefits-on-the-way/

10  Borthomieu, Y. (2014). Satellite lithium-ion batteries. *Lithium-Ion Batteries*, 311–344. https://doi.org/10.1016/b978-0-444-59513-3.00014-5; Meseguer, J., Pérez-Grande, I., & Sanz-Andrés, A. (2012). Keplerian orbits. *Spacecraft Thermal Control*, 39–57.

11  Allain, R. (2015, September 15). What's so special about low earth orbit? *WIRED*. Retrieved from www.wired.com/2015/09/whats-special-low-earth-orbit/

12  Ritchie, G. (2019, August 9). Why low-earth orbit satellites are the new space race. *Bloomberg*. Retrieved from www.bloomberg.com/news/articles/2019-08-09/why-low-earth-orbit-satellites-are-the-new-space-race-quicktake

13  Ritchie, G. (2019, August 9). Why low-earth orbit satellites are the new space race. *Bloomberg*. Retrieved from www.bloomberg.com/news/articles/2019-08-09/why-low-earth-orbit-satellites-are-the-new-space-race-quicktake

14  Avnet Silica. (2019, June 27). Low-earth-orbit satellites and IoT. *Avnet Silica*. Retrieved from www.avnet.com/wps/portal/silica/resources/article/low-earth-orbit-satellites-and-iot/

15  Ritchie, G. (2019, August 9). Why low-earth orbit satellites are the new space race. *Bloomberg*. Retrieved from www.bloomberg.com/news/articles/2019-08-09/why-low-earth-orbit-satellites-are-the-new-space-race-quicktake; Blackman, J. (2019, November 4). What is LEO, and how will LEO satellites transform the IoT sector? *Enterprise IoT Insights*. Retrieved from https://enterpriseiotinsights.com/20191104/channels/fundamentals/what-is-leo-and-how-will-leo-satellites-transform-iot

16  Blackman, J. (2019, November 4). What is LEO, and how will LEO satellites transform the IoT sector? *Enterprise IoT Insights*. Retrieved from https://enterpriseiotinsights.com/20191104/channels/fundamentals/what-is-leo-and-how-will-leo-satellites-transform-iot

17  Meseguer, J., Pérez-Grande, I., & Sanz-Andrés, A. (2012). Keplerian orbits. *Spacecraft Thermal Control*, 39–57

# CHAPTER 29

# NBIoT, LoRa, Sigfox and Other LPWAN Technologies Primer

DOI: 10.4324/9781003254614-34

# INTRODUCTION

This primer on low-power wide-area (LPWAN) technologies is the third of four primers that have an overarching focus on connectivity technologies. That is, technologies that enable people, systems, devices, and other things to pass and receive information from each other. It is the passing and receiving of this information, in combination with computation and storage, that is at the heart of, and extends, the power of other digital technologies like cloud computing, the Internet of Things, artificial intelligence, and robotics/drones. The primer provides an overview of LPWAN standards, data transmission speed, transmission range, the amount of data that can be sent, connectivity reliability, connection security, connection availability, and connection portability. It also discusses issues such as power consumption, infrastructure setup and maintenance costs, and connectivity equipment availability/reliability. The range of available connectivity technologies/standards require leaders, managers, and supporting professionals to understand how different technologies/standards work and what their strengths and shortcomings are. It also requires them to make important choices about which standards to go with for what purposes and when to experiment with a particular technology/standard, when to cut the cord on an existing connectivity technology/standard, and when to undertake large-scale adoption of a new standard.

---

**LEARNING OBJECTIVES**

- Develop knowledge of essential definitions and concepts relating LPWAN technologies
- Understand how these technologies and their related applications/practices/tools/methods/techniques can impact the efficiency, differentiation, adaptability, and agility of an organization
- Understand the roles leaders, managers, and supporting professionals can play in maximizing the leveraging of these

---

technologies and their related applications/practices/tools/
methods/techniques

- Analyze and evaluate the implications of these technologies
  and their related applications/practices/tools/methods/
  techniques, as well as related leadership or management roles
  in their optimal use, for organizations' digital transformation
  strategy and digital business strategy
- Apply knowledge and understanding of these technologies and
  their related applications/practices/tools/methods/techniques
  to participate in, support, or lead workstreams or initiatives
  related to the leveraging of these technologies to enhance
  organization digital transformation and digital business
  strategy

# LPWAN TECHNOLOGIES

Devices using cellular networks use a lot of power to send a lot of
data over medium distances, which is why they require constant
power access or regular recharging. But many IoT devices only need
to send a little bit of data over much longer distances, cannot be
regularly recharged, and thus they need to make the most of battery
life. Low-power wide-area (LPWA) and low-power wide-area network
(LPWAN) technologies provide a solution to this. They are a type of
wireless technology that allows for data to be sent at a low bit rate
(e.g., 0.3–50 Kbps) over long distances (e.g., a few kilometers to tens
of kilometers).[1] The technology for this type of network enables very
low power consumption so that an IoT device can use a standard AA
battery for many years (contrast this to a battery-powered device using
a cellular network; such a device typically needs to be recharged daily).[2]
LPWA technologies' simpler, lightweight protocols translate into less
complex/less costly hardware, less complex/less costly infrastructure
requirements, and thus significantly reduced IoT connectivity costs
(e.g., cents per device per month, as opposed to tens of dollars per

month).[3] Thus the technologies provide the ability for IoT devices to transfer data to each other over significantly longer distances, at significantly lower power consumption, and significantly lower cost. This makes the idea of an organization connecting hundreds, thousands, or even hundreds of thousands of devices a much more realistic proposition. There is a range of LPWA and LPWAN technologies including LTE-M, NBIoT, and LoRaWAN. These typically vary on dimensions such transmission speed, power consumption, latency, availability, mobility, extent of coverage, transmission distance, number of devices that can be connected per unit area, and cost. The right technology for an organization will depend on what the organization's use case is.

## NBIoT

The Narrowband Internet of Things (NBIoT) is a low-bandwidth LPWA cellular technology standard (low bandwidth meaning that very small amounts of data can be sent per second). NBIoT is classified as a 5G technology and has the proven security and privacy features of LTE mobile networks.[4] Key strengths of NBIoT over other standards include its super-low device power consumption, its capacity to have a massive number of devices connected per unit area, and its potential for ultra-cost-efficiency (it eliminates the need to aggregate sensor data before sending it to the primary server, thus reducing hardware costs).[5] Limitations of NBIoT include it being more suited to static devices than mobile ones, its low latency and its low speed (e.g., 26–159 Kbps). In fact, although low device power consumption is a strength of NBIoT, when large amounts of data have to be sent NBIoT can end up using more power, as a device has to be active for a longer period of time.[6] Given its current strengths and limitations, NBIoT has been viewed as being suited for use cases involving static devices that send minimal data and do so infrequently, thus maximizing battery life.[7] Examples of such use cases include smart power meters and battery-powered smart locks.

## LTE-M

LTE-M (also commonly referred to as LTE Machine Type Communication [LTE MTC], enhanced Machine Type Communication [eMTC], and LTE Cat-M1) is another cellular LPWA standard for IoT and machine-to-machine communication.[8] Although NBIoT is stronger than LTE-M on the low device power consumption dimension, LTE-M is stronger than NBIoT on mobility, speed (e.g., up to six times that of NBIoT), and latency dimensions.[9] LTE-M is also backward compatible with existing 4G LTE networks, making it more likely than NBIoT to be available/accessible in certain parts of the world.[10] LTE-M is seen as being suited for use cases involving mobility, sending lots of data, and doing so frequently. LTE-M use cases include wearable devices, connectivity with devices in thick walls or deep basements, and asset tracking/monitoring.

## LoRa/LoRaWAN

LoRa (long range) is an LPWAN technology, and LoRaWAN is a network protocol using LoRa that connects things (e.g., sensors) to the internet to enable bidirectional communication.[11] LoRa technology's key strengths are its long-range transmission (2–15 km) and low device power consumption, extending battery life by up to 10 years.[12] One of its limitations is the amount of data that can be sent per second (0.3–5 Kbps). As with NBIoT, this data transmission rate can result in high device power consumption if large amounts of data need to be sent. LoRa and LoRaWAN use cases include fleet tracking, livestock tracking, and sensors in very hard to reach places (e.g., in concrete or far away).[13]

## OTHER LPWAN TECHNOLOGIES

Other LPWAN technologies include Signfox and EC-GSM-IoT (extended coverage-GSM-Internet of Things). EC-GSM-IoT works over 4G, 3G, and even 2G mobile networks. This makes EC-GSM-IoT technology valuable in parts of the world that don't have access to the latest cellular networks. Still other technologies include Weightless, Wize, and Chirp.

# GOOGLE AND REFLECT

| Digital technology | Common terminology |
| --- | --- |
| LPWAN | Cellular LPWAN, cellular LPWA, EC-GSM-IoT, IoT stack, IoT gateway |

# EXAMPLE TOOLS AND VENDORS

| Digital technology | Tools and vendors |
| --- | --- |
| LPWAN | Ingenu RPMA, Sigfox 0G network, LoRa Alliance, Weightless (SIG), Wize, Chirp, Huawei NBIoT, Ericsson cellular IoT, Vodafone NBIoT, NBIoT Smart Locks, iMETOS NBIoT |

# DISCUSSION QUESTIONS

1   Which LPWA or LPWAN technology would you use if you frequently took customers on remote tours and relied on IoT devices to improve the tour experience?
2   Which LPWA or LPWAN is likely to be the most widely accepted, and why?
3   What advantages do LPWA or LPWAN technologies provide over other connectivity technologies?

# NOTES

1   Wedd, M. (2018, September 26). What is LPWANs and the LoRaWAN open standard? *IoT for All.* Retrieved from www.iotforall.com/what-is-lpwan-lorawan/
2   Upale, A. (2018). LTE cat M1 vs. NB-IoT vs. LoRa – comparing LPWANs. *Semiconductorstore.Com.* Retrieved from www.semiconductorstore.com/blog/2018/LTE-Cat-M1-vs-NB-IoT-vs-LoRa-Comparing-LPWANs-Symmetry-Blog/3496/

3  Wedd, M. (2018, September 26). What is LPWANs and the LoRaWAN
   open standard? *IoT for All*. Retrieved from www.iotforall.com/
   what-is-lpwan-lorawan/

4  Hwang, Y. (2020, January 17). Cellular IoT explained – NB-IoT vs. LTE-M
   vs. 5G and more. *IoT for All*. Retrieved from www.iotforall.com/cellular-iot-
   explained-nb-iot-vs-lte-m/; Øyvann, S. (2017, January 26). From parking
   to farming, applications for NB-IoT are heading out into the real world.
   *ZDNet*. Retrieved from www.zdnet.com/article/from-parking-to-farming-
   applications-for-nb-iot-are-heading-out-into-the-real-world/

5  Hwang, Y. (2020, January 17). Cellular IoT explained – NB-IoT vs. LTE-M
   vs. 5G and More. *IoT for All*. Retrieved from www.iotforall.com/cellular-
   iot-explained-nb-iot-vs-lte-m/; Gemalto.Com. (2020). Narrowband IoT
   overview (NB-IoT). Retrieved from www.gemalto.com/iot/resources/
   innovation-technology/nb-iot

6  Hwang, Y. (2020, January 17). Cellular IoT explained – NB-IoT vs. LTE-M
   vs. 5G and More. *IoT for All*. Retrieved from www.iotforall.com/cellular-iot-
   explained-nb-iot-vs-lte-m/; Øyvann, S. (2017, January 26). From parking
   to farming, applications for NB-IoT are heading out into the real world.
   *ZDNet*. Retrieved from www.zdnet.com/article/from-parking-to-farming-
   applications-for-nb-iot-are-heading-out-into-the-real-world/

7  Øyvann, S. (2017, January 26). From parking to farming, applications for NB-
   IoT are heading out into the real world. *ZDNet*. Retrieved from www.zdnet.
   com/article/from-parking-to-farming-applications-for-nb-iot-are-heading-
   out-into-the-real-world/

8  Hwang, Y. (2020, January 17). Cellular IoT explained – NB-IoT vs. LTE-M
   vs. 5G and more. *IoT for All*. Retrieved from www.iotforall.com/cellular-
   iot-explained-nb-iot-vs-lte-m/; SierraWireless. (2018, April 3). LTE-M vs.
   NB-IoT: Make the best choice for your needs. *SierraWireless*. Retrieved from
   www.sierrawireless.com/iot-blog/iot-blog/2018/04/lte-m-vs-nb-iot/

9  Hwang, Y. (2020, January 17). Cellular IoT explained – NB-IoT vs.
   LTE-M vs. 5G and More. *IoT for All*. Retrieved from www.iotforall.com/
   cellular-iot-explained-nb-iot-vs-lte-m/

10 SierraWireless. (2018, April 3). LTE-M vs. NB-IoT: Make the best choice for
   your needs. *SierraWireless*. Retrieved from www.sierrawireless.com/iot-blog/
   iot-blog/2018/04/lte-m-vs-nb-iot/

11 Wedd, M. (2018, September 26). What is LPWANs and the LoRaWAN
   open standard? *IoT for All*. Retrieved from www.iotforall.com/

what-is-lpwan-lorawan/; I-SCOOP. (2015). LoRa and LoRaWAN: The technologies, ecosystems, use cases and market. Retrieved from www.i-scoop. eu/internet-of-things-guide/lpwan/iot-network-lora-lorawan/

12 Maker.io Team. (2016, August 10). Introduction to LoRa technology – the game changer. *Digikey.Com*; Maker.io. Retrieved from www.digikey.com/en/ maker/blogs/introduction-to-lora-technology

13 Wedd, M. (2018, September 26). What is LPWANs and the LoRaWAN open standard? *IoT for All*. Retrieved from www.iotforall.com/what-is-lpwan-lorawan/; Pike, J. (2017, August 21). Understanding LoRa WAN Basics: A non-technical explanation. *Metova*. Retrieved from https://metova.com/ understanding-lora-basics-a-non-technical-explanation/

# CHAPTER 30

# NFC, Smart Bluetooth, iBeacon, and Other Communication Protocols Primer

DOI: 10.4324/9781003254614-35

# INTRODUCTION

This primer on NFC, Smart Bluetooth, iBeacon, and other communication protocols is the last of four primers that have an overarching focus on connectivity technologies. That is, technologies that enable people, systems, devices, and other things to pass and receive information from each other. It is the passing and receiving of this information, in combination with computation and storage, that is at the heart of, and extends, the power of other digital technologies like cloud computing, the Internet of Things, artificial intelligence, and robotics/drones. The primer provides an overview of NFC, Smart Bluetooth, iBeacon, and other communication protocol standards, data transmission speed, transmission range, the amount of data that can be sent, connectivity reliability, connection security, connection availability, and connection portability. It also discusses issues such as power consumption, infrastructure setup and maintenance costs, and connectivity equipment availability/reliability. The range of available connectivity technologies/standards require leaders, managers, and supporting professionals to understand how different technologies/ standards work and what their strengths and shortcomings are. It also requires them to make important choices about which standards to go with for what purposes and when to experiment with a particular technology/standard, when to cut the cord on an existing connectivity technology/standard, and when to undertake large-scale adoption of a new standard.

---

**LEARNING OBJECTIVES**

- Develop knowledge of essential definitions and concepts relating NFC, Smart Bluetooth, iBeacon, and other communication protocols technologies
- Understand how these technologies and their related applications/practices/tools/methods/techniques can impact the efficiency, differentiation, adaptability, and agility of an organization

---

- Understand the roles leaders, managers, and supporting professionals can play in maximizing the leveraging of these technologies and their related applications/practices/tools/methods/techniques
- Analyze and evaluate the implications of these technologies and their related applications/practices/tools/methods/techniques, as well as related leadership or management roles in their optimal use, for organizations' digital transformation strategy and digital business strategy
- Apply knowledge and understanding of these technologies and their related applications/practices/tools/methods/techniques to participate in, support, or lead workstreams or initiatives related to the leveraging of these technologies to enhance organization digital transformation and digital business strategy

# NFC, SMART BLUETOOTH, IBEACON, AND OTHER COMMUNICATION PROTOCOLS

## WHAT IS NFC, AND HOW DOES IT WORK?

NFC is short for near-field communication. It is a short-range wireless data transmission technology based on older RFID electromagnetic induction ideas. It enables two electronic devices to communicate with each other using electromagnetic waves when brought within 2–10 cm of each other.[1] NFC use cases include contactless payments (e.g., pay wave, pay pass, Apple Pay),[2] access control[3] (e.g., digital keys for smart locks), identification of objects via NFC tag scanning, speeding up pairing of Bluetooth objects, improved product authentication via scanning of NFC tags, provision of product on NFC tags, proof of compliance by checking if people with an NFC tag came in proximity with an area they were meant to inspect, and much more.[4] NFC technology enables devices or tags, or other things embedded with an NFC chip, to receive and/or transmit information that can be used in many different areas including customer engagement, product and supply chain management, marketing, asset management, and workflow management. Key benefits of NFC over similar Bluetooth or Wi-Fi are its much lower power consumption and ability to operate without a power source. A device with an NFC chip can create a magnetic field that is able to power or induce current in another NFC device, enabling that device to transmit data even if it has no power source of its own. This is referred to as inductive coupling. This is also how wireless chargers work (e.g., a charging device creates an electromagnetic field that induces charge in a wire connected to a rechargeable battery). An active NFC device (one with a power source and capable of both sending and receiving data, such as a smartphone) can interact with another active device so both can send and receive data. An active device can also interact with a passive device (one without a power source and only capable of transmitting data, such as an NFC tag or tag embedded with an NFC chip). In this case, the active device powers the passive device (see Figure 30.1).

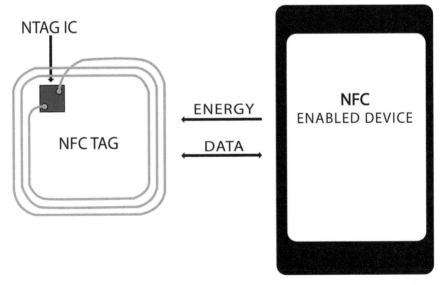

**Figure 30.1** *An NFC-enabled phone sets up a current, the NFC tag receives the "induced current," and – recognizing it is a valid signal – offers connection to the phone and begins data transfer*[5]

NFC chips transmit data at up to 424 Kbps, which is significantly less than Bluetooth's 2.1 Mbps, but this is still adequate for sending text, photos, and even audio. NFC is also considered high security given the need for devices to be right next to each other. This limits the opportunity for others to eavesdrop or intercept the data transfer. Other benefits, as far as access control, include limiting the ability for people to lend their access to others or have it stolen (e.g., if NFC access is via a smartphone). Regarding efficiency, smartphone-enabled NFC access minimizes instances of people forgetting their keys or keycards (they are less likely to forget their phone at home).

## WHAT ARE BLUETOOTH 5.0 AND BLUETOOTH LOW ENERGY (BLE), AND HOW DO THEY WORK?

Traditional or classic Bluetooth (Bluetooth 1.0 to 3.0) was often criticized for the difficulty in pairing devices and maintaining pairing, slow transmission speeds, and high device battery power consumption. Bluetooth 4.0 (also referred to as Bluetooth Smart or Smart Bluetooth) evolved as a response, offering high speed and low energy versions or categories of the technology. The low energy category (Bluetooth Low Energy, BLE, or Bluetooth LE) was designed for lower data rates (e.g., 1 Mbps) but much lower energy consumption. It allows Bluetooth devices to "sleep" while idle and only "wake up" or initiate Bluetooth functionality when data transmission is initiated. By reducing power consumption, BLE technology enables Bluetooth devices to operate for months or even years on a single coin cell battery. Reducing data transmission rates to lengthen battery life means that BLE is not suitable for devices that require a continuous stream of data (e.g., wireless headphones, speakers, radios). But the reduced transmission rate can work for devices that only need to send small bits of data or send data infrequently (e.g., wearable devices, periodic monitoring devices). Thus, these devices can benefit from longer battery life without a compromised ability to send data. BLE-enabled devices are capable of multi-point data transmission and coworking with different Bluetooth specifications (e.g., earlier versions of Bluetooth or Bluetooth high speed).[6] So, a device with both BLE and a high-speed

Bluetooth classic installed (Dual Mode Bluetooth) can switch between high speed or low energy uses as the situation demands. For example, if the device is a smartphone, BLE can take over the less intensive data tasks to preserve battery life, and classic Bluetooth can take over for tasks that require continuous connectivity or large data transmission.[7] If the device is a sphygmomanometer (blood pressure measuring device), it can use BLE to record blood pressure status and then use classic Bluetooth to transmit images or other larger data.[8]

As at the time of writing this book, Bluetooth 5.0 was the latest evolution in the Bluetooth standard. This version doubles the data transmission rate, making audio transmission possible and edging closer toward video. It quadruples the transmission range from 50 m to 200 m, which is enough to cover all the devices in a house or office. It enables the selection of 2 Mbps, 1 Mbps, 500 Kbps, and 125 Kbps transmission rates, so device use can be optimized for data rate and/or data range. Finally, Bluetooth 5.0 brings eight times the broadcast capacity.[9] The improvements in data transmission rate, range, and broadcast capability expand the longevity and connection capabilities of IoT devices both indoors and outdoors.[10]

## WHAT IS BEACON TECHNOLOGY, AND HOW DOES IT WORK?

Beacons are small devices that use BLE to send you data or content based on where you are (e.g., information about a sale at your favorite store as you walk into a shopping center).[11] Beacons are usually mounted or stuck in the particular location targeted users are likely to pass, and thus where location-based content is best served for the particular purpose it is aimed at. Apps on a user's phone pick up the beacon signals and execute response actions (e.g., you might receive a push notification from your favorite store's app, if it is installed on your phone, offering 50% off select items if you visit the store today).[12] Beacon technology has been seen as ideal for indoor settings where GPS can't reach. Beacon use cases range from location-based or proximity marketing (e.g., Best Buy serves up different ads to customers depending on which section of the store they are in).[13] But beacons can be put anywhere, even in novel outdoor locations, access control (e.g., smart locks that automatically unlock when an authorized user walks up to the front door), automated check-in (e.g., once a guest passes the front desk or arrives in their room), location-based content delivery (e.g., delivering information or other resources like emergency warnings, PowerPoint slides, directions), resource tracking (e.g., people, assets), ticketing/passes (e.g., tickets or passes purchased on your phone automatically present themselves as you walk in saving search and presentation time), and much more.[14] iBeacon is the Apple standard version of beacons first introduced in 2013.

## GOOGLE AND REFLECT

| Digital technology | Common terminology |
|---|---|
| NFC, Bluetooth Smart, and Beacons | NFC device, RFID, inductive coupling, proximity coupling device (PCD), host controller interface (HCI), inductive coupling, active NFC device, NFC tag, NFC card emulation, NFC encoding, ferrite sheet, passive NFC device, NFC forum, NFC-F, NFC-V, Bluetooth LE, Bluejacking,[15] Bluesnarfing, Bluespamming, Bluebugging, Bluecasting, Bluetooth douche, Bluetooth pairing, Bluetooth virus, Bluetooth personal area network, active slave broadcast (ASB), Bluetooth device address, Bluetooth host |

## EXAMPLE TOOLS AND VENDORS

| Digital technology | Tools and vendors |
|---|---|
| NFC, Bluetooth Smart and Beacons | Broadcom Topaz chip, DESFire MIFARE DESFire, NXP MIFARE Classic, Texas Instruments Bluetooth products, Nordic Semiconductor Bluetooth products, Silicon Labs Bluetooth products, Quuppa Bluetooth products, u-blox Bluetooth products, UnSeen Technologies Bluetooth products, Fanstel Bluetooth products, Laird Connectivity Bluetooth products |

# DISCUSSION QUESTIONS

1   What is an example of a product innovation opportunity presented by NFC, Bluetooth Smart, or beacons for your industry?
2   What is an example of a business model innovation opportunity presented by NFC, Bluetooth Smart, or beacons for your industry?
3   How could a competitor use NFC, Smart Bluetooth, or beacons to disrupt product/service offerings in your industry?

# NOTES

1   Triggs, R. (2019, June 30). What is NFC and how does it work. *Android Authority*. Retrieved from www.androidauthority.com/what-is-nfc-270730/; Joshi, C. (2019). What is NFC & how does it work? *Beaconstac.Com*. Retrieved from https://blog.beaconstac.com/2019/05/what-is-nfc-and-how-does-it-work/; Triggs, R. (2019, June 30). What is NFC and how does it work. *Android Authority*. Retrieved from www.androidauthority.com/what-is-nfc-270730/

2   Profis, S. (2014, September 9). Everything you need to know about NFC and mobile payments. *CNET*. Retrieved from www.cnet.com/how-to/how-nfc-works-and-mobile-payments/

3   Saritag. (2019). NFC tag authentication explained. *Seritag Learn NFC*. Seritag.Com. Retrieved from https://learn.seritag.com/tech/nfc-tag-authentication-explained

4   Ratna, S. (2019). Best use cases of NFC to implement in 2019: Proximity marketing without an app. *Beaconstac.Com*. Retrieved from https://blog.beaconstac.com/2019/01/proximity-marketing-without-an-app-best-use-cases-of-nfc-to-implement-in-2019/

5   Camperi, A. (2018). How to use an NFC Reader. Retrieved June 21, 2020, from Getkisi.com website: www.getkisi.com/lessons/how-to-use-an-nfc-reader

6   Allion Labs. (2012). The next bluetooth wave: High speed & low energy technology. Retrieved from www.allion.com/the-next-bluetooth-wave-high-speed-low-energy-technology/

7   Nguyen, A. (2018). When would you have BOTH bluetooth classic and low energy? *Semiconductorstore.Com*. Retrieved from www.semiconductorstore.

com/blog/2018/When-Would-You-Have-BOTH-Bluetooth-Classic-and-Low-Energy-Symmetry-Blog/3110

8 Technical Direct (an Allion Labs site). (2012). The next bluetooth wave: High speed & low energy technology. Retrieved from www.technical-direct.com/en/the-next-bluetooth-wave-high-speed-and-low-energy-technology/

9 Heukelman, C. (2017). Bluetooth 5 versus bluetooth 4.2, what's the difference? *Semiconductorstore.Com*. Retrieved from www.semiconductorstore.com/blog/2017/Bluetooth-5-versus-Bluetooth-4-2-whats-the-difference/2080

10 Heukelman, C. (2017). Bluetooth 5 versus Bluetooth 4.2, what's the difference? *Semiconductorstore.Com*. Retrieved from www.semiconductorstore.com/blog/2017/Bluetooth-5-versus-Bluetooth-4-2-whats-the-difference/2080

11 Ranger, S. (2014, June 10). What is Apple iBeacon? Here's what you need to know. *ZDNet*. Retrieved from www.zdnet.com/article/what-is-apple-ibeacon-heres-what-you-need-to-know/; Maycotte, H. O. (2015, September 1). Beacon technology: The where, what, who, how and why. *Forbes*. Retrieved from www.forbes.com/sites/homaycotte/2015/09/01/beacon-technology-the-what-who-how-why-and-where/#4fd0c53e1aaf

12 Ranger, S. (2014, June 10). What is Apple iBeacon? Here's what you need to know. *ZDNet*. Retrieved from www.zdnet.com/article/what-is-apple-ibeacon-heres-what-you-need-to-know/

13 Lighthouse.io. (2019). The beginners guide to beacons. Retrieved from https://lighthouse.io/beginners-guide-to-beacons/beacon-use-cases/

14 Lighthouse.io. (2019). The beginners guide to beacons. Retrieved from https://lighthouse.io/beginners-guide-to-beacons/beacon-use-cases/

15 PCMAG. (2020). Definition of bluetooth glossary. Retrieved from www.pcmag.com/encyclopedia/term/bluetooth-glossary

# INDEX

Page numbers in italics indicate a figure and page numbers in bold indicate a table on the corresponding page. Page numbers followed by 'n' indicate a note.